The Sphere Handbook

MW01030453

Humanitarian Charter and Minimum Standards
in Humanitarian Response

WHAT IS SPHERE?

THE HUMANITARIAN CHARTER

PROTECTION PRINCIPLES

CORE HUMANITARIAN STANDARD

WATER SUPPLY, SANITATION AND HYGIENE PROMOTION

FOOD SECURITY AND NUTRITION

SHELTER AND SETTLEMENT

HEALTH

Sphere Association
3 Rue de Varembé
1202 Geneva, Switzerland
Email: info@spherestandards.org
Website: www.spherestandards.org

First edition 2000
Second edition 2004
Third edition 2011
Fourth edition 2018

A catalogue record for this publication is available from The British Library and the US Library of Congress.

ISBN 978-1-908176-400 PBK
ISBN 978-1-908176-608 EPUB
ISBN 978-1-908176-707 PDF

Citation: Sphere Association. *The Sphere Handbook: Humanitarian Charter and Minimum Standards in Humanitarian Response*, fourth edition, Geneva, Switzerland, 2018. www.spherestandards.org/handbook

The Sphere Project was initiated in 1997 by a group of NGOs and the Red Cross and Red Crescent Movement to develop a set of universal minimum standards in core areas of humanitarian response: The Sphere Handbook. The aim of the Handbook is to improve the quality of humanitarian response in situations of disaster and conflict, and to enhance the accountability of humanitarian action to crisis-affected people. The Humanitarian Charter and Minimum Standards in Humanitarian Response are the product of the collective experience of many people and agencies. They should therefore not be seen as representing the views of any one agency. In 2016, the Sphere Project was registered as the Sphere Association.

Distributed for the Sphere Association by Practical Action Publishing and its agents and representatives throughout the world. Practical Action Publishing (UK Company Reg. No. 1159018) is the wholly owned publishing company of Practical Action and trades only in support of its parent charity objectives.

Practical Action Publishing, 27a, Albert Street, Rugby, CV21 2SG, United Kingdom
Tel +44 (0) 1926 634501; Fax +44 (0)1926 634502
Website: www.practicalactionpublishing.org/sphere

Designed by: Non-linear Design Studio, Milan, Italy
Printed by: Webcom, Canada.
Typeset by vPrompt eServices, India

Contents

Foreword

The Sphere Handbook is marking its 20th anniversary with the publication of this fourth edition. It is the result of an intense year-long mobilisation of humanitarian actors around the globe and reflects two decades of experience using the standards in front-line operations, policy development and advocacy to uphold principled quality and accountability.

With a clear, rights-based framework, the Handbook builds on the legal and ethical foundations of humanitarianism with pragmatic guidance, global good practice and compiled evidence to support humanitarian staff wherever they work.

Sphere holds a unique place in the sector and in the constantly evolving humanitarian landscape. This edition was clearly informed by the international commitments made at the first World Humanitarian Summit in 2016, the 2030 Agenda for Sustainable Development and other global initiatives.

However, even as the policy landscape continues to evolve, we know that the immediate survival needs of people in conflict and disasters remain largely the same wherever crisis strikes. Sphere supports and contributes to global and local policy processes by recalling the fundamental necessity to provide accountable assistance to help people survive, recover and rebuild their lives with dignity.

Sphere's strength and global reach lie in the fact that it belongs to all. This sense of ownership is renewed every few years, when the standards are reviewed and revised by the users themselves. It is a moment when we collectively restate our commitments and agree on improved action to make sure that practitioners have the best information available to them wherever they may work. This makes Sphere a core reference and a reminder of the fundamental importance of human dignity and the right of people to participate fully in decisions that affect them.

Sphere is one of the foundations of humanitarian work. It is the starting point for new humanitarian actors and a standing reference for experienced staff, providing guidance on priority actions and where to find more detailed technical information. Our standards partners provide even more support in specific sectors beyond Sphere to help people recover and thrive.

This edition benefits from the input of thousands of people working with more than 450 organisations in at least 65 countries around the world. The global reach reflects experience from diverse contexts, extraordinary challenges and different types of actors. These standards would not exist without the unwavering commitment of so many of you. You have the thanks of our sector for your contributions during the revision and, indeed, over the past two decades.

We look forward to continuing this important work and learning together with you as you use this Handbook.

Martin McCann
Sphere Board Chair

Christine Knudsen
Executive Director

Acknowledgements

This edition of The Sphere Handbook is the result of the most diverse and far-reaching consultation process in the history of Sphere. Nearly 4,500 online comments were received from 190 organisations, and more than 1,400 people participated in 60 in-person events hosted by partners in 40 countries. Sphere gratefully acknowledges the scale and breadth of the contributions made, including from national, local and international NGOs, national authorities and ministries, Red Cross and Red Crescent societies, universities, UN organisations and individual practitioners.

The Shelter and Settlement chapter is dedicated to the memory of **Graham Saunders**, author of this chapter in the 2004 and 2011 editions and advisor in the early development of the 2018 edition.

Graham was a true humanitarian and a champion of the Shelter sector. His vision, leadership and endless energy have been instrumental in putting humanitarian shelter issues on the map and shaping the field for future generations of shelter practitioners. He continuously strived to improve our practice and professionalise the sector. He will be greatly missed as a pioneer, professional and friend.

The revision process was coordinated by the Sphere office. Individual chapters were developed by lead authors with cross-sectoral support from designated thematic experts and resource persons from the humanitarian sector. The majority of the authors and thematic experts were put forward by their home organisations, dedicating their time and effort as an in-kind contribution to the sector.

Writing groups and reference groups were established to support the authors and thematic experts in their work. Sphere acknowledges the valuable contribution of all these individuals throughout 2017 and 2018. A full list of all working group and reference group members can be found on the Sphere website, spherestandards.org. Lead authors and experts are noted below.

Foundation chapters

- **Humanitarian Charter and Annex 1:** Dr Mary Picard
- **Protection Principles:** Simon Russell (Global Protection Cluster) and Kate Sutton (Humanitarian Advisory Group)
- **Core Humanitarian Standard:** Takeshi Komino (CWSA Japan) and Sawako Matsuo (JANIC)

Technical chapters

- **Water, Sanitation and Hygiene Promotion:** Kit Dyer (NCA) and Jenny Lamb (Oxfam GB)
- **Food Security:** Daniel Wang'ang'a (WVI)
- **Nutrition:** Paul Wasike (Save the Children USA)
- **Shelter and Settlement:** Seki Hirano (CRS) and Ela Serdaroglu (IFRC)
- **Health:** Dr Durgavasini Devanath (IFRC), Dr Julie Hall (IFRC), Dr Judith Harvie (International Medical Corps), Dr Unni Krishnan (Save the Children Australia), Dr Eba Pasha (independent)

Vulnerabilities, capacities and operational settings

- **Children and child protection:** Susan Wisniewski (Terre des Hommes)
- **Older people:** Irene van Horssen and Phil Hand (HelpAge)
- **Gender:** Mireia Cano (GenCap)
- **Gender-based violence:** Jeanne Ward (independent)
- **Persons with disabilities:** Ricardo Pla Cordero (Humanity and Inclusion)
- **People living with and affected by HIV:** Alice Fay (UNHCR)
- **Mental health and psychosocial support:** Dr Mark van Ommeren (WHO), Peter Ventevogel (UNHCR)
- **Protracted crises:** Sara Sekkenes (UNDP)
- **Urban settings:** Pamela Sitko (WVI)
- **Civil–military coordination:** Jennifer Jalovec and Mark Herrick (WVI)
- **Environment:** Amanda George and Thomas Palo (Swedish Red Cross)
- **Disaster risk reduction:** Glenn Dolcemascolo and Muthoni Njogu (UNISDR)
- **Cash-based assistance and markets:** Isabelle Pelly (CaLP)
- **Supply-chain management and logistics:** George Fenton (Humanitarian Logistics Association)
- **Monitoring, evaluation, accountability and learning:** Joanna Olsen (CRS)

Sphere Board (May 2018)

Action by Churches Together (ACT) Alliance (Alwynn Javier) * Aktion Deutschland Hilft (ADH) (Karin Settele) * CARE International (Phillipe Guiton) * CARITAS Internationalis (Jan Weuts) * Humanitarian Response Network, Canada (Ramzi Saliba) * InterAction (Julien Schopp) * The International Council of Voluntary Agencies (ICVA) (Ignacio Packer) * International Federation of Red Cross and Red Crescent Societies (IFRC) (David Fisher) * International Medical Corps (IMC) (Mary Pack) * The Lutheran World Federation (LWF) (Roland Schlott) * Office Africain pour le développement et la coopération (OFADEC) (Mamadou Ndiaje) * Oxfam International - Intermón (Maria Chalaux Freixa) * Plan International (Colin Rogers) * RedR International (Martin McCann) * Save the Children (Unni Krishnan) * Sphere India (Vikrant Mahajan) * The Salvation Army (Damaris Frick) * World Vision International (WVI) (Isabel Gomes).

Thanks also go to Board members who initiated and guided the revision have since left the Board: Sarah Kambarami (ACT Alliance) * Anna Garvander (Church of Sweden/LWF) * Nan Buzard (ICVA) * Barbara Mineo (Oxfam International – Intermón) * Maxime Vieille (Save the Children).

Donors

In addition to contributions from the Board organisations listed above, funding for the Handbook revision process was provided by:

Danish International Development Agency (DANIDA) * German Ministry of Foreign Affairs * Irish Aid * Australian Government – Department of Foreign Affairs and Trade (DFAT) * European Commission's Humanitarian Aid and Civil Protection Department (ECHO) through International Federation of Red Cross and Red Crescent Societies (IFRC) * USAID's Office of United States Foreign Disaster Assistance (OFDA) * Swedish International Development Cooperation Agency (SIDA) through Church of Sweden * Swiss Agency for Development and Cooperation (SDC) * United Nations High Commissioner for Refugees (UNHCR) * United States Department of State Bureau of Population, Refugees and Migration (US-PRM).

Handbook revision team

Christine Knudsen, Executive Director (Sphere)
Aninia Nadig, Advocacy and Networking Manager (Sphere)
Editors: Kate Murphy and Aimee Ansari (Translators without Borders)
Revision coordinators: Lynnette Larsen and Miro Modrusan

With support from Sphere staff:
Tristan Hale, Learning and Training Manager
Wassila Mansouri, Networking and Outreach Officer
Juan Michel, Communications Manager through September 2017
Barbara Sartore, Communications Manager from October 2017
Loredana Serban, Administration and Finance Officer
Kristen Pantano and Caroline Tinka, Interns
Online consultation support: Markus Forsberg, (PHAP)
Handbook design: Non-linear (www.non-linear.com)
Copy editing, layout and production: Practical Action Publishing (www.practicalactionpublishing.org)
Kimberly Clarke and Megan Lloyd-Laney (CommsConsult)

Significant thanks for additional support during the Handbook revision process go to James Darcy, Malcolm Johnston, Hisham Khogali, Ben Mountfield, Dr Alice Obrecht, Ysabeau Rycx, Panu Saaristo, Manisha Thomas and Marilise Turnbull.

Sphere Focal Points which organised in-person revision consultations:

ADRA Argentina (Regional consultation with ADRAs South America)
Agency Coordinating Body for Afghan Relief (Afghanistan)
Alliance of Sphere Advocates in the Philippines (ASAP)
Amity Foundation (member of The Benevolence Standards Working Group, Focal Point for China)
BIFERD (Democratic Republic of Congo)
Community World Service Asia (Thailand and Pakistan)
Daniel Arteaga Galarza* with Secretaría de Gestión de Riesgos (Ecuador)
Dr Oliver Hoffmann* with the Sphere Focal Point for Germany
Grupo Esfera Bolivia
Grupo Esfera El Salvador
Grupo Esfera Honduras
Illiassou Adamou* with the Child Protection sub-cluster (Niger)
Indonesian Society for Disaster Management (MPBI)
Institut Bioforce (France)
InterAction (United States)
Inter-Agency Accountability Working Group (Ethiopia)
Korea NGO Council for Overseas Development Cooperation (Korea, Republic of)
Sphere Community Bangladesh (SCB)
Sphere India
Ukraine NGO Forum
UNDP Chile

*Individual focal points

What is Sphere?

Handbook

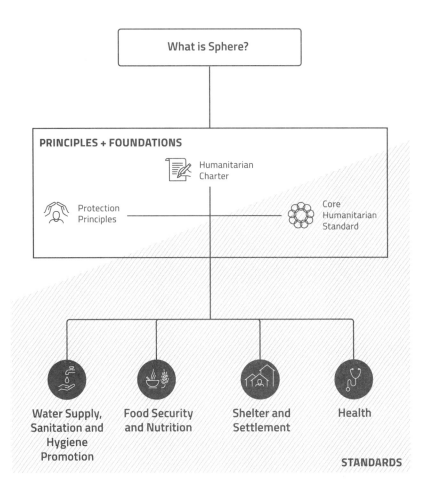

What is Sphere?

PRINCIPLES + FOUNDATIONS

Humanitarian Charter

Protection Principles

Core Humanitarian Standard

Water Supply, Sanitation and Hygiene Promotion

Food Security and Nutrition

Shelter and Settlement

Health

STANDARDS

ANNEX 1	Legal foundation to Sphere
ANNEX 2	Code of Conduct
ANNEX 3	Acronyms and Abbreviations

Contents

What is Sphere?

The Sphere Project, now known as Sphere, was created in 1997 by a group of humanitarian non-governmental organisations and the Red Cross and Red Crescent Movement. Its aim was to improve the quality of their humanitarian responses and to be accountable for their actions. The Sphere philosophy is based on two core beliefs:

- People affected by disaster or conflict have the right to life with dignity and, therefore, the right to assistance; and
- All possible steps should be taken to alleviate human suffering arising out of disaster or conflict.

The Humanitarian Charter and Minimum Standards put these core beliefs into practice. The Protection Principles inform all humanitarian action, and the Core Humanitarian Standard contains commitments to support accountability across all sectors. Together, they form The Sphere Handbook, which has developed into one of the most widely referenced humanitarian resources globally.

1. The Handbook

The principal users of The Sphere Handbook are practitioners involved in planning, managing or implementing a humanitarian response. This includes staff and volunteers of local, national and international humanitarian organisations responding to a crisis, as well as affected people themselves. The Handbook is also used for humanitarian advocacy to improve the quality and accountability of assistance and protection in line with humanitarian principles. It is increasingly used by governments, donors, military or the private sector to guide their own actions and allow them to work constructively with the humanitarian organisations that apply the standards.

The Handbook was first piloted in 1998, with revised editions published in 2000, 2004, 2011 and now 2018. Each revision process has relied on sector-wide consultations with individuals, non-governmental organisations (NGOs), governments and United Nations agencies. The resulting standards and guidance are informed by evidence and reflect 20 years of field testing by practitioners around the world.

This fourth edition marks the 20th anniversary of The Sphere Handbook and reflects changes in the humanitarian sector over that time. It includes new guidance for working in urban settings, for addressing Minimum Standards in protracted crises, and for delivering assistance through markets as a way to meet the standards. All technical chapters have been updated to reflect current practice, and the harmonised Core Humanitarian Standard replaces the previous Core Standards.

Four foundation chapters and four technical chapters

The Handbook reflects Sphere's commitment to a principled and rights-based humanitarian response. It is based on fundamental respect for people's right to be fully involved in decisions regarding their recovery.

The four foundation chapters outline the ethical, legal and practical basis for humanitarian response. They underpin all technical sectors and programmes. They describe commitments and processes to ensure a good quality humanitarian response, and encourage responders to be accountable to those affected by their actions. These chapters help the user apply the Minimum Standards more effectively in any context. Reading a technical chapter without also reading the foundation chapters risks missing essential elements of the standards. The foundation chapters are:

What is Sphere? (this chapter): Outlines the Handbook structure, its use and underlying principles. Importantly, it illustrates how to use the Handbook in practice.

The Humanitarian Charter: The cornerstone of The Sphere Handbook, expressing the shared conviction of humanitarian actors that all people affected by crisis have a right to receive protection and assistance. This right ensures the basic conditions for life with dignity. The Charter provides the ethical and legal backdrop to the Protection Principles, the Core Humanitarian Standard and the Minimum Standards. It builds on the 1994 Code of Conduct for the International Red Cross and Red Crescent Movement and Non-Governmental Organisations (NGOs) in Disaster Relief. The Code of Conduct remains an integral component of The Sphere Handbook ⊕ *see Annex 2.*

For a list of key documents constituting the legal foundation to the Humanitarian Charter ⊕ *see Annex 1.*

Protection Principles: A practical translation of the legal principles and rights outlined in the Humanitarian Charter into four principles that inform all humanitarian response.

The Core Humanitarian Standard: Nine commitments that describe essential processes and organisational responsibilities to enable quality and accountability in achieving the Minimum Standards.

The four technical chapters include Minimum Standards in key response sectors:

- Water Supply, Sanitation and Hygiene Promotion (WASH)
- Food Security and Nutrition
- Shelter and Settlement
- Health

In practice, humanitarian needs do not fall neatly into specific sectors. Effective humanitarian response must address people's needs holistically, and sectors should coordinate and collaborate with each other to do so. In the context of a

---

The Code of Conduct: 10 Core Principles

1. The humanitarian imperative comes first.
2. Aid is given regardless of the race, creed or nationality of the recipients and without adverse distinction of any kind. Aid priorities are calculated on the basis of need alone.
3. Aid will not be used to further a particular political or religious standpoint.
4. We shall endeavour not to act as instruments of government foreign policy.
5. We shall respect culture and custom.
6. We shall attempt to build disaster response on local capacities.
7. Ways shall be found to involve programme beneficiaries in the management of relief aid.
8. Relief aid must strive to reduce future vulnerabilities to disaster as well as meeting basic needs.
9. We hold ourselves accountable to both those we seek to assist and those from whom we accept resources.
10. In our information, publicity and advertising activities, we shall recognise disaster victims as dignified human beings, not hopeless objects.

The Code of Conduct: Principles of Conduct for the International Red Cross and Red Crescent Movement and NGOs in Disaster Response Programmes for full text ⊕ see Annex 2

---

protracted crisis, this may also expand beyond the humanitarian response with a need to work closely with development actors. The Handbook contains cross-references to help make these links. Readers should familiarise themselves with all chapters to support a holistic response.

The Minimum Standards promote a consistent approach

The standards are informed by available evidence and humanitarian experience. They present best practice based on broad consensus. Because they reflect inalienable human rights, they apply universally.

However, the context in which a response is taking place must be understood, monitored and analysed in order to apply the standards effectively.

The structure of the standards

The standards share a common structure to support the reader in understanding the universal statement, followed by a series of key actions, key indicators and guidance notes to achieve them.

- **The standards** are derived from the principle of the right to life with dignity. These are general and qualitative in nature, stating the minimum to be achieved in any crisis. The equivalents in the Core Humanitarian Standard (CHS) are the "commitment" and "quality criterion".
- **Key actions** outline practical steps to attain the Minimum Standard. These are suggestions and may not be applicable in all contexts. The practitioner should select the most relevant for the situation.

- **Key indicators** serve as signals to measure whether the standard is being attained. They provide a way to capture process and programme results against the standard and over the life of the response. Minimum quantitative requirements are the lowest acceptable level of achievement for indicators and are only included where there is sectoral consensus.
- **Guidance notes** provide additional information to support the key actions, with cross-references to the Protection Principles, the Core Humanitarian Standard and other standards within the Handbook. Cross-references are also given to other standards of the Humanitarian Standards Partnership.

Working with the key indicators

The Sphere key indicators are a way to measure whether a standard is being achieved; they should not be confused with the standard itself. The standard is universal, but the key indicators, like the key actions, should be considered in light of both the context and phase of the response. There are three types of Sphere indicator:

- **Process indicators** check whether a minimum requirement has been achieved. For example: standardised protocols are used to analyse food security, livelihoods and coping strategies ⊕ *see Food security and nutrition assessments standard 1.1: Food security assessment.*
- **Progress indicators** provide the unit of measurement to monitor achievement of the standard. It should be used to determine baseline, set targets with partners and stakeholders, and monitor changes towards that target. For example: percentage of households observed to store water safely in clean and covered containers at all times ⊕ *see Water supply standard 2.2: Water quality.* While the optimal target is 100 per cent, practitioners should associate the indicator with the reality on the ground, monitoring improvements against the baseline and progress towards the agreed target over time.
- **Target indicators** are specific, quantifiable targets which represent the quantifiable minimum below which the standard is not being met. Those targets should be reached as soon as possible, as falling short of the target will compromise the overall programme. For example: percentage of children aged six months to 15 years who have received measles vaccination: target is 95 per cent ⊕ *see Essential healthcare – child health standard 2.2.1: Childhood vaccine-preventable diseases.*

Links with other standards

The Sphere Handbook does not cover all aspects of humanitarian assistance that support the right to life with dignity. Partner organisations have developed complementary standards in several sectors, based on the same philosophy and commitments as Sphere's. These are available through Sphere, the Humanitarian Standards Partnership and their partner organisations' own websites.

- Livestock Emergency Guidelines and Standards (LEGS): LEGS Project
- Minimum Standards for Child Protection in Humanitarian Action (CPMS): Alliance for Child Protection in Humanitarian Action
- Minimum Standards for Education: Preparedness, Response, Recovery: Inter-Agency Network for Education in Emergencies (INEE)
- Minimum Economic Recovery Standards (MERS): Small Enterprise Education and Promotion (SEEP) Network
- Minimum Standard for Market Analysis (MISMA): Cash Learning Partnership (CaLP)
- Humanitarian Inclusion Standards for Older People and People with Disabilities: Age and Disability Consortium

2. Using the standards in context

Humanitarian responses take place in many different contexts. Several factors will influence how the Minimum Standards can be applied in the operating environment to support the right to life with dignity. These factors include:

- the setting in which humanitarian response is being delivered;
- the differences across populations and diversity among individuals;
- operational and logistical realities that will affect how and what kind of humanitarian response is delivered; and
- accurate baselines and indicators in different contexts, including defining key terms and setting targets.

Culture, language, the capacity of responders, security, access, environmental conditions and resources will influence the response. It is also important to anticipate any potential negative effects of the response and act to limit these ⊕ *see Protection Principles 1 and 2,* and *Core Humanitarian Standard Commitment 3.*

The Sphere Handbook is a voluntary code for quality and accountability, designed to encourage the broadest possible use and ownership of the standards. It is not a "how to" guide but a description of what must be in place as a minimum for people to survive and recover from crisis with dignity.

Conforming to the Sphere standards does not mean implementing all key actions or meeting all key indicators of all standards. The degree to which an organisation can meet the standards will depend on a range of factors, some of which are beyond their control. Access to the affected population, or political or economic insecurity, may make achieving the standards impossible in some contexts.

In cases where the minimum requirements exceed the living conditions of the host community, consider how to reduce potential tension, such as by offering community-based services. In some situations, national authorities may establish minimum requirements that are higher than the Sphere Minimum Standards.

The Sphere standards are an expression of the fundamental rights related to life with dignity, and remain constant. The indicators and minimum requirements may need to be adapted to be meaningful in context. In cases where the standards are not met, any proposal to reduce the minimum requirements should be considered carefully. Agree any changes collectively and report the shortfall in actual progress against the minimums widely. In addition, humanitarian organisations must assess the negative impact on the population of not meeting a standard and take steps to minimise any harm. Use this response gap for advocacy and strive to reach the indicators as soon as possible.

The standards apply throughout the programme cycle

The Sphere standards should be used throughout the programme cycle, from assessment and analysis, through strategy development, planning and programme design, implementation and monitoring, to evaluation and learning.

Assessment and analysis

The Sphere Minimum Standards provide a basis for needs assessment and analysis in each sector, with assessment checklists available in each chapter. At the onset of a crisis, Sphere standards help to identify immediate needs and prioritise activities that will address these needs. Planning figures and minimum assistance levels are outlined globally to help formulate minimum response-wide outcomes. The standards therefore also serve to improve coordination across organisations and sectors.

Strategy development and programme design

The Core Humanitarian Standard and the Minimum Standards support the planning of responses to provide the right humanitarian assistance at the right time to those most in need. The full participation of the affected population and coordination with national and local authorities is essential to achieve this across all sectors.

The key actions and indicators provide a framework to identify priorities, determine planning figures and coordinate across sectors. This helps to ensure that sectoral responses reinforce each other and support the population's own capacity to meet their needs. The key actions and indicators outline the quality of assistance that should be attained. They also provide a basis for conducting a response analysis that identifies the best way to meet identified needs and minimise potential harmful side-effects.

Programme planning usually involves analysis of several response options, such as in-kind provision of goods, cash-based assistance, direct service provision, technical assistance or a mix of these. The specific combination of response options chosen usually evolves over time. The Minimum Standards focus on what must be done, rather than how the assistance should be delivered.

Cash-based assistance, a form of market-based programming, is increasingly used to meet humanitarian needs. Considerations for using cash-based assistance have been integrated throughout the Handbook, in all chapters. Cash-based assistance can be used to meet multi-sector needs as well as sector-specific needs. It can also be used to address discriminatory practices that restrict women's access to assets and their decision-making around the management of assets. Multi-purpose grants can be an effective way to provide assistance and meet standards across sectors. All cash-based assistance should be informed by a multi-sectoral analysis of needs, dynamics in the context, market functionality and a feasibility assessment.

Not all sectors are well adapted to market-based programming. This is the case particularly for providers of direct services or technical assistance. Health and nutrition providers may choose to support access to existing health service providers and local public health interventions that do not operate as markets.

To determine the way in which assistance can best be delivered, consultations with the population, analysis of the markets, knowledge of the ways services are provided, and an understanding of the supply chain and logistics capacities will be needed. This response analysis should be reviewed over time as the situation changes ⊕ *see Appendix: Delivering assistance through markets.*

Implementation

If the Sphere standards cannot be met for all or some groups from the affected population, investigate why and explain the gaps, as well as what needs to change. Assess the negative implications, including protection and public health risks. Document these issues and work actively with other sectors and the affected population to identify appropriate ways to minimise potential harm.

Monitoring, evaluation, accountability and learning

Monitoring, evaluation, accountability and learning (MEAL) supports timely and evidence-based management decisions. It allows humanitarian programmes to adjust to changing contexts. All of the Minimum Standards have indicators that can be monitored to determine whether they are being achieved, whether they are being achieved equitably for all segments of a population, or how much more needs to be done. Evaluation supports learning to improve policy and future practice, and promotes accountability. MEAL systems also contribute to broader learning efforts related to effective humanitarian action.

Understanding vulnerabilities and capacities

Throughout the Handbook, the term "people" has been used in a broad sense, to reflect Sphere's belief that all individuals have a right to a life with dignity and therefore a right to assistance. "People" should be read as including women, men, boys and girls, regardless of their age, disability, nationality, race, ethnicity, health status, political affiliation, sexual orientation, gender identity or any other characteristic that they may use to define themselves.

Not all people have equal control of power and resources. Individuals and groups within a population have different capacities, needs and vulnerabilities, which

Assess current situation and trends over time

– Who is affected? – Needs and vulnerabilities – Coping strategies and capacities – Displaced? Mobile? – What are affected people's priorities?	– Protection threats and risks – Security situation and rule of law – Access to assistance – Access to people in need? – Seasonal variations in hazards	– Stakeholders and power relationships – Capacity and intent of responders – Response plans of authorities and other actors – Role of host population	– Available goods and services – Market systems and supply chains – Capacity of infrastructure – Service providers (financial and others) – Logistics capacities, constraints

↓

Analyse and prioritise

What problems must be addressed? For which groups of people? In what geographic area? Over what timeframe? Against which standards?

↓

Review options and decide how the response will be delivered

Consider available options in your context:	From these, select response options based on your assessment of:	
– Direct service delivery – Commodity distribution – Technical assistance – Market-based programming – Cash-based assistance	– Urgency and timeliness – Feasibility – Capacities – Dignity – Protection threats, risks	– Efficiency, cost-effectiveness – Resilience – National ownership – Government policy

↓

Design a programme built on quality and accountability

Essential lenses	Communication and accountability	Monitoring context, process, progress and results	Transition and exit strategies
– Disaggregate data by sex, age and disability – Vulnerabilities and protection – Sustainability or transition	– Feedback and complaints mechanisms – Coordination – Systematic community engagement	– Selection of indicators – Appropriate data disaggregation	– Local engagement and ownership – National systems and ownership – Partnerships

Understanding context to apply the standards (Figure 1)

change over time. Individual factors such as age, sex, disability and legal or health status can limit access to assistance. These and other factors may also be the basis of intentional discrimination. Systematic dialogue with women, men, girls and boys of all ages and backgrounds – both separately and in mixed groups – is fundamental to good programming. To be young or old, a woman or girl, a person with a disability or of a minority ethnicity does not in itself make an individual universally vulnerable. Rather, it is the interplay of factors in a given context that can strengthen capacities, build resilience or undermine access to assistance for any individual or group.

In many contexts, entire communities and groups may also be vulnerable because they live in remote, insecure or inaccessible areas, or because they are geographically dispersed with limited access to assistance and protection. Groups may be under-served and discriminated against because of nationality, ethnicity, language, or religious or political affiliation, which requires special attention to reflect the principle of impartiality.

When diverse groups are involved in programme design, humanitarian responses are more comprehensive, inclusive and can have more sustainable results. Inclusion of, and participation by, the affected population is fundamental to life with dignity.

Data disaggregation

In many situations, population-level data is difficult to find or determine. However, disaggregated data will show the distinct needs and impact of actions on different groups. Disaggregated data can help to identify those people most at risk, indicate whether they are able to access and use humanitarian assistance, and where more needs to be done to reach them. Disaggregate data to the extent possible and with categories appropriate to the context to understand differences based on sex or gender, age, disability, geography, ethnicity, religion, caste or any other factors that may limit access to impartial assistance.

For general data on age, use the same cohorts as in national data-collection systems. If there are no national age cohorts, use the table below. More refined disaggregation may be needed to target specific groups such as infants, children, youth, women or older people.

Children

Children comprise a significant proportion of any crisis-affected population but are often less visible. Children's capacities and needs vary according to their biological age and stage of development. Special measures must be taken to ensure they are protected from harm and have equitable access to basic services.

During crises, children face specific life-threatening risks, including malnutrition, separation from their families, trafficking, recruitment into armed groups, and physical or sexual violence and abuse, all of which require immediate action.

Protection risks are often compounded by many factors. For example, adolescent and young boys are more likely to be recruited as soldiers by armed forces

Sex	Disability status	Age									
		0–5	6–12	13–17	18–29	30–39	40–49	50–59	60–69	70–79	80+
Female	Without disabilities										
	With disabilities										
Male	Without disabilities										
	With disabilities										

and groups or to participate in the worst forms of child labour. Adolescent girls are more likely to be recruited as sex slaves or trafficked. Children with disabilities are more likely to be abandoned or neglected. Girls with disabilities require particular attention because they face greater risk of sexual violence, sexual exploitation and malnutrition.

Actively seek the views of girls and boys of all ages and backgrounds, so they can influence how assistance is delivered, monitored and evaluated. The Convention on the Rights of the Child states that "child" means every person under the age of 18. Analyse how the affected population defines children, to ensure that no child or young person is excluded from assistance.

Older people

Older people are a fast-growing proportion of the population in most countries, but often neglected in humanitarian responses.

In many cultures, being considered old is linked to circumstances (such as being a grandparent) or physical signs (such as white hair), rather than age. While many sources define old age as 60 years and older, 50 years may be more appropriate in contexts where humanitarian crises occur.

Older people bring knowledge and experience of coping strategies and act as caregivers, resource managers, coordinators and income generators. Older people often embody traditions and history and act as cultural reference points. Isolation, physical weakness, disruption of family and community support structures, chronic illness, functional difficulties and declining mental capacities can all increase the vulnerability of older people in humanitarian contexts.

Ensure that older people are consulted and involved at each stage of humanitarian response. Consider age-appropriate and accessible services, environments and information, and use age-disaggregated data for programme monitoring and management.

Gender

"Gender" refers to the socially constructed differences between women and men throughout their life cycle. This may change over time and within and across cultures and context. Gender often determines the different roles, responsibilities, power and access to resources of women, girls, boys and men. Understanding these differences and how they have changed during the crisis is critical to effective humanitarian programming and the fulfilment of human rights. Crises can be an opportunity to address gender inequalities and empower women, girls, boys and men.

Gender is not the same as sex, which refers to the biological attributes of a person.

"Gender" does not mean "women only". While women and girls most often face constraints within gender roles, men and boys are also influenced by strict expectations of masculinity. Gender equality programming requires their inclusion for the development of more equitable relationships and equal participation of women, girls, men and boys.

Gender-based violence

"Gender-based violence" describes violence based on gender differences between males and females. It underscores how inequality between males and females is the foundation of most forms of violence perpetrated against women and girls across the world. Crises can intensify many forms of gender-based violence, including intimate partner violence, child marriage, sexual violence and trafficking.

Organisations are responsible for taking all necessary steps to prevent the sexual exploitation and abuse of people affected by crises, including in their own activities. When allegations of misconduct are found to be true, it is important that the competent authorities hold the perpetrator to account and that cases are dealt with in a transparent way.

Persons with disabilities

About 15 per cent of the world's population lives with some form of disability. Persons with disabilities include those who have long-term physical, mental, intellectual or sensory impairments which, in interaction with various barriers, may hinder their full and effective participation in society on an equal basis with others.

In humanitarian contexts, persons with disabilities are more likely to face barriers and obstacles to the physical environment, transportation, information and communications, and humanitarian facilities or services. Response and preparedness programming should consider the capacities and needs of all persons with disabilities and make deliberate efforts to remove physical, communication and attitudinal barriers to their access and participation. Risks to women and girls with disabilities can be compounded by gender inequality and discrimination.

⊕ *See References: Washington Group Questions* for disaggregation of data by disability status, and the ⊕ *Humanitarian inclusion standards for older people and people with disabilities,* for more information.

People living with and affected by HIV

Knowing the HIV prevalence in a specific context is important in order to under-stand vulnerabilities and risks and to inform an effective response. Displacement may lead to increased HIV vulnerabilities, and crises are likely to cause disruption in prevention, testing, care, treatment and support services. Specific measures are often needed to protect against violence and discrimination among high-risk populations. This can be compounded by gender inequality and discrimination based on disability status, gender identity and sexual orientation. In turn, this may discourage people living with HIV to seek services in a crisis, if any are available. Violence, discrimination and negative coping strategies such as transactional sex increase vulnerability to HIV transmission, especially for women, girls and LGBTQI communities. Those at the highest risk include men who have sex with men, people who inject drugs, sex workers, transgender people, persons with disabilities, and people in prisons and other closed settings ⊕ *see Essential healthcare – sexual and reproductive health standard 2.3.3: HIV.*

Factors such as a reduction in mobility over time and greater access to services for crisis-affected populations can decrease the risk of HIV. Dispel any possible misconceptions about the presence of people living with HIV and an increased HIV prevalence to avoid discriminatory practices. People living with HIV are entitled to live their lives in dignity, free from discrimination, and should enjoy non-discriminatory access to services.

LGBTQI people

People who identify as lesbian, gay, bisexual, transgender, queer or intersex (LGBTQI) are often at heightened risk of discrimination, stigma, and sexual and physical violence. They may face barriers to accessing healthcare, housing, educa-tion, employment, information and humanitarian facilities. For example, LGBTQI people often face discrimination in assistance programmes that are based on "conventional" family units, such as for emergency accommodation or food distribution. Such barriers affect their health and survival and may have long-term consequences on integration. Include specific, safe and inclusive protection responses in preparedness and planning. Ensure meaningful consultation with LGBTQI individuals and organisations at each stage of humanitarian response.

Mental health and psychosocial support

People react differently to the stress of a humanitarian crisis. Some are more likely to be overwhelmed by distress, especially if they have been forcibly displaced, separated from family members, survived violence or experienced previous mental health conditions. Providing basic services and security in a socially and culturally appropriate way is essential to both prevent distress among affected populations and address discrimination.

Strengthening community psychosocial support and self-help creates a protec-tive environment, allowing those affected to help each other towards social and emotional recovery. Focused individual, family or group interventions – including clinical interventions – are important, but do not necessarily have to be provided by mental health professionals. They can also be provided by trained and supervised lay people ⊕ *see Essential healthcare standard 2.5: Mental healthcare.*

Affected populations often express a spiritual or religious identity and may associate themselves with a faith community. This is often an essential part of their coping strategy and influences an appropriate response across a wide range of sectors. There is growing evidence that affected populations benefit when humanitarians take account of their faith identity. Existing faith communities have great potential to contribute to any humanitarian response. A people-centred approach requires humanitarian workers to be aware of the faith identity of affected populations. There is a growing body of tools to help achieve this.

Understanding the operational setting

Humanitarian response takes place in vastly different contexts, ranging from urban to rural, and conflict to rapid-onset disaster, and often a combination of these over time. The effectiveness of the response in meeting the needs of the affected population will depend on geographic, security, social, economic, political and environmental factors. While the Minimum Standards have been developed to focus on immediate life-saving assistance, they are applicable in humanitarian responses that last a few days, weeks, months or even years. The humanitarian response should change and adapt over time and avoid creating aid dependency. A continuous analysis of the context and situation will signal when programmes should adapt to a changing environment, such as new security issues or seasonal constraints such as flooding.

An ongoing evaluation of how the response affects local dynamics such as procurement of goods and services or hiring of transport is essential to make sure humanitarian action does not fuel conflict dynamics ⊕ *see Protection Principle 2.* When crises become protracted, underlying systemic weaknesses may intensify needs and vulnerabilities, requiring additional protection and resilience-building efforts. Some of these will be better addressed through or in cooperation with development actors.

Coordination mechanisms such as the cluster system are required to establish a clear division of labour and responsibility and to identify gaps in coverage and quality. It is important to prevent the duplication of efforts and the waste of resources. The sharing of information and knowledge between stakeholders, along with joint planning and integrated activities, can also ensure that organisations manage risk better and improve the outcomes of a response.

Supporting national and local actors

Recognising the primary role and responsibility of the host state, the Handbook guides all those involved in humanitarian response and the role that humanitarian organisations can play in supporting this responsibility. In a conflict, the willingness of state or non-state actors to facilitate access to the population will have a determining effect.

The state's role in leading or coordinating a response will be shaped by many factors, including:

- the existence of a government body specifically charged with the coordination or implementation of humanitarian response (often referred to as a National Disaster Management Authority or Organisation);
- the role and strength of line ministries to set standards such as nutrition standards and standards for essential drugs and medical staff; and
- the lack of functioning state institutions, such as in contested areas. In such extraordinary cases, humanitarian actors may need to set up their own coordination mechanisms.

Protracted crises

When it is evident that a humanitarian response will last more than several months or years, consider different means of meeting needs and supporting life with dignity. Explore opportunities to work with existing service providers, local authorities, local communities, social protection networks or development actors to help meet needs. Assessments need to consider the context and the protection concerns, and how the rights of the affected population will be impacted. Involve individuals of both sexes and all ages, disabilities and backgrounds, including self-defined communities, in the analysis, assessment, decision-making and monitoring and evaluation. Pursue long-term and permanent solutions as early as possible. When humanitarian actors have the opportunity to establish long-term solutions, those should take precedence over temporary measures.

Recognise that affected people are often the first to respond to their own needs and protect themselves. National and local authorities, civil society organisations, faith-based organisations and others provide critical assistance. Be aware of these pre-existing assistance networks and identify ways to support rather than undermine or duplicate them.

Urban settings

As more and more of the world's population moves to towns and cities, humanitarians must be prepared to respond in urban contexts. Urban areas typically differ from other contexts in terms of:

- **Density:** a higher density of people, houses, infrastructure, laws and cultures in a relatively small area;
- **Diversity:** social, ethnic, political, linguistic, religious and economically diverse groups live in close proximity; and
- **Dynamics:** urban environments are fluid and changing, with high mobility and rapidly shifting power relationships.

The municipality will often be the key government authority, with links to other government actors and departments, such as line ministries. Access to basic services, food security and livelihoods should be carefully assessed, including any discrimination. People in cities and towns use cash to pay rent, buy food and access healthcare. The Minimum Standards for life with dignity apply, regardless of how the assistance is provided.

The Sphere Minimum Standards can be used to support multiple entry points for providing assistance in urban areas, including through settlement, neighbourhood or area-based approaches. Established groups with shared interests, such as schools, clubs, women's groups and taxi drivers, can provide useful entry points. Working with local actors (such as the private sector, local government, neighbourhood leaders and community groups) can be vital in restarting, supporting and strengthening existing services instead of replacing them. Be mindful of how humanitarian assistance may support municipal investment planning, creating value during the crisis and in the longer term.

As in any setting, a context analysis in urban environments should look at the existing resources and opportunities, such as commerce, cash, technology, public spaces, people with specialised skill sets, and social and cultural diversity, alongside risks and protection aspects. The analysis should inform response options and the final choice of delivery mode, such as deciding to provide in-kind or cash-based assistance (and the best way for doing so). The cash-based economy of towns and cities provides opportunities for partnerships with actors in markets and technology, which may facilitate the use of cash-based assistance.

Communal settlements

Planned communal settlements and camps, as well as collective centres and spontaneous settlements, are home to millions of people who have been forcibly displaced. The Sphere standards can be used to ensure the quality of assistance in community settings. They can also help identify priorities for multi-sectoral programmes to address public health concerns, and for access to basic services in spontaneous settlements.

In communal settlements, dedicated camp management capacity can contribute to greater accountability and coordinated service delivery. However, communal settlements also pose specific protection risks. For example, when the right to freedom of movement to leave the settlement is denied, people may not be able to access markets or pursue livelihoods. Special attention should also be paid to host communities, because real or perceived differences in treatment may lead to escalating tensions or conflict. In such cases, advocating for an alternative to camp-like settings and addressing host community needs too can help to ensure that affected populations are able to live with dignity.

Settings with domestic or international military forces

When humanitarian organisations respond in the same area as domestic or international military forces, it is important to be aware of each other's mandates, modus operandi, capacities and limits. In disaster and conflict settings, humanitarian organisations may find themselves working closely with a range of militaries, including host government forces, non-state armed groups and international peacekeepers. Humanitarian actors should note that host governments are obliged to provide assistance and protection to people affected by crisis in their territory. Domestic military forces are often mandated to do this.

Humanitarian principles must guide all humanitarian–military dialogue and coordination at all levels and stages of interaction. Information sharing, planning and task division are three essential elements of effective civil–military coordination. While information sharing between humanitarian and military actors can occur, it must depend on the context of operational activities. Humanitarian agencies must not share information that gives one party to a conflict a tactical advantage or endangers civilians.

At times, humanitarian organisations may need to use the unique capabilities of militaries to support humanitarian operations. Military support to humanitarian organisations should be limited to infrastructure support and indirect assistance; direct assistance is a last resort.

Cooperation with militaries has an actual or perceived impact on a humanitarian organisation's neutrality and operational independence, so must be carefully considered in advance. Internationally agreed guidance documents should inform any humanitarian–military coordination arrangements ⊕ *see Core Humanitarian Standard Commitment 6* and *References.*

Environmental impact in humanitarian response

The environment in which people live and work is essential for their health, well-being and recovery from crisis. Understanding how affected people are dependent on the environment for their own recovery can also inform programme design and lead to more sustainable responses to cope with future shocks and reduce future risk.

Humanitarian operations affect the environment both directly and indirectly. Effective humanitarian response should therefore carefully assess environmental risk alongside wider assessments and situational analysis. Programmes should minimise their environmental impact and consider how procurement, transport, choice of materials, or land and natural resource use may protect or degrade the environment further ⊕ *see Shelter and settlement standard 7: Environmental sustainability.*

Countries and regions facing poverty as well as fragile institutional capacity and ecology are at higher risk of natural disasters and instability, creating a vicious circle of social and environmental degradation. This has an impact on health, education, livelihoods and other dimensions of security, dignity and well-being. Environmental sustainability is an important component of a good quality humanitarian response ⊕ *see Core Humanitarian Standard Commitments 3, 9* and *Shelter and settlement standard 7: Environmental sustainability.*

Appendix
Delivering assistance through markets

This appendix complements The Sphere Handbook introduction, providing further information and guidance on using markets to attain the Minimum Standards and help people meet their needs in the aftermath of a crisis. It builds on the foundation chapters and is referenced in the technical chapters. As such, it is an integral component of The Sphere Handbook. To respond effectively, humanitarian actors should understand what the needs are as well as how to practically meet them. Part of this analysis is understanding how markets are functioning and what goods and services are available at the local, national, regional and international level. This understanding also allows humanitarian programmes to support – or at least not disrupt – markets during the response.

Market analysis as part of response analysis

Once needs and capacities have been assessed to identify priorities, the different ways to respond and meet those needs should be analysed. Response analysis should ensure that operational, programmatic and contextual risks and opportunities are systematically considered when determining how assistance will be provided. This is sometimes called the "choice of modality".

Identifying the best way for assistance to meet needs requires:

- disaggregated information on priorities and how people want to access assistance, across sectors and over time; and
- an understanding of economic vulnerabilities, both pre-existing and those created by the crisis.

As part of response analysis, market analysis helps to identify what may be the most effective way to meet priority needs: in-kind assistance, service provision, cash-based assistance or a mix of these in context. Market analysis will help identify any constraints on markets, including supply and demand issues, or policies, norms, rules or infrastructure that limit market functioning.

Whichever response option is chosen, it should be market-sensitive and strive to protect livelihoods, local jobs and businesses. Sphere is based on a fundamental respect for people affected by crisis and on supporting their choices for their own recovery. By considering how people interact with local markets to get goods, services and income, market analysis supports a people-centred approach.

Programming and markets

Assistance can be delivered through markets in many ways at the local, national or regional level. Market-based programming can be used directly to deliver assistance, or markets can be supported to better serve the affected population.

- Local and regional procurement of commodities and non-food items supports the supply side of markets.
- Cash-based assistance, helping people to buy locally available goods or services, supports the demand side of markets.
- Support to infrastructure, such as improving road access to markets, or reforms such as laws to prevent price fixing, support the market so it can better serve the affected population.

Sex, ethnicity or disability often directly influence physical, financial and social access to markets. How do men, women, youth and older people access markets differently? Are traders from a specific ethnicity able to access credit facilities? These and other factors influence the degree to which individuals can actively participate in markets.

Ethical and environmental considerations should be weighed when developing market-based programmes. Ensure that markets that over-exploit natural resources, ecosystems and the environment are not developed in a way that puts people at further risk.

Goods, services and markets: When responding to priority humanitarian needs, consider both goods and services. Most Sphere standards involve providing some kind of commodity or access to goods. Social sectors such as health and education, however, are characterised by providing or improving access to services, and delivering through markets may not be an option. When working with third-party service providers or sub-contractors, take steps to closely monitor the quality of services and products with them ⊕ *see Health systems standard 1.4: Health financing.*

In some cases, market-based programmes that indirectly support access to services are appropriate. Cash-based assistance can support transport to healthcare facilities or access to education (buying uniforms and materials). Tracking household expenditures provides clear data on the cost of accessing services, including those that should be free. Household expenditure monitoring should always be supported by outcome monitoring of cash assistance.

Service-based sectors can also consider market-based programming for goods such as insecticide-treated bednets, supplementary feeding supplies and pharmaceuticals if they meet quality criteria ⊕ *see Health systems standard 1.3: Essential medicines and medical devices.*

In most contexts, a combination of market-based interventions will be needed. Market-based programmes will likely need to be supported by other activities such as those providing technical assistance. This combination will also evolve over the course of the programme and may shift from in-kind to cash or vouchers or vice versa. Along with programme monitoring, market monitoring is important to confirm or adjust the form of assistance.

Collaboration between supply chain, logistics and programme functions is needed at all times. For further guidance on tools that support this choice and analysis ⊕ *see References.*

Checklists

Checklist for cash-based assistance

This section presents a list of considerations for delivering assistance through markets. It follows the programme management cycle and includes other important elements to consider when adopting this approach to meet the Minimum Standards. Each context will be different, and the options for delivery mechanisms will vary based on infrastructure, data protection, cost-effectiveness and financial inclusion.

Programme design

- Base targeting criteria on programme objectives and include cash-based-assistance-specific considerations.
- Carefully consider who within the household should receive cash-based assistance, informed by a clear risk assessment and weighing any protection concerns.
- Identify safe, accessible and effective mechanisms to deliver assistance based on the context, objectives and size of the programme as well as on recipients' financial literacy and preferences.
- Calculate the transfer amount based on the needs to be covered and the cost of meeting these needs.
- Set the transfer frequency and duration based on needs, seasonality, the financial service provider's capacity and protection risks.
- Where possible and feasible, adopt a multi-sector perspective.
- Define key issues and related indicators to monitor process, activity, output and outcome levels.

Implementation

- Include context-specific considerations and any other relevant dimensions in financial service provider tenders and establish clear criteria for selection.
- Consider using existing familiar delivery mechanisms already in place for social protection.
- Set up recipient registration and identification systems that are appropriate to the delivery mechanism and for the protection of personal data.
- Ensure that registration and identification cover data required by the financial service provider.
- Apply and document data protection measures.
- Set up mechanisms for digital data in collaboration with different organisations to the extent possible ("inter-operable systems").

- Clearly define the procedures, roles and responsibilities for the cash delivery process, as well as risk management mechanisms.
- Ensure that the process delivering cash-based assistance is accessible and effective.
- Make sure all affected groups can access the chosen delivery mechanism throughout the project's lifespan.
- Ensure recipients have information on programme objectives and the duration of cash-based assistance, so they can make informed spending decisions.
- Ensure financial service providers are accountable to recipients through contractual management and monitoring ⊕ *see Core Humanitarian Standard Commitments 4 and 5.*

Monitoring, evaluation and learning

- Monitor cash-based-assistance-related processes, activities, outputs and risks, including through post-distribution monitoring.
- Monitor whether the cash or vouchers were received by the right person, safely, on time and in the correct amount.
- Monitor markets and their supply chains consistently, beyond price monitoring.
- Monitor household expenditure and triangulate with market monitoring data to assess whether needs can indeed be met through cash-based assistance and negative coping strategies reduced.
- Monitor potential risks of cash-based assistance, including protection risks and any negative impact on natural resources.
- Evaluate outcomes related to cash-based assistance.
- Regularly evaluate whether the choice of cash-based assistance is effective in meeting changing needs, adapt the programme accordingly and support continuous learning for future programmes.

Checklist for supply chain management and logistics

This section presents a list of considerations for supply-chain management and logistics. It follows the programme management cycle and includes other important elements to consider.

Supply chain management (SCM) starts with the choice of commodity or service. It includes identifying the source of what is needed, procurement, quality management, risk management (including insurance), packaging, shipping, transportation, warehousing, inventory management, delivery and distribution. SCM involves many different partners, and it is important to coordinate activities ⊕ *see Core Humanitarian Standard Commitment 6.*

Specific SCM expertise is required. Particular types of relevant expertise include contract management, transportation and warehouse management, inventory management, pipeline analysis and information management, shipment tracking and import management. Management and monitoring practices should ensure that commodities are safeguarded to distribution points. However, humanitarian organisations are also responsible for ensuring that products and services (including cash-based assistance services) reach the people who need assistance.

Local and regional purchasing stimulates local markets, which may give farmers and manufacturers an incentive to produce more and may in turn boost the local economy. However, when supplies are already relatively limited, local or regional purchasing could cause problems in other markets or disrupt existing commercial networks. Conversely, importing can crowd out local or regional producers and also disrupt existing commercial networks.

Programme design

- Assess the local availability of needed goods and services before sourcing them from outside the area.
- Consider working with reputable local or regional transporters who have valuable knowledge of local regulations, procedures and facilities and can help to ensure compliance with the laws of the host country and to expedite deliveries.
- In a conflict environment, apply a particularly rigorous vetting process to service providers.
- Carefully ensure that sourcing locally does not cause or exacerbate hostilities.
- Consider whether any use of natural resources is sustainable and whether use may lead to further conflict over resources.
- Establish a transparent, fair and open procedure for awarding contracts, considering local, national and international options.
- If several organisations are involved, coordinate local sourcing to the extent possible.

Implementation

- Build good relationships with suppliers, local traders and service providers.
- Enforce the appropriate quality of goods and services through contracts as well as ethical and environmentally sustainable practices.
- Train and supervise staff at all levels of the supply chain to maintain product quality and adhere to, safety procedures (for recipients and staff) as well as ethical and environmentally sustainable practices.
- Include staff of partner organisations and service providers in training and conduct training in the local language.
- Set up accountability procedures, including supply, transport and storage planning, inventory management, reporting and financial systems.
- Avoid using food to pay for logistics operations such as unloading at warehouses. Such costs should be included in the core budget.
- Separate warehouses for food and non-food items are recommended. When selecting a warehouse, establish that it has not been used to store hazardous goods and that there is no danger of contamination. Factors to

consider include: security, capacity, ease of access, structural solidity and absence of any threat of flooding.

- Assess and manage risks to the security of transport routes and warehouses.
- In conflict situations, establish control systems and supervise all stages of the supply chain to minimise the risk of looting or requisitioning by warring parties.
- Analyse and address broader political and security implications, such as the possibility of diverted stocks fuelling an armed conflict ⊕ *see Protection Principle 2.*
- Minimise and report product losses at all levels of the supply chain.
- Have damaged or unsuitable commodities inspected by qualified inspectors (such as food safety experts and public health laboratories) and certified for disposal.

- Dispose of damaged commodities quickly, before they become a health or security hazard. Methods of commodity disposal include sale (for example or food for animal feed) and burial or incineration that is author-ised and should be witnessed by relevant authorities. In all cases, unfit commodities must not re-enter the supply chain, harm the environment or contaminate water sources ⊕ *see WASH Solid waste management standards 5.1 to 5.3.*
- Day-to-day management needs include prompt and transparent reporting of any delays or deviations in the supply chain. Make sufficient documentation and forms available in the local language at all locations where goods are received, stored and/or dispatched. Doing so maintains a documented audit trail of transactions.

Monitoring, evaluation and learning

- Monitor and manage commodity pipelines to avoid diversion of and interrup-tion to distributions, as well as to avoid market distortion.
- Inform stakeholders regularly about the performance of supply chain efforts.
- Share relevant information on stock levels, expected arrivals and distribu-tions among supply chain stakeholders. Use the tracking of stock levels to highlight anticipated shortfalls and problems in time. Information sharing among partners may facilitate loans that prevent pipeline breaks. If there are insufficient resources, commodities will need to be prioritised. Consult stakeholders when considering solutions.
- Ensure that accountability and communication mechanisms reflect the specificities of delivery processes.
- Ensure commodity tracking and information management systems are in place from the beginning of the intervention.
- Evaluate regularly if the assistance is effective in meeting changing needs, adapt the programme accordingly and support continuous learning for future programmes.

References and further reading

Understanding vulnerabilities and capacities
Humanitarian Inclusion Standards for Older People and People with Disabilities. Age and Disability Consortium as part of the ADCAP programme. HelpAge, 2018. www.helpage.org

Faith-based programming
A faith-sensitive approach in humanitarian response: Guidance on mental health and psychosocial programming. The Lutheran World Federation and Islamic Relief Worldwide, 2018. https://interagencystandingcommittee.org

Market analysis and market-based programming
Minimum Economic Recovery Standards (MERS): Core Standard 2 and Assessment and Analysis Standards. The Small Enterprise Education and Promotion Network (SEEP), 2017. https://seepnetwork.org

Minimum Standard for Market Analysis (MISMA). The Cash Learning Partnership (CaLP), 2017. www.cashlearning.org

Cash-based assistance
CBA Programme Quality Toolbox. CaLP. http://pqtoolbox.cashlearning.org

Supply chain management and logistics
Cargo Tracking: Relief Item Tracking Application (RITA). Logistics Cluster. www.logcluster.org

HumanitarianResponse.info: Logistics references page. UNOCHA. https://www.humanitarianresponse.info

Logistics Operational Guide (LOG). Logistics Cluster. http://dlca.logcluster.org

Oxfam Market Systems and Scenarios for CTP – RAG Model 2013. Logistics Cluster. www.logcluster.org

Toolkit for Logistics in C&V. Logistics Cluster. www.logcluster.org

Further reading
For further reading suggestions please go to www.spherestandards.org/handbook/online-resources

The
Humanitarian
Charter

The Humanitarian Charter

The Humanitarian Charter provides the ethical and legal backdrop to the Protection Principles, the Core Humanitarian Standard and the Minimum Standards that follow in the Handbook. It is in part a statement of established legal rights and obligations, in part a statement of shared belief.

In terms of legal rights and obligations, the Humanitarian Charter summarises the core legal principles that have most bearing on the welfare of those affected by disaster or conflict. With regard to shared belief, it attempts to capture a consensus among humanitarian agencies on the principles which should govern the response to disaster or conflict, including the roles and responsibilities of the various actors involved.

The Humanitarian Charter forms the basis of a commitment by humanitarian agencies that endorse Sphere and an invitation to all those who engage in humanitarian action to adopt the same principles.

Our beliefs

1. The Humanitarian Charter expresses our shared conviction as humanitarian agencies that all people affected by disaster or conflict have a right to receive protection and assistance to ensure the basic conditions for life with dignity. We believe that the principles described in this Humanitarian Charter are universal, applying to all those affected by disaster or conflict, wherever they may be, and to all those who seek to assist them or provide for their security. These principles are reflected in international law, but derive their force ultimately from the fundamental moral principle of **humanity**: that all human beings are born free and equal in dignity and rights. Based on this principle, we affirm the primacy of the **humanitarian imperative**: that action should be taken to prevent or alleviate human suffering arising out of disaster or conflict, and that nothing should override this principle.

As local, national and international humanitarian agencies, we commit to promoting and adhering to the principles in this Charter and to meeting Minimum Standards in our efforts to assist and protect those affected. We invite all those who engage in humanitarian activities, including governmental and private sector actors, to endorse the common principles, rights and duties set out below as a statement of shared humanitarian belief.

Our role

2. We acknowledge that it is firstly through their own efforts, and through the support of community and local institutions, that the basic needs of people affected by disaster or conflict are met. We recognise the primary role and responsibility of the affected state to provide timely assistance to those affected, to

ensure people's protection and security and to provide support for their recovery. We believe that a combination of official and voluntary action is crucial to effective prevention and response, and in this regard National Societies of the Red Cross and Red Crescent Movement and other civil society actors have an essential role to play in supporting public authorities. Where national capacity is insufficient, we affirm the role of the wider international community, including governmental donors and regional organisations, in assisting states to fulfil their responsibilities. We recognise and support the special roles played by the mandated agencies of the United Nations and the International Committee of the Red Cross.

3. As humanitarian agencies, we interpret our role in relation to the needs and capacities of affected populations and the responsibilities of their governments or controlling powers. Our role in providing assistance reflects the reality that those with primary responsibility are not always fully able to perform this role themselves, or may be unwilling to do so. As far as possible, consistent with meeting the humanitarian imperative and other principles set out in this Charter, we will support the efforts of the relevant authorities to protect and assist those affected. We call upon all state and non-state actors to respect the impartial, independent and non-partisan role of humanitarian agencies and to facilitate their work by removing unnecessary legal and practical barriers, providing for their safety and allowing them timely and consistent access to affected populations.

Common principles, rights and duties

4. We offer our services as humanitarian agencies on the basis of the principle of humanity and the humanitarian imperative, recognising the rights of all people affected by disaster or conflict – women and men, boys and girls. These include the rights to protection and assistance reflected in the provisions of international humanitarian law, human rights and refugee law. For the purposes of this Charter, we summarise these rights as follows:

- **the right to life with dignity;**
- **the right to receive humanitarian assistance; and**
- **the right to protection and security.**

While these rights are not formulated in such terms in international law, they encapsulate a range of established legal rights and give fuller substance to the humanitarian imperative.

5. The **right to life with dignity** is reflected in the provisions of international law, and specifically the human rights measures concerning the right to life, to an adequate standard of living and to freedom from torture or cruel, inhuman or degrading treatment or punishment. The right to life entails the duty to preserve life where it is threatened. Implicit in this is the duty not to withhold or frustrate the provision of life-saving assistance. Dignity entails more than physical well-being; it demands respect for the whole person, including the values and beliefs of individuals and affected communities, and respect for their human rights, including liberty, freedom of conscience and religious observance.

6. The **right to receive humanitarian assistance** is a necessary element of the right to life with dignity. This encompasses the right to an adequate standard of living, including adequate food, water, clothing, shelter and the requirements for good health, which are expressly guaranteed in international law. The Core Humanitarian Standard and the Minimum Standards reflect these rights and give practical expression to them, specifically in relation to the provision of assistance to those affected by disaster or conflict. Where the state or non-state actors are not providing such assistance themselves, we believe they must allow others to help do so. Any such assistance must be provided according to the principle of **impartiality**, which requires that it be provided solely on the basis of need and in proportion to need. This reflects the wider principle of **non-discrimination**: that no one should be discriminated against on any grounds of status, including age, gender, race, colour, ethnicity, sexual orientation, language, religion, disability, health status, political or other opinion, and national or social origin.

7. The **right to protection and security** is rooted in the provisions of international law, in resolutions of the United Nations and other intergovernmental organisations, and in the sovereign responsibility of states to protect all those within their jurisdiction. The safety and security are of particular humanitarian concern, including the protection of refugees and internally displaced persons. As the law recognises, some people may be particularly vulnerable to abuse and adverse discrimination due to their status, for example their age, gender or race, and may require special measures of protection and assistance. To the extent that a state lacks the capacity to protect people in these circumstances, we believe it must seek international assistance to do so.

The law relating to the protection of civilians and displaced people demands particular attention here:

i. During **armed conflict** as defined in international humanitarian law, specific legal provision is made for protection and assistance to be given to those not engaged in the conflict. In particular, the 1949 Geneva Conventions and the Additional Protocols of 1977 impose obligations on the parties to both international and non-international armed conflicts. We stress the general immunity of the civilian population from attack and reprisals, and in particular the importance of:

    - the principle of **distinction** between civilians and combatants, and between civilian objects and military objectives;
    - the principles of **proportionality** in the use of force and **precaution** in attack;
    - the duty to refrain from the use of weapons that are indiscriminate or that, by their nature, cause superfluous injury or unnecessary suffering; and
    - the duty to permit impartial relief to be provided.

    Much of the avoidable suffering caused to civilians in armed conflicts stems from a failure to observe these basic principles.

ii.   The **right to seek asylum or sanctuary** remains vital to the protection
       of those facing persecution or violence. Those affected by disaster or
       conflict are often forced to flee their homes in search of security and the
       means of subsistence. The provisions of the 1951 Convention Relating to
       the Status of Refugees (as amended) and other international and regional
       treaties provide fundamental safeguards for those unable to secure
       protection from the state of their nationality or residence who are forced
       to seek safety in another country. Chief among these is the principle of
       non-refoulement: the principle that no one shall be sent back to a country
       where their life, freedom or physical security would be threatened or
       where they are likely to face torture or other cruel, inhuman or degrading
       treatment or punishment. The same principle applies by extension to
       internally displaced persons, as reflected in international human rights law
       and elaborated in the 1998 Guiding Principles on Internal Displacement and
       related regional and national law.

Our commitment

8. We offer our services in the belief that the affected population is at the centre
of humanitarian action, and recognise that their active participation is essential to
providing assistance in ways that best meet their needs, including those of vulnerable and socially excluded people. We will endeavour to support local efforts to
prevent, prepare for and respond to disaster and to the effects of conflict, and to
reinforce the capacities of local actors at all levels.

9. We are aware that attempts to provide humanitarian assistance may sometimes
have unintended adverse effects. In collaboration with affected communities and
authorities, we aim to minimise any negative effects of humanitarian action on the
local community or on the environment. With respect to armed conflict, we recognise that the way in which humanitarian assistance is provided may potentially
render civilians more vulnerable to attack, or may on occasion bring unintended
advantage to one or more of the parties to the conflict. We are committed to
minimising any such adverse effects, in so far as this is consistent with the
principles outlined above.

10. We will act in accordance with the principles of humanitarian action set out
in this Charter and with the specific guidance in the Code of Conduct for the
International Red Cross and Red Crescent Movement and Non-Governmental
Organisations (NGOs) in Disaster Relief (1994).

11. The Core Humanitarian Standard and the Minimum Standards give practical substance to the common principles in this Charter, based on agencies'
understanding of the basic minimum requirements for life with dignity and their
experience of providing humanitarian assistance. Though the achievement of
the standards depends on a range of factors, many of which may be beyond our
control, we commit ourselves to attempting consistently to achieve them and we
expect to be held to account accordingly. We invite all parties, including affected
and donor governments, international organisations, and private and non-state

actors, to adopt the Core Humanitarian Standard and the Minimum Standards as accepted norms.

12. By adhering to the Core Humanitarian Standard and the Minimum Standards, we commit to making every effort to ensure that people affected by disasters or conflict have access to at least the minimum requirements for life with dignity and security, including adequate water, sanitation, food, nutrition, shelter and healthcare. To this end, we will continue to advocate that states and other parties meet their moral and legal obligations towards affected populations. For our part, we undertake to make our responses more effective, appropriate and accountable through sound assessment and monitoring of the evolving local context, through transparency of information and decision-making, and through more effective coordination and collaboration with other relevant actors at all levels, as detailed in the Core Humanitarian Standard and the Minimum Standards. In particular, we commit to working in partnership with affected populations, emphasising their active participation in the response. We acknowledge that our fundamental accountability must be to those we seek to assist.

Protection
Principles

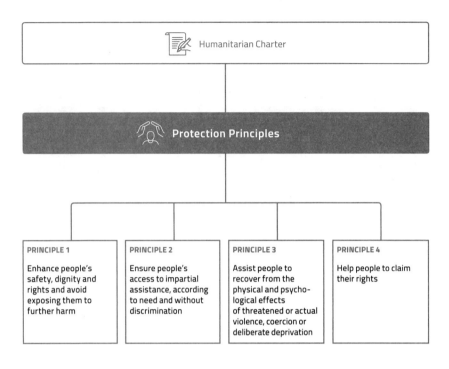

Humanitarian Charter

Protection Principles

PRINCIPLE 1	PRINCIPLE 2	PRINCIPLE 3	PRINCIPLE 4
Enhance people's safety, dignity and rights and avoid exposing them to further harm	Ensure people's access to impartial assistance, according to need and without discrimination	Assist people to recover from the physical and psycho-logical effects of threatened or actual violence, coercion or deliberate deprivation	Help people to claim their rights

APPENDIX Summary of Professional Standards for Protection Work

Contents

Protection Principles

Four Protection Principles apply to all humanitarian action and all humanitarian actors.

1. Enhance the safety, dignity and rights of people, and avoid exposing them to harm.
2. Ensure people's access to assistance according to need and without discrimination.
3. Assist people to recover from the physical and psychological effects of threatened or actual violence, coercion or deliberate deprivation.
4. Help people claim their rights.

The Protection Principles support the rights set out in the Humanitarian Charter: the right to life with dignity, the right to humanitarian assistance and the right to protection and security. The Principles articulate the role that all humanitarian actors can play in helping protect people. The roles and responsibilities of humanitarian actors are, however, secondary to those of the state. The state or other authorities hold legal responsibility for the welfare of people within their territory or control and for the safety of civilians in armed conflict. Ultimately, it is these authorities that have the duty to ensure people's security and safety through action or restraint. The role of humanitarian actors may be to encourage and persuade the authorities to fulfil their responsibilities and, if they fail to do so, assist people in dealing with the consequences.

This chapter provides guidance on how humanitarian organisations can contribute to protection by helping people stay safe, access assistance, recover from violence and claim their rights.

Protection is concerned with the safety, dignity and rights of people affected by disaster or armed conflict. The Inter-Agency Standing Committee (IASC) defines protection as:

"... all activities aimed at obtaining full respect for the rights of the individual in accordance with the letter and the spirit of the relevant bodies of law (i.e. international human rights law, international humanitarian law, international refugee law)."

In a broad sense, protection encompasses all efforts pursued by humanitarian and human rights actors to ensure that the rights of affected persons and the obligations of duty bearers under international law are understood, respected, protected and fulfilled without discrimination.

Protection is about taking action to keep people safe from violence, coercion and deliberate deprivation. There is often a priority set of protection concerns affecting whole communities in any given humanitarian context, where concerted action is essential if these are to be effectively tackled. For a humanitarian response to be protection-oriented, it is vital to understand and address the key risks to those affected, including serious harm arising from the failure to respect international humanitarian, refugee or human rights law.

Putting the Principles into practice

Anyone applying the Sphere Minimum Standards should be guided by the Protection Principles, even if they do not have a distinct protection mandate or specialised capacity in protection. This includes understanding the context and taking steps to prevent, limit or end violations and risks to people's safety. Providing information and supporting the ability of people to make informed decisions about their own situation and recovery is essential.

Specialised protection actors should fulfil these Principles in addition to meeting specific complementary standards. Specialised protection actors carry out stand-alone work focusing on specific areas of concern such as:

- child protection;
- gender-based violence;
- housing, land and property rights;
- mine action;
- rule of law and justice;
- legal counselling;
- human rights advocates and defenders;
- internally displaced populations; and
- refugee rights.

⊕ *See References* and *Appendix: Professional Standards for Protection Work*, which cover family tracing, renewal of documents, data protection and other areas.

Protection activities

Protection-related activities can be preventive, responsive, remedial and environment-building. Upholding the Protection Principles requires a combination of these activities.

- **Preventive:** Preventing threats to safety, dignity or rights from occurring, or reducing exposure or vulnerability to these threats.
- **Responsive:** Stopping ongoing violations or abuse by immediate response to incidents of violence, coercion and deprivation.
- **Remedial:** Providing remedies for ongoing or past abuses by offering healthcare (including psychosocial support), legal assistance or other support, to help people restore their dignity.
- **Environment-building:** Contributing to a policy, social, cultural, institutional and legal environment that supports the full respect of the rights of the affected population. This includes encouraging respect for rights in accordance with international law.

Advocacy, whether public or private, is common to all four activity types. Where threats to the affected population come from deliberate decisions, actions or policies, humanitarian or human rights organisations should advocate for changes to decisions, actions or policies that threaten the rights of the affected population. This may include influencing or changing the behaviour of a person or organisation that poses a threat, as well as seeking change in discriminatory policies or legal frameworks. It may also include supporting people's own efforts to stay safe and reducing people's exposure to risk.

Protection Principle 1:
Enhance people's safety, dignity and rights and avoid exposing them to further harm

Humanitarian actors take steps to reduce overall risks and vulnerability of people, including to the potentially negative effects of humanitarian programmes.

This Principle includes:

- Understanding protection risks in context;
- Providing assistance that reduces risks that people may face in meeting their needs with dignity;
- Providing assistance in an environment that does not further expose people to physical hazards, violence or abuse; and
- Supporting the capacity of people to protect themselves.

Central to this principle is the importance of avoiding negative effects caused by humanitarian programming ⊕ *see Core Humanitarian Standard Commitment 3.*

....

Guidance notes

Context analysis: Understand the context and anticipate the consequences of humanitarian action that may affect the safety, dignity and rights of the affected population. Work with partners and groups of affected women, men, boys and girls to do regular risk analysis as the situation changes over time.

The following list is not exhaustive but can form a basis for such an analysis:

- What are the protection threats, risks and vulnerabilities across the whole population? What capacities does the population have to minimise those?
- Are there groups that face specific risks? Why? Consider, for example, ethnicity, caste, class, gender, sex, age, disability or sexual orientation.
- Are there obstacles preventing people from accessing assistance or participating in decisions? These may include security, social or physical barriers, or how information is provided.
- What are local communities doing to protect themselves? How can humanitarian organisations support and not undermine these efforts? Are there risks to people protecting themselves?
- Are people engaged in negative coping mechanisms such as transactional sex, early marriage, child labour or risky migration? What can be done to mitigate the underlying vulnerabilities?

- Are humanitarian activities having unintended negative consequences, such as putting people at risk at distribution points or causing division within the community or with host communities? What can be done to reduce this risk?
- Are there punitive laws that pose a protection risk, such as mandatory testing for HIV, criminalisation of same-sex relationships, or other?

Set up and maintain information exchange and accountability mechanisms with communities, including those at risk, to identify and address protection issues.

Avoid becoming complicit in violations of people's rights through activities that give legitimacy to the policies and practices that cause the problem. Examples may include activities that enable the forced relocation of populations for political or military reasons, or indirectly increasing conflict through careless choice of partners or commercial contractors. This analysis may involve difficult choices and decisions, but it should be explicitly considered and reviewed as circumstances change.

Humanitarian assistance: The way that assistance is provided, and the environment in which it is provided, can make people more vulnerable to harm, violence or coercion.

- Provide assistance in the safest possible environment and actively look for ways to minimise threats and vulnerabilities. For instance, provide education and healthcare in locations that all people can safely access ⊕ *see INEE Handbook*.
- Take all reasonable steps when providing and managing assistance to protect people from physical and sexual assault. For example, valuable commodities or cash-based assistance can be subject to looting, putting recipients at risk of harm.
- Help people find safe options for meeting basic needs in a way that reduces exposure to risks. For example, provide fuel alternatives that reduce the need to collect firewood in dangerous environments.
- Design activities that protect girls and boys, and do not create additional risks, such as child recruitment, abduction or separation from family ⊕ *see CPMS Handbook*.
- Coordinate with government authorities and specialised organisations on the removal of landmines and unexploded ordnance from areas where assistance is provided ⊕ *see International Mine Action Standards*.
- Consider any unintended impact on the environment that could affect people's safety, dignity and rights.
- Consult with different parts of the community, including at-risk groups and organisations they trust, to understand the best way to provide assistance. For example, work with persons with disabilities to determine how to provide assistance. There should be no additional risks to their well-being or to the well-being of the people they trust to receive assistance on their behalf.

Community protection mechanisms: Understand the means by which people try to protect themselves, their families and communities. Support community-led self-help initiatives. Humanitarian interventions should not compromise people's capacity to protect themselves and others.

Sensitive information: Ensure that people are not put at risk as a result of the way that humanitarian actors record and share information. Establish a policy on collecting and referring sensitive information. It should define the circum-stances under which information may be referred and respect the principle of informed consent. Failure to do so may compromise the safety of survivors and of staff.

Protection Principle 2:
Ensure people's access to impartial assistance, according to need and without discrimination
Humanitarian actors identify obstacles to accessing assistance and take steps to ensure it is provided in proportion to need and without discrimination.

This Principle includes:

- Challenging any actions that deliberately deprive people of their basic needs, using humanitarian principles and relevant law ⊕ *see Humanitarian Charter*;
- Ensuring people receive support on the basis of need, and that they are not discriminated against on any other grounds; and
- Ensuring access to assistance for all parts of the affected population.

Central to this principle is the idea that communities should have access to the humanitarian assistance they need ⊕ *see Core Humanitarian Standard Commitment 2.*

Guidance notes

Impartiality: Prioritise assistance on the basis of need alone and provide assis-tance in proportion to need. This is the principle of impartiality affirmed in the Code of Conduct for the International Red Cross and Red Crescent Movement and NGOs in Disaster Relief ⊕ *see Annex 2* and *Humanitarian Charter.* Humanitarian organ-isations should not focus uniquely on a particular group (for example, displaced people in a campsite or specific minority groups) if this focus is to the detriment of another group in the affected population that is in need.

Right to receive humanitarian assistance: Advocate for the right of people affected by crisis to receive humanitarian assistance. Where people are unable to meet their basic needs and the relevant authorities are unable to provide assistance, the authorities should not deny access to impartial humanitarian organisations.

Such denial may violate international law, particularly in situations of armed conflict. People affected by crisis do not need to have a special legal status in order to receive humanitarian assistance and protection.

Authorities should not deny the existence of humanitarian needs or use bureaucratic barriers to restrict movement of humanitarian workers.

Barriers to access: Monitor people's access to humanitarian assistance to identify and understand any barriers they may face. Take steps to address these where possible.

- Consider barriers that reduce people's freedom of movement or their physical access to humanitarian assistance. This includes blockades, landmines and checkpoints. In armed conflict, parties may establish checkpoints, but these should not discriminate between categories of affected people or unduly hinder people's access to humanitarian assistance.
- Address barriers that may restrict access by some groups and individuals, resulting in inequitable assistance. Barriers may lead to discrimination against women and children, older people, persons with disabilities or minorities. They may also prevent people accessing assistance on the basis of ethnic, religious, political, sexual orientation, gender identity, language or other considerations.
- Provide information, in accessible formats and languages, about entitlements and feedback mechanisms. Promote outreach with "hidden" at-risk groups, such as persons with disabilities, children living on the streets, or those living in less accessible regions, to facilitate their safe access to assistance.

Protection Principle 3:
Assist people to recover from the physical and psychological effects of threatened or actual violence, coercion or deliberate deprivation

Humanitarian actors provide immediate and sustained support to those harmed by violations, including referral to additional services as appropriate.

This Principle includes:

- Referring survivors to relevant support services;
- Taking all reasonable steps to ensure that the affected population is not subject to further violence, coercion or deprivation; and
- Supporting people's own efforts to recover their dignity and rights within their communities and be safe.

Central to this Principle is the idea that communities and people affected by crisis receive coordinated, complementary assistance ⊕ *see Core Humanitarian Standard Commitment 6.*

Guidance notes

Referrals: Be aware of the existing referral systems and help people affected by violence to safely access appropriate services. Some people may not seek assistance after a violation. Take steps to understand the barriers that stop people from seeking assistance and adapt the referral system accordingly.

Support survivors of physical or gender-based violence to access services such as healthcare, police assistance, mental health and psychosocial support, and other services. These services should be sensitive to the people's sex, age, disability, sexual orientation and other relevant factors ⊕ *see Guidelines for Integrating Gender-based Violence Interventions in Humanitarian Action.*

Set up and use safe and effective referral mechanisms to child protection services that support children who are survivors of violence, exploitation, abuse and neglect.

Community action: Support community action and self-help activities that help to restore people's sense of agency and improve their protection.

Support family, community and individual response mechanisms of protection, and mental health and psychosocial support. This can include creating opportunities where people can discuss their situation, choose particular protection threats to be addressed, and develop and implement steps for addressing them.

Help local groups such as youth groups, women's groups or religious groups to implement non-violent means of self-protection, and support vulnerable people.

Wherever possible, keep families together, including non-traditional families, and enable people from a particular village or support network to live in the same area.

Support positive communal coping mechanisms such as culturally appropriate burials, religious ceremonies and practices, and non-harmful cultural and social practices.

Ongoing violations, monitoring and reporting: Be aware of mechanisms to report on human rights violations and follow the procedures and policies in place for safe sharing of sensitive information ⊕ *see Protection Principle 1* and *Appendix: Professional Standards for Protection Work.*

Ongoing violations must also be considered and addressed with partners and specialised agencies. The primary responsibility to protect people resides with the government and other relevant authorities. Work with specialised agencies to identify those parties who have the legal responsibility or capacity to provide protection and remind them of their obligations.

Security and law enforcement agencies, police, and military and peacekeeping forces play an important role in ensuring the physical security of people. When appropriate and safe to do so, alert police or law enforcement or military actors to violations of human rights.

During armed conflict, consider monitoring the institutions that provide essential services and are specifically protected under international humanitarian law, such as schools and hospitals, and reporting any attacks on them. Make specific efforts to reduce the risks and threats of abductions or forced recruitment that may happen in these locations.

Managing sensitive information: Humanitarian organisations should have clear policies and procedures to guide staff on how to respond if they become aware of or witness abuses, and on how to make referrals to specialists or specialised agencies. The confidentiality of the information should be explained in those policies.

Evidence such as witness statements, population profiles and images that allow people to be identified may be highly sensitive and can put people at risk. Sensitive information on specific abuses or violations should be collected by specialised agencies with the necessary skills, systems, capacity and protocols in place ⊕ *see Appendix: Professional Standards for Protection Work.*

Protection Principle 4:
Help people to claim their rights
Humanitarian actors help affected communities claim their rights through information and documentation, and support efforts to strengthen respect for rights.

This Principle includes:

- Supporting people to assert their rights and to access remedies from government or other sources;
- Assisting people to secure the documentation they need to demonstrate their entitlements; and
- Advocating for full respect of people's rights and international law, contributing to a stronger protective environment.

Central to this Principle is that people affected by crisis should know their rights and entitlements ⊕ *see Core Humanitarian Standard Commitment 4.*

....

Guidance notes

Accessible information: Provide education and information that enable people to understand and advocate for their rights. Inform people of their entitlements, for example in relation to return and resettlement options. Work with specialised organisations providing legal aid to inform people of their rights under the laws and regulations of the country.

Provide information in languages that affected people can understand. Use multiple formats (such as written, graphic or audio) to make information as widely accessible as possible. Test message comprehension with different groups, considering variations in age, gender, education level and mother tongue.

Documentation: People generally have rights, regardless of whether they possess particular documentation. However, without some form of documentation such as a birth certificate, marriage certificate, death certificate, passport, land title or education certificate, people may face barriers to accessing their rights or entitlements. Refer them to agencies that can provide or replace these documents.

Legal documentation recognised by the relevant authorities should not be confused with documents issued by humanitarian organisations, such as ration cards or registration documents. Documentation issued by authorities should not determine who is eligible for assistance from humanitarian organisations.

Access to legal support and justice systems: People are entitled to seek legal and other redress from the government and relevant authorities for violations of their rights. This can include compensation for loss or restitution of property. People are also entitled to expect that the perpetrators of violations will be brought to justice.

Assist those who choose legal remedies to access justice mechanisms in a safe manner. Effective referral requires an understanding of which agencies can provide legal support.

Avoid promoting access to justice in situations where the judicial process might cause further harm to victims. For instance, healthcare providers and gender-based violence referral networks should be aware of the national medico-legal system and the relevant laws on sexual violence. Inform survivors about any mandatory reporting laws that could limit the confidentiality of the information patients disclose. This may influence the survivor's decision to continue care or reporting, but must be respected ⊕ *see Health: Sexual and reproductive health standard 2.3.2.*

During crises, affected communities may be able to use alternative and informal dispute-resolution mechanisms, such as community-level mediation. Where these exist, inform people and explain how they can access the services.

Land access and ownership can be major points of contention. Encourage authorities and communities to work together to resolve issues relating to access or ownership of land.

Appendix
Summary of Professional Standards for Protection Work

In armed conflict or other situations of violence, the protection of civilians who may be exposed to harm and suffering is critical. An effective protection response requires professional competence and adherence to commonly agreed professional Minimum Standards that are applicable to all protection actors.

The Professional Standards for Protection Work were established to create a shared basis for protection work among humanitarian and human rights actors, and to maximise the effectiveness of that work for the affected population. They complement the Protection Principles.

The standards reflect the view that people must be at the centre of action taken on their behalf. People have a meaningful role to play in analysing, developing and monitoring protection responses to the threats and risks they face. Beyond improving people's physical security, protection efforts should promote respect of the rights, dignity and integrity of those at risk or subject to violations and abuse.

The range of activities implemented by humanitarian actors varies greatly, and it is essential for all actors to integrate protection concerns into their practice in line with the Protection Principles. The Professional Standards are primarily intended for protection professionals and organisations implementing dedicated protection work in armed conflict and other situations of violence.

The professional standards offer organisations a solid basis from which to review and develop internal policies, guidelines and training materials. They offer a practical reference for practitioners who design and implement protection strategies at field level. They can also serve as a source of inspiration. They are a useful reference point to help other actors and stakeholders understand how specialised protection actors safely implement activities to enhance the protection of individuals and communities.

These standards do not seek to regulate protection work or restrict diversity, but rather complement other professional principles and encourage protection actors to integrate them into their own practices, guidelines and training.

The 2018 Professional Standards are organised as follows:

1. Overarching principles in protection work
2. Managing protection strategies
3. Outlining the protection architecture
4. Building on the legal base of protection
5. Promoting complementarity
6. Managing data and information for protection outcomes
7. Ensuring professional capacities

The standards include a view on the implications of information and communication technology (ICT) and the growing body of law on data protection, with specific guidance on protection information management.

Dialogue and interaction between humanitarian and human rights actors and United Nations peacekeeping operations and other internationally mandated military and police forces are often necessary to secure protection outcomes. The Professional Standards provide guidance on upholding a principled approach in these interactions.

National, regional and international efforts to tackle "violent extremism" through counter-terrorism legislation are also addressed in the Professional Standards, clarifying how this kind of legislation may affect the activities of protection actors.

Download the Professional Standards for Protection Work from the International Committee of the Red Cross (ICRC) e-Book store:
https://shop.icrc.org/e-books/icrc-activities-ebook.html.

References and further reading

General protection: background and tools
Minimum Agency Standards for Incorporating Protection into Humanitarian Response – Field Testing Version. Caritas Australia, CARE Australia, Oxfam Australia and World Vision Australia, 2008. http://sitap.org

Policy on Protection in Humanitarian Action. IASC, 2016. www.interagencystanding-committee.org

Professional Standards for Protection Work Carried Out by Humanitarian and Human Rights Actors in Armed Conflict and Other Situations of Violence. ICRC, 2018. https://shop.icrc.org

Gender-based violence
Guidelines for Integrating Gender-based Violence Interventions in Humanitarian Action: Reducing risk, promoting resilience, and aiding recovery. IASC, 2015. gbvguidelines.org

Housing, land and property rights
Principles on Housing and Property Restitution for Refugees and Displaced Persons. OHCHR, 2005. www.unhcr.org

Internally displaced persons
Handbook for the Protection of Internally Displaced Persons. Global Protection Cluster, 2010. www.globalprotectioncluster.org

Mental health and psychosocial support
IASC Guidelines on Mental Health and Psychosocial Support in Emergency Settings. IASC, 2007. https://interagencystandingcommittee.org

Mine action
International Mine Action Standards. www.mineactionstandards.org

Older persons and persons with disabilities
Humanitarian Inclusion Standards for Older People and People with Disabilities. Age and Disability Consortium as part of the ADCAP programme. HelpAge, 2018. www.helpage.org

Children and child protection
INEE Minimum Standards for Education: Preparedness, Response, Recovery. INEE, 2010. www.ineesite.org/en/minimum-standards

Minimum Standards for Child Protection in Humanitarian Action: Alliance for Child Protection in Humanitarian Action, 2012. http://cpwg.net

Further reading
For further reading suggestions please go to
www.spherestandards.org/handbook/online-resources

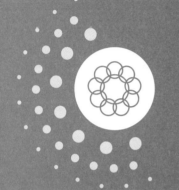

Core
Humanitarian
Standard

The Humanitarian Charter and Protection Principles directly support the Core Humanitarian Standard. Together, these three chapters constitute the principles and foundations of the Sphere standards.

The Core Humanitarian Standard (Figure 2)

APPENDIX: Guiding questions for monitoring Key actions and Organisational requirements (online)

Contents

One core standard with nine commitments

Many organisations and individuals are typically involved in a humanitarian response. Some common elements and ways of working are therefore useful for promoting an effective response. Without a common approach, outcomes may be inconsistent and unpredictable.

The Core Humanitarian Standard on Quality and Accountability (CHS) sets out nine Commitments that organisations and individuals involved in humanitarian response can use to improve the quality and effectiveness of the assistance they provide. It also facilitates greater accountability to communities and people affected by crisis, staff, donors, governments and other stakeholders. Knowing what humanitarian organisations have committed to will enable them to hold those organisations to account. It is a voluntary framework for both individuals and organisations.

The Standard applies both at the response and programme levels and in all phases of a response. However, the nine Commitments are not intended to correspond to any particular phase of the programme cycle. Some are more relevant to a certain phase of the cycle, while others, such as communication with affected people, are intended to apply throughout all phases.

The Core Humanitarian Standard, along with the Humanitarian Charter and Protection Principles, forms a strong foundation within The Sphere Handbook and supports all technical standards. Throughout the Handbook, there are cross-references between the technical chapters and these foundations.

More detailed information on the Core Humanitarian Standard, including resources to help users apply it in practice, can be found at corehumanitarian-standard.org.

A unique structure

The Core Humanitarian Standard was developed through a collective effort by the humanitarian sector to harmonise the core standards from Sphere, the Humanitarian Accountability Partnership (HAP), People In Aid, and Groupe URD into a single framework. It is now managed on behalf of the sector by Sphere, the CHS Alliance and Groupe URD, who jointly hold the copyright.

Each of the nine commitments concentrates on a specific aspect of response. Taken together, they form a solid approach to effective and accountable humanitarian action.

The structure of the Core Humanitarian Standard differs slightly from that of the other Sphere standards:

- The **Commitment** states what communities and people affected by crisis can expect from organisations and individuals delivering humanitarian assistance.
- **The Quality criterion** describes a situation where the Commitment is met and how humanitarian organisation and staff should be working to meet the Commitment.
- **Performance indicators** measure progress in meeting the Commitment, drive learning and improvement and allow for comparison across time and location.
- **Key actions** and **Organisational responsibilities** describe what staff should deliver and the policies, processes and systems that organisations need to have in place to ensure their staff provide high-quality, accountable humanitarian assistance.
- **Guidance notes** support the Key actions and Organisational responsibilities with examples and additional information.
- **Guiding questions** support planning, evaluation and review activities ⊕ *see Appendix 1 (available online).*
- **References** provide additional learning on specific issues.

The following chart shows how the Core Humanitarian Standard can be used at different levels. Sphere, Groupe URD and the CHS Alliance propose complementary tools which can be found at corehumanitarianstandard.org.

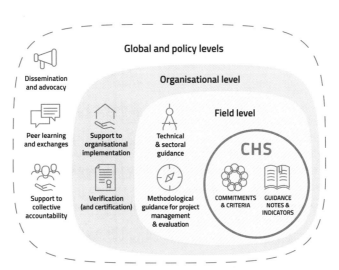

Using the Core Humanitarian Standard (Figure 3)

Commitment 1

Communities and people affected by crisis receive assistance appropriate to their needs.

Quality criterion
Humanitarian response is appropriate and relevant.

Performance indicators

1. Communities and people affected by crisis consider that the response takes account of their specific needs, culture, and preferences.
2. The assistance and protection provided correspond with assessed risks, vulnerabilities and needs.
3. The response takes account of the capacities, skills and knowledge of people requiring assistance and protection.

Key actions

1.1 Conduct a systematic, objective and ongoing analysis of the context and stakeholders.

- Assess the role and capacity of local government and other political and non-political actors, as well as the impact of the crisis on them.
- Assess existing local capacities (material, human, markets) to meet priority assistance and protection needs, understanding that these will change over time.
- Cross-check and verify information, acknowledging that assessment data will initially be imperfect, but should not impede life-saving actions.
- Assess the safety and security of affected, displaced and host populations to identify threats of violence and any forms of coercion, denial of subsistence or denial of basic human rights.
- Assess gender-related and power dynamics, as well as social marginalisation, to define a more effective and sustainable response.
- Coordinate with others to avoid burdening communities with multiple assessments. Joint assessments and findings should be shared with interested agencies, government and affected populations.

1.2 Design and implement appropriate programmes based on an impartial assessment of needs and risks and an understanding of the vulnerabilities and capacities of different groups.

- Assess the protection and assistance needs of women, men, children and adolescents, of those in hard-to-reach locations and at-risk groups such as persons with disabilities, older people, socially isolated individuals, female-headed households, ethnic or linguistic minorities and stigmatised groups (for example, people living with HIV).

1.3 **Adapt programmes to changing needs, capacities and context.**

- Monitor the political situation and adapt stakeholder analysis and security.
- Monitor epidemiological and other data regularly to inform ongoing decision-making and prioritise life-saving interventions.
- Remain flexible enough to redesign any intervention in response to changing needs. Confirm that donors agree with programme changes as needed.

Organisational responsibilities

1.4 **Policies commit to providing impartial assistance based on the needs and capacities of communities and people affected by crisis.**

- Organisations maintain policies, processes and systems that support a commitment to humanitarian principles and inclusiveness.
- All staff understand their responsibilities and how they may be held to account.
- Organisations share these policies transparently with other stakeholders.

1.5 **Policies set out commitments which take into account the diversity of communities, including disadvantaged or marginalised people, and to collect disaggregated data.**

- Required levels of data disaggregation for assessment and reporting are clearly outlined.

1.6 **Processes are in place to ensure an appropriate ongoing analysis of the context.**

- Humanitarian workers have management support to acquire the knowledge, skills, behaviours and attitudes necessary to manage and carry out assessments.

Guidance notes

Assessment and analysis is a process, not a single event. As time allows, in-depth analysis should be carried out. The capacities and needs of affected people and communities should not be assumed but identified through assessments that engage them in an ongoing discussion to find appropriate responses.

Consider providing basic training in psychological first aid for staff involved in assessments. This can help the staff manage people who become distressed during an assessment.

Ensure specialised assessments for groups potentially facing protection risks. Specific assessments with women, men, boys and girls to understand their exposure to violence, discrimination and other harms are an example.

Impartial assessment: Acting impartially does not mean treating all people the same. Providing rights-based assistance requires an understanding of differing capacities, needs and vulnerabilities. People may be vulnerable because of discrimination based on individual factors such as age, sex, disability, health status, sexual orientation or gender identity, or because they are caring for others who are vulnerable.

Vulnerability: Social and contextual factors also contribute to people's vulnerability. These include discrimination and marginalisation, social isolation, environmental degradation, climate variability, poverty, lack of land tenure, poor governance, ethnicity, class, caste and religious or political affiliations.

Existing capacity: People, communities, organisations and authorities affected by crisis already possess relevant skills, knowledge and capacity to cope with, respond to and recover from crises. To uphold the right to life with dignity, actively engage affected people in decisions that affect them. Targeted efforts may need to be undertaken to strengthen participation of typically under-represented groups, such as women, children, older people, people with disabilities, and linguistic or ethnic minorities.

Data disaggregation: This is important to understand the impact of actions or events on different groups. At a minimum, good practice encourages disaggregation by sex, age and disability. Additional factors should be based on context.

Analysis of disaggregated data is necessary to using standards in context and to monitoring. Good use of disaggregated data can show who has been most affected, who is able to access assistance and where more needs to be done to reach an at-risk population ⊕ *see What is Sphere?*.

Ongoing analysis and effective use of the data: Human resources systems should be flexible enough to recruit and deploy assessment teams rapidly. Allocate programme budgets and resources according to need. Funding should support ongoing analysis of assistance and protection needs and the adaptation and correction of programmes, including measures to facilitate access (such as outreach mechanisms, accessibility of facilities and communication).

Commitment 2
Communities and people affected by crisis have access to the humanitarian assistance they need at the right time.

Quality criterion
Humanitarian response is effective and timely.

Performance indicators

1. Communities and people affected by crisis, including the most vulnerable groups, consider that the timing of the assistance and protection they receive is adequate.

2. Communities and people affected by crisis consider that the response meets their needs.
3. Monitoring and evaluation reports show that the humanitarian response meets its objectives in terms of timing, quality and quantity.

Key actions

2.1 ⟩ Design programmes that address constraints so that the proposed action is realistic and safe for communities.

- Clearly identify and state any limitations if it is not possible to assess and meet the needs of a specific area or population group, including hard-to-reach locations.
- Prioritise support to local response capacity in advance where contingency planning shows areas or populations are vulnerable and may prove hard to access in the future.

2.2 ⟩ Deliver humanitarian response in a timely manner, making decisions and acting without unnecessary delay.

- Be aware of living conditions, cultural practices, seasons, agricultural calendars and other factors that influence providing the right services at the right time.
- Include time frames for delivery and monitoring systems in programme plans; anticipate and flag delays.
- Acknowledge that decisions will be made based on imperfect knowledge in the early stages of an acute crisis and refine decisions as information becomes available.
- Coordinate with others to develop shared strategies to address collective issues that block timely assistance.

2.3 ⟩ Refer any unmet needs to those organisations with the relevant technical expertise and mandate, or advocate for those needs to be addressed.

- This includes unmet information needs as well as protection and assistance needs.

2.4 ⟩ Use relevant technical standards and good practice employed across the humanitarian sector to plan and assess programmes.

- Apply national technical standards, where these exist, adapted to the humanitarian context.
- Coordinate with relevant stakeholders to advocate for the use of globally agreed standards to complement national ones (including Sphere and partner standards in related sectors).

2.5 **Monitor the activities, outputs and outcomes of humanitarian responses in order to adapt programmes and address poor performance.**

- Define time-bound and context-specific performance indicators. Review them on a regular basis to measure progress towards meeting assistance and protection needs.
- Include progress against objectives and performance indicators, in addition to activities and outputs (such as number of facilities built). Monitor project outcomes and desired results such as use of facilities or changes in practice.
- Review systems regularly so that only useful information is collected, with updated contextual information (such as local market function, change in security).

Organisational responsibilities

2.6 **Programme commitments are in line with organisational capacities.**

- Policies reflect the importance of using agreed humanitarian technical quality standards and developing expertise in chosen areas of intervention.
- Acknowledge the conditions under which the organisation may need to provide services outside this area of expertise until others can do so.

2.7 **Policy commitments ensure:**

    a.   **systematic, objective and ongoing monitoring and evaluation of activities and their effects;**

    b.   **evidence from monitoring and evaluations is used to adapt and improve programmes; and**

    c.   **timely decision-making, with resources allocated accordingly.**

Guidance notes

Addressing constraints and realistic programming: Where an organisation cannot access a population or meet identified needs, it has a responsibility to refer these needs to appropriate actors (including government, non-government actors) ⊕ *see Protection Principle 3.*

Use forecasts and early warning systems for contingency planning before a crisis to help communities, authorities and agencies respond quickly when needed. This will also allow affected people to protect their assets before their lives and livelihoods are at risk.

Develop decision-making processes that are flexible enough to respond to new information from ongoing assessments. Within an organisation, delegate decisions and resources as close to the implementation site as possible.

Document decisions and decision-making processes to demonstrate transparency. Base the processes on consultation, meaningful participation and coordination with others ⊕ *see Commitment 6.*

Monitoring activities, outputs and outcomes: Monitoring informs project revisions, verifies application of selection criteria and confirms whether aid is reaching the people most in need. Document any programme changes that result from monitoring and establish monitoring systems that involve and rely on affected people and key stakeholders ⊕ *see Commitment 7.*

Use common response-wide monitoring indicators where available.

Organisational decision-making: Both the responsibilities and processes for decision-making within organisations must be clearly defined and understood, including who is responsible, who will be consulted and what information is needed to inform decision-making.

Organisational policies, processes and systems: Organisations should document how humanitarian action improves outcomes, using systematic and rigorous monitoring and evaluation. Show how data from monitoring and evaluation is used to adapt programmes, policies and strategies, strengthen preparedness and improve performance in a timely manner ⊕ *see Commitment 7.* This may include an emergency response fund or being able to recruit or deploy qualified staff quickly when needed.

Commitment 3

Communities and people affected by crisis are not negatively affected and are more prepared, resilient and less at-risk as a result of humanitarian action.

Quality criterion
Humanitarian response strengthens local capacities and avoids negative effects.

Performance indicators

1. Communities and people affected by crisis consider themselves better able to withstand future shocks and stresses, as a result of humanitarian action.
2. Local authorities, leaders and organisations with responsibilities for responding to crises consider that their capacities have been increased.
3. Communities and people affected by crisis, including vulnerable and marginalised individuals, do not identify negative effects resulting from humanitarian action.

Key actions

3.1 **Ensure programmes build on local capacities and work towards improving the resilience of communities and people affected by crisis.**

- Design services (for example, drought management and flood-, hurricane- or earthquake-resistant structures) that reduce the impact of hazards.
- Support self-help initiatives and community preparedness actions.

3.2 **Use the results of any existing community hazard and risk assessments and preparedness plans to guide activities.**

- Understand and address needs and capacities of different groups who are exposed to different levels of risk.

3.3 **Enable the development of local leadership and organisations in their capacity as first responders in the event of future crises, taking steps to ensure that marginalised and disadvantaged groups are appropriately represented.**

- Work with municipal authorities and local government as much as possible.
- Advocate that local actors are treated as equal partners with autonomy to design and/or lead a response.
- Support the initiatives of local groups and organisations, as the platform for learning and capacity-building to strengthen first response in future crises.
- Hire local and national staff, considering diversity within the population, instead of expatriates wherever possible.

3.4 **Plan a transition or exit strategy in the early stages of the humanitarian programme that ensures longer-term positive effects and reduces the risk of dependency.**

- Provide support to strengthen existing state and community systems, rather than establish parallel efforts that will not last beyond the duration of the response.

3.5 **Design and implement programmes that promote early disaster recovery and benefit the local economy.**

- Take steps to restore social services, education, markets, transfer mechanisms and livelihood opportunities that cater to the needs of vulnerable groups.
- Fully consider market conditions when analysing which form of assistance (cash, voucher, or in-kind) will have the greatest positive outcome.
- Buy goods and services locally when possible.
- Mitigate negative repercussions on the market to the extent possible.

3.6 **Identify and act upon potential or actual unintended negative effects in a timely and systematic manner, including in the areas of:**
   a. **people's safety, security, dignity and rights;**
   b. **sexual exploitation and abuse by staff;**
   c. **culture, gender, and social and political relationships;**
   d. **livelihoods;**
   e. **the local economy; and**
   f. **the environment.**

Organisational responsibilities

3.7 **Policies, strategies and guidance are designed to:**

a. **prevent programmes having any negative effects such as, for example, exploitation, abuse or discrimination by staff against communities and people affected by crisis; and**

b. **strengthen local capacities.**

3.8 **Systems are in place to safeguard any personal information collected from communities and people affected by crisis that could put them at risk.**

- Establish clear and comprehensive policies on data protection, including electronic registration and distribution systems.
- Inform those receiving aid about their rights in relation to data protection, how they can access the personal information that an organisation holds about them and how to raise concerns they have about misuse of information.

Guidance notes

Community resilience and local leadership: Communities, local organisations and authorities are the first to act in a crisis and have in-depth knowledge of the situation and specific needs. These local actors should be equal partners and given autonomy in designing or leading a response. This requires a commitment by international and local agencies to adapt their way of working and engage in open dialogue and constructive criticism. Local financial infrastructure/services should be used wherever possible, instead of creating new parallel systems.

Transition and exit strategy: In collaboration with the authorities and affected population, design services as soon as possible that will continue after the emergency programme has finished (for example, introduce cost-recovery measures, use locally available materials or strengthen local management capacity).

Negative effects and "do no harm": The high value of aid resources and the powerful position of humanitarian workers can lead to exploitation and abuse, competition, conflict, and misuse or misappropriation of aid. Aid can undermine livelihoods and market systems, drive resource conflict and amplify unequal power relations between different groups. Anticipate these potential negative effects, monitor and take actions to prevent them if possible.

Be aware of cultural practices that may have negative effects on some groups. Examples include: biased targeting of girls, boys or specific castes; unequal education opportunities for girls; refusing immunisations; and other forms of discrimination or preferential treatment.

Safe and responsive feedback and complaints mechanisms can reduce abuse and misuse. Staff should welcome and seek out suggestions and complaints. Staff should be trained in how to exercise confidentiality and refer sensitive information, such as disclosures of exploitation and abuse.

Sexual exploitation and abuse by staff: All staff share a responsibility to prevent exploitation and abuse. Staff members have a responsibility to report any abuse they suspect or witness, whether within their own organisation or outside. Note that children (girls in particular) are often highly vulnerable, and policies should explicitly protect children from exploitation and abuse ⊕ *see Commitment 5.*

Environmental concerns: Humanitarian response can cause environmental degradation (for example, soil erosion, depletion or pollution of groundwater, overfishing, waste production and deforestation). Environmental degradation can amplify a crisis or levels of vulnerability and reduces people's resilience to shocks.

Measures to reduce environmental degradation include reforestation, rainwater harvesting, efficient use of resources and ethical procurement policies and practices. Major construction activities should only be performed following an environmental assessment ⊕ *see Commitment 9.*

Organisational policies to prevent negative effects and strengthen local capacities: Organisations are encouraged to have a clearly documented risk management policy and system in place. Non-governmental organisations (NGOs) that fail to systematically tackle unethical behaviour or corruption via their own anti-bribery policies and procedures and through collective action with other NGOs increase corruption risks for other actors.

Policies and procedures should reflect a commitment to the protection of vulnerable people and outline ways to prevent and investigate the abuse of power. Careful recruitment, screening and hiring practices can help to reduce the risk of staff misconduct, and codes of conduct should make it clear what practices are forbidden. Staff should formally agree to adhering to these codes and be made aware of the sanctions they will face if they fail to do so ⊕ *see Commitment 8.*

Safeguarding personal information: All personal information collected from individuals and communities must be treated as confidential. This is particularly the case in handling protection-related data, reported violations, complaints of abuse or exploitation, and gender-based violence. Systems that ensure confidentiality are essential to prevent further harm ⊕ *see Protection Principles* and *Commitments 5 and 7.*

The increasing use of electronic registration and distribution systems in humanitarian response highlights the need for clear and comprehensive policies on data protection. Agreements obliging third parties such as banks and commercial organisations to safeguard information are essential. Clear guidance about the collection, storage, use and disposal of data, aligned with international standards and local data protection laws, is important. Systems to mitigate the risk of data being lost should be put in place. Data should be destroyed once no longer required.

Commitment 4

Communities and people affected by crisis know their rights and entitlements, have access to information and participate in decisions that affect them.

Quality criterion
Humanitarian response is based on communication, participation and feedback.

Performance indicators

1. Communities and people affected by crisis are aware of their rights and entitlements.
2. Communities and people affected by crisis consider that they have timely access to clear and relevant information, including about issues that may put them at further risk.
3. Communities and people affected by crisis are satisfied with the opportunities they have to influence the response.
4. All staff are trained and provided with guidance on the rights of the affected population.

Key actions

4.1 Provide information to communities and people affected by crisis about the organisation, the principles it adheres to, how it expects its staff to behave, the programmes it is implementing and what they intend to deliver.

- Consider information itself as a key element of protection. Without accurate information about the assistance and their entitlements, people may become vulnerable to exploitation and abuse ⊕ *see Protection Principle 1.*
- Communicate clearly what behaviour people can expect from humanitarian workers and how they can complain if they are not satisfied.

4.2 Communicate in languages, formats and media that are easily understood, respectful and culturally appropriate for different members of the community, especially vulnerable and marginalised groups.

- Use existing communication systems and consult with people on their communications preferences. Consider the degree of privacy required for different formats and media.
- Ensure that communications technology, new and old, is used effectively and safely.

4.3 Ensure representation is inclusive, involving the participation and engagement of communities and people affected by crisis at all stages of the work.

- Give attention to groups or individuals historically excluded from power and decision-making processes. Systematically consider ethical ways of engaging with these individuals and groups to respect dignity and avoid any increased stigma.

- Consider the balance between direct community participation and indirect representation by elected representatives through the various stages of response.

4.4 **Encourage and facilitate communities and people affected by crisis to provide feedback on their level of satisfaction with the quality and effectiveness of the assistance received, paying particular attention to the gender, age and diversity of those giving feedback.**

- Train staff to gain and maintain people's trust, know how to respond to both positive and negative feedback and observe the reactions of different community members to the way services are provided.
- Integrate feedback collection into a broader approach across organisations or sectors to review, analyse and act on the feedback.
- Share response to the feedback with the community.

Organisational responsibilities

4.5 **Policies for information sharing are in place, and promote a culture of open communication.**

- Define and document processes for sharing information.
- Strive to share organisational information about successes and failures openly with a range of stakeholders to promote a system-wide culture of openness and accountability.

4.6 **Policies are in place for engaging communities and people affected by crisis, reflecting the priorities and risks they identify in all stages of the work.**

- Outline how staff members are trained and encouraged to facilitate community engagement and decision-making, listen to diverse communities of affected people and manage negative feedback.
- Design policies and strategies to help create space and time for community dialogues, decision-making and self-help.

4.7 **External communications, including those used for fundraising purposes, are accurate, ethical and respectful, presenting communities and people affected by crisis as dignified human beings.**

- Share information based on risk assessment. Consider potential harm to the population, such as when sharing information about cash distributions or demographics of specific settlements, which can put people at risk of being attacked.
- Exercise care when making use of stories and images that discuss and depict affected people, as this can be an invasion of their privacy and a breach of confidentiality if their permission is not sought ⊕ *see Protection Principle 1 on informed consent.*

Guidance notes

Sharing information with communities: Sharing accurate, timely, understandable and accessible information strengthens trust, deepens levels of participation and improves the impact of a project. It is key to being transparent. Sharing financial information with communities can improve cost-effectiveness and help communities to identify and highlight waste or fraud.

If an organisation does not share information appropriately with the people it aims to assist, misunderstandings and delays, inappropriate projects that waste resources, and negative perceptions about the organisation can develop. This can generate anger, frustration and insecurity.

Effective, safe, accessible and inclusive communication: Different groups have different communication and information needs and sources. They may need time talking among themselves in a safe, private setting to process the information and its implications.

Informed consent: Be aware that some people may express consent without fully understanding the implications. This is not ideal, but a degree of consent and participation may initially have to be assumed based on expressed willingness to take part in project activities, observation, knowledge, or legal or other documents (such as contractual agreements with the community) ⊕ *see Protection Principle 1.*

Participation and engagement: Consult affected people and local institutions early in the response to build on existing knowledge and develop positive, respectful relations. Early consultation can be a better use of time than fixing inappropriate decisions later. In the early stages of an acute response, consultation might only be possible with limited numbers of affected people. Over time, there will be more opportunities for more people and groups to become involved in decision-making.

Be aware that in some conflict settings, encouraging group discussions and decision-making could be seen as a form of political organising and could harm local people. Consider various methods to enhance community engagement with the feedback system, including the use of community scorecards.

Feedback: Formal feedback can be sought through specific assessments (using group discussions or interviews), post-distribution monitoring, or questionnaires. Informal feedback received during daily interaction should also be used to develop trust and improve programmes on an ongoing basis. Obtain feedback on whether women, men, girls and boys feel respected and satisfied with their influence over decision-making. People may be satisfied with the aid delivered, but dissatisfied with their influence on decision-making.

People may fear that critical feedback will have negative repercussions. There may also be cultural reasons why criticism of an intervention is unacceptable. Explore different methods of providing informal and formal feedback, including methods for confidentially sharing the feedback.

Design feedback mechanisms with other agencies and ensure they are accessible to all people. They should be seen as separate from complaints mechanisms that address serious infringements of practice or behaviour ⊕ *see Commitment 5*, although in practice there is usually an overlap in the types of feedback and complaints received. Acknowledge and follow up on the feedback received and adapt the programme when appropriate. Integrate feedback mechanisms into organisations' monitoring and evaluation systems.

Promoting a culture of open communication: Organisations should publicly state (on their website or in promotional material that is accessible by affected people) any specific interests such as political or religious identity. This allows stakeholders to better understand the nature of the organisation and its likely affiliations and policies.

Organisational commitment to participation and listening to communities: Gender and diversity policies can help to promote the values and commitments of the organisation and provide concrete examples of expected behaviour. Feedback from affected people should also inform strategy and programme development.

Restricting information, confidentiality and non-disclosure: Not all information can or should be shared with all stakeholders. Consider how the collection of information that can identify groups (demographics) or individuals may cause or increase people's vulnerability or create new threats to their protection ⊕ *see Protection Principles.*

An ethical approach to external communications: Fundraising material and photographs taken out of context can often be misleading and can also increase protection risks. Policies and guidelines relating to external communications should be available to all staff and can help to ensure that mistakes are not made.

Details attached to images and included in stories must not allow people (particularly children) to be traced to his or her home or community. Geotagging of images should be disabled when taking photographs.

Commitment 5
Communities and people affected by crisis have access to safe and responsive mechanisms to handle complaints.

Quality criterion
Complaints are welcomed and addressed.

Performance indicators

1. Communities and people affected by crisis, including vulnerable and marginalised groups, are aware of complaints mechanisms established for their use.

2. Communities and people affected by crisis consider the complaints response mechanisms accessible, effective, confidential and safe.
3. Complaints are investigated, resolved and results fed back to the complainant within the stated time frame.

Key actions

5.1 **Consult with communities and people affected by crisis on the design, implementation and monitoring of complaints processes.**

- Disaggregate by sex, age and disability, as these criteria may influence people's views on access and obstacles to complaints mechanisms.
- Agree on how complaints can be submitted, what may prevent people and staff from complaining, and how they wish to receive the response to complaints. Consider how complaints will be recorded and tracked and how what is learned from them will be incorporated into future planning.
- Explore joint complaints mechanisms with other agencies, partners and third-party contractors.
- Train staff on the complaints mechanism.

5.2 **Welcome and accept complaints, and communicate how the mechanism can be accessed and the scope of issues it can address.**

- Consider an information campaign to help raise awareness of the system and procedures, during which people can ask further questions about how it will work.

5.3 **Manage complaints in a timely, fair and appropriate manner that prioritises the safety of the complainant and those affected at all stages.**

- Deal with each complaint individually, even if many cover similar issues.
- Provide a response within a specified time frame. The complainant should know when to expect a response.
- Consider community management or engagement in the complaints-handling system.

Organisational responsibilities

5.4 **The complaints response process for communities and people affected by crisis is documented and in place. The process should cover programming, sexual exploitation and abuse, and other abuses of power.**

- Keep records of how the complaints mechanism is set up, decision criteria, all complaints made, how they were responded to and within what time frame.
- Take care to ensure that information on complaints is kept confidential, in strict accordance with data protection policies.
- Work with other organisations on complaints mechanisms, as this may be less confusing for communities and staff.

5.5 An organisational culture in which complaints are taken seriously and acted upon according to defined policies and processes has been established.

- Publicly share policies which relate to an organisation's duty of care to the people it aims to assist, its codes of conduct and how it will protect potentially vulnerable groups such as women, children and people with disabilities.
- Establish formal investigation procedures that adhere to the principles of confidentiality, independence and respect. Conduct investigations in a thorough, timely and professional manner, meeting legal standards and local labour law requirements. Provide training to designated managers on investigations and on handling staff misconduct, or provide access to specialist advice.
- Include a grievance procedure and whistleblowing policy to deal with staff complaints, and make staff aware of them.

5.6 Communities and people affected by crisis are fully aware of the expected behaviour of humanitarian staff, including organisational commitments made on the prevention of sexual exploitation and abuse.

- Explain the complaints process to communities and staff. Include mechanisms for both sensitive issues (such as those relating to corruption, sexual exploitation and abuse, gross misconduct or malpractice) and non-sensitive information (such as challenges to the use of selection criteria).

5.7 Complaints that do not fall within the scope of the organisation are referred to a relevant party in a manner consistent with good practice.

- Clarify guidance on which complaints fall within the organisation's remit, and when and how to refer to other service providers.

Guidance notes

Designing a complaints mechanism: Social and power dynamics must be assessed before deciding on the best way to interact with communities. Pay attention to the needs of older people, women and girls, boys and men, persons with disabilities and others who might be marginalised. Ensure they have a say in the design and implementation of complaints systems.

Raising awareness about how to make a complaint: Time and resources will be needed to ensure that affected people know what services, staff attitudes and behaviour they can expect from humanitarian organisations. They should also know what to do and where to make a complaint if a humanitarian organisation has failed to meet these commitments.

The mechanism should be designed so that people may be assured that they can always make a complaint confidentially and without fear of retaliation.

Manage expectations, as communities may believe that the complaints process can solve all their problems. This can generate frustration and disappointment if the expected changes are outside the control of the agency.

Managing complaints: Explain clearly to the complainant when the complaint falls outside the control and responsibility of the organisation. Where possible and in agreement with the complainant, refer the complaint to the appropriate organisation. Coordinate with other agencies and sectors to ensure this functions effectively.

Only trained staff should investigate allegations of sexual exploitation and abuse by humanitarian workers.

Confidential referral for additional care and support (such as mental health and psychosocial support, or other healthcare) should be provided for complainants according to their wishes.

Anonymous and malicious complaints present specific challenges because their source is unknown. They may be a warning signal to the organisation of underlying discontent, and any follow-up will need to investigate whether there is any previously unacknowledged cause for complaint.

Protecting complainants: Take care when deciding who needs to know what information within the organisation. People reporting sexual abuse may face social stigma and real danger from perpetrators and their own families. Design a mechanism which ensures that complaints will be treated confidentially. A whistleblowing policy should be in place to protect staff who highlight concerns about programmes or the behaviour of colleagues.

Data protection policies should cover how long specific types of information should be kept, in accordance with relevant data protection laws.

Complaints-handling process: Ensure that both the organisation's staff and the communities it serves have the opportunity to report complaints. Such complaints can be seen as an opportunity to improve the organisation and its work. Complaints can indicate the impact and appropriateness of an intervention, potential risks and vulnerabilities, and the degree to which people are satisfied with the services provided.

Sexual exploitation and abuse (SEA) of people affected by crisis: An organisation and its senior management are responsible for ensuring that complaints mechanisms and procedures are in place, and are safe, transparent, accessible and confidential. Where appropriate, organisations should consider including specific statements about cooperating with investigations into SEA cases in their partnership agreements.

Organisational culture: Managers and senior staff should model and promote a culture of mutual respect between all staff, partners, volunteers and people affected by crisis. Their support for the implementation of community complaints mechanisms is vital. Staff should be aware of how to handle complaints or allegations of abuse. In the case of criminal activity or where international law has been broken, staff should know how to contact the appropriate authorities. Organisations working with partners should agree on how they will raise and handle complaints (including against each other).

Staff behaviour and codes of conduct: Organisations should have a staff code of conduct that is endorsed by senior management and made public. A child safeguarding policy should apply to all staff and partners, and inductions and training should be provided on expected standards of behaviour. Staff should know and understand the consequences of breaching the code of conduct ⊕ *see Commitments 3 and 8.*

Commitment 6

Communities and people affected by crisis receive coordinated, complementary assistance.

Quality criterion
Humanitarian response is coordinated and complementary.

Performance indicators

1. Organisations minimise gaps and overlaps identified by affected communities and partners through coordinated action.
2. Responding organisations – including local organisations – share relevant information through formal and informal coordination mechanisms.
3. Organisations coordinate needs assessments, delivery of humanitarian aid and monitoring of aid implementation.
4. Local organisations report adequate participation and representation in coordination mechanisms.

....

Key actions

6.1〉 **Identify the roles, responsibilities, capacities and interests of different stakeholders.**

- Consider collaboration to optimise the capacity of communities, host governments, donors, private sector and humanitarian organisations (local, national, international) with different mandates and expertise.
- Suggest and lead joint assessments, trainings and evaluations across organisations and other stakeholders to ensure a more coherent approach.

6.2〉 **Ensure humanitarian response complements that of national and local authorities and other humanitarian organisations.**

- Recognise that the overall planning and coordination of relief efforts is ultimately the responsibility of the host government. Humanitarian organisations have an essential role to play in supporting the state's response and coordination function.

6.3 Participate in relevant coordination bodies and collaborate with others in order to minimise demands on communities and maximise the coverage and service provision of the wider humanitarian effort.

- Advocate for the application of and adherence to recognised quality standards and guidelines through coordination. Use coordination bodies to contextualise humanitarian standards, especially the indicators, to collectively monitor and evaluate activities and the overall response.
- Determine the scope of activities and commitments, as well as any overlap with other coordination bodies and how this will be managed, for example in relation to accountability, gender and protection coordination.

6.4 Share necessary information with partners, coordination groups and other relevant actors through appropriate communication channels.

- Respect the use of local language(s) in meetings and other communications. Examine barriers to communication so that local stakeholders are enabled to participate.
- Communicate clearly and avoid jargon and colloquialisms, especially when other participants do not speak the same language.
- Provide interpreters and translators if needed.
- Consider the location of meetings to allow local actors to participate.
- Work with networks of local civil society organisations to ensure their members' contributions are included.

Organisational responsibilities

6.5 Policies and strategies include a clear commitment to coordination and collaboration with others, including national and local authorities, without compromising humanitarian principles.

- Include coordination in organisational policies and resourcing strategies. The organisation should provide a statement on how it will engage with partners, host authorities and other humanitarian or non-humanitarian actors.
- Staff representing agencies in coordination meetings should have the appropriate information, skills and authority to contribute to planning and decision-making. Clearly articulate coordination responsibilities in staff job descriptions.

6.6 Work with partners is governed by clear and consistent agreements that respect each partner's mandate, obligations and independence, and recognises their respective constraints and commitments.

- Local and national organisations engage or collaborate with partners with a shared understanding of each other's organisational mandate and mutual roles and responsibilities, for effective and accountable action.

Guidance notes

Working with the private sector: The private sector can bring commercial efficiencies, complementary expertise and resources to humanitarian organisations. At the very least, information sharing is required to avoid duplication and to promote humanitarian good practice. Ensure that the partnering businesses have committed to core human rights and do not have a history of perpetuating inequalities or discriminatory practices. Partnerships with the private sector should ensure explicit benefits for people affected by crisis, while recognising that private sector actors may have additional objectives of their own.

Civil–military coordination: Humanitarian organisations must remain clearly distinct from the military to avoid any real or perceived association with a political or military agenda that could compromise the agencies' impartiality, independence, credibility, security and access to affected populations.

The military has particular expertise and resources, including those associated with security, logistics, transport and communication. However, any association with the military must be in the service of and led by humanitarian agencies and according to endorsed guidelines ⊕ *see What is Sphere? Humanitarian Charter* and *Protection Principles*. Some organisations will maintain minimum dialogue to ensure operational efficiency, while others may establish stronger links.

The three key elements of civil–military coordination are information sharing, planning and division of tasks. Dialogue should take place throughout, in every context and at all levels.

Complementary assistance: Local organisations, local authorities and civil society networks have a significant amount of context-specific experience. They may need support in re-establishing themselves following the effects of a crisis and need to be engaged and represented in coordination of the response effort.

Where authorities are a party to the conflict, humanitarian actors should use their judgement regarding the authorities' independence, keeping the interests of the affected populations at the centre of their decision-making.

Coordination: Cross-sectoral coordination can address people's needs holistically rather than in isolation. For example, coordination on mental health and psychosocial supports must be done across the health, protection and education sectors, such as through a technical working group made up of these specialists.

Coordination leaders have a responsibility to ensure that meetings and information sharing are well managed, efficient and results-orientated. Local actors may not participate in coordination mechanisms if they seem to be relevant only to international agencies, due to language or location. National and sub-national coordination mechanisms may be required and should have clear reporting lines.

Participation in coordination mechanisms before a disaster establishes relationships and enhances coordination during a response. Link emergency coordination structures with longer-term development plans and coordination bodies where they exist.

International interagency mechanisms for the coordination of emergencies should support national coordination mechanisms. In refugee assistance, the refugee coordination mechanism should be that used by UNHCR.

Sharing information (including financial): between different stakeholders and different coordination mechanisms makes it more likely that programme gaps or duplication will be identified.

Working with partners: Different types of arrangements may exist with partners, ranging from the purely contractual to shared decision-making and shared resources. Respect the mandate and vision of the partner organisation and its independence. Identify opportunities for mutual learning and development. Identify what both parties stand to gain from the partnership as they increase their knowledge and capacities and ensure better response preparedness and more varied response options.

Longer-term collaborations between local and national civil society organisations and international organisations can allow all partners to increase their knowledge and capacities, and ensure better response preparedness and more varied response options.

Commitment 7

Communities and people affected by crisis can expect delivery of improved assistance as organisations learn from experience and reflection.

Quality criterion
Humanitarian actors continuously learn and improve.

Performance indicators

1. Communities and people affected by crisis identify improvements to the assistance and protection they receive over time.
2. Improvements are made to assistance and protection interventions as a result of the learning generated in the current response.
3. The assistance and protection provided reflects learning from other responses.

Key actions

7.1 Draw on lessons learned and prior experience when designing programmes.

- Design monitoring systems that are simple and accessible, recognising that information should be representative of different groups, clearly articulating who benefited from previous programmes and who did not.
- Consider failures as well as successes.

7.2 **Learn, innovate and implement changes on the basis of monitoring and evaluation, and feedback and complaints.**

- Use open-ended listening and other qualitative participatory approaches. People affected by crisis are the best sources of information about needs and changes in the situation.
- Share and discuss learning with communities, asking them what they would like to do differently and how to strengthen their role in decision-making or management.

7.3 **Share learning and innovation internally, with communities and people affected by crisis, and with other stakeholders.**

- Present the information collected through monitoring and evaluation in an accessible format that allows sharing and decision-making ⊕ *see Commitment 4.*
- Identify ways to support system-wide learning activities.

Organisational responsibilities

7.4 **Evaluation and learning policies are in place, and means are available to learn from experiences and improve practices.**

- Organisations include a performance review and improvement plan that is based on measurable, objective indicators in their learning cycle.
- All staff understand their responsibilities in relation to monitoring the progress of their work and how learning can contribute to their professional development.

7.5 **Mechanisms exist to record knowledge and experience and make it accessible throughout the organisation.**

- Organisational learning leads to practical changes (such as improved strategies for carrying out assessments, reorganisation of teams for more cohesive response, and clearer articulation of decision-making responsibilities).

7.6 **The organisation contributes to learning and innovation in humanitarian response among peers and within the sector.**

- Compile and publish reports on humanitarian responses, including key lessons learned and recommendations for revised practices during future responses.

Guidance notes

Learning from experience: Different approaches and methods suit different performance, learning and accountability purposes:

Monitoring – collection of regular data sets of project activities and performance can be used for course correction. Use qualitative and quantitative data to monitor and evaluate; triangulate data and maintain consistent records. Consider the ethics of how data is collected, managed and reported. Determine what data is collected and how it is presented based on the intended use and users of the data. Do not collect data that will not be analysed or used.

Real-time reviews – one-off assessment exercises, involving people working on the project, can be used for course correction.

Feedback – information received from affected people, not necessarily structures, can be used for course correction. People affected by crisis are the best judges of changes in their lives.

After-action reviews – one-off exercises, involving people working on project, occurring after project completion. Identifies elements to retain and change in future projects.

Evaluations – formal activities to objectively determine the value of an activity, project or programme, normally conducted by people external to the project, can be real time (to allow for course correction) or occur after project completion, to provide learning for similar situations and to inform policy.

Research – this involves systematic investigation into specific defined questions related to humanitarian action, generally used to inform policy.

Innovation: Crisis response often leads to innovation as people and organisations adapt to changing environments. People affected by crisis are innovating as they adapt to their own changing circumstances; they may benefit from support that involves them more systematically in innovation and development processes.

Collaboration and sharing of lessons: Collaborative learning with other agencies, governmental and non-governmental bodies and academic bodies is a professional obligation and can introduce fresh perspectives and ideas, as well as maximise the use of limited resources. Collaboration also helps to reduce the burden of repeated evaluations in the same community.

Peer-learning exercises have been used by a variety of organisations and can be undertaken to monitor progress in real time or as a reflective exercise post-crisis.

Networks and communities of practice (including academia) can create opportunities to learn from peer groups, both in the field and in after-action reviews or learning forums. This can make an important contribution to organisational practice and system-wide learning. Sharing challenges as well as successes among peers can enable humanitarians to identify risks and avoid future mistakes.

Evidence that is available across sectors is particularly useful. Learning and reviewing evidence among organisations is more likely to contribute to organisational change than lessons learned within a single organisation.

Monitoring performed by the people affected by crisis themselves can enhance transparency and quality and encourage ownership of the information.

Evaluation and learning policies: Key lessons and areas identified for improvement are not always addressed systematically, and lessons cannot be considered learned unless they have brought about demonstrable changes in current or subsequent responses.

Knowledge management and organisational learning: Knowledge management involves collecting, developing, sharing, storing and effectively using organisational knowledge and learning. Longer-term national staff are often key to preserving local knowledge and relationships. Learning should also extend to national, regional and local actors and help them develop or update their own crisis-preparedness plans.

Commitment 8
Communities and people affected by crisis receive the assistance they require from competent and well-managed staff and volunteers.

Quality criterion
Staff are supported to do their job effectively and are treated fairly and equitably.

Performance indicators

1. All staff feel supported by their organisation to do their work.
2. Staff satisfactorily meet their performance objectives.
3. Communities and people affected by crisis assess staff to be effective in terms of their knowledge, skills, behaviours and attitudes.
4. Communities and people affected by crisis are aware of humanitarian codes of conduct and how to raise concerns about violations.

Key actions

8.1 **Staff work according to the mandate and values of the organisation and to agreed objectives and performance standards.**

- Different terms and conditions may apply to staff of different types or levels. National employment law often dictates the status of an individual and must be respected. All staff members must be made aware of their legal and organisational status, whether national or international.

8.2 **Staff adhere to the policies that are relevant to them and understand the consequences of not adhering to them.**

- The need for induction and training on organisational mandate, policies and codes of conduct applies in all situations, including a rapid deployment or scale-up.

8.3 **Staff develop and use the necessary personal, technical and management competencies to fulfil their role and understand how the organisation can support them to do this.**

- Opportunities for formal staff development may be limited in the first phase of response, but managers should provide an induction and on-the-job training as a minimum.

Organisational responsibilities

8.4 **The organisation has the management and staff capacity and capability to deliver its programmes.**

- Hire people who will increase the accessibility of services and avoid any perception of discrimination, considering language, ethnicity, gender, disability and age.
- Consider how the organisation will address peaks in demand for qualified staff in advance. Clarify country-level roles and responsibilities as well as internal decision-making responsibilities and communication.
- Avoid deploying staff for short periods of time which leads to high staff turnover, undermines continuity and programme quality and may lead to staff avoiding personal responsibility for assignments.
- Adopt ethical recruitment practices to avoid the risk of undermining local NGO capacity.
- Develop locally recruited staff who are likely to stay for longer periods of time. In multi-mandated agencies, development staff should be trained and available for humanitarian response.

8.5 **Staff policies and procedures are fair, transparent, non-discriminatory and compliant with local employment law.**

- Organisational policy and practice promotes the role of national staff at management and leadership level to ensure continuity, institutional memory and more contextually appropriate responses.

8.6 **Job descriptions, work objectives and feedback processes are in place so that staff have a clear understanding of what is required of them.**

- Job descriptions are accurate and kept up to date.
- Staff develop individual objectives for work aspirations and competencies which are documented in a development plan.

8.7 **A code of conduct is in place that establishes, at a minimum, the obligation of staff not to exploit, abuse or otherwise discriminate against people.**

- The organisation's code of conduct is understood, signed and upheld, making it clear to all representatives of the organisation (including staff, volunteers, partners and contractors) what standards of behaviour are expected and what the consequences will be if they breach the code.

8.8 **Policies are in place to support staff to improve their skills and competencies.**

- Organisations should have mechanisms to review staff performance, assess capacity gaps and develop talent.

8.9 **Policies are in place for the security and the well-being of staff.**

- Agencies exercise a duty of care to their workers. Managers make humanitarian workers aware of risks and protect them from exposure to unnecessary threats to their physical and emotional health.
- Measures that can be adopted include effective security management, preventative health advice, active support for working reasonable hours and access to psychological support.
- Establish a policy that expresses zero tolerance for harassment and abuse, including sexual harassment and abuse, in the workplace.
- Establish holistic prevention and response strategies to address incidents of sexual harassment and violence as experienced or perpetrated by their staff.

Guidance notes

Staff and volunteers: Any designated representative of the organisation, including national, international, permanent or short-term employees, as well as volunteers and consultants, is considered to be a member of staff.

Organisations should sensitise staff and volunteers to raise awareness of marginalised groups and avoid stigmatising and discriminatory attitudes and practices.

Adhering to organisational mandates, values and policies: Staff are expected to work within the legal scope, mission, values and vision of the organisation, which should be defined and communicated to them. Beyond this wider understanding of the role and ways of working of the organisation, an individual should work to a set of personal objectives and the performance expectations agreed with their manager.

Policies should make explicit commitments to gender balance with staff and volunteers.

Policies should promote a work environment that is open, inclusive and accessible to persons with disabilities. This might include: identifying and eliminating barriers to accessibility in the workplace; prohibiting discrimination on the basis of disability; promoting equal opportunities and equal remuneration for work of equal value; and providing reasonable adjustments for persons with disabilities in the workplace.

External partners, contractors and services providers should also know the policies and codes of conduct that apply to them, as well as the consequences of non-compliance (such as termination of contracts).

Performance standards and development of competencies: Staff and their employers are mutually accountable for their skills development – including management skills. With the help of clear objectives and performance standards, they should understand what skills, competencies and knowledge are required to perform their current role. They should also be made aware of the opportunities for growth and development that might be available or required. Competencies can be improved through experience, training, mentoring or coaching.

There are various methods that can be used to assess a staff member's skills and behaviours, including observation, reviewing work output, direct discussions with them and interviewing their colleagues. Regular documented performance appraisals should allow managers to identify areas for support and training.

Staff capacity and capability: Personnel management systems differ by agency and context but should be informed by good practice. They need to be considered and planned at a strategic level with the support of senior management. Organisation and project plans must consider staff capacity and gender balance. There must be the right number of staff with the right skills in the right place at the right time to deliver short- and long-term organisational objectives.

Organisations should ensure that staff have the competencies needed to support community listening, decision-making and action. Staff should also be trained in how to apply standard operating procedures, as this allows for higher levels of delegation and faster responses.

Performance review schedules must be flexible enough to cover staff who work short-term, as well as those on open-ended contracts. Adequate attention should be given to competencies of listening, enabling inclusion, facilitating community dialogue and enabling community decision-making and initiatives. Partner organisations should agree on the competencies required for staff to meet the agreed commitments.

Staff policies and procedures: The style and complexity of staff policies and procedures will depend on the size and context of each agency. However simple or complex the agency may be, staff should participate in the development and review of policies where possible to ensure that their views are represented. A staff manual facilitates knowledge of and consultation on policies and the consequences of non-adherence.

Staff guidance: Each staff member should identify individual objectives that cover their work aspirations and the competencies they hope to develop, and document these in a development plan.

An effective response is not simply about ensuring that skilled staff are present, but also depends on the way that individuals are managed. Research from emergency contexts shows that effective management, frameworks and procedures are as important, if not more important than, the skills of personnel in ensuring an effective response.

Security and well-being: Staff often work long hours in risky and stressful conditions. An agency's duty of care to its national and international staff includes actions to promote mental and physical well-being and avoid long-term exhaustion, burnout, injury or illness.

Managers can promote a duty of care through modelling good practice and personally complying with policy. Humanitarian workers also need to take personal responsibility for managing their well-being. Psychological first aid should be immediately available to workers who have experienced or witnessed extremely distressing events.

Train staff to receive information on incidents of sexual violence experienced by their colleagues. Provide access to robust investigative and deterrence measures that promote trust and accountability. When incidents do occur, adopt a survivor-centred approach to medical and psychosocial support, which includes recognition of vicarious trauma. Support should be responsive to and inclusive of the needs of expatriate and national staff.

A culturally and linguistically appropriate mental health professional should contact all national and international staff and volunteers one to three months after they have survived a potentially traumatic event. The professional should assess the survivor and refer them for clinical treatment if appropriate.

Commitment 9

Communities and people affected by crisis can expect that the organisations assisting them are managing resources effectively, efficiently and ethically.

Quality criterion
Resources are managed and used responsibly for their intended purpose.

Performance indicators

1. Communities and people affected by crisis are aware of community-level budgets, expenditures and results achieved.
2. Communities and people affected by crisis consider that the available resources are being used:
    a. for what they were intended; and
    b. without diversion or wastage.
3. The resources obtained for the response are used and monitored according to agreed plans, targets, budgets and time frames.
4. Humanitarian response is delivered in a way that is cost-effective.

Key actions

9.1 **Design programmes and implement processes to ensure the efficient use of resources, balancing quality, cost and timeliness at each phase of the response.**

- Adapt procedures in rapid-onset crises to enable faster financial decision-making and cope with challenges (for example, a lack of available suppliers to carry out competitive tenders).

9.2 **Manage and use resources to achieve their intended purpose, minimising waste.**

- Ensure staff with specific skills and systems are in place to manage risks related to procurement, cash-based assistance and stock management.

9.3 **Monitor and report expenditure against budget.**

- Establish financial planning and monitoring systems to ensure that programme objectives are met, including procedures to mitigate key financial management risks.
- Track all financial transactions.

9.4 **When using local and natural resources, consider their impact on the environment.**

- Conduct a rapid environmental impact assessment to determine risk and put mitigating measures in place as early as possible in the response or programme.

9.5 **Manage the risk of corruption and take appropriate action if it is identified.**

- Document funding criteria and sources of funding. Be open and transparent with project information.
- Encourage stakeholders to report abuses of power.

Organisational responsibilities

9.6 **Policies and processes governing the use and management of resources are in place, including how the organisation:**

   a.   **accepts and allocates funds and gifts-in-kind ethically and legally;**
   b.   **uses its resources in an environmentally responsible way;**
   c.   **prevents and addresses corruption, fraud, conflicts of interest and misuse of resources;**
   d.   **conducts audits, verifies compliance and reports transparently;**
   e.   **assesses, manages and mitigates risk on an ongoing basis; and**
   f.   **ensures that the acceptance of resources does not compromise its independence.**

Guidance notes

Efficient use of resources: The term "resources" refers to the inputs an organisation needs to deliver its mission. This includes but is not limited to funds, staff, goods, equipment, time, land and the environment in general.

In high-profile acute crises, there is often pressure to respond quickly and to demonstrate that agencies are doing something to address the situation. This can lead to poor project planning and insufficient emphasis on exploring different potential programme and financial options (for example, the use of cash-based assistance) that may offer better value for money. However, the elevated risk of corruption in these contexts means it is important to provide training and support to staff and establish complaints mechanisms to prevent corruption within the systems ⊕ *see Commitments 3 and 5*.

Deploying experienced senior staff during this time can help to mitigate the risks and strike a balance between providing a timely response, maintaining standards and limiting waste.

Collaboration and coordination between organisations (and communities) can also contribute to a more efficient response (for example, by conducting joint assessments or evaluations and supporting interagency registration and logistics systems).

At the end of the project, the assets and resources that remain will need to be donated, sold or returned responsibly.

Using resources for their intended purpose: All humanitarian actors are accountable to both donors and affected people and should be able to demonstrate that resources have been used wisely, efficiently and to good effect.

Accounting records should satisfy accepted national and/or international standards and should be applied systematically within the organisation.

Fraud, corruption and waste divert resources away from those who need them most. However, an intervention that is not effective because it is understaffed or under-resourced cannot be said to be accountable. Economical does not always equal value for money. A balance will often need to be struck between economy, effectiveness and efficiency.

Monitoring and reporting on expenditure: All staff members share responsibility for ensuring that finances are well managed. Staff are encouraged to report any suspected fraud, corruption or misuse of resources.

Environmental impact and use of natural resources: Humanitarian responses can have negative impacts on the environment. For example, they can produce large amounts of waste, degrade natural resources, contribute to the depletion or contamination of the water table and cause deforestation and other environmental hazards. Ecosystems are essential to human well-being and buffer against natural hazards. Any impact on the environment must be addressed as a cross-sectoral issue, as this may cause further and lasting damage to lives, health and livelihoods. Involving affected people and their concerns in this process is key. Support for the local management of natural resources should be integrated into programming.

Managing corruption risks: The definition and understanding of corrupt practices is not the same in all cultures. A clear definition of the behaviour that is expected of staff (including volunteers) and partners is fundamental in addressing this risk ⊕ *see Commitment 8*. Engaging respectfully with community members, and establishing on-site monitoring mechanisms and transparency with stake-holders can help to reduce corruption risks.

Gifts-in-kind may create ethical dilemmas. Giving gifts in many cultures is an important social norm, and refusing a gift would appear rude. If receiving the gift causes a sense of indebtedness, the receiver should politely refuse it. If it is accepted, it is important to declare this and discuss it with a manager if concerns remain. Mitigate risks for operational independence and organisational impartiality by producing guidance for staff and encouraging transparency. Staff should be made aware of such policies and possible dilemmas.

Natural resources and environmental impact: Organisations should commit to environmentally sound policies and practices (including a plan of action and rapid environmental impact assessment) and make use of existing guidelines to help address environmental issues in an emergency. Green procurement policies help reduce the impact on the environment but need to be managed in a way that minimises delay in the provision of assistance.

Corruption and fraud: Fraud includes theft, diversion of goods or property and the falsification of records such as expense claims. Every organisation must keep an accurate record of financial transactions to show how funds have been used. Establish systems and procedures to ensure internal control of financial resources and to prevent fraud and corruption.

Organisations should support recognised good practice in financial management and reporting. Organisational policies should also ensure that procurement systems are transparent and robust and incorporate counter-terrorism measures.

Conflicts of interest: Staff must ensure that there is no conflict between the aims of the organisation and their own personal or financial interests. For example, they must not award contracts to suppliers, organisations or individuals if they or their family stand to gain financially.

There are various forms of conflict of interest, and people do not always recognise that they are contravening organisational codes and policies. For example, using the organisation's resources without permission or taking gifts from a supplier might be construed as a conflict of interest.

Creating a culture where people feel that they can openly discuss and declare any potential or actual conflicts of interest is key to managing them.

Auditing and transparency: Audits can take several forms. Internal audits check that procedures are being followed. External audits verify whether the organisation's financial statements are true and fair. An investigative audit is executed when an organisation suspects a specific problem, usually fraud.

References and further reading

Additional resources for the Core Humanitarian Standard: corehumanitarianstandard.org

CHS Alliance: www.chsalliance.org

CHS Quality Compass: www.urd.org

Overseas Development Institute (ODI): www.odi.org

Accountability

Child Protection Minimum Standards (CPMS). Global Child Protection Working Group, 2010. http://cpwg.net

Complaints Mechanism Handbook. ALNAP, Danish Refugee Council, 2008. www.alnap.org

Guidelines on Setting Up a Community Based Complaints Mechanism Regarding SexualExploitation and Abuse by UN and non-UN Personnel. PSEA Task Force, IASC Taskforce, 2009. www.pseataskforce.org

Humanitarian inclusion standards for older people and people with disabilities. Age and Disability Consortium, 2018. www.refworld.org

Lewis, T. Financial Management Essentials: Handbook for NGOs. Mango, 2015. www.mango.org

Livestock Emergency Guidelines and Standards (LEGS). LEGS Project, 2014. https://www.livestock-emergency.net

Minimum Economic Recovery Standards (MERS). SEEP Network, 2017. https://seepnetwork.org

Minimum Standards for Education: Preparedness, Recovery and Response. The Inter-Agency Network for Education in Emergencies INEE, 2010. www.ineesite.org

Minimum Standard for Market Analysis (MISMA). The Cash Learning Partnership (CaLP), 2017. www.cashlearning.org

Munyas Ghadially, B. *Putting Accountability into Practice.* Resource Centre, Save the Children, 2013. http://resourcecentre.savethechildren.se

Top Tips for Financial Governance. Mango, 2013. www.mango.org

Aid worker performance

A Handbook for Measuring HR Effectiveness. CHS Alliance, 2015. http://chsalliance.org

Building Trust in Diverse Teams: The Toolkit for Emergency Response. ALNAP, 2007. www.alnap.org

Protection Against Sexual Exploitation and Abuse (PSEA). OCHA. https://www.unocha.org

Protection from Sexual Exploitation and Abuse. CHS Alliance.
https://www.chsalliance.org

Rutter, L. *Core Humanitarian Competencies Guide: Humanitarian Capacity Building Throughout the Employee Life Cycle.* NGO Coordination Resource Centre, CBHA, 2011.
https://ngocoordination.org

World Health Organization, War Trauma Foundation and World Vision International. Psychological First Aid: Guide for Field Workers. WHO Geneva, 2011.www.who.int

Assessments
Humanitarian Needs Assessment: The Good Enough Guide. ACAPS and ECB, 2014.
www.acaps.org

Multi-sector Initial Rapid Assessment Manual (revised July 2015). IASC, 2015.
https://interagencystandingcommittee.org

Participatory assessment, in *Participation Handbook for Humanitarian Field Workers* (Chapter 7). ALNAP and Groupe URD, 2009. http://urd.org

Cash-based response
Blake, M. Propson, D. Monteverde, C. *Principles on Public-Private Cooperation in Humanitarian Payments.* CaLP, World Economic Forum, 2017.
www.cashlearning.org

Cash or in-kind? Why not both? Response Analysis Lessons from Multimodal Programming. Cash Learning Partnership, July 2017. www.cashlearning.org

Martin-Simpson, S. Grootenhuis, F. Jordan, S. *Monitoring4CTP: Monitoring Guidance for CTP in Emergencies.* Cash Learning Partnership, 2017.
www.cashlearning.org

Children
Child Safeguarding Standards and how to implement them. Keeping Children Safe, 2014. www.keepingchildrensafe.org

Coordination
Knox Clarke, P. Campbell, L. *Exploring Coordination in Humanitarian Clusters.* ALNAP, 2015. https://reliefweb.int

Reference Module for Cluster Coordination at the Country Level. Humanitarian Response, IASC, 2015. www.humanitarianresponse.info

Design and response
The IASC Humanitarian Programme Cycle. Humanitarian Response.
www.humanitarianresponse.info

Persons with Disability
Convention on the Rights of Persons with Disabilities. United Nations.
https://www.un.org

Washington Group on Disability Statistics and sets of disability questions. Washington Group. www.washingtongroup-disability.com

Environment
Environment and Humanitarian Action: Increasing Effectiveness, Sustainability and Accountability. UN OCHA/UNEP, 2014. www.unocha.org

The Environmental Emergencies Guidelines, 2nd edition. Environment Emergencies Centre, 2017. www.eecentre.org

Training toolkit: Integrating the environment into humanitarian action and early recovery. UNEP, Groupe URD. http://postconflict.unep.ch

Gender
Mazurana, D. Benelli, P. Gupta, H. Walker, P. *Sex and Age Matter: Improving Humanitarian Response in Emergencies.* ALNAP, 2011, Feinstein International Center, Tufts University.

Women, Girls, Boys and Men: Different Needs, Equal Opportunities, A Gender Handbook for Humanitarian Action. IASC, 2006. https://interagencystandingcommittee.org

Gender-based violence
Guidelines for Integrating Gender-based Violence Interventions in Humanitarian Action: Reducing risk, promoting resilience, and aiding recovery. GBV Guidelines, IASC, 2015. http://gbvguidelines.org

Handbook for Coordinating Gender-based Violence Interventions in Humanitarian Settings. United Nations, UNICEF, November 2010. https://www.un.org

People-centred humanitarian response
Bonino, F. Jean, I. Knox Clarke, P. *Closing the Loop – Effective Feedback in Humanitarian Contexts.* ALNAP, March 2014, London. www.alnap.org

Participation Handbook for Humanitarian Field Workers. Groupe URD, ALNAP, 2009. www.alnap.org

What is VCA? An Introduction to Vulnerability and Capacity Assessment. IFRC, 2006, Geneva. www.ifrc.org

Performance, monitoring and evaluation
Catley, A. Burns, J. Abebe, D. Suji, O. *Participatory Impact Assessment: A Design Guide.* Tufts University, March 2014, Feinstein International Center, Somerville. http://fic.tufts.edu

CHS Alliance and Start, A. *Building an Organisational Learning & Development Framework: A Guide for NGOs.* CHS Alliance, 2017. www.chsalliance.org

Hallam, A. Bonino, F. *Using Evaluation for a Change: Insights from Humanitarian Practitioners.* ALNAP Study, October 2013, London. www.alnap.org

Project/Programme Monitoring and Evaluation (M&E) Guide. ALNAP, IRCS, January 2011. https://www.alnap.org

Sphere for Monitoring and Evaluation. The Sphere Project, March 2015. www.sphereproject.org

Protection
Slim, H. Bonwick, A. *Protection: An ALNAP Guide for Humanitarian Agencies.* ALNAP, 2005. www.alnap.org

Recovery
Minimum Economic Recovery Standards. SEEP Network, 2017. https://seepnetwork.org

Resilience
Reaching Resilience: Handbook Resilience 2.0 for Aid Practitioners and Policymakers in Disaster Risk Reduction, Climate Change Adaptation and Poverty Reduction. Reaching Resilience, 2013. www.reachingresilience.org

Turnbull, M. Sterret, C. Hilleboe, A. *Toward Resilience, A Guide to Disaster Risk Reduction and Climate Change Adaptation.* Catholic Relief Services, 2013. www.crs.org

Further reading
For further reading suggestions please go to www.spherestandards.org/handbook/online-resources

Water Supply, Sanitation and Hygiene Promotion

Humanitarian
Charter

Protection
Principles

Core
Humanitarian
Standard

Water Supply, Sanitation, and Hygiene Promotion (WASH)

Hygiene promotion	Water supply	Excreta management	Vector control	Solid waste management	WASH in disease outbreaks and healthcare settings
Standard 1.1 Hygiene promotion	**Standard 2.1** Access and water quantity	**Standard 3.1** Environment free from human excreta	**Standard 4.1** Vector control at settlement level	**Standard 5.1** Environment free from solid waste	**Standard 6** WASH in healthcare settings
Standard 1.2 Identification, access and use of hygiene items	**Standard 2.2** Water quality	**Standard 3.2** Access to and use of toilets	**Standard 4.2** Household and personal actions to control vectors	**Standard 5.2** Household and personal actions to safely manage solid waste	
Standard 1.3 Menstrual hygiene management and incontinence		**Standard 3.3** Management and main-tenance of excreta collection, transport, disposal and treatment		**Standard 5.3** Solid waste management systems at community level	

APPENDIX 1 Water supply, sanitation and hygiene promotion initial needs assessment checklist
APPENDIX 2 The F diagram: Faecal–oral transmission of diarrhoeal diseases
APPENDIX 3 Minimum water quantities: survival figures and quantifying water needs
APPENDIX 4 Minimum numbers of toilets: community, public places and institutions
APPENDIX 5 Water- and sanitation-related diseases
APPENDIX 6 Household water treatment and storage decision tree

Contents

Essential concepts in water supply, sanitation and hygiene promotion

Everyone has the right to water and sanitation

The Sphere Minimum Standards for water supply, sanitation and hygiene promotion (WASH) are a practical expression of the right to access water and sanitation in humanitarian contexts. The standards are grounded in the beliefs, principles, duties and rights declared in the Humanitarian Charter. These include the right to life with dignity, the right to protection and security, and the right to receive humanitarian assistance on the basis of need.

For a list of the key legal and policy documents that inform the Humanitarian Charter ⊕ *see Annex 1: Legal foundation to Sphere.*

People affected by crises are more susceptible to illness and death from disease, particularly diarrhoeal and infectious diseases. Such diseases are strongly related to inadequate sanitation and water supplies and poor hygiene. WASH programmes aim to reduce public health risks.

The main pathways for pathogens to infect humans are faeces, fluids, fingers, flies and food. The main objective of WASH programmes in humanitarian response is to reduce public health risks by creating barriers along those pathways ⊕ *see Appendix 2: The F diagram.* The key activities are:

- promoting good hygiene practices;
- providing safe drinking water;
- providing appropriate sanitation facilities;
- reducing environmental health risks; and
- ensuring conditions that allow people to live with good health, dignity, comfort and safety.

In WASH programmes, it is important to:

- manage the entire water chain: water sourcing, treatment, distribution, collection, household storage and consumption;
- manage the entire sanitation chain in an integrated manner;
- enable positive healthy behaviours; and
- ensure access to hygiene items.

Community engagement is crucial

Community engagement in WASH is a dynamic process connecting the community and other stakeholders so that people affected by the crisis have more control over the response and its impact on them. Effective engagement links communities and response teams to maximise community influence to reduce public health risks, provide appropriate, accessible services, improve programme quality and establish accountability. It explores the capacity and willingness of the community to manage and maintain WASH systems ⊕ *see Figure 4 WASH Community Engagement*.

Engaging with the community creates an essential understanding of perceptions, needs, coping mechanisms, capacities, existing norms, leadership structures and priorities, as well as the appropriate actions to take. Monitoring and evaluation, including feedback mechanisms, demonstrate whether WASH responses are appropriate or need to be adjusted. ⊕ *see Core Humanitarian Standard Commitments 4 and 5.*

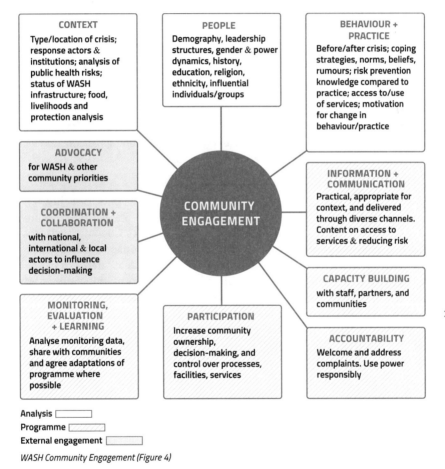

CONTEXT
Type/location of crisis; response actors & institutions; analysis of public health risks; status of WASH infrastructure; food, livelihoods and protection analysis

PEOPLE
Demography, leadership structures, gender & power dynamics, history, education, religion, ethnicity, influential individuals/groups

BEHAVIOUR + PRACTICE
Before/after crisis; coping strategies, norms, beliefs, rumours; risk prevention knowledge compared to practice; access to/use of services; motivation for change in behaviour/practice

ADVOCACY
for WASH & other community priorities

COORDINATION + COLLABORATION
with national, international & local actors to influence decision-making

COMMUNITY ENGAGEMENT

INFORMATION + COMMUNICATION
Practical, appropriate for context, and delivered through diverse channels. Content on access to services & reducing risk

CAPACITY BUILDING
with staff, partners, and communities

MONITORING, EVALUATION + LEARNING
Analyse monitoring data, share with communities and agree adaptations of programme where possible

PARTICIPATION
Increase community ownership, decision-making, and control over processes, facilities, services

ACCOUNTABILITY
Welcome and address complaints. Use power responsibly

Analysis ▭
Programme ▭
External engagement ▭

WASH Community Engagement (Figure 4)

WASH requires particular considerations in urban areas

Community engagement can be harder in urban areas, where the population density is higher and at-risk groups are less visible. However, in urban areas, public spaces, media and technology can provide the opportunity for broader and more efficient dialogue. Diverse ownership of assets (household in rural areas, public–private mix in urban areas) affects the choice of response options and methods of delivery.

A combination of approaches is needed

Market-based assistance can efficiently and effectively meet WASH needs, such as by ensuring access to hygiene items. Cash-based assistance (direct cash and/or vouchers) should be complemented by other WASH activities, including technical assistance and community engagement. For implementation, options vary from infrastructure construction to hygiene promotion and community mobilisation. Generators or temporary toilets can be provided immediately, while an overhaul of water treatment services is a long-term project. Quality control and technical assistance are critical to ensure health and safety. Technical assistance should be timely and appropriate. It should be consistent, accessible and achievable to deliver sustainably.

WASH responses should enhance long-term community goals and minimise environmental impact. Integrated water and sanitation management should meet human needs and protect the ecosystem. This can influence the choice of technology, timing and phasing of activities, community engagement, private sector and market engagement, and financing options.

These Minimum Standards should not be applied in isolation

The right to adequate water and sanitation is linked to the rights to shelter, food and health. Effective progress in achieving the Minimum Standards in one area influences progress in other areas. Close coordination and collaboration with other sectors as well as coordination with local authorities and other responding agencies helps ensure that needs are met, that efforts are not duplicated, and that the quality of WASH responses is optimised. For example, where nutritional standards are not met, the urgency to meet the water and sanitation standards is higher because people's vulnerability to disease has increased. The same applies to populations where HIV prevalence is high. Cross-references throughout the Handbook suggest some potential linkages.

Where national standards are lower than the Sphere Minimum Standards, humanitarian organisations should work with the government to progressively raise them.

International law specifically protects the right to water and sanitation

The right includes access to a sufficient, safe and affordable water supply for personal and domestic use, and private, safe and clean sanitation facilities. States are obliged to ensure this right during crises ⊕ see Annex 1: Legal foundation to Sphere.

Safe water and appropriate sanitation facilities are essential to:

- sustain life, health and dignity;
- prevent death from dehydration;

- reduce the risk of water-, sanitation- and hygiene-related diseases; and
- allow for adequate consumption, cooking, and personal and domestic hygienic requirements.

The right to water and sanitation is part of the universal rights essential for human survival and dignity, and state and non-state actors have responsibilities to fulfil the right. During armed conflict, for example, attacking, destroying, removing or making water installations or irrigation works useless is prohibited.

Links to the Protection Principles and the Core Humanitarian Standard

Water use affects protection. Armed conflict and inequity affect water security for individuals and groups. Multiple demands for water for consumption and domestic and livelihoods purposes can cause protection concerns if short- and long-term activities are not designed appropriately. Protection in WASH responses is often considered from the perspective of personal protection and safety, recognising particular vulnerability during water collection, defecation or menstrual hygiene management. Such personal protection elements are essential, but wider protection concerns are fundamental, too. Simple measures from the start, such as locks on toilet doors, adequate lighting and facilities segregation can reduce the risk of abuse or violence.

Adapted and inclusive programming is essential to avoid discrimination, reduce potential risks and improve usage or quality of services. For example, ensure that persons with disabilities can access hygiene facilities, and that women or children have appropriately sized containers in which to carry water. Engaging individuals and communities in all stages of the response can help incorporate protection considerations into WASH programmes.

Aid workers should be trained on child safeguarding and know how to use referral systems for suspected cases of violence, abuse or exploitation, including of children.

Civil–military cooperation and coordination should be carefully considered for humanitarian organisations, particularly in conflicts. Perceptions of neutrality and impartiality may affect community acceptance. Humanitarian organisations may have to accept military help in some situations, for example in transportation and distribution. However the impact on humanitarian principles must be carefully considered and efforts made to mitigate protection risks ⊕ *see Humanitarian Charter,* and *Settings with domestic and international military forces* in *What is Sphere?*

In applying the Minimum Standards, all nine Commitments in the Core Humanitarian Standard should be respected as a foundation for providing an accountable WASH programme.

1. Hygiene promotion

Diseases related to water, sanitation and hygiene cause significant preventable sickness and death in crises. Hygiene promotion that supports behaviours, community engagement, and actions to reduce the risk of disease is fundamental to a successful WASH response.

A standardised approach that relies mostly on teaching messages and distributing hygiene items is unlikely to be very effective. Risks–and the perception of risks–vary across contexts. People have different life experiences, coping strategies, and cultural and behavioural norms. It is important to adapt approaches based on analysis of these factors as well as context. Effective hygiene promotion relies on:

- working with the community to mobilise action and contribute to decision-making;
- two-way communication and feedback on risks, priorities and services; and
- access to and use of WASH facilities, services and materials.

Hygiene promotion should build on people's own knowledge of risk and disease prevention to promote positive health-seeking behaviour.

Monitor activities and outcomes regularly to ensure that hygiene promotion and WASH programmes evolve. Coordinate with health actors to monitor the incidence of WASH-related diseases such as diarrhoeal disease, cholera, typhoid, trachoma, intestinal worms and schistosomiasis ⊕ *see Essential healthcare – communicable diseases standards 2.1.1 to 2.1.4* and *Health systems standard 1.5.*

Hygiene promotion standard 1.1:
Hygiene promotion
People are aware of key public health risks related to water, sanitation and hygiene, and can adopt individual, household and community measures to reduce them.

Key actions

1 ⟩ Identify the main public health risks and the current hygiene practices that contribute to these risks.

- Develop a community profile to determine which individuals and groups are vulnerable to which WASH-related risks and why.
- Identify factors that can motivate positive behaviours and preventive action.

2 〉 Work with the affected population to design and manage hygiene promotion and the wider WASH response.

- Develop a communications strategy using both mass media and community dialogue to share practical information.
- Identify and train influential individuals, community groups and outreach workers.

3 〉 Use community feedback and health surveillance data to adapt and improve hygiene promotion.

- Monitor access to and use of WASH facilities, and how hygiene promotion activities affect behaviour and practice.
- Adapt activities and identify unmet needs.

Key indicators

Percentage of affected households who correctly describe three measures to prevent WASH-related diseases

Percentage of target population who correctly cite two critical times for handwashing

Percentage of target population observed to use handwashing stations on leaving communal toilets

Percentage of affected households where soap and water are available for handwashing

Percentage of affected population who collect water from improved water sources

Percentage of households that store drinking water in clean and covered containers

Percentage of carers who report that they dispose of children's excreta safely

Percentage of households using incontinence products (pads, urinal bottles, bed pans, commode chairs) who report that they dispose of excreta from adult incontinence safely

Percentage of affected households who dispose of solid waste appropriately

Percentage of people who have provided feedback and say that their feedback was used to adapt and improve WASH facilities and services

Local environment is free of human and animal faeces

Guidance notes

Understanding and managing WASH risks: Prioritising and reducing WASH risks in the initial phase of a crisis can be challenging. Focus on the use of safe water, excreta management and handwashing, as these are likely to have the greatest impact on preventing disease transmission. Assessing WASH-related public health risks and steps to reduce them will require an understanding of:

- current use of WASH facilities and services;
- access to essential household hygiene items ⊕ *see Hygiene promotion standards 1.2 and 1.3*;
- current coping strategies, local customs and beliefs;
- social structures and power dynamics in the community;
- where people go for healthcare (including traditional healers, pharmacies, clinics);
- who is responsible for operating and maintaining WASH infrastructure;
- disease surveillance data linked to WASH;
- social, physical and communication barriers to accessing WASH facilities and services, particularly for women and girls, older people and persons with disabilities;
- income-level variations; and
- environmental conditions and seasonal trends for diseases.

To maintain motivation, behavioural change and practice need to be easy. Facilities should be convenient and accessible for all users, safe, dignified, clean and culturally appropriate. Include both men and women in hygiene promotion activities, as active hygiene support by men may have a decisive influence on behaviours in the family.

Community mobilisation: Work with existing structures, ensuring that paid or voluntary opportunities are equally available to both women and men. Respected community and faith-based leaders, outreach workers and trusted local actors such as women's or youth groups can facilitate mobilisation and preventive action.

Allocating two outreach workers per 1,000 people is common. Outreach workers and volunteers should have good communication skills, be able to build respectful relationships with local communities, and have a thorough understanding of local needs and concerns. If needed, incentives for outreach workers should be agreed through a local coordination forum to promote equity and avoid disruption.

Community health workers may have similar roles to WASH outreach workers, but different responsibilities ⊕ *see Health systems standard 1.2: Health workforce*.

Working with children: Children can promote healthy behaviours to their peers and family. The department of education or social services can identify opportunities to promote hygiene in schools, residential care and child-headed households, and to children living on the street. Involve the children in developing the messages ⊕ *see INEE and CPMS Handbooks*.

Communication channels and approaches: Provide information in multiple formats (written, graphic, audio) and languages to make it as widely accessible as possible. Adapt for children and persons with disabilities and develop and test messages to ensure they are understandable across differences in age, sex, education level and language.

Community-level dialogue is useful for problem solving and action planning. Mass media can reinforce general information with a broader reach. Both are useful if targeted at specific audiences. Design appropriate feedback mechanisms with users and monitor their effectiveness. Communicate feedback to the community, encouraging them to respond in turn ⊕ *see Core Humanitarian Standard Commitment 5.*

Handwashing with soap is an important way to prevent transmission of diarrhoeal diseases. Handwashing facilities need a regular supply of water, soap and safe drainage. Position facilities so that handwashing happens before touching food (eating, preparing food or feeding a child) and after contact with excreta (after using the toilet or cleaning a child's bottom) ⊕ *see Water supply standard 2.2: Water quality.*

Promoting the use of toilets: A key issue for hygiene promotion staff is the inclusive use of excreta disposal facilities and materials. In addition to concerns about cleanliness and smell, major deterrents for people using toilets are embarrassment, cultural taboos, physical accessibility and concerns about privacy and safety ⊕ *see Excreta management standard 3.2: Access to and use of toilets.*

Collecting, transporting and storing drinking water safely is key to reducing contamination risks. Households need separate containers for collecting and storing drinking water ⊕ *see Hygiene promotion standard 1.2* and *Water supply standards 2.1 and 2.2.*

People on the move: Find opportunities to engage with people on the move, either by travelling with them temporarily or meeting them at rest areas. Use communication channels such as radio, SMS, social media groups and free hotlines to provide hygiene information and solicit feedback. Design the "household items" package to support this by including mobile phones or solar chargers, which will also enable people to communicate with their families, access information and provide feedback.

Hygiene promotion standard 1.2:
Identification, access to and use of hygiene items

Appropriate items to support hygiene, health, dignity and well-being are available and used by the affected people.

Key actions

1 ⟩ Identify the essential hygiene items that individuals, households and communities need.

- Consider different needs of men and women, older people, children and persons with disabilities.

- Identify and provide additional communal items for maintaining environmental hygiene, such as solid waste receptacles and cleaning equipment.

2 ⟩ Provide timely access to essential items.

- Assess availability of items through local, regional or international markets.

3 ⟩ Work with affected populations, local authorities and other actors to plan how people will collect or buy hygiene items.

- Provide information about timing, location, content and intended recipients of cash-based assistance and/or hygiene items.
- Coordinate with other sectors to provide cash-based assistance and/or hygiene items and decide on distribution mechanisms.

4 ⟩ Seek feedback from affected people on the appropriateness of the hygiene items chosen and their satisfaction with the mechanism for accessing them.

Key indicators

All affected households have access to the minimum quantity of essential hygiene items:

- two water containers per household (10–20 litres; one for collection, one for storage);
- 250 grams of soap for bathing per person per month;
- 200 grams of soap for laundry per person per month;
- Soap and water at a handwashing station (one station per shared toilet or one per household); and
- Potty, scoop or nappies to dispose of children's faeces.

Percentage of affected people who report/are observed using hygiene items regularly after distribution

Percentage of household income used to purchase hygiene items for identified priority needs

Guidance notes

Identify essential items: Adapt hygiene items and hygiene kits to the culture and context. Prioritise essential items in the initial phase (such as soap, water containers, and menstruation and incontinence materials) over the "nice to have" items (such as hair brush, shampoo, toothpaste, toothbrush). Some groups will have specific requirements ⊕ *see Guidance notes - At-risk groups* (below).

Water containers: Identify 10–20-litre water containers for collecting and storing drinking and domestic water. The size and type of containers should be appropriate for the age and carrying capacity of those who usually collect water.

Containers should have lids, be clean and covered. Storage containers should have a narrow neck or tap to ensure safe collection, storage and consumption of drinking water.

If the water supply is intermittent, provide larger storage containers. In urban settings or where supplies are centralised, household storage should be enough for ordinary consumption (including peak consumption, where relevant) between refills.

At-risk groups: Some people will need different or greater quantities of personal hygiene items because of their age, health status, disability, mobility or incontinence. Persons with disabilities or who face barriers to mobility may need additional items. This includes extra soap, incontinence items, water containers, bed pans, a commode chair or plastic covers for mattresses. Ask people or their carers if they need help collecting and disposing of their waste in a way that respects their dignity. Consult with them and their families or carers on the most appropriate support.

Market-based programming for hygiene items: Provision of hygiene items should support local markets where possible (for example by providing cash or vouchers or improving warehouse infrastructure). A market assessment and household income analysis, including gender roles in expenditure decisions, should inform the plans for access and use of hygiene items. Monitor whether or not the market is providing the quantity and quality of products, and adjust if necessary ⊕ *see Delivering assistance through markets.*

Distribution: Prioritise the safety and security of the population when organising any distribution ⊕ *see Protection Principle 1.*

Set up a dedicated distribution team. Inform people in advance of the timing, location, list of items and any eligibility criteria. Counter discrimination or stigmatisation and, if necessary, distribute to households or through separate distribution lines. Identify and address any barriers to accessing distribution locations or distribution systems, specifically for women and girls, older people and persons with disabilities.

Replenish consumables: Establish a reliable regular supply of consumables such as soap and menstruation and incontinence materials.

Coordination of joint distributions: Plan shared community consultations to understand needs and coping mechanisms across sectors. Address multiple needs at the same time for the convenience of the target population and to save time and money across sectors. Ensure that households can safely transport home all their items following distribution.

People on the move: Where people are on the move, confirm transportability of hygiene items (such as travel-sized soap). Let people select the items they want, rather than issuing standardised kits. Establish a system to collect and dispose of packaging waste where people are on the move.

Hygiene promotion standard 1.3:
Menstrual hygiene management and incontinence

Women and girls of menstruating age, and males and females with incontinence, have access to hygiene products and WASH facilities that support their dignity and well-being.

Key actions

1 > Understand the practices, social norms and myths concerning menstrual hygiene management and incontinence management, and adapt hygiene supplies and facilities.

2 > Consult women, girls and people with incontinence on the design, siting and management of facilities (toilets, bathing, laundry, disposal and water supply).

3 > Provide access to appropriate menstrual hygiene management and incontinence materials, soap (for bathing, laundry and handwashing) and other hygiene items.

- For distributions, provide supplies in discrete locations to ensure dignity and reduce stigma, and demonstrate proper usage for any unfamiliar items.

Key indicators

Percentage of women and girls of menstruating age provided with access to appropriate materials for menstrual hygiene management

Percentage of recipients who are satisfied with menstrual hygiene management materials and facilities

Percentage of people with incontinence that use appropriate incontinence materials and facilities

Percentage of recipients that are satisfied with incontinence management materials and facilities

Guidance notes

Addressing menstrual hygiene management and incontinence in crises: Successfully managing menstrual hygiene and incontinence helps people to live with dignity and engage in daily activities. In addition to providing access to hygiene items, it is important to consult with users about disposal mechanisms at home as well as in communal facilities and institutions such as schools. Toilet facilities should be adapted and space provided for laundry and drying facilities ⊕ *see Excreta management standards 3.1 and 3.2.*

Taboos about menstruation: Menstruation beliefs, norms and taboos will affect the success of the response. Investigating these issues may not be possible during the initial or acute phase of the crisis, but it should be done as soon as possible.

Incontinence may not be a widely used term in some contexts, even within the medical profession. Incontinence is a complex health and social issue that occurs when a person is unable to control the flow of their urine or faeces. It can lead to a high level of stigma, social isolation, stress and an inability to access services, education and work opportunities. Prevalence may seem low, as many people will keep it a secret, yet a wide range of people may live with incontinence. This includes:

- older people;
- persons with disabilities and those facing mobility barriers;
- women who have given birth—including girls, who are at increased risk of fistula;
- people with chronic illnesses such as asthma, diabetes, stroke or cancer;
- girls and women who have experienced gender-based violence or have undergone female genital mutilation;
- people who have had surgery such as removal of the prostate;
- women going through the menopause; and
- young children and children psychologically affected by conflict or disaster.

Poor incontinence hygiene management can be a major source of disease transmission in emergencies. Access to much higher amounts of water and soap is critical. People with incontinence and their carers each need five times as much soap and water as others. People who are incontinent and immobile need to consult health or disability specialists to learn how to prevent and manage infections and bed sores, which can be fatal.

Supplies and facilities: Discuss options with affected people to understand their preferences for: disposable or reusable materials; disposal mechanisms in homes, schools, health centres and communal facilities; laundry and drying facilities; and toilet and bathing facilities. Consider age-specific norms and preferences, as the type and quantity of supplies may change over time. Provide demonstrations for unfamiliar materials.

Different types of pads are required for faecal and urine incontinence, and for different levels of severity of incontinence. Sizing is important for safe use. Supply both urine and faecal incontinence pads in a range of sizes and types.

Consider proximity to toilets for people with incontinence. Some people may be able to prevent incontinence episodes if they can access the toilet quickly. A toilet commode chair, bed pan and/or urinal bottle may need to be supplied.

Minimum supplies: *For both menstrual hygiene management and incontinence:*

- a dedicated container with lid for soaking cloths and storing pads/cloths; and
- rope and pegs for drying.

For menstrual hygiene:

- either absorbent cotton material (4 square metres per year), disposable pads (15 per month) or reusable sanitary pads (six per year), as preferred by women and girls;
- underwear (six per year);
- extra soap (250 grams per month) ⊕ *see Hygiene promotion standard 1.2: Identification, access to and use of hygiene items.*

For incontinence, supplies will depend on the severity and type of incontinence and people's preferences. A suggested minimum is:

- either absorbent soft cotton material (8 square metres per year), disposable incontinence pads (150 per month) or reusable incontinence underwear (12 per year);
- underwear (12 per year);
- extra soap (500 grams bathing and 500 grams laundry per month);
- two washable leak-proof mattress protectors;
- additional water containers;
- bleach or similar disinfectant cleaning product (3 litres of non-diluted product per year);
- bed pan and urinal bottles (male and female), toilet commode chair (as appropriate).

Replenishment of supplies: Plan how and when to replenish materials. Cash-based assistance or in-kind distributions may be used in different ways over time. Explore options for small enterprises to provide materials or for people to make their own protection materials ⊕ *see Delivering assistance through markets.*

Schools, safe spaces and learning centres: Support for WASH in schools and safe spaces should consider the WASH infrastructure and the training provided to teachers. Facilities should have a discrete disposal mechanism a container with a lid, with collection and disposal system or a chute from the toilet to an incinerator. Install well-maintained and sex-segregated WASH facilities with hooks and shelves for menstrual hygiene supplies.

Encourage teachers to adopt menstrual hygiene management education as part of standard lessons. Train teachers to:

- support girls' menstrual hygiene practices;
- keep menstrual hygiene supplies at school;
- support students who experience incontinence due to the psychological effects of the crisis ⊕ *see INEE Handbook.*

Shelter: Work with the shelter sector to ensure there is adequate privacy for menstrual hygiene and incontinence management in the household or communal shelter. This may include using privacy screens or separate areas for changing.

People on the move: Offer menstrual hygiene and incontinence management supplies as people pass through supply points.

2. Water supply

Inadequate water quantity and quality is the underlying cause of most public health problems in crisis situations. There may not be sufficient water available to meet basic needs, so supplying a survival level of safe drinking water is essential. The priority is to provide an adequate quantity of water, even if it is of intermediate quality. This may be necessary until Minimum Standards for both water quantity and quality are met.

Taps, wells and pipes often fall into disrepair due to conflict, natural disaster or lack of functional maintenance systems. In conflict, depriving access to water may be used as an intentional strategy by parties to the conflict. This is strictly prohibited in international humanitarian law.

Consult community members and relevant stakeholders to understand how they use and access water, whether there are any access limitations, and how these may change seasonally.

Water supply standard 2.1:
Access and water quantity

People have equitable and affordable access to a sufficient quantity of safe water to meet their drinking and domestic needs.

Key actions

1 > Identify the most appropriate groundwater or surface water sources, taking account of potential environmental impacts.

- Consider seasonal variations in water supply and demand, and mechanisms for accessing drinking water, domestic water and water for livelihoods.
- Understand different sources of water, suppliers and operators, and access to water within communities and households.

2 > Determine how much water is required and the systems needed to deliver it.

- Work with stakeholders to locate waterpoints that allow safe and equitable access for all community members.
- Establish operation and maintenance systems that assign clear responsibilities and include future needs for sustainable access.

3 > Ensure appropriate waterpoint drainage at household and communal washing, bathing and cooking areas and handwashing facilities.

- Look for opportunities to reuse water, such as for vegetable gardens, brick-making or irrigation.

Key indicators

Average volume of water used for drinking and domestic hygiene per household

- Minimum of 15 litres per person per day
- Determine quantity based on context and phase of response

Maximum number of people using water-based facility

- 250 people per tap (based on a flow rate of 7.5 litres/minute)
- 500 people per hand pump (based on a flow rate of 17 litres/minute)
- 400 people per open hand well (based on a flow rate of 12.5 litres/minute)
- 100 people per laundry facility
- 50 people per bathing facility

Percentage of household income used to buy water for drinking and domestic hygiene

- Target 5 per cent or less

Percentage of targeted households who know where and when they will next get their water

Distance from any household to the nearest waterpoint

- <500 metres

Queuing time at water sources

- <30 minutes

Percentage of communal water distribution points free of standing water

Percentage of water systems/facilities that have functional and accountable management system in place

Guidance notes

Water source selection should consider:

- availability, safety, proximity and sustainability of a sufficient quantity of water;
- need for and feasibility of water treatment, whether bulk or at household level; and
- social, political or legal factors affecting the source control of water sources might be controversial, especially during conflicts.

A combination of approaches and sources is often required in the initial phase of a crisis to meet survival needs. Surface water sources, despite requiring more treatment, may be the quickest solution. Groundwater sources and/or gravity-flow supplies from springs are preferable. They require less treatment, and gravity-flow does not require pumping. Monitor all sources regularly to avoid over-extraction ⊕ *see Shelter and settlement standard 2: Location and settlement planning.*

Needs: The quantity of water needed for drinking, hygiene and domestic use depends upon the context and phase of a response. It will be influenced by factors such as pre-crisis use and habits, excreta containment design and cultural habits ⊕ *see Understanding and managing WASH risks* in *Hygiene promotion standard 1.1* and *Excreta management standard 3.2.*

A minimum of 15 litres per person per day is established practice. It is never a "maximum" and may not suit all contexts or phases of a response. For example, it is not appropriate where people may be displaced for many years. In the acute phase of a drought, 7.5 litres per person per day may be appropriate for a short time. In an urban middle-income context, 50 litres per person per day may be the minimum acceptable amount to maintain health and dignity.

The consequences of providing different quantities of water should be reviewed against morbidity and mortality rates for WASH-related diseases. Coordinate with other WASH actors to agree on a common minimum for quantity in context. For guidance on determining water quantities for human, livestock, institutional and other uses ⊕ *see Essential healthcare – communicable diseases standards 2.1.1 to 2.1.4* and *WASH Appendix 3.* For emergency livestock water needs ⊕ *see LEGS Handbook*

Needs	Quantity (litres/person/day)	Adapt to context based on
Survival: water intake (drinking and food)	2.5–3	Climate and individual physiology
Hygiene practices	2–6	Social and cultural norms
Basic cooking	3–6	Food type and social and cultural norms
Total basic water	7.5–15	

Minimum basic survival water needs: Water needs will vary within the population, particularly for persons with disabilities or facing mobility barriers, and among groups with different religious practices.

Measurement: Do not simply divide the quantity of delivered water by the population served. Household surveys, observation and community discussion groups are more effective methods of collecting data on water use and consumption than measuring the volume of water trucked or pumped, or handpump use. Triangulate water system reports with household reports.

Access and equity: Waterpoints include communal bathing, cooking and laundry facilities and toilets, as well as institutional settings such as schools or health facilities.

The minimum quantity targets (see key indicators above) assume that the waterpoint is accessible for about 8 hours a day of constant water supply. Use these targets with caution, as they do not guarantee a minimum quantity of water or equitable access.

Water and sanitation responses should address the needs of both host and displaced populations equitably to avoid tension and conflict.

During design, consider that needs vary across age groups and sex, as well as for persons with disabilities or those facing mobility barriers. Locate accessible waterpoints sufficiently close to households to limit exposure to any protection risks.

Inform the affected population of when and where to expect the delivery of water, their entitlement to equitable distribution, and how to give feedback.

Round-trip and queuing time: Excessive round-trip and queuing times indicate an inadequate number of waterpoints or inadequate yields at water sources. This can lead to reduced individual water consumption and increased consumption from unprotected surface sources, and result in less time for tasks such as education or income-generating activities. Queuing time also affects the risk of violence at the tap stand ⊕ *see Protection Principle 1* and *Core Humanitarian Standard Commitment 1*.

Appropriate water containers: ⊕ *See Hygiene promotion standard 1.2: Identification, access to and use of hygiene items*. Where household-level water treatment and safe storage (HWTSS) is used, adjust the number and size of containers. For example, a coagulant, flocculation and disinfection process will require two buckets, a straining cloth and a stirrer.

Market-based programming for water: Analyse how households accessed water and containers before and after the crisis. This simple market assessment should inform decisions about how to provide sustainable access to water in the short and long term. Determine how to use, support and develop the water market, considering a combined approach of household cash-based assistance, grants and technical capacity building with vendors or suppliers, or other means. Track the monthly market prices (water, fuel) for household expenditure over time, and use these trends to inform changes in programme design ⊕ *see Delivering assistance through markets*.

Payment: Water costs should be no more than 3–5 per cent of household income. Be aware of how households are covering higher costs during the crisis and take steps to counter negative coping mechanisms ⊕ *see Protection Principle 1*. Ensure that finance systems are managed in a transparent way.

Management of the water systems and infrastructure: Work with the community and other stakeholders to decide on the siting, design and use of waterpoints (both immediate and long-term plans). This includes bathing, cooking and laundry facilities, toilets, and institutions such as schools, markets and health facilities. Use feedback to adapt and improve access to water facilities.

Consider the previous and current water governance structures, the ability and willingness of people to pay for water and sanitation services, and cost-recovery mechanisms. Consider capital investment in water supply systems that offer longer-term savings or economies of scale. Compare alternatives such as solar pumping or a piped water system with water trucking, especially in protracted crises in urban areas and communal settlements.

Provide people with the means to operate and maintain water systems through WASH committees or partnerships with the private or public sector.

Use of bottled water: Treated water is more cost-effective, appropriate and technically sound than bottled water, because of transport, cost, quality and waste generation. Exceptions can be made for the short term (for example, people on the move). Establish an appropriate plastic waste management system.

Laundry, washing and bathing facilities: If household private bathing is not possible, provide separate facilities for men and women that ensure safety, privacy and dignity.

Consult with the users, particularly women, girls and persons with disabilities, to decide the location, design and safety of facilities. Consider access to hot water for bathing and laundry during specific contexts, such as responding to scabies, and during climatic variations.

Drainage from waterpoints, laundry areas, bathing facilities and handwashing stations: In constructing and rehabilitating water distribution and usage points, ensure that wastewater does not pose a health hazard or breeding ground for problem vectors. Establish an overall drainage plan in coordination with site planners, the shelter sector and/or municipal authorities.

Design WASH systems and infrastructure to comply with the drainage requirements. For instance, the pressure rating at tap stands, the size of the waterpoint and/or laundry apron, and the height from the tap to the bottom of the water containers should be appropriate ⊕ *see Shelter and settlement standard 2: Location and settlement planning.*

Water supply standard 2.2: Water quality

Water is palatable and of sufficient quality for drinking and cooking, and for personal and domestic hygiene, without causing a risk to health.

Key actions

1 ⟩ Identify public health risks associated with the water available and the most appropriate way to reduce them.

- Protect water sources and regularly renew sanitary surveys at source and water points.

2 〉 Determine the most appropriate method for ensuring safe drinking water at point of consumption or use.

- Treatment options include bulk water treatment and distribution, with safe collection and storage at the household level, or household-level water treatment and safe storage.

3 〉 Minimise post-delivery water contamination at point of consumption or use.

- Equip households with safe containers to collect and store drinking water, and the means to safely draw water for drinking.
- Measure water quality parameters (free residual chlorine (FRC) and coliform-forming units (CFU)) at point of delivery and point of consumption or use.

Key indicators

Percentage of affected people who collect drinking water from protected water sources

Percentage of households observed to store water safely in clean and covered containers at all times

Percentage of water quality tests meeting minimum water quality standards

- <10 CFU/100ml at point of delivery (unchlorinated water)
- ≥0.2–0.5mg/l FRC at point of delivery of delivery (chlorinated water)
- Turbidity of less than 5 NTU

Guidance notes

Maintaining a safe water chain: Water-related diseases pose a risk to the integrity of the water chain. The barriers to faecal–oral transmission include excreta containment, covering food, handwashing at key times, and safe collection and storage of water ⊕ _see Hygiene promotion standard 1.1; Excreta management standard 3.2_ and _Appendix 2: The F diagram._

A risk assessment of the water chain, from the water source to the drinking water storage container, includes:

1. sanitary survey of the waterpoint;
2. observation of use of separate containers for water collection and storage;
3. observation of clean and covered drinking water containers; and
4. water quality testing.

Where there is a high likelihood of unsafe water, these actions can highlight apparent risks without carrying out labour-intensive household water-quality testing.

A sanitary survey assesses conditions and practices that may constitute a public health risk at the water point. It considers the structure of the water point, drainage, fencing, defaecation practices and solid waste management practices as possible sources of contamination. The survey also examines water containers in the household.

Water quality: When commissioning a new water source, test the water for physical, bacteriological and chemical parameters. Do this before and after local seasonal fluctuations. Do not neglect the analysis of chemical parameters (such as fluoride and arsenic levels) that can lead to long-term health issues.

Faecal coliform bacteria (>99 per cent of which are *E. coli*) indicate the level of human and animal waste contamination in water and the possible presence of other harmful pathogens. If any faecal coliforms are present, treat the water. Even if *E. coli* is not found, water is prone to recontamination without a residual disinfectant.

Where water is chlorinated (prior to distribution or household-level treatment) carry out spot checks in households by measuring FRC and treat where necessary. The frequency of water delivery, temperature and length of time water is stored all affect household FRC measurements (chlorine dissipation).

Promoting protected sources: People may prefer unprotected water sources such as rivers, lakes and unprotected wells for reasons of taste, proximity and social convenience. Understand their rationale and develop messages and activities that promote protected water sources.

Palatable water: If safe drinking water does not taste good (due to salinity, hydrogen sulfide or chlorine levels that people are not used to), users may drink from better-tasting but unsafe sources. Use community engagement and hygiene activities to promote safe drinking water.

Water disinfection: Water should be treated with a residual disinfectant such as chlorine if there is a significant risk of source or post-delivery contamination. The risk will be determined by population density, excreta disposal arrangements, hygiene practices and the prevalence of diarrhoeal disease. Turbidity should be below 5 NTU. If it is higher, train users to filter, settle and decant the water to reduce turbidity before treatment. Consider short-term double-dose chlorination if there is no alternative. Be aware that chlorine dissipation varies depending on the length of storage and temperature range, so factor this into dosing and contact times ⊕ *see Appendix 6: Household water treatment and storage decision tree.*

Quantity versus quality: If it is not possible to meet Minimum Standards for both water quantity and quality, prioritise quantity over quality. Even water of intermediate quality can be used to prevent dehydration, decrease stress and prevent diarrhoeal diseases.

Post-delivery contamination: Water that is safe at the point of delivery can become contaminated during collection, storage and drawing of drinking water. Minimise this through safe collection and storage practices. Clean household or settlement storage tanks regularly and train the community to do so ⊕ *see Hygiene promotion standards 1.1* and *1.2.*

Household-level water treatment and safe storage (HWTSS): Use HWTSS when a centrally operated water treatment system is not possible. HWTSS options that reduce diarrhoea and improve the microbiological quality of stored household water include boiling, chlorination, solar disinfection, ceramic filtration, slow sand filtration, membrane filtration, and flocculation and disinfection. Work with other sectors to agree household fuel requirements and access for boiling water. Avoid introducing an unfamiliar water treatment option in crises and in epidemics. Effective use of HWTSS options requires regular follow-up, support and monitoring, and is a prerequisite to adopting HWTSS as an alternative water treatment approach ⊕ *see Appendix 6: Household water treatment and storage decision tree.*

Water quality for institutions: Treat all water supplies for schools, hospitals, health centres and feeding centres with chlorine or another residual disinfectant ⊕ *see Appendix 3: Minimum water quantities: survival figures and quantifying water needs.*

Chemical and radiological contamination: Where hydrogeological records or knowledge of industrial or military action suggest that water supplies may carry chemical or radiological public health risks, carry out a chemical analysis. A decision to use possibly contaminated water for longer-term supplies should only follow a thorough analysis of the health implications and validation with the local authorities.

3. Excreta management

An environment free of human excreta is essential for people's dignity, safety, health and well-being. This includes the natural environment as well as the living, learning and working environments. Safe excreta management is a WASH priority. In crisis situations, it is as important as providing a safe water supply.

All people should have access to appropriate, safe, clean and reliable toilets. Defaecation with dignity is a highly personal matter. Appropriateness is determined by cultural practices, people's daily customs and habits, perceptions, and whether individuals have used sanitation facilities before. Uncontrolled human defaecation constitutes a high risk to health, particularly where population density is high, where people are displaced, and in wet or humid environments.

Different terms are used in the WASH sector to define excreta management facilities. In this Handbook, "toilet" means any facility or device that immediately contains excreta and creates the first barrier between people and the waste ⊕ *see Appendix 2: The F diagram*. The word "toilet" is used in place of the word "latrine" throughout the Handbook.

Containment of human excreta away from people creates an initial barrier to excreta-related disease by reducing direct and indirect routes of disease transmission ⊕ *see Appendix 2: The F diagram*. Excreta containment should be integrated with collection, transport, treatment and disposal to minimise public health risks and environmental impact.

Evidence of human faeces in the living, learning and working environment can indicate protection issues. People may not feel safe using facilities, especially in densely populated areas.

For this chapter, "human excreta" is defined as waste matter discharged from the body, especially faeces, urine and menstrual waste. The standards in this section cover the whole excreta chain, from initial containment to ultimate treatment.

Excreta management standard 3.1: Environment free from human excreta

All excreta is safely contained on-site to avoid contamination of the natural, living, learning, working and communal environments.

Key actions

1 〉 Establish facilities in newly constructed communal settlements or those with substantially damaged infrastructure to immediately contain excreta.

2 ⟩ Decontaminate any faeces-contaminated living, learning and working spaces or surface water sources immediately.

3 ⟩ Design and construct all excreta management facilities based on a risk assessment of potential contamination of any nearby surface water or groundwater source.

- Assess the local topography, ground conditions and groundwater and surface water (including seasonal variations) to avoid contaminating water sources and inform technical choices.

4 ⟩ Contain and dispose of children's and babies' faeces safely.

5 ⟩ Design and construct all excreta management facilities to minimise access to the excreta by problem vectors.

Key indicators

There are no human faeces present in the environment in which people live, learn and work

All excreta containment facilities are sited appropriately and are an adequate distance from any surface or groundwater source

Guidance notes

Phasing: Immediately after a crisis, control indiscriminate open defaecation as a matter of urgency. Establish defaecation areas, site and build communal toilets, and start a concerted hygiene campaign. Prevent defaecation near all water sources (whether used for drinking or not) and water storage and water treatment facilities. Do not establish defaecation areas uphill or upwind of settlements. Do not establish them along public roads, near communal facilities (especially health and nutrition facilities) or near food storage and preparation areas.

Conduct a hygiene promotion campaign that encourages safe excreta disposal and creates a demand for more toilets.

In urban crises, assess the extent of damage to existing sewerage systems. Consider installing portable toilets or use septic or containment tanks that can be regularly desludged.

Distance from water sources: Ensure faecal material from containment facilities (trench latrines, pits, vaults, septic tanks, soakaway pits) does not contaminate water sources. Faecal contamination is not an immediate public health concern unless the water source is consumed, but environmental damage must be avoided.

Where possible, conduct soil permeability tests to determine the speed at which waste moves through the soil (infiltration rate). Use this to determine the minimum distance between containment facilities and water sources.

The infiltration rate will depend on soil saturation levels, any extraction from the source, and the nature of the excreta (more watery excreta will travel faster than less watery excreta).

If soil permeability tests cannot be conducted, the distance between containment facilities and water sources should be at least 30 metres, and the bottom of pits should be at least 1.5 metres above the groundwater table. Increase these distances for fissured rocks and limestone, or decrease them for fine soils.

In high groundwater table or flood situations, make the containment infrastructure watertight to minimise groundwater contamination. Alternatively, build elevated toilets or septic tanks to contain excreta and prevent it from contaminating the environment. Prevent drainage or spillage from septic tanks from contaminating surface water or groundwater sources.

If contamination is suspected, immediately identify and control the source of contamination and initiate water treatment. Some water contaminants can be managed with purification treatment methods such as chlorination. However, the source of contaminants such as nitrates needs to be identified and controlled. Methaemoglobinaemia is an acute but reversible condition associated with high nitrate levels in drinking water, for instance ⊕ *see Water supply standard 2.2: Water quality.*

Containment of children's faeces: Infants' and children's faeces are commonly more dangerous than those of adults. Excreta-related infection among children is frequently higher, and children may not have developed antibodies to infections. Provide parents and caregivers with information about safe disposal of infants' faeces, laundering practices and the use of nappies (diapers), potties or scoops to manage safe disposal.

Excreta management standard 3.2: Access to and use of toilets

People have adequate, appropriate and acceptable toilets to allow rapid, safe and secure access at all times.

Key actions

1 ⟩ Determine the most appropriate technical options for toilets.

- Design and construct toilets to minimise safety and security threats to users and maintenance workers, especially women and girls, children, older people and persons with disabilities.
- Segregate all communal or shared toilets by sex and by age where appropriate.

2 ⟩ Quantify the affected population's toilets requirements based on public health risks, cultural habits, water collection and storage.

3 ⟩ Consult representative stakeholders about the siting, design and implementation of any shared or communal toilets.

- Consider access and use by age, sex and disability; people facing mobility barriers; people living with HIV; people with incontinence; and sexual or gender minorities.
- Locate any communal toilets close enough to households to enable safe access, and distant enough so that households are not stigmatised by proximity to toilets.

4 ⟩ Provide appropriate facilities inside toilets for washing and drying or disposal of menstrual hygiene and incontinence materials.

5 ⟩ Ensure that the water supply needs of the technical options can be feasibly met.

- Include adequate supply of water for handwashing with soap, for anal cleansing, and for flush or hygienic seal mechanisms if selected.

Key indicators

Ratio of shared toilets

- Minimum 1 per 20 people

Distance between dwelling and shared toilet

- Maximum 50 metres

Percentage of toilets that have internal locks and adequate lighting

Percentage of toilets reported as safe by women and girls

Percentage of women and girls satisfied with the menstrual hygiene management options at toilets they regularly use

Guidance notes

What is adequate, appropriate and acceptable? The type of toilet adopted will depend on the phase of the response, preferences of the intended users, existing infrastructure, the availability of water for flushing and water seals, the soil formation and the availability of construction materials.

Generally, toilets are adequate, appropriate and acceptable if they:

- are safe to use for all of the population, including children, older people, pregnant women and persons with disabilities;
- are located to minimise security threats to users, especially to women and girls and people with other specific protection concerns;

- are no more than 50 metres from dwellings;
- provide privacy in line with users' expectations;
- are easy to use and keep clean (generally, clean toilets are used more frequently);
- do not present a hazard to the environment;
- have adequate space for different users;
- have inside locks;
- are provided with easy access to water for handwashing, anal cleansing and flushing;
- allow for the dignified cleaning, drying and disposal of women's menstrual hygiene materials, and child and adult incontinence materials;
- minimise fly and mosquito breeding; and
- minimise smell.

Provide people who have chronic illnesses, such as HIV, with easy access to a toilet. They frequently suffer from chronic diarrhoea and reduced mobility.

Monitor use and the percentage of people who report that the toilets meet their requirements. Use this information to understand which groups are not satisfied and how to improve the situation. Consider access and use by sex and age, persons with disabilities or facing mobility barriers, people living with HIV and people with incontinence.

Accessibility: The technical option chosen should respect the right of all people, including persons with disabilities, to safely access sanitation facilities. Accessible toilets, or additions to existing toilets, may need to be constructed, adapted or bought for children, older people and persons with disabilities or incontinence. As a guide, single-access gender-neutral toilets with ramps or level entries, with enhanced accessibility inside the superstructure, should also be made available at a **minimum ratio of 1 per 250 people**.

Safe and secure facilities: Inappropriate siting of toilets may make women and girls more vulnerable to attack, especially at night. Ensure that all at-risk groups, including women and girls, boys, older people and others with specific protection concerns feel and are safe when using the toilets during both day and night. Adequately light facilities and consider providing at-risk groups with torches. Ask the community, especially those most at risk, how to enhance their safety. Consult stakeholders from schools, health centres and clinics, child-friendly spaces, marketplaces and nutrition feeding centres.

Note that it is not sufficient to consult only with women and children about safe and dignified WASH facilities, as in many contexts men control what women and children are allowed to do. Be aware of these social hierarchies and power dynamics, and actively engage with decision-makers to reinforce the right of women and children to safely access toilets and showers.

Lighting at communal facilities can improve access but can also attract people to use the lighting for other purposes. Work with the community, especially those most at risk of threats to their safety, to find additional ways to reduce their exposure to risks.

Quantifying toilet requirements: Consider how to adapt toilet requirements in context to reflect changes in the living environment before and after the crisis, requirements in public areas and any specific public health risks. During the first phases of a rapid-onset crisis, **communal toilets are an immediate solution with a minimum ratio of 1 per 50 people**, which must be improved as soon as possible. A **medium-term minimum ratio is 1 per 20 people**, with a ratio of 3:1 for female to male toilets. For planning figures and number of toilets ⊕ *see Appendix 4.*

Household, shared or communal? Household toilets are considered the ideal in terms of user safety, security, convenience and dignity, and the demonstrated links between ownership and maintenance. Sometimes shared facilities for a small group of dwellings may be the norm. Communal or shared toilets can be designed and built with the aim of ensuring household toilets in future. For example, leaving sanitation corridors in settlements provides the space to build communal facilities close to shelters and then build household facilities as budgets allow. Sanitation corridors ensure access for desludging, maintenance and decommissioning.

Communal toilets will also be necessary in some public or communal spaces such as health facilities, market areas, feeding centres, learning environments and reception or administrative areas ⊕ *see Appendix 4: Minimum numbers of toilets: community, public places and institutions.*

Communal sanitation facilities built during a rapid response will have specific operation and maintenance requirements. Payment for toilet cleaners may be agreed with communities as a temporary measure, with a clear exit strategy.

Water and anal cleansing material: In designing the facility, ensure enough water, toilet paper or other anal cleansing material is available. Consult users about the most appropriate cleansing material and ensure safe disposal and sustainability of supply.

Handwashing: Ensure that the facility allows for handwashing, including water and soap (or an alternative such as ash) after using toilets, cleaning the bottom of a child who has defecated, and before eating and preparing food.

Menstrual hygiene management: Toilets should include appropriate containers for the disposal of menstrual materials in order to prevent blockages of sewerage pipes or difficulties in desludging pits or septic tanks. Consult with women and girls on the design of toilets to provide space, access to water for washing, and drying areas.

Excreta management standard 3.3:
Management and maintenance of excreta collection, transport, disposal and treatment

Excreta management facilities, infrastructure and systems are safely managed and maintained to ensure service provision and minimum impact on the surrounding environment.

Key actions

1 〉 Establish collection, transport, treatment and disposal systems that align with local systems, by working with local authorities responsible for excreta management.

- Apply existing national standards and ensure that any extra load placed on existing systems does not adversely affect the environment or communities.
- Agree with local authorities and landowners about the use of land for any off-site treatment and disposal.

2 〉 Define systems for short- and long-term management of toilets, especially sub-structures (pits, vaults, septic tanks, soakage pits).

- Design and size sub-structures to ensure that all excreta can be safely contained and the pits desludged.
- Establish clear and accountable roles and responsibilities and define sources of finance for future operation and maintenance.

3 〉 Desludge the containment facility safely, considering both those doing the collection and those around them.

4 〉 Ensure that people have the information, means, tools and materials to construct, clean, repair and maintain their toilets.

- Conduct hygiene promotion campaigns on the use, cleaning and maintenance of toilets.

5 〉 Confirm that any water needed for excreta transport can be met from available water sources, without placing undue stress on those sources.

Key indicator

All human excreta is disposed of in a manner safe to public health and the environment

Guidance notes

Desludging is the removal of (untreated and partially treated) excreta from the pit, vault or tank, and transport to an off-site treatment and disposal facility.

If desludging is required, it must be designed into operation and maintenance processes and budgets from the start.

Sullage or domestic wastewater is classified as sewage when mixed with human excreta. Unless the settlement is sited where there is an existing sewerage system, domestic wastewater should not be allowed to mix with human excreta. Sewage is difficult and more expensive to treat than domestic wastewater.

Planning: Initially, plan for an excreta volume of 1–2 litres per person per day. Long term, plan for 40–90 litres per person per year; excreta reduces in volume as it decomposes. Actual volume will depend on whether water is used for flushing or not, whether material or water is used for anal cleansing, whether water and other material is used for cleaning toilets, and the diet of the users. Ensure that household water from cleaning and cooking or from laundry and bathing does not enter the containment facilities, as the excess water will mean more desludging. Allow 0.5 metres at the top of the pit for backfill.

For specific public health situations such as cholera outbreaks ⊕ *see WASH standard 6: WASH in healthcare settings.*

Local markets: Use locally available materials and labour for toilet construction where appropriate. This enhances participation in the use and maintenance of the facilities.

Excreta containment in difficult environment: In floods or urban crises, appropriate excreta containment facilities can be especially difficult to provide. In these situations, consider raised toilets, urine diversion toilets, sewage containment tanks and temporary disposable plastic bags with appropriate collection and disposal systems. Support these different approaches with hygiene promotion activities.

Excreta as a resource: Excreta is also a potential resource. Technology is available to convert processed sludge into energy, for example as combustible bricks or as biogas. Ecological sanitation or composting processes recover organic fractions and nutrients from a combination of human waste and organic kitchen waste. The resulting compost can be used as a soil conditioner or fertiliser for household gardens.

4. Vector control

A vector is a disease-carrying agent. Vectors create a pathway from the source of a disease to people. Vector-borne diseases are a major cause of sickness and death in many humanitarian settings. Most vectors are insects such as mosquitoes, flies and lice, but rodents can also be vectors. Some vectors can also cause painful bites. Vectors can be symptomatic of solid waste, drainage or excreta management problems, inappropriate site selection, or broader safety and security problems.

Vector-borne disease can be complex, and solving vector-related problems may require specialist advice. However, simple and effective measures can prevent the spread of such diseases.

Vector control programmes may have no impact if they target the wrong vector, use ineffective methods, or target the right vector in the wrong place or at the wrong time. Controls must be targeted and based on the life cycles and ecologies of the vectors.

Control programmes should aim to reduce vector population density, vector breeding sites, and contact between humans and vectors. In developing control programmes, consult existing studies and seek expert advice from national and international health organisations. Seek local advice on disease patterns, breeding sites and seasonal variations in vector numbers and disease incidence.

The standards in this section focus on reducing or eliminating problem vectors to prevent vector-borne disease and reduce nuisance. Vector control across multiple sectors is required ⊕ *see Shelter and settlement standard 2, Essential healthcare – communicable diseases standard 2.1.1* and *Food assistance standard 6.2.*

Vector control standard 4.1: Vector control at settlement level

People live in an environment where vector breeding and feeding sites are targeted to reduce the risks of vector-related problems.

Key actions

1 ⟩ Assess vector-borne disease risk for a defined area.

- Establish whether the area's incidence rate is greater than the World Health Organization (WHO) or national established norm for the disease.
- Understand the potential vector breeding sites and life cycle, especially feeding, informed by local expertise and knowledge of important vectors.

2 ⟩ Align humanitarian vector control actions with local vector control plans or systems, and with national guidelines, programmes or policies.

3 ⟩ Determine whether chemical or non-chemical control of vectors outside households is relevant based on an understanding of vector life cycles.

- Inform the population about potential risks that originate from chemical control of vectors and about the schedule for chemical application.
- Train and equip all personnel handling chemicals with personal protective equipment (PPE) and clothing.

Key indicator

Percentage of identified breeding sites where the vector's life cycle is disrupted

Guidance notes

Communal settlements: Site selection is important to minimising the exposure of the affected population to the risk of vector-borne disease. This should be one of the key factors when considering possible sites. To control malaria, for example, locate communal settlements 1–2 kilometres upwind from large breeding sites such as swamps or lakes, but ensure the availability of an additional clean water source. Consider the impact a new settlement site can have on the presence of problem vectors in neighbouring host communities ⊕ *see Shelter and settlement standard 2: Location and settlement planning.*

Assessing risk factors: Base decisions about vector control responses on an assessment of potential disease and other risks, as well as on epidemiological and clinical evidence of vector-borne disease problems. Review suspected and confirmed cases during the previous two years in the defined area. Other factors influencing this risk include:

- immunity status of the population, including previous exposure and nutritional and other stresses;
- movement of people from a non-endemic to an endemic area during displacement;
- pathogen type and prevalence, in both vectors and humans;
- vector species, numbers, behaviours and ecology (season, breeding sites) and how they potentially interact; and
- increased exposure to vectors as a result of proximity, settlement pattern, shelter type, existing individual protection and avoidance measures.

Removing or modifying vector breeding and feeding sites: Many WASH activities can have a major impact on breeding and feeding sites, including:

- eliminating stagnant water or wet areas around water distribution points, bathing areas and laundries;

- managing solid waste storage at household level, during collection and transportation, and at treatment and disposal sites;
- providing lids for water containers;
- managing excreta;
- cleaning toilet slabs and superstructures to dissuade vector presence;
- sealing offset toilet pits to ensure no faeces enters the environment and problem vectors do not enter the pits;
- running hygiene promotion programmes on general cleanliness; and
- keeping wells covered and/or treating them with larvicide, for example where dengue fever is endemic.

The three main species of mosquitoes responsible for transmitting disease are:

- *Culex* (filariasis and West Nile virus), which breed in stagnant water with organic matter, such as in toilets;
- *Anopheles* (malaria and filariasis), which breed in relatively unpolluted surface water such as puddles, slow-flowing streams and wells; and
- *Aedes* (dengue, yellow fever, chikungunya and Zika virus), which breed in water containers such as bottles, buckets and tyres.

Biological and non-chemical control: Biological control introduces organisms that prey on, parasitise, compete with or reduce populations of the target vector species. For example, larvivorous fish and freshwater crustaceans can control *Aedes* mosquitoes (vectors of dengue). One of the most promising strategies is the use of *Wolbachia* endosymbiotic bacteria, which has been targeted towards reducing dengue virus transmission. Biological control has been effective in certain operational environments, and evidence points to it being effective at scale.

While biological control avoids chemical contamination of the environment, there may be operational limitations and undesired ecological consequences. Biological control methods are only effective against the immature stages of vector mosquitoes and are typically restricted to use in large concrete or glazed clay water-storage containers or wells. The willingness of local communities to accept the introduction of organisms into water containers is essential. Community involvement is desirable when distributing the control organisms and in monitoring and restocking containers when necessary.

Environmental engineering responses: Several basic environmental engineering measures reduce vector breeding, including:

- proper disposal of human and animal excreta, properly functioning toilets, and keeping lids on the squatting hole of pit toilets;
- proper disposal of solid waste to control insects and rodents;
- ensuring good drainage in settlements; and
- draining standing water and clearing vegetation around open canals and ponds to control mosquitoes.

Such measures will reduce the population density of some vectors. It may not be possible to have sufficient impact on all the vector breeding, feeding and resting sites within or near a settlement, even in the longer term. If so, consider local-ised chemical control or individual protection measures. Spraying infected spaces may reduce the number of adult flies and prevent a diarrhoea epidemic or help to minimise the disease burden if employed during an epidemic. Indoor residual spraying will reduce the adult density of mosquitoes transmitting malaria or dengue. Toxic baits will reduce rodent populations.

National and international protocols: The WHO has published clear interna-tional protocols and norms that address both the choice and the application of chemicals in vector control, as well as the protection of personnel and training requirements. Vector control measures should address two principal concerns: efficacy and safety. If national norms regarding the choice of chemicals fall short of international standards, then consult with and lobby the relevant national authority for permission to adhere to the international standards.

Protect all personnel handling chemicals by providing training, protective clothing and bathing facilities and restricting the number of hours they spend handling chemicals.

Coordination with malaria treatment: Implement malaria vector control strategies simultaneously with early diagnosis and treatment with anti-malarials ⊕ *see Essential healthcare – communicable diseases standard 2.1.1: Prevention.*

Vector control standard 4.2:
Household and personal actions to control vectors
All affected people have the knowledge and means to protect themselves and their families from vectors that can cause a significant risk to health or well-being.

Key actions

1 ⟩ Assess current vector avoidance or deterrence practices at the household level as part of an overall hygiene promotion programme.

- Identify barriers to adopting more effective behaviours and motivators.

2 ⟩ Use participatory and accessible awareness campaigns to inform people of problem vectors, high-risk transmission times and locations, and preventive measures.

- Follow up specifically with high-risk groups.

3 ⟩ Conduct a local market assessment of relevant and effective preventive measures.

- Consider strengthening markets to provide a sustainable source of preven-tive measures.

- Make a procurement, distribution and implementation plan for vector control items in collaboration with the community, local authorities and other sectors if local markets are unable to meet the demand.

4 〉 Train communities to monitor, report and provide feedback on problem vectors and the vector control programme.

Key indicators

Percentage of affected people who can correctly describe modes of transmission and effective vector control measures at the household level

Percentage of people who have taken appropriate action to protect themselves from relevant vector-borne diseases

Percentage of households with adequate protection for stored food

Guidance notes

Individual malaria protection measures: Timely, systematic protection measures such as insecticidal tents, curtains and bed nets help protect against malaria. Long-lasting insecticidal nets also give some protection against body and head lice, fleas, ticks, cockroaches and bedbugs. Use other protection methods like long-sleeved clothing, household fumigants, burning coils, aerosol sprays and repellents against mosquitoes. Support the use of such methods for those most at risk, such as children under five years, people with immune deficiencies and pregnant women.

High-risk groups: Some sections of the community will be more vulnerable to vector-related diseases than others, particularly babies and infants, older people, persons with disabilities, sick people, and pregnant and breastfeeding women. Identify high-risk groups and take specific action to reduce that risk. Take care to prevent stigmatisation.

Social mobilisation and communication: Behavioural change is required at both individual and community levels to reduce both vector larval habitats and the adult vector population. Social mobilisation and communication activities should be fully integrated into vector prevention and control efforts, using a wide variety of channels.

Individual protection measures for other vectors: Good personal hygiene and regular washing of clothes and bedding are the most effective protection against body lice. Control infestations by personal treatment (powdering), mass laundering or delousing campaigns. Develop and use treatment protocols for new arrivals in the settlement. A clean household environment, effective waste disposal and appropriate storage of cooked and uncooked food will deter rats, other rodents and insects (such as cockroaches) from entering houses or shelters ⊕ *see Hygiene promotion standard 1.1: Hygiene promotion.*

5. Solid waste management

Solid waste management is the process of handling and disposing of organic and inorganic solid waste. This involves:

- planning solid waste management systems;
- handling, separating, storing, sorting and processing waste at source;
- transferring to a collection point; and
- transporting and final disposal, reuse, re-purposing or recycling.

Waste can be generated at the household, institutional or community level and includes medical waste. It may be hazardous or non-hazardous. Inadequate solid waste management poses a public health risk as it can create favourable habitats for insects, rodents and other disease vectors ⊕ *see Vector control standard 4.1: Vector control at settlement level*. Untreated waste can pollute surface water and groundwater. Children may play in poorly managed solid waste, risking injury or sickness. Waste pickers, who earn money from collecting reusable materials from waste dumps, may be at risk of injury or infectious disease.

Solid waste can block drainage systems, generating stagnant and polluted surface water, which may be a habitat for vectors and create other public health risks.

These standards do not cover treatment or disposal of chemical effluents or leachates. For sources of advice on handling and treating hazardous waste ⊕ *see References and further reading.* For sources of advice on handling and treating hazardous waste. For medical waste ⊕ *see WASH standard 6: WASH in healthcare settings.*

Solid waste management standard 5.1:
Environment free from solid waste
Solid waste is safely contained to avoid pollution of the natural, living, learning, working and communal environments.

Key actions

1 ⟩ Design the solid waste disposal programme based on public health risks, assessment of waste generated by households and institutions, and existing practice.

- Assess capacities for local reuse, re-purposing, recycling or composting.
- Understand the roles of women, men, girls and boys in solid waste management to avoid creating additional protection risks.

2 > Work with local or municipal authorities and service providers to make sure existing systems and infrastructure are not overloaded, particularly in urban areas.

- Ensure new and existing off-site treatment and disposal facilities can be used by everyone.
- Establish a timeline for complying as quickly as possible with local health standards or policies on solid waste management.

3 > Organise periodic or targeted solid waste clean-up campaigns with the necessary infrastructure in place to support the campaign.

4 > Provide protective clothing for and immunise people who collect and dispose of solid waste and those involved in reuse or re-purposing.

5 > Ensure that treatment sites are appropriately, adequately and safely managed.

- Use any safe and appropriate treatment and disposal methods, including burying, managed landfill and incineration.
- Manage waste management sites to prevent or minimise protection risks, especially for children.

6 > Minimise packing material and reduce the solid waste burden by working with organisations responsible for food and household item distribution.

....

Key indicator

There is no solid waste accumulating around designated neighbourhood or communal public collection points

....

Guidance notes

People on the move will discard items that are heavy or no longer needed. Solid waste generation at distribution points may increase tensions with host populations. The volume of solid waste will increase if distributed household items do not meet real needs. This solid waste is likely to be of different materials to that generated locally and may need to be treated or disposed of differently.

Urban areas: Urban solid waste management infrastructure may be integrated with other service systems. Work with existing authorities and systems to accommodate the extra solid waste burden.

Protection for waste handlers: Provide protective clothing for everyone involved in solid waste management. At a minimum, provide gloves. Ideally, also provide boots and protective masks. When necessary, provide immunisation against tetanus and hepatitis B. Ensure soap and water is available for washing hands and face. Inform and train staff on the correct ways to transport and dispose of waste and of the risks associated with improper management ⊕ *see Essential healthcare – communicable diseases standard 2.1.1: Prevention.*

Waste handlers can be stigmatised as dirty or poor. Community consultation can help to change attitudes. Ensuring waste handlers have appropriate equipment and are able to maintain cleanliness will also help.

Communal settlements and rural areas: Household solid waste disposal may be possible, and even preferred, in communal settlements and areas with lower population densities. Base the size of domestic solid waste burial or burning pits on household size and an assessment of the waste stream. Household pits should be properly fenced to prevent children and animals accessing them, and ideally be located at least 15 metres from dwellings.

For neighbourhood or communal collection points, initially provide a 100-litre container for every 40 households. Provide one container per ten households in the longer term, as household waste production is likely to increase over time. As a guide, a 2.5-person maintenance team should be available per 1,000 persons.

Reuse, re-purpose and recycle: Encourage reuse, re-purposing or recycling of solid waste by the community, unless doing so presents a significant public health risk. Consider the potential for small-scale business opportunities or supplementary income from waste recycling, and the possibility of household or communal composting of organic waste.

Solid waste management standard 5.2:
Household and personal actions to safely manage solid waste

People can safely collect and potentially treat solid waste in their households.

Key actions

1 ⟩ Provide households with convenient, adequately sized and covered storage for household waste or containers for small clusters of households.

■ Consider household preference for the number and size of containers for reuse and recycling.

2 ⟩ Provide clearly marked and fenced public neighbourhood collection points where households can deposit waste on a daily basis.

3 ⟩ Organise a system to regularly remove household and other waste from designated public collection points.

4 ⟩ Ensure that solid waste burial or burning pits at household or communal levels are safely managed.

Key indicators

Percentage of households with access to a designated neighbourhood or communal solid waste collection point at an acceptable distance from their dwelling

Percentage of households reporting appropriate and adequate waste storage at household level

Guidance note

Planning: The amount of solid waste that people generate depends on how food is obtained and cooked, and which activities are carried out within or near the household. Variations can be seasonal and often reflect distribution or market schedules. Assume that one person generates 0.5 kilograms of solid waste per day. This equates to 1–3 litres per person per day, based on a typical solid waste density of 200 to 400kg/m^3.

Solid waste management standard 5.3:
Solid waste management systems at community level

Designated public collection points do not overflow with waste, and final treatment or disposal of waste is safe and secure.

Key actions

1 〉 Ensure that institutions such as schools and learning spaces, child-friendly spaces and administrative offices have clearly marked, appropriate and adequate covered on-site storage for waste generated at that location.

2 〉 Provide clearly marked and fenced storage for waste generated in communal areas, especially formal or informal marketplaces, transit centres and registration centres.

Key indicators

Percentage of schools and learning centres with appropriate and adequate waste storage

Percentage of public markets with appropriate and adequate waste storage

Percentage of solid waste pits or incinerators at schools, learning centres, public markets and other public institutions that are managed safely

Guidance notes

Market waste: Marketplaces need particular attention, as communal areas often lack designated ownership and responsibility for solid waste management. Treat most market waste in the same manner as domestic solid waste.

Abattoir waste: Ensure that slaughtering is hygienic and complies with local laws. Much of the solid waste produced by abattoirs and fish markets can be treated as domestic solid waste but pay special attention to their liquid waste. If appropriate, dispose of this waste in a covered pit next to the abattoir or fish processing plant. Run blood and other liquid waste into the pit through a slab-covered channel to reduce insect access to the pit. Make water available for cleaning purposes.

6. WASH in disease outbreaks and healthcare settings

WASH and health actors both work to reduce public health risks, prevent disease transmission and control disease outbreaks. Strong coordination with government structures and partners – across the two sectors – is needed to address public health risks in the community and in healthcare settings. This standard builds on WASH standards 1–5 and the Health chapter, which should be consulted in their entirety and guide all technical interventions.

Infection prevention and control (IPC) is a key activity in disease prevention in any situation as well as for outbreak response. It is critical for the patient, the healthcare worker and the community. It is the responsibility of health agencies to ensure Minimum Standards are met in healthcare settings, but doing so often requires structured collaboration and support from WASH actors.

Good and consistently applied WASH practices, in both the community and healthcare settings, will reduce transmission of infectious diseases and help control outbreaks. Minimum actions in this standard apply to ongoing response and highlight areas to scale up in the event of an outbreak.

Community-based outbreak response

It is not always practical to respond to every component of WASH. Focus on the immediate public health risk and build trust and accountability with the communities. Prioritise response based on epidemiological findings, assessment of risk factors, transmission routes (especially beyond faecal–oral), expected impact of each intervention and available resources.

Community engagement remains a key component of outbreak response in order to prevent the spread of disease. Existing community perceptions and beliefs can support or hinder a response, so it is important to understand and address them. Some social norms may need to be modified to prevent disease transmission. For example, work with the community to find alternative forms of greeting to replace handshaking.

Encourage specific disease prevention and treatment measures within the affected community. This can include using mosquito nets to prevent malaria, or oral rehydration salts and zinc (for children) for diarrhoea.

If community outreach workers perform active case finding or related tasks, they must be trained. Integrate all data into the overall outbreak investigation and response. Quick tracking of the spread of the outbreak and who it affects is critical for a timely response, and integrated data in a common system will prevent double counting or missing key areas ⊕ *see Essential healthcare – communicable diseases standard 2.1.4: Outbreak preparedness and response.*

During any disease outbreak always follow up-to-date technical guidance, as emerging diseases will have different risks and impact. Extensive guidance exists on IPC in specific disease prevention and control, and this must be followed as a priority ⊕ *see References below.* This standard provides a minimum of issues to be considered and describes the collaboration between WASH and health sectors. The diagram below provides an overview of key community-based WASH actions during an outbreak. For health actions, ⊕ *see Essential healthcare – communicable diseases standards 2.1.1 to 2.1.4.*

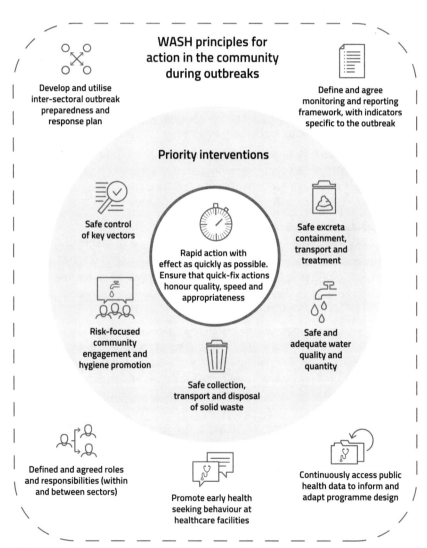

WASH principles for action in the community during outbreaks (Figure 5)

Standard 6:
WASH in healthcare settings

All healthcare settings maintain minimum WASH infection prevention and control standards, including in disease outbreaks.

Key actions

1 ⟩ Provide a reliable water supply of sufficient quantity and quality, appropriate to the healthcare setting.

- Store at least 48 hours' worth of safe water (0.5mg/l free residual chlorine) to ensure a constant supply.
- **Outbreaks:** Increase water quantities and adapt chlorine solutions according to disease type, risk and needs.

2 ⟩ Provide sufficient excreta disposal facilities to limit disease transmission.

- Provide commode chairs and bucket toilets for those facing mobility barriers.
- Clean sanitation facilities (toilets, showers, washing area) with water and detergent. Avoid using strong detergents in toilets.
- **Outbreaks:** Provide excreta disposal facilities in each zone of the healthcare setting.
- **Outbreaks:** Adapt materials and supplies for the specific disease, such as cholera beds and excreta or vomit buckets.
- **Outbreaks:** Determine any extra precautions needed for cleaning, decommissioning and desludging excreta facilities and equipment.

3 ⟩ Provide enough cleaning materials and equipment for healthcare workers, patients and visitors to maintain hygiene.

- Provide handwashing stations at key locations with safe water, soap or alcohol rub. Air dry or use "once only" towels.
- **Outbreaks:** Provide handwashing stations in each zone.
- **Outbreaks:** Set up additional hygiene practices, such as chlorine foot baths or spraying (depending on the disease) and handwashing before putting on or removing personal protective equipment (PPE).
- **Outbreaks:** Provide patients with specific hygiene items and training before discharge.

4 ⟩ Maintain a clean and hygienic environment.

- Clean floors and horizontal work surfaces daily with water and detergent.
- Clean and disinfect potentially contaminated surfaces with a 0.2 per cent chlorine solution.
- Clean, disinfect or sterilise reusable medical devices depending on risk before each use.

- Disinfect all linen with 0.1 per cent chlorine solution after soaking if visibly soiled; sterilise all linens for operating theatres.
- **Outbreaks:** Increase disinfectant strengths for cleaning floors and contaminated surfaces. Consider special mechanisms for disinfecting linen.

5 〉 Handle, treat and dispose of waste correctly.

- Segregate healthcare waste at point of generation using the three-bin method.
- Train all healthcare workers in waste segregation and management.
- Ensure that designated teams should wear PPE to collect, treat and dispose of waste (minimum: gloves and boots).
- **Outbreaks:** Increase waste-handling precautions, using full PPE based on disease type.

6 〉 Ensure all healthcare workers, patients and carers use appropriate PPE.

- Provide PPE for the type of exposure and category of isolation precautions.
- Train healthcare workers, patients and others in the facility to select, use and remove PPE.
- **Outbreaks:** Assess the type of anticipated exposure and adapt PPE to type of transmission.

7 〉 Manage and bury the dead in a way that is dignified, culturally appropriate and safe according to public health practices.

- Consider local traditions as well as the need for identification and return of deceased to families.
- **Outbreaks:** Identify alternatives with the community if usual practices are unsafe.
- **Outbreaks:** Train and equip teams with appropriate PPE to carry out burials.

Key indicators

All healthcare workers clean their hands, using soap or alcohol rub, before and after every patient contact

All patients and carers wash their hands before handling or eating food and after going to the toilet

All handwashing stations have soap or alcohol rub (or 0.05 per cent chlorine solution in outbreaks)

Number of handwashing stations

- Minimum: one station for every ten inpatients

Drinking water quality at point of delivery

- Minimum: 0.5–1mg/l FRC

Quantity of safe water available

- Minimum: 5 litres per outpatient per day

- Minimum: 60 litres per patient per day in cholera treatment centre
- Minimum: 300–400 litres per patient per day in viral haemorrhagic fever treatment centre

Number of accessible toilets

- Minimum: four in outpatient facilities (separated for men, women, children and healthcare workers)
- Minimum: 1 per 20 inpatients (separated for men, women, children and healthcare workers)

Guidance notes

Infection prevention and control programming is essential in all healthcare settings, including ambulances and community health programmes. It requires development of guidelines on standard precautions, transmission-based precautions and clinical aseptic techniques. Include a dedicated infection prevention and control team in each setting and training for healthcare workers. Surveillance systems should monitor healthcare-associated infections and antimicrobial resistance. Settings should have appropriate staffing and workload. Beds should contain one patient only. Healthcare should be provided in a safe and appropriate environment, built with sufficient WASH infrastructure and equipment to maintain safe hygiene practices ⊕ *see Health systems standards 1.1 and 1.2.*

Water quantity and quality: When calculating amounts of water required, refer to the values in Appendix 3 and adjust for the situation, ⊕ *see Appendix 3: Minimum water quantities.* Mobile clinics should aim to provide the same WASH standards as for outpatients, including access to a safe water source and toilets. Ensure at least a 48-hour supply (and storage) per facility. For outbreaks such as Ebola and cholera, allow for 72 hours' supply. For the foundations of community WASH programmes ⊕ *see Water supply standards 2.1 and 2.2.*

The following chlorine solutions are required for different uses in healthcare settings.

Chlorine solution	Healthcare facility activity
0.05%	Handwashing Laundry (after cleaning)
0.2% (cholera) 0.5% (Ebola)	Wiping horizontal work surfaces after cleaning (for cholera only) Cleaning materials, aprons, boots, cooking utensils and dishes Rinsing bedpans, buckets Cleaning surfaces contaminated with body fluid Preparing dead bodies (Ebola)
2%	Preparing dead bodies (cholera) Added to excreta and vomit buckets (cholera)
1%	Mother solution for chlorinating water

Excreta management: ⊕ *See Excreta management standards 3.1 to 3.3* for guidance on excreta management generally and *Hygiene promotion standard 1.3: Menstrual hygiene management and incontinence* for specific information on materials.

Provide technically and culturally appropriate toilet facilities with separate locked and well-lit toilets with sufficient space for carers to assist patients. All sanitation facilities (toilets, showers, washing area) should be cleaned with water and detergent. Avoid using strong disinfectants inside toilets (particularly for septic tanks), as it disrupts the natural biodegradation processes of some pathogens.

During outbreaks, take extra precautions when cleaning, decommissioning or desludging excreta facilities and equipment (for example, chlorine solution for cleaning, treatment with quicklime or chlorine).

Greywater: As a minimum dispose of greywater using a grease trap and soakaway pit. Ensure it is fenced off to prevent tampering by the public.

Healthcare waste contains infectious organisms such as HIV and hepatitis B, which can also contaminate soil and water sources. Use a minimum three-bin method to collect and segregate waste as soon as it is created:

Category	Example	Container colour/label
General waste Not hazardous	Paper	Black
Used sharps Hazardous, infectious	Needles, scalpels, infusion sets, broken glass, empty vials	Yellow, labelled "SHARPS", leak-proof and puncture-proof
Not sharps Hazardous, infectious	Materials contaminated with body fluids, such as swabs, dressings, sutures, laboratory cultures	Yellow, labelled and leak-proof

Further segregation may be needed, including for pathological (human tissue), pharmaceutical and chemical (laboratory reagents) waste. Collect segregated waste from the medical area at least daily, and immediately if highly infectious. Use trolleys to transport waste using a fixed route to designated areas with restricted public access. Waste containers, trolleys and storage areas must be disinfected regularly. Vaccinate all healthcare waste handlers for hepatitis B and tetanus.

Treat and dispose of waste depending on the available facilities:

Category	Treatment and disposal
General	Recycle, burn, or bury Municipal landfill
Used sharps	Sharps pit Encapsulate and bury in landfill Incinerate (not vials) then bury in ash pit (with caution, as sharps may not be blunted)

Category	Treatment and disposal
Infectious (not sharps)	Burial pit (cover waste with quicklime) Incinerate then bury in ash pit Autoclave or chemically treat
Pathological	Depends on socio-cultural norms: Burial pits (for example, placenta pit) or burial sites Cremation
Pharmaceutical	Follow national guidelines if possible or return to supplier Encapsulate and dispose in landfill Special incinerators (>1,200 degrees Celsius)
Chemical waste	Follow national guidelines if possible or return to supplier Small amounts can be incinerated or encapsulated Treat in treatment plant or rotary kiln

Incinerators should exceed 900 degrees Celsius and have dual chambers. Low-quality incinerators produce toxic emissions and air pollutants and do not completely sterilise. All pits and incinerators should be built to existing national and international standards and be safely operated, maintained and decommissioned.

Personal protective equipment (PPE) is mandatory for compliance with IPC protocols and to ensure that patients, families and staff are not put at further risk.

Assess the type of exposure anticipated (splash, spray, contact or touch) and the disease transmission category. Use equipment that is well-fitted, durable and appropriate (such as fluid-resistant or fluid-proof).

Basic PPE protects wearers from exposure to blood, body fluid, secretions or excretions. It includes: gloves when touching infectious material; gowns/aprons when clothes or exposed skin is in contact with infectious material; face protection such as masks, goggles or shields to protect from splashes, droplets or sprays. Additional PPE (or basic PPE at additional times) may also have to be worn depending on type of disease transmission: contact (e.g. gown and gloves when in patient environment); droplet (surgical masks within 1 metre of patient); and airborne (particulate respirators).

Place single-use PPE in waste bins (such as 220-litre barrels) at the entrance to the undressing area. Collect and take bins to a designated waste management area. Place reusable PPE such as heavy-duty gloves and goggles in bins containing a 0.5 per cent chlorine solution. Clean, launder, repair and store appropriately.

A 0.5 per cent chlorine solution should be available for washing gloved hands after each undressing step. Provide a separate 0.05 per cent chlorine solution hand-washing stand as the final step in the undressing process.

Management of the dead: Promote safe, dignified and culturally appropriate burial of dead persons, including identification of all persons. Let people identify their family members and conduct funerals. Do not dispose of bodies unceremoniously in mass graves. Mass burial may be a barrier to obtaining the death certificates necessary for making legal claims. Consider potential legal issues when burying the victims of violence ⊕ *see Health systems standard 1.1: Health service delivery.*

Special precautions, such as preparing the dead with chlorine solution, may be needed during outbreaks, depending on the disease pathogen and its transmission. Rituals for cleansing and caring for the dead can increase the possibility of disease transmission, but failure to respect cultural sensitivities could lead to burials happening in secret and being unreported.

Healthcare workers and burial teams should wear PPE at all times. Support community burial workers with psychosocial services. Work with community leaders to prevent stigmatisation of people performing this role.

Decommissioning: Consult the community, local authorities and humanitarian actors to decide how to decommission a temporary healthcare setting during a response.

Appendix 1
Water supply, sanitation and hygiene promotion initial needs assessment checklist

This list of questions is primarily for use to assess needs, identify resources and describe local conditions. It does not include questions that will determine the external resources needed to supplement those immediately and locally available.

General

- How many people are affected and where are they? Disaggregate the data by sex, age, disability and so on.
- What are people's likely movements? What are the security factors for the affected people and for potential relief responses?
- What are the current, prevalent or possible WASH-related diseases?
- Who are the key people to consult or contact?
- Who are the vulnerable people in the population and why?
- Is there equal access for all to existing facilities, including at public places, health centres and schools?
- What special security risks exist for women, girls, boys and men? At-risk groups?
- What water, sanitation and hygiene practices were the population accustomed to before the crisis?
- What are the formal and informal power structures (for example, community leaders, elders, women's groups)?
- How are decisions made in households and in the community?
- Is there access to local markets? What key WASH goods and services were accessible in the market before the crisis and are accessible during the crisis?
- Do people have access to cash and/or credit?
- Are there seasonal variations to be aware of that may restrict access or increase demands on labour during harvesting time, for example?
- Who are the key authorities to liaise and collaborate with?
- Who are the local partners in the geographical area, such as civil society groups that have similar capacity in WASH and community engagement?

Hygiene promotion

- What water, sanitation and hygiene practices were people accustomed to before the crisis?
- What existing practices are harmful to health, who practises these and why?

- Who still practises positive hygiene behaviour and what enables and motivates them to do this?
- What are the advantages and disadvantages of any proposed changes in practice?
- What are the existing formal and informal channels of communication and outreach (such as community health workers, traditional birth attendants, traditional healers, clubs, cooperatives, churches and mosques)?
- What access to the mass media is there in the area (for example, radio, television, video, newspapers)?
- What local media organisations and/or non-governmental organisations (NGOs) are there?
- Which segments of the population can and should be targeted (for example, mothers, children, community leaders, religious leaders)?
- What type of outreach system would work in this context (for example, community hygiene volunteers or workers or promoters, school health clubs, WASH committees) for both immediate and medium-term mobilisation?
- What are the learning needs of hygiene promotion staff and community outreach workers?
- What non-food items are available and what are the most urgently needed based on preferences and needs?
- Where do people access markets to buy their essential hygiene items? Has this access (cost, diversity, quality) changed since the crisis?
- How do households access their essential hygiene items? Who makes the decisions regarding which items to buy and prioritise?
- How effective are hygiene practices in healthcare settings (particularly important in epidemic situations)?
- What are the needs and preferences of women and girls for menstrual hygiene practices?
- What are the needs and preferences of people living with incontinence?

Water supply

- What is the current water supply source and who are the present users?
- How much water is available per person per day?
- What is the daily and weekly frequency of the water supply availability?
- Is the water available at the source sufficient for short-term and longer-term needs for all groups?
- Are water collection points close enough to where people live? Are they safe?
- Is the current water supply reliable? How long will it last?
- Do people have enough water containers of the appropriate size and type (collection and storage)?
- Is the water source contaminated or at risk of contamination (microbiological, chemical or radiological)?

- Is there a water treatment system in place? Is treatment necessary? Is treatment possible? What treatment is necessary?
- Is disinfection necessary? Does the community have problems with water palatability and acceptance associated with chlorine taste and smell?
- Are there alternative sources of water nearby?
- What traditional beliefs and practices relate to the collection, storage and use of water?
- Are there any obstacles to using the available water supply sources?
- Is it possible to move the population if water sources are inadequate?
- What are the alternatives if water sources are inadequate?
- Are there any traditional beliefs and practices related to hygiene (for example, during the Haiti cholera outbreak the disease was associated with voodoo culture)? Are any of these beliefs or practices either useful or harmful?
- What are the key hygiene issues related to water supply?
- Do people buy water? If so where, at what cost and for what purposes? Has this access (the cost, quality, regularity of delivery) changed?
- Do people have the means to use water hygienically?
- Are waterpoints and laundry and bathing areas well drained?
- Are soil conditions suitable for on-site or off-site management of problem water from waterpoints and laundry and bathing areas? Has a soil percolation test been carried out?
- In the event of rural displacement, what is the usual source of water for livestock?
- Will there be any environmental effects due to possible water supply intervention, abstraction and use of water sources?
- What other users are currently using the water sources? Is there a risk of conflict if the sources are utilised for new populations?
- What opportunities are there to collaborate with the private and/or public sector in water provision? What bottlenecks and opportunities exist that could inform the response analysis and recommendations?
- What operation and maintenance duties are necessary? What capacity is there to fulfil them in the short and long term? Who shall be accountable for them?
- Is there an existing or potential finance mechanism or system that can recover the operation and maintenance costs?
- How does the host population access water and ensure that its water is safe at the point of use?

Excreta disposal

- Is the environment free of faeces?
- If there is open defecation, is there a designated area?
- Are there any existing facilities? If so, are they used? Are they sufficient? Are they operating successfully? Can they be extended or adapted?

- Are the facilities safe and dignified: lighted, equipped with locks, privacy screens? Can people access the toilet facilities during the day and night? If not at night, what are the alternatives?
- What excreta management practices does the host population practice?
- Is the current defecation practice a threat to water supplies (surface or groundwater) or living areas and to the environment in general?
- Are there any social – cultural norms to consider in the design of the toilet?
- Are people familiar with the design, construction and use of toilets?
- What local materials are available for constructing toilets?
- Is there an existing acceptance of and practice for composting?
- From what age do children start to use the toilet?
- What happens to the faeces of infants and young children?
- What is the slope of the terrain?
- What is the level of the groundwater table?
- Are soil conditions suitable for on-site excreta disposal?
- Do current excreta disposal arrangements encourage vectors?
- Are there materials or water available for anal cleansing? How do people normally dispose of these materials?
- Do people wash their hands after defecation and before food preparation and eating? Are soaps or other cleansing materials with water available next to the toilet or within the household?
- How do women and girls manage menstruation? Are there appropriate materials or facilities available for this?
- Are there any specific facilities or equipment available for making sanitation accessible for persons with disabilities, people living with HIV, people living with incontinence or people immobile in medical facilities?
- Have environmental considerations been assessed: for example, the extraction of raw materials such as sand and gravel for construction purposes, and the protection of the environment from faecal matter?
- Are there skilled workers in the community, such as masons or carpenters and unskilled labourers?
- Are there available pit emptiers or desludging trucks? Currently, is the collected faecal waste disposed of appropriately and safely?
- What is the appropriate strategy for management of excreta – inclusive of containment, emptying, treatment and disposal?

Vector-borne diseases

- What are the vector-borne disease risks and how serious are they?
- What daily or seasonal patterns do local vectors follow in relation to reproduction, resting and feeding?
- Are there traditional beliefs and practices (for example, the belief that dirty water causes malaria) that relate to vectors and vector-borne disease? Are any of these beliefs or practices either useful or harmful?

- If vector-borne disease risks are high, do people at risk have access to individual protection?
- Is it possible to make changes to the local environment (especially by, for example, drainage, scrub clearance, excreta disposal, solid waste disposal) to inhibit vector breeding?
- Is it necessary to control vectors by chemical means? What programmes, regulations and resources exist regarding the use of chemicals for vector control?
- What information and safety precautions need to be provided to households?

Solid waste management

- Is accumulated solid waste a problem?
- How do people dispose of their waste? What type and quantity of solid waste is produced?
- Can solid waste be disposed of on-site or does it need to be collected and disposed of off-site?
- What is the normal solid waste disposal practice for affected people (for example, compost and/or refuse pits, collection system, bins)?
- Are there medical facilities and activities producing waste? How is it disposed of? Who is responsible?
- Where are disposable sanitary materials disposed of (for example, children's nappies, menstruation hygiene materials and incontinence materials)? Is their disposal discreet and effective?
- What is the effect of the current solid waste disposal on the environment?
- What solid waste management capacity do the private and public sectors have?

Appendix 2
The F diagram: faecal–oral transmission of diarrhoeal diseases

W WATER

S SANITATION

H HYGIENE

Barriers can stop the transmission of disease; these can be primary (preventing the initial contact with the faeces) or secondary (preventing it being ingested by a new person). They can be controlled by water, sanitation and hygiene interventions.

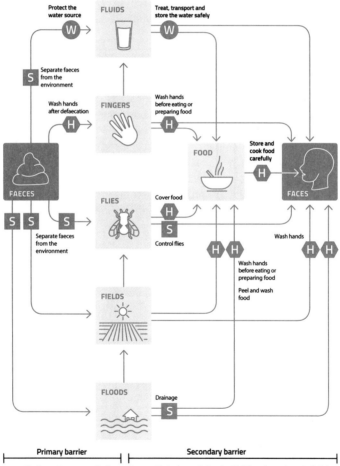

NOTE The diagram is a summary of pathways; other associated routes may be important. Drinking water may be contaminated by a dirty water container, for example, or food may be infected by dirty cooking utensils. © WEDC

The 5 Fs: faeces, fluids, fingers, flies, food (Figure 6)

Source: Water, Engineering and Development Centre (WEDC)

Appendix 3
Minimum water quantities: survival figures and quantifying water needs

Surviving needs: water intake (drinking and food)	2.5–3 litres per person per day (depends on climate and individual physiology)
Basic hygiene practices	2–6 litres per person per day (depends on social and cultural norms)
Basic cooking needs	3–6 litres per person per day (depends on food type, social and cultural norms)
Health centres and hospitals	5 litres per outpatient 40–60 litres per in-patient per day 100 litres per surgical intervention and delivery Additional quantities may be needed for laundry equipment, flushing toilets and so on
Cholera centres	60 litres per patient per day 15 litres per carer per day
Viral haemorrhagic fever centre	300–400 litres per patient per day
Therapeutic feeding centres	30 litres per in-patient per day 15 litres per carer per day
Mobile clinic with infrequent visits	1 litre per patient per day
Mobile clinic with frequent visits	5 litres per patient per day
Oral rehydration points (ORPs)	10 litres per patient per day
Reception/transit centres	15 litres per person per day if stay is more than one day 3 litres per person per day if stay is limited to day-time
Schools	3 litres per pupil per day for drinking and hand washing (Use for toilets not included: see Public toilets below)
Mosques	2–5 litres per person per day for washing and drinking
Public toilets	1–2 litres per user per day for hand washing 2–8 litres per cubicle per day for toilet cleaning
All flushing toilets	20–40 litres per user per day for conventional flushing toilets connected to a sewer 3–5 litres per user per day for pour-flush toilets
Anal washing	1–2 litres per person per day
Livestock	20–30 litres per large or medium animal per day 5 litres per small animal per day

Appendix 4
Minimum numbers of toilets:
community, public places and institutions

Location	Short term	Medium and long term
Community	1 toilet for 50 persons (communal)	1 toilet for 20 persons (shared family) 1 toilet for 5 persons or 1 family
Market areas	1 toilet for 50 stalls	1 toilet for 20 stalls
Hospitals/medical centres	1 toilet for 20 beds or 50 outpatients	1 toilet for 10 beds or 20 outpatients
Feeding centres	1 toilet for 50 adults 1 toilet for 20 children	1 toilet for 20 adults 1 toilet for 10 children
Reception/transit centres	1 toilet for 50 individuals 3:1 female for male	
Schools	1 toilet for 30 girls 1 toilet for 60 boys	1 toilet for 30 girls 1 toilet for 60 boys
Offices		1 toilet for 20 staff

Source: Adapted from Harvey, Baghri and Reed (2002)

Note: Where the context allows, aim for shared family toilets or, even better, household toilets from the onset in order to build acceptance, ownership and culturally appropriate sanitation interventions.

Note: the community, the same number of bathing facilities as toilets per 50 persons (short-term) or 20 persons (long-term) should be provided.

Appendix 5
Water- and sanitation-related diseases

1 . Environmental classification of water-related infections

Category	Infection	Pathogenic agent
1) Faecal–oral (water-borne or water-washed)		
a) Diarrhoeas and dysenteries	Amoebic dysentery	Protozoon
	Balantidiasis	Protozoon
	Campylobacter enteritis	Bacterium
	Cholera	Bacterium
	Cryptosporidiosis	Protozoon
	E. coli diarrhoea	Bacterium
	Giardiasis	Protozoon
	Rotavirus diarrhoea	Virus
	Salmonellosis	Bacterium
	Shigellosis	Bacterium
	Yersiniosis	Bacterium
b) Enteric fevers	Typhoid	Bacterium
	Paratyphoid	Bacterium
	Poliomyelitis	Virus
	Hepatitis A	Virus
	Leptospirosis	Spirochaete
	Ascariasis	Helminth
	Trichuriasis	Helminth
2) Water-washed		
a) Skin and eye infections	Infectious skin diseases	Miscellaneous
	Infectious eye diseases	Miscellaneous
b) Other	Louse-borne typhus	Rickettsia
	Louse-borne relapsing fever	Spirochaete
3) Water-based		
a) Penetrating skin	Schistosomiasis	Helminth
b) Ingested	Guinea worm	Helminth
	Clonorchiasis	Helminth
	Diphyllobothriasis	Helminth
	Paragonimiasis	Helminth
	Others	Helminth
4) Water-related insect vector		
a) Biting near water	Sleeping sickness	Protozoon
b) Breeding in water	Filariasis	Helminth
	Malaria	Protozoon
	River blindness	Helminth
	Mosquito-borne viruses	Virus
	Yellow fever	Virus
	Dengue	Virus
	Others	

Source: ACF: Water, Sanitation and Hygiene for Populations at Risk, Annex 5, page 675

2. Environmental classification of excreta-related infections

Category	Infection	Pathogenic agent	Dominant transmission mechanisms	Major control measure (engineering measures in italics)
1) Faecal–oral (non-bacterial) Non-latent, low infection dose	Poliomyelitis Hepatitis A Rotavirus diarrhoea Amoebic dysentery Giardiasis Balantidiasis Enterobiasis Hymenolepiasis	Virus Virus Virus Protozoon Protozoon Protozoon Helminth Helminth	Person to person contact Domestic contamination	Domestic water supply Improved housing Provision of toilets Health education
2) Faecal–oral (bacterial) Non-latent, medium, or high infectious dose Moderately persistent and able to multiply	Diarrhoeas and dysenteries Campylobacter enteritis Cholera E. coli diarrhoea Salmonellosis Shigellosis Yersiniosis Enteric fevers Typhoid Paratyphoid	 Bacterium Bacterium Bacterium Bacterium Bacterium Bacterium Bacterium Bacterium	Person to person contact Domestic contamination Water contamination Crop contamination	Domestic water supply Improved housing Provision of toilets Excreta treatment before reuse or discharge Health education
3) Soil-transmitted helminths Latent and persistent with no intermediate host	Ascariasis (roundworm) Trichuriasis (whipworm) Hookworm Strongyloidiasis	Helminth Helminth Helminth Helminth	Yard contamination Ground contamination in communal defaecation area Crop contamination	Provision of toilets with clean floors Excreta treatment before land application
4) Beef and pork tapeworms Latent and persistent with cow or pig intermediate host	Taeniasis	Helminth	Yard contamination Field contamination Fodder contamination	Provision of toilets Excreta treatment before land application Cooking and meat inspection
5) Water-based helminths Latent and persistent with aquatic intermediate host(s)	Schistosomiasis Clonorchiasis Diphyllobothriasis Paragonimiasis	Helminth Helminth Helminth Helminth	Water contamination	Provision of toilets Excreta treatment before discharge Control of animals harbouring infection Cooking

Category	Infection	Pathogenic agent	Dominant transmission mechanisms	Major control measure (engineering measures in italics)
6) Excreta-related insect vectors	Filariasis (transmitted by *Culex pipiens* mosquitoes) infections	Helminth	Insects breed in various faecally contaminated sites	Identification and elimination of potential breeding sites
	Infections in categories 1–4, especially I and II, which may be transmitted by flies and cockroaches	Miscellaneous		Use of mosquito netting

Appendix 6
Household water treatment and storage decision tree

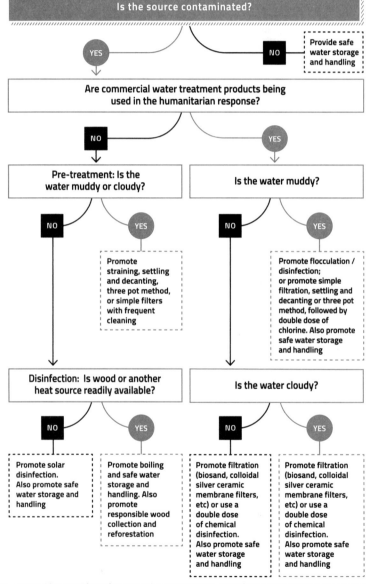

Source: *Adapted from IFRC (2008) Household water treatment and safe storage in emergencies manual*

References and further reading

General/right to water
The Rights to Water and Sanitation (Information Portal). www.righttowater.info

United Nations General Assembly Resolution 64/292 The human right to water and sanitation. 2010. www.un.org

Impact of WASH on health
Bartram, J. Cairncross, S. *"Hygiene, sanitation, and water: forgotten foundations of health."* PLoS Med, vol. 7, 2010, e1000367.

Blanchet, K. et al. *An Evidence Review of Research on Health Interventions in Humanitarian Crises.* LSHTM, Harvard School of Public Health, 2013. www.elrha.org

Campbell, O.M. Benova, L. et al. *"Getting the basic rights: the role of water, sanitation and hygiene in maternal and reproductive health: a conceptual framework."* Trop Med Int Health, vol. 20, 2015, pp. 252-67.

Fewtrell, L. Kaufmann, et al. *"Water, sanitation, and hygiene interventions to reduce diarrhoea in less developed countries: a systematic review and meta-analysis."* Lancet Infectious Diseases, vol. 5, 2005, pp. 42-52. www.thelancet.com

Ramesh, A. Blanchet, K. et al. *"Evidence on the Effectiveness of Water, Sanitation, and Hygiene (WASH) Interventions on Health Outcomes in Humanitarian Crises: A Systematic Review."* PLoS One, vol. 10, 2015, e0124688.

Wolf, J. Pruss-Ustun, A. et al. *"Assessing the impact of drinking water and sanitation on diarrhoeal disease in low- and middle-income settings: systematic review and meta-regression."* Trop Med Int Health, vol. 19, no. 9, 2014.

Effective WASH programming
Compendium of accessible WASH technologies. WaterAid and WEDC, 2014. www.wateraid.org

Davis, J. Lambert, R. *Engineering in Emergencies* (2nd ed). ITDG Publishing & RedR UK, 2002.

Efficacy and effectiveness of water, sanitation, and hygiene interventions in emergencies in low- and middle-income countries: a systematic review. https://www.developmentbookshelf.com

Public Health Engineering in Precarious Situations. MSF, 2010. http://refbooks.msf.org

WASH Manual for Refugee Settings: Practical Guidance for Refugee Settings. UNHCR, 2017. http://wash.unhcr.org

Water, Sanitation and Hygiene for Populations at Risk. ACF, 2005. www.actionagainsthunger.org

Protection and WASH

House, S. Ferron, S. Sommer, M. Cavill, S. *Violence, Gender & WASH: A Practitioner's Toolkit - Making water, sanitation and hygiene safer through improved programming and services.* WaterAid/SHARE, 2014. http://violence-WASH.lboro.ac

Humanitarian Inclusion Standards for older people and people with disabilities. Age and Disability Consortium, 2018. https://www.cbm.org

INEE Minimum Standards for Education: Preparedness, Response, Recovery. INEE, 2010.www.inees ite.org

Jones, H.E. Reed, R. *Water and sanitation for disabled people and other vulnerable groups: Designing services to improve accessibility.* Loughborough University, UK, 2005. wedc-knowledge.lboro.ac

Minimum Standards for Child Protection in Humanitarian Action: Alliance for Child Protection in Humanitarian Action, 2012. http://cpwg.net

Hygiene promotion/behaviour change

Curtis, V. Cairncross, S. *"Effect of washing hands with soap on diarrhoea risk in the community: a systematic review." Lancet Infect Dis*, vol. 3, 2003, pp. 275-81.

De Buck, E. Hannes, K. et al. *Promoting handwashing and sanitation behaviour change in low- and middle income countries. A mixed method systematic review. Systematic Review 36.* International Initiative for Impact Evaluation, June 2017. www.3ieimpact.org

Ferron, S. Morgan, J. O'Reilly, M. *Hygiene Promotion: A Practical Manual from Relief to Development.* ITDG Publishing, Rugby, UK, 2000 and 2007.

Freeman, M.C. Stocks, M.E. et al. *"Hygiene and health: systematic review of hand-washing practices worldwide and update of health effects." Trop Med Int Health*, vol. 19, 2014, pp. 906-16.

Harvey, P. Baghri, S. Reed, B. Emergency Sanitation: Assessment and Programme Design. WEDC, 2002. https://wedc-knowledge.lboro.ac

Hygiene Promotion in Emergencies. Training package. WASH Cluster. http://washcluster.net

Hygiene Promotion Guidelines. UNHCR, 2017. http://wash.unhcr.org

Rabie, T. Curtis, V. *"Handwashing and risk of respiratory infections: a quantitative systematic review." Trop Med Int Health*, vol. 11, 2006, pp. 258-67.

Watson, J.A. Ensink, J.H. Ramos, M. Benelli, P. Holdsworth, E. Dreibelbis, R. Cumming, O. *"Does targeting children with hygiene promotion messages work? The effect of handwashing promotion targeted at children, on diarrhoea, soil-transmitted helminth infections and behaviour change, in low- and middle-income countries." Trop Med Int Health*, 2017.

Menstrual hygiene

Mahon, T. Cavill, S. *Menstrual Hygiene Matters: Training guide for practitioners.* WaterAid. https://washmatters.wateraid.org

Sommer, M. Schmitt, M. Clatworthy, D. *A Toolkit for integrating Menstrual Hygiene Management (MHM) into Humanitarian Response.* Colombia University, Mailman

School of Public Health and International Rescue Committee. New York, 2017. www.rescue.org

Incontinence

Groce, N. Bailey, N. Land, R. Trani, J.F. Kett, M. *"Water and sanitation issues for persons with disabilities in low- and middle-income countries: a literature review and discussion of implications for global health and international development."* Journal of Water and Health, vol. 9, 2011, pp. 617-27.

Hafskjold, B. Pop-Stefanija, B. et al. *"Taking stock: Incompetent at incontinence - why are we ignoring the needs of incontinence sufferers?"* Waterlines, vol. 35, no. 3, 2016. www.developmentbookshelf.com

Excreta management

Clasen, T.F. Bostoen, K. Schmidt, W.P. Boisson, S. Fung, I.C. Jenkins, M.W. Scott, B. Sugden, S. Cairncross, S. *"Interventions to improve disposal of human excreta for preventing diarrhoea."* Cochrane Database Syst Rev, 2010, CD007180.

Freeman, M.C. Garn, J.V. Sclar, G.D. Boisson, S. Medlicott, K. Alexander, K.T. Penakalapati, G. Anderson, D. Mahtani, A.G. Grimes, J.E.T. Rehfuess, E.A. Clasen, T.F. *"The impact of sanitation on infectious disease and nutritional status: A systematic review and meta-analysis."* Int J Hyg Environ Health, vol. 220, 2017, pp. 928-49.

Gensch, R. Jennings, A. Renggli, S. Reymond, Ph. *Compendium of Sanitation Technologies in Emergencies.* German WASH Network and Swiss Federal Institute of Aquatic Science and Technology (Eawag), Berlin, Germany, 2018.

Graham, J.P. Polizzotto, M.L. "Pit latrines and their impacts on groundwater quality: A systematic review." *Environmental Health Perspectives,* vol. 121, 2013. http://hsrc.himmelfarb.gwu

Harvey, P., *Excreta Disposal in Emergencies: A Field Manual.* An Inter-Agency Publication, WEDC, 2007. http://wash.unhcr.org

Simple Pit Latrines. WASH Fact sheet 3.4. WHO. www.who.int

Water treatment

Branz, A. Levine, M. Lehmann, L. Bastable, A. Imran Ali, S. Kadir, K. Yates, T. Bloom, D. Lantagne, D. *"Chlorination of drinking water in emergencies: a review of knowledge to develop recommendations for implementation and research needed."* Waterlines, vol. 36, no. 1, 2017. https://www.developmentbookshelf.com

Lantagne, D.S. Clasen, T.F. *"Point-of-use water treatment in emergencies."* Waterlines, vol. 31, no. 1-2, 2012.

Lantagne, D.S. Clasen, T.F. *"Use of household water treatment and safe storage methods in acute emergency response: Case study results from Nepal, Indonesia, Kenya, and Haiti."* Environmental Science and Technology, vol. 46, no. 20, 2012.

Rayner, J. Murray, A. Joseph, M. Branz, A.J. Lantagne, D. *"Evaluation of household drinking water filter distributions in Haiti."* Journal of Water, Sanitation and Hygiene for Development, vol. 6, no. 1, 2016.

Water quality

Bain, R. Cronk, R. Wright, J. Yang, H. Slaymaker, T. Bartram, J. *"Fecal Contamination of Drinking-Water in Low- and Middle-Income Countries: A Systematic Review and Meta-Analysis."* PLoS Med, vol. 11, 2014, e1001644.

Guidelines for Drinking-Water Quality. WHO, 2017. www.who.int

Kostyla, C. Bain, R. Cronk, R. Bartram, J. *"Seasonal variation of fecal contamination in drinking water sources in developing countries: a systematic review."* PubMed, 2015.

Vector control

Dengue: Guidelines for Diagnosis, Treatment, Prevention and Control. New Edition. World Health Organization, Geneva, 2009. Chapter 3, Vector management and delivery of vector control services. www.who.int

Handbook for Integrated Vector Management. WHO, 2012. www.who.int

Lacarin, C.J. Reed, R.A. *Emergency Vector Control Using Chemicals.* WEDC, Loughborough University, 1999. UK. https://wedc-knowledge.lboro.ac

Malaria Control in Humanitarian Emergencies: An Inter-agency Field Handbook. WHO, 2005. www.who.int

Thomson, M. *Disease Prevention Through Vector Control: Guidelines for Relief Organisations.* Oxfam GB, 1995. https://policy-practice.oxfam.org

Vector Control: Aedes aegypti vector control and prevention measures in the context of Zika, Yellow Fever, Dengue or Chikungunya: Technical Guidance. WASH WCA Regional Group, 2016. http://washcluster.ne

Solid waste management

Disaster Waste Management Guidelines. UNOCHA, MSB and UNEP, 2013. www.eecentre.org

Technical Notes for WASH in Emergencies, no. 7: Solid waste management in emergencies. WHO/WEDC, 2013. www.who.int

WASH in disease outbreaks

Brown, J. Cavill, S. Cumming, O. Jeandron, A. *"Water, sanitation, and hygiene in emergencies: summary review and recommendations for further research."* Waterlines, vol. 31, 2012.

Cholera Toolkit. UNICEF, 2017. www.unicef.org

Essential environmental health standards in health care. WHO, 2008. http://apps.who.int

Guide to Community Engagement in WASH: A practitioners guide based on lessons from Ebola. Oxfam, 2016. https://policy-practice.oxfam.org

Infection prevention and control (IPC) guidance summary: Ebola guidance package. WHO, 2014. www.who.int

Lantagne, D. Bastable, A. Ensink, J. Mintz, E. *"Innovative WASH Interventions to Prevent Cholera."* WHO Wkly Epid Rec. October 2, 2015.

Management of a Cholera Epidemic. MSF, 2017. https://sherlog.msf.org

Rapid Guidance on the Decommissioning of Ebola Care Facilities. WHO, 2015. http://apps.who.int

Taylor, D.L. Kahawita, T.M. Cairncross, S. Ensink, J.H. *"The Impact of Water, Sanitation and Hygiene Interventions to Control Cholera: A Systematic Review."* PLoS One, vol. 10, e0135676. Doi: 10.1371/journal.pone.0135676, 2015. http://journals.plos.org

Yates, T. Allen, J. Leandre Joseph, M. Lantagne, D. *WASH interventions in disease outbreak response. Humanitarian Evidence Programme.* Oxfam GB, 2017. https://policy-practice.oxfam.org

Yates, T. Vujcic, J.A. Joseph, M.L. Gallandat, K. Lantagne, D. *"Water, sanitation, and hygiene interventions in outbreak response: a synthesis of evidence."* Waterlines, vol. 37, no. 1, pp. 5–30. https://www.developmentbookshelf.com

Infection prevention and control

Aide Memoire for infection prevention and control in a healthcare facility. WHO, 2011. http://www.who.int

Essential water and sanitation requirements for health structures. MSF, 2009.

Guidelines on Core Components of Infection Prevention and Control Programmes at the National and Acute Health Care Facility Level. WHO, 2016. www.who.int

Guidelines for Safe Disposal of Unwanted Pharmaceuticals in and after Emergencies. WHO, 1999. www.who.int

Hand Hygiene Self-Assessment Framework. WHO, 2010. www.who.int

Incineration in Health Structures of Low-Income Countries. MSF, 2012. https://sherlog.msf.org

Laundries for Newbies. MSF, 2016. https://sherlog.msf.org

Management of Dead Bodies after Disasters: A Field Manual for First Responders. Second Edition. ICRC, IFRC, 2016. https://www.icrc.org

Medical Waste Management. ICRC, 2011. https://www.icrc.org

Safe management of wastes from health-care activities. Second edition. WHO, 2014. www.who.int

Sterilisation Guidelines. ICRC, 2014. http://icrcndresourcecentre.org

WASH in health care facilities. UNICEF, WHO, 2015. www.who.int

Waste Zone Operators Manual. MSF, 2012. https://sherlog.msf.org

WASH and nutrition

Altmann, M. et al. *"Effectiveness of a household water, sanitation and hygiene package on an outpatient program for severe acute malnutrition: A pragmatic cluster - randomized controlled trial in Chad."* The American Journal of Tropical Medicine and Hygiene, vol. 98, no. 4, Apr 2018, pp. 1005-12. https://www.ajtmh.org

BABYWASH and the 1,000 days: a practical package for stunting reduction. Action Against Hunger (ACF), 2017. https://www.actionagainsthunger.org

Null, C. et al. (2018) *"Effects of water quality, sanitation, handwashing, and nutritional interventions on diarrhoea and child growth in rural Kenya: a cluster randomised control trial."* The Lancet: Global Health, vol. 6, no. 3, March 2018, pp. e316–e329. https://www.sciencedirect.com

Oxfam and Tufts University WASH and Nutrition Series: Enteric Pathogens and Malnutrition. Technical memorandum 1. Oxfam, Tufts.
https://oxfamintermon.s3.amazonaws.com

WASH'NUTRITION 2017 Guidebook: Integrating water, sanitation, hygiene and nutrition to save lives. Action Against Hunger (ACF), 2017. www.actionagainsthunger.org

WASH, cash and markets
CaLP CBA quality toolbox. http://pqtoolbox.cashlearning.org

Further reading
For further reading suggestions please go to
www.spherestandards.org/handbook/online-resources

Food Security
and Nutrition

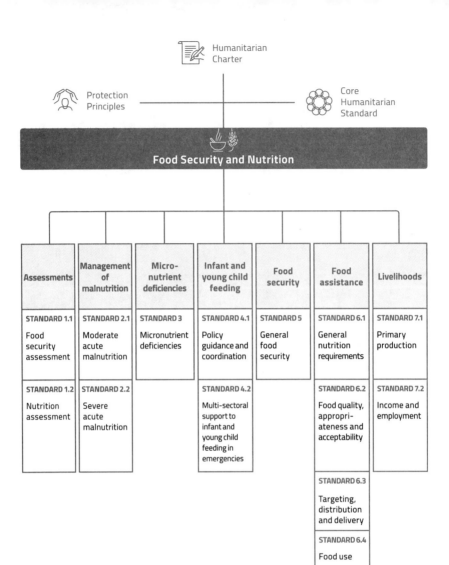

Humanitarian Charter

Protection Principles

Core Humanitarian Standard

Food Security and Nutrition

Assessments	Management of malnutrition	Micro-nutrient deficiencies	Infant and young child feeding	Food security	Food assistance	Livelihoods
STANDARD 1.1 Food security assessment	**STANDARD 2.1** Moderate acute malnutrition	**STANDARD 3** Micronutrient deficiencies	**STANDARD 4.1** Policy guidance and coordination	**STANDARD 5** General food security	**STANDARD 6.1** General nutrition requirements	**STANDARD 7.1** Primary production
STANDARD 1.2 Nutrition assessment	**STANDARD 2.2** Severe acute malnutrition		**STANDARD 4.2** Multi-sectoral support to infant and young child feeding in emergencies		**STANDARD 6.2** Food quality, appropriateness and acceptability	**STANDARD 7.2** Income and employment
					STANDARD 6.3 Targeting, distribution and delivery	
					STANDARD 6.4 Food use	

APPENDIX 1   Food security and livelihoods assessment checklist
APPENDIX 2   Seed security assessment checklist
APPENDIX 3   Nutrition assessment checklist
APPENDIX 4   Measuring acute malnutrition
APPENDIX 5   Measures of the public health significance of micronutrient deficiencies
APPENDIX 6   Nutritional requirements

Contents

Essential concepts
in food security and nutrition

Everyone has the right to be free from hunger and to have adequate food

The Sphere Minimum Standards for food security and nutrition are a practical expression of the right to adequate food in humanitarian contexts. The standards are grounded in the beliefs, principles, duties and rights declared in the Humanitarian Charter. These include the right to life with dignity, the right to protection and security, and the right to receive humanitarian assistance on the basis of need.

For a list of the key legal and policy documents that inform the Humanitarian Charter, with explanatory comments for humanitarian workers, ⊕ *see Annex 1.*

Undernutrition reduces people's ability to recover after a crisis. It impairs cognitive functions, reduces immunity to disease, increases susceptibility to chronic illness, limits livelihoods opportunities and reduces the ability to engage within the community. It undermines resilience and may increase dependence on ongoing support.

The causes of undernutrition are complex

The immediate causes of undernutrition are inadequate food intake and repeated disease ⊕ *see Figure 7.* The underlying causes are household food insecurity, poor feeding and care practices, unhealthy household environment and inadequate healthcare.

These underlying causes are inter-connected. So, although food insecurity is one cause of undernutrition, providing food assistance is unlikely to lead to a lasting solution unless other causes are addressed at the same time. Food and nutrition responses should work with WASH, shelter and settlement, and healthcare responses in a coordinated approach. For example, people require an adequate quantity and quality of water to prepare nutritious food and to adopt safe feeding practices. Having access to sanitation and hygiene facilities will reduce the risk of disease outbreaks. Having access to adequate shelter provides access to cooking facilities and protects people from extreme weather, which further reduces the risk of disease. When people have access to good healthcare, they are likely to have a higher nutritional status. This in turn increases their ability to pursue livelihood opportunities.

Control of the underlying causes will prevent and reduce undernutrition. Retaining people's livelihood assets is fundamental to this, because it increases their ability to manage other potential causes of undernutrition. Livelihoods assets include equipment and machinery, raw materials, land, knowledge and access to functioning markets. Food security and nutrition responses should contribute to protecting

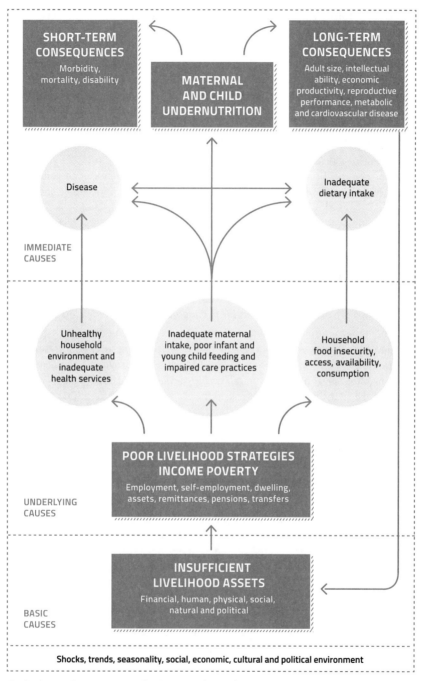

Food security and nutrition: causes of undernutrition (Figure 7)

and developing these assets, and therefore supporting different livelihood strategies, whether there are high malnutrition rates or not.

Social, economic, cultural and political changes in the post-crisis environment will affect a household's coping strategies and access to livelihoods or livelihood assets. Stabilising those external factors will contribute to increased opportunities for income and ultimately reduce people's exposure to the causes of undernutrition.

Working in urban areas brings specific challenges

Increasing urbanisation is creating new challenges for the food security and nutrition sector. Urban environments potentially offer increased employment and income-generating opportunities. However, as urban populations increase, demand for housing and services in those areas also increases. In many cases, existing land use planning policies and strategies cannot meet the unanticipated demand. Overcrowding, air pollution, poor waste management and lack of sanitation facilities in slums increase the chance of contracting acute illnesses. This reduces people's ability to take advantage of livelihoods opportunities and often triggers the underlying causes of undernutrition.

Some groups are particularly vulnerable to undernutrition

Developing an appropriate food response requires a full understanding of the unique nutritional needs of pregnant and breastfeeding women, infants and children, older people and persons with disabilities. Improving food security at the household level also requires an understanding of different roles. Women, for instance, often play a greater role in the planning and preparation of food for their households.

It is important to disaggregate data by sex, age and disability at a minimum. This shows who needs what kind of food and who may be missing important nutritional elements. Disaggregate post-distribution monitoring in the same way, to confirm that programme interventions are providing equitable access to adequate and appropriate food and nutrition.

Preventing undernutrition is just as important as treating acute malnutrition. Food security and nutrition interventions may determine nutrition and health status in the short term, and survival and well-being in the long term.

These Minimum Standards should not be applied in isolation

The Minimum Standards in this chapter reflect the core content of the right to food and contribute to the progressive realisation of this right globally.

The right to adequate food is linked to the rights to water and sanitation, health, and shelter. Progress in achieving the Sphere Minimum Standards in one area influences progress in other areas. Therefore, an effective response requires close coordination and collaboration with other sectors, local authorities and other responding agencies. This helps ensure that needs are met, that efforts are not duplicated and that the quality of food security and nutrition responses is optimised. Cross-references throughout the Handbook suggest potential linkages.

For example, if nutritional requirements are not being met, the need for WASH is greater, because people's vulnerability to disease increases. The same applies to populations where HIV is prevalent or where there is a large proportion of older people or persons with disabilities. In those circumstances, healthcare resources will also need to be adjusted. Decide priorities based on information shared between sectors, and review it as the situation evolves.

Where national standards are lower than the Sphere Minimum Standards, humanitarian organisations should work with the government to raise them progressively.

International law specifically protects the right to adequate food

The right to be free from hunger and to have adequate food is protected by international law. It requires physical and economic access to adequate food at all times. States are obliged to ensure this right when individuals or groups, including refugees and internally displaced persons, are unable to access adequate food, including in crises ⊕ *see Annex 1.*

States may request international assistance if their own resources are insufficient. In doing so they should:

- respect existing access to adequate food, and allow continued access;
- protect individuals' access to adequate food by ensuring that organisations or individuals do not deprive them of such access; and
- actively support people to ensure secure livelihoods and food security by providing them with the resources they need.

Withholding adequate food from civilians as a method of warfare is prohibited under the Geneva Conventions. It is also prohibited to attack, destroy, remove or render useless crops, livestock, foodstuffs, irrigation works, drinking water installations and supplies, and agricultural areas that produce foodstuffs.

In the case of occupation, international humanitarian law obliges an occupying power to ensure adequate food for the population, including importing supplies if those in the occupied territory are inadequate.

Links to the Protection Principles and Core Humanitarian Standard

Food and nutrition assistance has the potential to lead to serious rights violations if it is misused, particularly in exploitation or abuse of programme participants. Programmes must be designed with the affected population and implemented in ways that contribute to their safety, dignity and integrity. Proper management and strong oversight of staff and resources are required, along with strict adherence and enforcement of a code of conduct for all those involved in delivering assistance programmes. Establish clear feedback mechanisms with the affected population and respond quickly to any concerns. Aid workers should be trained on child safe-guarding and know how to use referral systems for suspected cases of violence, abuse or exploitation, including of children ⊕ *see Protection Principle 1* and *Core Humanitarian Standard Commitment 5*.

Civil-military cooperation and coordination, such as logistical support, should be carefully evaluated in all situations, and especially in conflict settings ⊕ *see What is Sphere* and *Protection Principles*.

In applying the Minimum Standards, all nine Commitments in the Core Humanitarian Standard should be respected as a foundation for providing an accountable food security and nutrition programme.

1. Food security and nutrition assessments

Food security and nutrition assessments are required throughout a crisis. They show how the context evolves and enable responses to be adjusted appropriately. Ideally food security and nutrition assessments should overlap, as they identify the barriers to adequate nutrition and to the availability, access to and use of food. Joint food security and nutrition assessments can increase cost-effectiveness and link nutrition to food security programming.

Assessments should adhere to widely accepted principles, use internationally accepted methods, and be impartial, representative and well-coordinated between humanitarian organisations and governments. Assessments must be complementary, consistent and comparable. Stakeholders must agree on a suitable methodology. It should include a cross-section of the affected population, with attention given to at-risk groups. Multi-sectoral assessments can help in assessing large-scale crises and wide geographical areas.

The objective of food security and nutrition assessments can be to:

- understand the situation, current needs and how to meet those needs;
- estimate how many people need assistance;
- identify groups at highest risk; and/or
- provide a baseline to monitor the impact of a humanitarian response.

The assessments can be conducted at various stages of a crisis. For example:

- an initial assessment within the first two to three days to start immediate distribution of food assistance;
- a rapid assessment within two to three weeks, relying on assumptions and estimates to provide a basis for designing programmes;
- a detailed assessment within 3 to 12 months if the situation seems to be deteriorating or more information is required to develop recovery programmes.

Detailed **food security assessments** identify livelihood strategies, assets and coping strategies. They consider how these have changed as a result of the crisis, and the consequences for household food security. A detailed assessment should identify how best to protect and/or promote these livelihood strategies in order to achieve food security.

Detailed **nutrition assessments** involve collecting and analysing representative data to establish prevalence rates of acute malnutrition, infant and young child feeding, and other care practices. This data, combined with analysis of the other underlying causes of malnutrition, and assessments of health and food security, presents a nutrition causal analysis. This is useful in planning, implementing and monitoring nutrition programmes.

Markets play a crucial role in food security and nutrition in both urban and rural environments. All assessments should include an analysis of markets that meets the Minimum Standard for Market Analysis (MISMA) and/or the Minimum Economic Recovery Standard (MERS) Assessment and Analysis standards ⊕ *see Delivering assistance through markets.*

The following food security and nutrition assessment standards build on Core Humanitarian Standard Commitment 1 to design appropriate food security and nutrition responses for the affected people ⊕ *see Appendices 1, 2 and 3* and the *LEGS Handbook* for assessment checklists.

Food security and nutrition assessments standard 1.1: Food security assessment

Where people are at risk of food insecurity, assessments are conducted to determine the degree and extent of food insecurity, identify those most affected and define the most appropriate response.

Key actions

1 ⟩ Collect and analyse information on food security at the initial stage and during the crisis.

- Include analysis of critical issues linked to food security, such as environmental degradation, security and market access.

2 ⟩ Analyse the impact of food security on the nutritional status of the affected population.

- Include a review of the underlying causes of undernutrition, including inadequate care, unhealthy household environments, lack of healthcare or access to social protection systems.
- Collect data more frequently in urban contexts, where the situation can change more rapidly and be more difficult to observe than in rural contexts.

3 ⟩ Identify possible responses that can help to save lives and protect and promote livelihoods.

- Include market assessments and capacities of government and other actors to respond to needs.

4 ⟩ Analyse available cooking resources and methods, including the type of stove and fuel and availability of pots and utensils.

- Analyse how people got and stored food and cooking fuel before the crisis, their pre-crisis income, and how they cope now.

- Pay attention to the rights and protection needs of women and girls, who are most commonly responsible for fuel collection and food preparation.

Key indicators

Standardised protocols are used to analyse food security, livelihoods and coping strategies

Percentage of analytical reports that synthesise findings, including assessment methodology and constraints encountered

Guidance notes

Pre-crisis data combined with geographical information systems data can provide an overview of the potential impact of a crisis. However, it is unlikely to be disaggregated sufficiently to give a clear picture in an urban situation.

Assessment sources, tools and information systems: Information sources include crop assessments, satellite images, household assessments, focus group discussions and interviews with key informants. Useful tools include the Food Consumption Score, Household Dietary Diversity Score and Reduced Coping Strategies Index for rapid measurement of household food security. There are many local and regional food security information systems, including famine early warning systems. Use the Integrated Food Security Phase Classification where available and use standardised protocols to classify the severity and causes of acute food insecurity in the areas of concern. The design of food security programmes should be based on a clear response analysis using the findings of assessments.

Environmental degradation can cause food insecurity, and food insecurity can lead to environmental degradation. For example, collecting firewood and producing traditional charcoal make it possible to cook food and generate income from its sale. However, it can also result in deforestation. Responses should protect and support food security while limiting negative environmental impact.

At-risk groups: Disaggregate data by sex, age, disability, wealth group and other relevant factors. Women and men may have different complementary roles in securing household nutritional well-being. Consult with both, separately if necessary, about practices related to food security, food preparation and household resources. Be aware that older people and people with disabilities may be excluded in intra-household distribution of food assistance.

Include girls and boys, especially child-headed households, separated or unaccompanied children, children with disabilities and children living in alternative care. Be mindful of children in different crisis contexts. During infectious disease outbreaks, for example, include children in observation, interim care and treatment centres. In conflict settings, include children in demobilisation centres.

Coping strategies: Consider the different types of coping strategy, their effectiveness and any negative effects. Some coping strategies, such as the sale of land, migration of whole families or deforestation, may permanently undermine future food security. Some coping strategies used by, or forced on, women, girls and boys may impact their health, psychological well-being and social integration. These coping strategies include transactional or "survival" sex, marrying daughters for bride price, women and girls eating last and least, child labour, risky migration, and sale and trafficking of children.

Proxy measures: Food consumption reflects the energy and nutrient intake of individuals in households. It is not practical to measure actual energy and nutrient intake during initial assessments, so use proxy indicators. For example the number of food groups consumed by an individual or household and the frequency of consumption over a given period reflect dietary diversity. Changes in the daily number of meals consumed and dietary diversity are good proxy measures of food security, especially when correlated with a household's socio-economic status.

Tools for measuring food consumption patterns include the Household Dietary Diversity Score, the Household Food Insecurity Access Scale and the Food Consumption Score. The Household Hunger Scale is another good proxy indicator of food insecurity. Some commonly used indicators such as the Food Consumption Score may not adequately reflect food insecurity in an urban context. Triangulate selected measures with coping strategy measures to understand different constraints in accessing food.

The Food Expenditure Share and its established thresholds may be too complex to implement in urban households. This is because several people may be in charge of the food basket, household members consume food sourced outside of the house, and many people may contribute to household income.

Market analysis and cost of diet: Capture information about access to markets, financial capital, livelihoods and economic vulnerability. These elements are linked to commodity prices, income-earning opportunities and wage rates, which affect food security. Market systems, both formal and informal, can protect livelihoods by supplying productive items such as seeds and tools ⊕ *see Food security and nutrition – livelihoods standards 7.1 and 7.2.*

Include a market analysis as part of initial and subsequent context assessments. Market analyses should assess whether local markets can support nutritional needs and establish the minimum cost and affordability of foods that meet the nutrient needs of a typical household ⊕ *see Delivering assistance through markets.*

Increasingly in rural areas, and regularly in urban areas, responses are market-based. They use vendors, market spaces, local food products and transportation services to address the needs of affected people. It is therefore important to understand market access for at-risk groups ⊕ *see MISMA Handbook.*

Food security and nutrition assessments standard 1.2: Nutrition assessment

Nutrition assessments use accepted methods to identify the type, degree and extent of undernutrition, those most at risk and the appropriate response.

Key actions

1 ⟩ Compile pre-crisis information and conduct initial assessments to establish the nature and severity of the nutrition situation.

- Assess national and local capacity to lead or support a response, as well as other nutrition actors.

2 ⟩ Conduct rapid mid upper arm circumference (MUAC) screening and infant and young child feeding in emergencies (IYCF-E) assessments to assess the nutritional situation at the onset of the crisis.

3 ⟩ Identify groups that have the greatest need for nutritional support.

- Gather information on the causes of undernutrition from primary or secondary sources, including the community's perceptions and opinions.
- Engage with communities to identify at-risk groups, paying attention to age, sex, disability, chronic illness or other factors.

4 ⟩ Determine an appropriate response based on an understanding of the context and the emergency.

- Determine whether the situation is stable or declining, reviewing trends in nutritional status over time rather than the prevalence of malnutrition at a specific time.
- Consider both prevention and treatment options.

Key indicators

Standardised protocols are used to assess malnutrition and identify causes

Percentage of assessment reports that include the assessment methodology and constraints encountered

Guidance notes

Contextual information: Information on the causes of undernutrition can be gathered from primary and secondary sources, including health and nutrition profiles, research reports, early warning information, health facility records, food security reports and other sources. Examples include:

- demographic health surveys;
- multi-indicator cluster surveys;
- national nutrition information databases;

- other national health and nutrition surveys;
- national nutrition surveillance systems;
- admission rates and coverage in existing programmes for managing malnutrition; and
- HIV prevalence, incidence and mortality data, including groups at higher risk or with higher burden ⊕ *see Essential healthcare – sexual and reproductive health standard 2.3.3: HIV.*

Local institutions and communities themselves should actively contribute to assessment, interpreting findings and planning responses wherever possible.

Rapid response: In the first phase of a crisis, decisions on general food distributions or immediate treatment of malnutrition should be based on a rapid assessment, initial findings and the existing capacity to respond. An in-depth analysis should be conducted at a later stage but should not delay response in the acute phase.

Scope of analysis: In-depth assessments should be conducted where information gaps are identified and if additional information is needed for programme design, to measure programme outcomes or for advocacy. Determine whether population-wide qualitative or quantitative assessments are needed to understand anthropometric status, micronutrient status, infant and young child feeding, maternal care practices and associated potential determinants of undernutrition. Coordinate with health, WASH and food security sectors to design and prepare for the assessments.

Anthropometric surveys: These are used to examine physical proportions of the body and provide an estimate of the rates of chronic and acute malnutrition. They can be based on random sampling or specific screening. Surveys should report weight-for-height Z scores according to World Health Organization (WHO) standards. Use weight-for-height Z scores reported against the National Center for Health Statistics (NCHS) reference to compare with past surveys. Include wasting and severe wasting measured by MUAC data. The most widely accepted practice is to assess malnutrition levels in children aged 6–59 months as a proxy for the entire population. However, where there are other groups that face greater nutritional risks, consider including them in the assessment as well ⊕ *see Appendix 4: Measuring acute malnutrition.*

Establish the rates of nutrition oedema and record them separately. Report confidence intervals for the rates of malnutrition and demonstrate survey quality assurance. Use existing tools such as the Standardised Monitoring and Assessment of Relief and Transitions (SMART) methodology manual, Standardised Expanded Nutrition Survey (SENS) for Refugee Populations, Emergency Nutrition Assessment software, or Epi Info software.

Infant and young child feeding assessments: Assess the needs and priorities for IYCF-E and monitor the impact of humanitarian action and inaction on infant and young child feeding practices. Pre-crisis data can be used to inform early decision-making. Work with other sectors to include IYCF-E questions in other sectoral assessments and draw on available multi-sectoral data to inform the assessment ⊕ *see Appendix 3: Nutrition assessment checklist.*

Include the number of available breastfeeding counsellors, trained health workers and other support services and their capacity. For more in-depth assessment, conduct random sampling, systematic sampling or cluster sampling. This may be through a stand-alone IYCF-E survey or an integrated survey. However, an integrated survey may result in limited sample size, which may reduce the representativeness of the survey.

Other indicators: Additional information can be carefully considered to inform the overall assessment of nutritional status. This includes immunisation and nutrition programme coverage rates, especially measles, vitamin A, iodine or other micronutrient deficiencies, disease morbidity and health-seeking behaviour. Crude infant and under-5 mortality rates, with cause of death, can also be considered where available.

Interpreting levels of undernutrition: Detailed analysis of the reference population size and density, as well as mortality and morbidity rates, is needed to decide whether levels of undernutrition require intervention. Information is also needed on health status, seasonal fluctuations, IYCF-E indicators, pre-crisis levels of undernutrition, the proportion of severe acute malnutrition in relation to global acute malnutrition, and levels of micronutrient deficiencies ⊕ *see Essential health-care standard 2.2.2: Management of newborn and childhood illness* and *Appendix 5: Measures of the public health significance of micronutrient deficiencies.*

A combination of complementary information systems may be the most cost-effective way to monitor trends. Decision-making models and approaches that consider several variables, such as food security, livelihoods, and health and nutrition may be appropriate ⊕ *see Food security and nutrition assessments standard 1.1: Food security assessment.*

2. Management of malnutrition

The prevention and treatment of malnutrition are both important considerations in humanitarian crises. Chronic malnutrition can be prevented, but there is limited evidence that it can be reversed or treated. On the other hand, acute malnutrition – which may be triggered during a crisis – can be prevented and treated with the right nutrition responses.

Nutrition responses are key in reducing morbidity and mortality in affected populations. However, they require an understanding of the complex underlying causes of malnutrition. A multi-sectoral approach is essential to addressing all the causes and their interactions.

Management of moderate acute malnutrition: In crises, supplementary feeding is often the primary strategy for preventing and treating moderate acute malnutrition.

Two types of supplementary feeding programmes are common: blanket supplementary feeding programmes for prevention, and targeted supplementary feeding programmes for treatment of moderate acute malnutrition and prevention of severe acute malnutrition. The use of each depends on the levels of acute malnutrition, vulnerable population groups and the risk of an increase in acute malnutrition.

Blanket supplementary feeding programmes are recommended where food insecurity is high and there is a need to expand interventions beyond only moderate acute malnutrition cases. They should be accompanied by general food distributions targeting affected households. There are no defined impact indicators for blanket supplementary feeding programmes, but it is important to monitor coverage, adherence, acceptability and rations provided. The indicators for managing moderate acute malnutrition primarily refer to targeted supplementary feeding.

The main aim of a targeted supplementary feeding programme is to prevent the moderately malnourished becoming severely malnourished and to rehabilitate them. These types of programmes usually provide a food supplement to the general ration for moderately malnourished individuals, pregnant and nursing mothers, and other at-risk individuals.

Management of severe acute malnutrition: A variety of approaches are used for therapeutic care. Community-based management of acute malnutrition is the preferred approach where conditions allow. This includes:

- inpatient care for people with medical complications who present with severe acute malnutrition;
- inpatient care for all infants under six months old who present with severe acute malnutrition;
- outpatient care for people with severe acute malnutrition but without medical complications;

- community outreach; and
- other context-specific services or programmes for individuals with moderate acute malnutrition.

Programmes addressing severe acute malnutrition should be supported by supplementary feeding programmes and community mobilisation to support outreach, active case-finding, referral and follow-up.

Management of malnutrition standard 2.1: Moderate acute malnutrition

Moderate acute malnutrition is prevented and managed.

Key actions

1 > Establish clearly defined and agreed strategies, objectives and criteria for set-up and closure of interventions from the outset of the programme.

2 > Maximise access to coverage of moderate acute malnutrition interventions through community engagement and involvement from the beginning.

- Work with community stakeholders to identify vulnerable individuals and households.

3 > Establish admission and discharge protocols, based on nationally and internationally accepted anthropometric criteria.

- Specify the discharge criteria when reporting performance indicators.
- Investigate and act on causes of default and non-response, or an increase in deaths.

4 > Link the management of moderate acute malnutrition to the management of severe acute malnutrition and to existing health services.

5 > Provide take-home dry or suitable ready-to-use supplementary food rations unless there is a clear rationale for on-site feeding.

- Provide rations on a weekly or every two weeks basis. Consider household composition and size, household food security, and the likelihood of sharing when setting the size and composition of the ration.
- Provide clear information on how to hygienically prepare and store supplementary food, and how and when to consume it.

6 > Emphasise protecting, supporting and promoting breastfeeding, complementary feeding and hygiene.

- Provide clear information on the importance of exclusive breastfeeding in children up to six months, and continued breastfeeding for children from 6 to 24 months, for both the physical and psychological health of mother and child.

- Admit breastfeeding mothers of acutely malnourished infants under six months to supplementary feeding programmes, independent of maternal nutrition status.

Key indicators

Percentage of target population that can access dry ration supplementary feeding sites within one day's return walk (including time for treatment)

- >90 per cent

Percentage of target population that can access on-site programmes within one hour

- >90 per cent

Percentage of moderate acute malnutrition (MAM) cases with access to treatment services (coverage)

- >50 per cent in rural areas
- >70 per cent in urban areas
- >90 per cent in formal camps

The proportion of discharges from targeted supplementary feeding programmes who have died, recovered or defaulted

- Died: <3 per cent
- Recovered: >75 per cent
- Defaulted: <15 per cent

Guidance notes

Programme design: Design programmes that build on and support existing health system capacity and consider access to health facilities, the geographical spread of the population and security. Maintain links to inpatient and outpatient therapeutic care, ante-natal care, malaria prevention, childhood illness and screening, HIV and tuberculosis care, and food security programmes including food, cash or voucher transfers.

Supplementary feeding programmes are not meant to replace the diet but to complement it. It is key to design programmes as part of a multi-sectoral approach with complementary services such as WASH, health, IYCF and general food distribution. Assess availability of supplementary foods on national or international markets and factor potential pipeline constraints into programme planning ⊕ *see Delivering assistance through markets.*

Prevention or treatment: Adopt a blanket approach to prevent malnutrition, or a targeted approach to treat it. The decision will depend on:

- levels of acute malnutrition and numbers of affected people;
- risk of increased morbidity;

- risk of decreased food security;
- population displacement and density;
- capacity to screen and monitor the affected population using anthropometric criteria; and
- available resources and access to the affected people.

Targeted supplementary feeding generally requires more time and effort to screen and monitor individuals with acute malnutrition, but it also requires fewer special-ised food resources. A blanket approach generally requires less staff expertise but more specialised food resources.

Effective community mobilisation: Community mobilisation and involvement will improve people's understanding of the programme and its likely effectiveness. Work with the target population in deciding where to locate programme sites. Consider at-risk groups who may face difficulties in accessing sites. Share clear and compre-hensive information on the available support in accessible languages using multiple information-sharing channels, including audio, visual and written forms.

Coverage refers to the number of individuals receiving treatment as a proportion of the number of people who need treatment. Coverage can be affected by the:

- acceptability of the programme, including location and accessibility of programme sites;
- security situation;
- frequency of distributions;
- waiting time;
- extent of mobilisation, home visits and screening;
- availability of male and female nutrition staff;
- alignment of admission criteria and coverage; and
- caregivers' ability to identify signs of malnutrition.

Coverage assessment methodologies are costly and require specially trained staff. If coverage surveys are not feasible, consult national guidance when deciding on alternative methods. Use routine programme data such as screening, referrals and admissions to estimate coverage.

There may be no need to conduct regular coverage assessments unless there have been significant changes in the programme area, such as population movements or a new treatment product or protocol.

Admission criteria should be consistent with national and international guidance. Admission criteria for infants below six months and for groups whose anthropomet-ric status is difficult to determine should include clinical and breastfeeding status ⊕ *see Appendix 4: Measuring acute malnutrition* and *References and further reading*.

Individuals who are (or are suspected to be) HIV-positive or who have tuberculosis or another chronic illness should not be discriminated against and should have equal access to care if they meet the admission criteria. Some individuals who do not meet anthropometric criteria for acute malnutrition may benefit from supplementary feeding. This may include, for example people living with HIV, tuberculosis or other chronic diseases, people discharged from care but requiring therapeutic support to avoid relapse, or persons with disabilities. Adjust monitoring and reporting systems if such individuals do not meet anthropo-metric criteria.

People living with HIV who do not meet admission criteria often require nutri-tional support. Such support is better offered outside the context of treatment for severe acute malnutrition in crises. Provide these individuals and their families with a range of services, including community and home-based care, tuberculosis treatment centres and prevention of mother-to-child-transmission programmes.

Discharge criteria and monitoring: The number of discharged individuals includes those who have recovered, died, defaulted or not recovered. Individuals referred for complementary services, such as healthcare, have not ended the treat-ment and will either continue treatment or return to the treatment later. Do not include individuals transferred to other sites or who have not ended the treatment.

If individuals join a nutrition programme after discharge from therapeutic care, report them as a separate category to avoid biased results. If an individual develops acute malnutrition symptoms as a result of other factors such as disability, cleft or surgical problems, include them in programme reporting. Investigate how the gender of the individual may influence access to treatment, treatment default, and recovery.

Calculate discharge statistics as follows:

- Percentage of discharges recovered = number of individuals recovered/total number of discharged x 100
- Percentage of discharges died = number of deaths/total number of discharged x 100
- Percentage of discharges defaulted = number of defaulters/total number of discharged x 100
- Percentage of discharges not recovered = number of individuals not recov-ered/total number of discharged x 100

In addition to the indicators outlined above, monitoring systems should include:

- the population's participation;
- acceptability of the programme (the default and coverage rate could be used as a proxy measure of this);
- the quantity and quality of food;
- coverage;
- reasons for transfers to other programmes (particularly of children whose nutritional status deteriorates to severe acute malnutrition); and
- number of individuals admitted and in treatment.

Consider external factors such as:

- morbidity patterns;
- levels of undernutrition in the population;
- level of food insecurity in households and in the population;
- complementary interventions available to the population (including general food assistance or equivalent programmes); and
- the capacity of existing systems for service delivery.

Links to health and other sectors: Both targeted and blanket supplementary feeding programmes can be used as a platform for delivering complementary services. In many situations, a blanket supplementary feeding programme for prevention can support crisis response. For example, it can provide access to the target population through a census registration, community screening and referral for severe acute malnutrition and moderate acute malnutrition management. It can also allow for child survival interventions such as:

- anthelmintics;
- vitamin A supplementation;
- iron and folic acid combined with malaria screening and treatment;
- zinc for treatment of diarrhoea; and
- immunisations.

⊕ *See Essential healthcare – communicable diseases standards 2.1.1 to 2.1.4 and Essential healthcare – child health standards 2.2.1 and 2.2.2.*

Populations with high levels of vulnerability, such as high HIV prevalence and people with difficulties moving or feeding, may require programme adaptations to meet their needs. This could include adjusting the quality and quantity of the supplementary food ration ⊕ *see Infant and young child feeding standard 4.1.*

Management of malnutrition standard 2.2: Severe acute malnutrition
Severe acute malnutrition is treated.

Key actions

1 ⟩ Establish clearly defined and agreed strategies, objectives and criteria for set-up and closure of interventions from the outset of the programme.

- Include adequate staffing and relevant capacity, expertise and skills.

2 ⟩ Include inpatient care, outpatient care, referral and community mobilisation components in the management of severe acute malnutrition.

3 ⟩ Provide nutrition and healthcare according to nationally and internationally recognised guidelines for the management of severe acute malnutrition.

4 ⟩ Establish discharge criteria that include anthropometric and other indices.

5 ⟩ Investigate and act on causes of default and non-response, or an increase in deaths.

6 ⟩ Protect, support and promote breastfeeding, complementary feeding, hygiene promotion, and good mother and child interaction.

- Provide clear information on the importance of exclusive breastfeeding in children up to six months, and continued breastfeeding for children from 6 to 24 months, for both the physical and psychological health of mother and child.

Key indicators

Percentage of the target population less than a one day's return walk (including time for treatment) to the programme site

- >90 per cent of the target population

Percentage of severe acute malnutrition (SAM) cases with access to treatment services (coverage)

- >50 per cent in rural areas
- >70 per cent in urban areas
- >90 per cent in a camp

Proportion of discharges from therapeutic care who have died, recovered or defaulted

- Died: <10 per cent
- Recovered: >75 per cent
- Defaulted: <15 per cent

Guidance notes

Programme components: Inpatient care may be provided directly or through referral. Programmes should provide decentralised outpatient care for children with no medical complications. Outpatient programme sites should be close to the targeted population, to reduce the risks and costs associated with travelling with young children, and the risk of further displacement. ⊕ *See Child health standard 2.2.2: Management of newborn and childhood illness.*

Link programmes with other relevant services, such as:

- supplementary feeding;
- HIV and tuberculosis networks;
- rehabilitation;
- primary health services; and
- food security programmes including food or cash-based assistance.

Coverage assessment methodologies are similar in severe acute malnutrition and moderate acute malnutrition programmes ⊕ *see Management of malnutrition standard 2.1: Moderate acute malnutrition.*

Admission criteria should be consistent with national and international guidance. Admission criteria for infants below six months and for groups whose anthropometric status is difficult to determine, should include clinical and breastfeeding status ⊕ *see Appendix 4: Measuring acute malnutrition* and *References and further reading.*

Individuals who are (or are suspected to be) HIV-positive or who have tuberculosis or another chronic illness should not be discriminated against and should have equal access to care if they meet the admission criteria. Some individuals who do not meet anthropometric criteria for acute malnutrition may benefit from supplementary feeding. For example people living with HIV, tuberculosis or other chronic diseases, people discharged from care but requiring therapeutic support to avoid relapse, or persons with disabilities. Adjust monitoring and reporting systems if such individuals do not meet anthropometric criteria.

People living with HIV who do not meet admission criteria often require nutritional support. Such support is better offered outside the context of treatment for severe acute malnutrition in crises. Provide these individuals and their families with a range of services, including community and home-based care, tuberculosis treatment centres and prevention of mother-to-child-transmission programmes.

Discharge criteria and recovery: Discharged individuals must be free from medical complications. In addition, they should have regained their appetite and have achieved and maintained appropriate weight gain without nutrition-related oedema (for example, for two consecutive weighings). Calculate mean weight gain separately for individuals with and without nutritional oedema. Breastfeeding is especially important for infants under six months, as well as for children aged 6 to 24 months. Non-breastfed infants will need close follow-up. Adhere to discharge criteria in order to avoid the risks associated with premature discharge.

Guidelines for community management of acute malnutrition specify the average length of stay for treatment and aim to shorten the recovery periods. Adhere to the existing national guidelines when calculating the average length of stay, as these depend on the context. HIV, tuberculosis and other chronic conditions may result in some malnourished individuals failing to respond to treatment. Work with health services and other social and community support services to identify longer-term treatment options for those people ⊕ *see Essential healthcare – sexual and reproductive health standard 2.3.3: HIV.*

Performance indicators for managing severe acute malnutrition: The population of discharged individuals for severe acute malnutrition is made up of those who have recovered, died, defaulted or not recovered ⊕ *see Guidance notes for Management of malnutrition standard 2.1: Moderate acute malnutrition.*

Performance indicators for managing severe acute malnutrition should combine inpatient and outpatient care outcomes without double-counting those that transfer from one to the other. If this is not possible, adjust the interpretation of outcome rates. For example, programmes should expect better performance when only providing outpatient care. When only providing inpatient care, programmes should aim for the results outlined for combined care.

Individuals who are referred to other services, such as health services, have not ended treatment. When assessing performance of outpatient treatment, report transfers to inpatient care in order to accurately represent programme performance.

Performance indicators do not factor in HIV clinical complexity. HIV clinical complexity will affect mortality rates. In these situations, interpretation of programme performance must take this into consideration.

In addition to discharge indicators, review disaggregated data of new admissions (sex, age, disability), number of children in treatment and coverage rates when monitoring performance. Investigate and document the proportion and causes of readmission, deterioration of clinical status, defaulting and failure to respond on an ongoing basis. Adapt the definition of these to guidelines in use.

Health inputs: All severe acute malnutrition programmes should include systematic treatments according to national or international guidance. It is essential that they include effective referral mechanisms for managing underlying illnesses such as tuberculosis and HIV. In areas of high HIV prevalence, malnutrition programmes should consider interventions that seek to avoid HIV transmission and that support maternal and child survival. In settings where HIV infection is common (HIV prevalence more than 1 per cent), test children with malnutrition to establish their HIV status and to determine their need for anti-retroviral drug treatment.

Breastfeeding support: Mothers of infant inpatients need skilled breastfeeding support as part of nutritional rehabilitation and recovery. This is particularly important for children below six months and for mothers with disabilities. Provide sufficient time and resources, such as a designated private breastfeeding area, to target skilled support and enable peer support. Breastfeeding mothers of severely malnourished infants under six months should receive a supplementary food ration regardless of their nutritional status. If those mothers meet the anthropometric criteria for severe acute malnutrition, admit them for treatment.

Psychosocial support: Emotional and physical stimulation through play is important during the rehabilitation period for children with severe acute malnutrition. It promotes attachment and positive maternal mood. Caregivers of such children often require social and psychosocial support to bring their children for treatment. Some mothers may also need to be supported to access mental health care services for perinatal depression. This may be achieved through mobilisation programmes. Programmes should emphasise the importance of stimulation and interaction in treating and preventing future disability and cognitive impairment in children. Enable all caregivers of severely malnourished children to feed and care for their children during treatment; provide them with advice, demonstrations and health and nutrition information. Pay attention to the impact of treatment on the caregivers and siblings to ensure adequate childcare arrangements, avoid family separation, minimise psychosocial distress and maximise the potential treatment adherence.

Linkage with other actors: Coordinate with child protection and gender-based violence partners to establish referral pathways and information sharing protocols. Train nutrition staff in how to provide supportive and confidential referrals for caregivers of children exposed to physical, sexual or emotional violence, exploitation or abuse.

3. Micronutrient deficiencies

Micronutrient deficiencies are a constraint to socio-economic development in many countries. They have a great impact on people's health, learning ability and productivity. These deficiencies contribute to a vicious cycle of malnutrition, underdevelopment and poverty, affecting already underprivileged groups.

Micronutrient deficiencies are difficult to identify in many contexts. While clinical signs of severe deficiencies may be easy to diagnose, the greater burden on the health and survival of populations may be subclinical deficiencies. Assume that a crisis will worsen any existing micronutrient deficiencies in a population. Address these deficiencies using population-wide interventions and individual treatment.

There are three approaches to controlling micronutrient deficiencies:

- **Supplementation:** Providing micronutrients in highly absorbable form normally results in the fastest control of the micronutrient status of individuals or targeted populations. Examples include supplementation programmes targeting anaemia through iron supplementation, folic acid supplementation in pregnant women and vitamin A supplementation in children younger than five years.
- **Fortification:** Fortifying food products with micronutrients can be an effective strategy for controlling micronutrient deficiencies. Examples of this include iodised salt, micronutrient powders or vitamin A fortified vegetable oil.
- **Food-based approaches:** The vitamins and minerals needed to prevent micronutrient deficiencies are present in a variety of foods. Policies and programmes should ensure improved year-round consumption of an adequate variety, quantity and quality of safe, micronutrient-rich foods.

While all three approaches are used in crises, the most common and widely used is supplementation.

Micronutrient deficiencies standard 3: Micronutrient deficiencies
Micronutrient deficiencies are corrected.

Key actions

1 ⟩ Collect information on the pre-crisis situation to determine the most common micronutrient deficiencies.

2 ⟩ Train health staff in identifying and treating micronutrient deficiencies.

3 ⟩ Establish procedures to respond to micronutrient deficiency risks.

4 > Link micronutrient responses with public health responses to reduce diseases commonly associated with crises, such as vitamin A to manage measles and zinc to manage diarrhoea.

Key indicators

There are no cases of scurvy, pellagra, beriberi or riboflavin deficiency

- ⊕ *See Appendix 5: Measures of the public health significance of micronutrient deficiencies* for a definition of public health significance by age group and whole population.
- Use national or context-specific indicators where they exist.

Rates of xerophthalmia, anaemia and iodine deficiency are not of public health significance

- ⊕ *See Appendix 5: Measures of the public health significance of micronutrient deficiencies* for a definition of public health significance by age group and whole population.
- Use national or context-specific indicators where they exist.

Guidance notes

Diagnosing clinical micronutrient deficiencies: Clinical micronutrient deficiencies should always be diagnosed by qualified medical staff. When clinical indicators of these deficiencies are incorporated into health or nutritional surveillance systems, train staff to conduct the basic assessment and refer accordingly. Case definitions are problematic; in crises, determine them through the response to supplementation.

Subclinical micronutrient deficiencies are those that are not severe enough to present readily identifiable symptoms. However, they can have adverse health outcomes. Identification requires specialised biochemical examination. An exception is anaemia, for which a basic test is available and easily undertaken in the field.

Indirect indicators can be used to assess the risk of micronutrient deficiencies and determine when supplements or an improved dietary intake may be required. Indirect assessment involves estimating nutrient intakes at the population level and extrapolating deficiency risk. To do this, review available data on food access, availability and utilisation, and assess food ration adequacy.

Prevention: Strategies for micronutritient deficiency prevention are addressed in section 6 below (⊕ see *Food assistance standard 6.1: General nutrition requirements*). Disease control is critical in preventing micronutrient deficiencies. Acute respiratory infection, measles, parasitic infections such as malaria, and diarrhoea are examples of diseases that deplete micronutrient stores. Preparedness for treatment will involve developing case definitions and guidelines for treatment, and systems for active case-finding ⊕ see *Essential healthcare – child health standards 2.2.1 and 2.2.2.*

Treatment of micronutrient deficiencies: Case-finding and treatment should occur within the health system and within feeding programmes. Where micronutrient deficiency rates exceed public health thresholds, blanket treatment of the population with supplements may be appropriate. Scurvy (vitamin C deficiency), pellagra (niacin deficiency), beriberi (thiamine deficiency) and ariboflavinosis (riboflavin deficiency) are the most commonly observed illnesses resulting from micronutrient deficiencies ⊕ *see Appendix 5: Measures of the public health significance of micronutrient deficiencies.*

Public health measures to control micronutrient deficiencies include:

- providing vitamin A supplementation with vaccination for children aged 6–59 months;
- de-worming all children aged 12–59 months;
- adding iodised salt and other fortified commodities such as vitamin A and D fortified vegetable oil in the food basket and providing micronutrient powders or iodised oil supplements;
- providing iron-containing multiple micronutrient products for children aged 6–59 months;
- providing daily iron-containing multiple micronutrient supplements, including folic acid, for pregnant and lactating women.

If multiple micronutrient products containing iron are not available, provide daily iron and folic acid supplements to pregnant women and those who have given birth in the past 45 days.

Use sex-disaggregated indirect indicators to assess the risk of micronutrient deficiecies in the affected population and determine the need for improved dietary intake or the use of supplements. For example, indirect indicators for vitamin A deficiency can include low birth weight, wasting or stunting. Assess the risk of micronutrient deficiencies in affected people and determine the need for improved dietary intake or the use of supplements ⊕ *see Food Security and Nutrition assessment standard 1.2: Nutrition assessment.*

4. Infant and young child feeding

Appropriate and timely support of infant and young child feeding in emergencies (IYCF-E) saves lives and protects children's nutrition, health and development. Inappropriate infant and young child feeding practices increase vulnerability to undernutrition, disease and death, and undermine maternal health. Crises increase those risks. Some infants and young children are particularly vulnerable, including:

- low birth-weight infants;
- separated and unaccompanied children;
- infants and children of depressed mothers;
- children under two years not breastfeeding;
- those from populations with medium or high HIV prevalence;
- children with disabilities, particularly those with feeding difficulties; and
- infants and young children with acute malnutrition, stunting or micronutrient deficiencies.

IYCF-E addresses actions and interventions to protect and support the nutritional needs of both breastfed and non-breastfed infants and young children aged 0–23 months. Priority interventions include:

- breastfeeding protection and support;
- appropriate and safe complementary feeding; and
- management of artificial feeding for infants with no possibility to breastfeed.

Support of pregnant and breastfeeding women is central to the well-being of their children. "Exclusive breastfeeding" means an infant receives no liquids other than breastmilk, and no solids except for necessary micronutrient supplements or medicines. It guarantees food and fluid security in infants for the first six months and provides active immune protection. Breastfeeding ensures optimal brain development and continues to protect the health of older infants and children, especially in contexts where WASH conditions are lacking. Breastfeeding also protects maternal health by delaying menstruation and protecting against breast cancer. It promotes psychological well-being by enhancing attachment and responsiveness.

The key actions in this section reflect the Operational Guidance on Infant and Young Child Feeding in Emergencies (Operational Guidance). The Operational Guidance is a product of an interagency working group whose aim is to provide concise, practical guidance on how to ensure appropriate IYCF-E and on the International Code of Marketing of Breastmilk Substitutes ("the Code").

Infant and young child feeding standard 4.1: Policy guidance and coordination

Policy guidance and coordination ensure safe, timely and appropriate infant and young child feeding.

Key actions

1 > Establish an IYCF-E coordination authority within the crisis coordination mechanism, and ensure collaboration across sectors.

- Assume the government is the coordination authority, wherever possible.

2 > Include the specifications of the Operational Guidance in relevant national and humanitarian organisation policy guidance on preparedness.

- Develop guidance and a joint statement with national authorities in situations where there is no policy.
- Strengthen relevant national policies wherever possible.

3 > Support strong, harmonised, timely communication on IYCF-E at all response levels.

- Inform humanitarian organisations, donors and media as soon as possible about any IYCF-E policies and practices that are in place.
- Communicate with affected people about available services, IYCF-E practices and feedback mechanisms.

4 > Avoid accepting or soliciting donations of breastmilk substitutes, other liquid milk products, feeding bottles and teats.

- Donations that do arrive should be managed by the designated authority, in accordance with the Operational Guidance and the Code.
- Ensure strict targeting and use, procurement, management and distribution of breastmilk substitutes. This must be based on needs and risk assessment, data analysis and technical guidance.

Key indicators

Percentage of adopted IYCF policies in emergencies that reflect the specifications of the Operational Guidance

No Code violations reported

Percentage of Code violations donations of breastmilk substitutes (BMS), liquid milk products, bottles and teats dealt with in a timely manner

Guidance notes

Communication with the affected people, responders and media: Communicating about available services and healthy infant and young child feeding practices will require adapted messages for different groups providing assistance and for the public. Consider the need to support caregivers who are grandparents, single parents, child-headed households or siblings as well as caregivers with disabilities, and people living with HIV when generating messages.

International Code of Marketing of Breastmilk Substitutes: The Code protects artificially fed babies by ensuring safe use of breastmilk substitutes. It is based on impartial, accurate information and applies in all contexts. It should be included in legislation during the preparedness phase and enforced during the crisis response. In the absence of national legislation, implement the Code provisions at a minimum.

The Code does not restrict the availability or prohibit the use of breastmilk substitutes, feeding bottles or teats. It only restricts their marketing, procurement and distribution. Common Code violations in crises derive from labelling issues and untargeted distribution. During crises, monitor and report Code violations to UNICEF, WHO and local authorities.

Use standard indicators where they exist and develop context-specific indicators where they do not. Define IYCF-E benchmarks to determine progress and achievement, considering intervention time frames. Encourage consistent IYCF-E indicator use across implementing partners and in surveys. Repeat assessments or parts of a baseline assessment as part of monitoring IYCF-E interventions. Use annual surveys to determine the impact of these interventions.

Artificial feeding: All breastmilk substitutes must comply with Codex Alimentarius and the Code. Access to adequate WASH services is essential to minimise the risks of artificial feeding in emergencies. The distribution system for breastmilk substitutes will depend on the context, including the scale of intervention. Do not include infant formula and other breastmilk substitutes in general or blanket food distributions. Do not distribute dried liquid milk products and liquid milk as a single commodity. Indications for and management of artificial feeding should be in accordance with the Operational Guidance and the Code, under the guidance of the designated IYCF-E coordinating authority.

Infant and young child feeding standard 4.2: Multi-sectoral support to infant and young child feeding in emergencies

Mothers and caregivers of infants and young children have access to timely and appropriate feeding support that minimises risks, is culturally sensitive and optimises nutrition, health and survival outcomes.

Key actions

1 ⟩ Prioritise pregnant and breastfeeding women for access to food, cash or voucher transfers and other supportive interventions.

2 › Provide access to skilled breastfeeding counselling for pregnant and breast-feeding mothers.

3 › Target mothers of all newborns with support for early initiation of exclusive breastfeeding.

- Provide simple guidance for exclusive breastfeeding in maternity services.
- Protect, promote and support exclusive breastfeeding in infants aged 0–5 months, and continued breastfeeding in children aged six months to two years.
- Where mixed feeding is practised in infants aged 0–5 months, support transitioning to exclusive breastfeeding.

4 › Provide appropriate breastmilk substitutes, feeding equipment and associated support to mothers and caregivers whose infants require artificial feeding.

- Explore the safety and viability of relactation and wet nursing where infants are not breastfed by their mother. Consider the cultural context and service availability in such situations.
- If breastmilk substitutes are the only acceptable options, include an essential package of support with cooking and feeding equipment, WASH support and access to healthcare services.

5 › Support timely, safe, adequate and appropriate complementary food support.

- Assess household foods to assess whether they are suitable as complementary foods for children and provide context-specific advice and support on complementary feeding.
- Ensure access to feeding equipment and cooking supplies, with considerations for children with feeding difficulties.

6 › Provide feeding support to particularly vulnerable infants and young children.

- Support infant stimulation activities and early child development care practices within nutrition programmes.

7 › Provide micronutrient supplements as necessary.

- Provide daily supplements to pregnant and breastfeeding women, including one daily requirement of multiple micronutrients to protect maternal stores and breastmilk content, whether the women receive fortified rations or not.
- Continue iron and folic acid supplements when already provided.

Key indicators

Percentage of breastfeeding mothers who have access to skilled counselling

Percentage of caregivers who have access to Code-compliant supplies of appropriate breastmilk substitutes (BMS) and associated support for infants who require artificial feeding

Percentage of caregivers who have access to timely, appropriate, nutritionally adequate and safe complementary foods for children aged 6 to 23 months

....

Guidance notes

IYCF-E assessment and monitoring: Assess the needs and priorities for IYCF-E response and monitor the impact of IYCF-E interventions ⊕ *see Food security and nutrition assessments standard 1.2: Nutrition assessment.*

Multi-sectoral collaboration: Sectoral entry points to identify and support IYCF-E include:

- ante-natal and post-natal care;
- immunisation points;
- growth monitoring;
- early childhood development;
- HIV treatment services (including prevention of mother-to-child transmission);
- acute malnutrition treatment;
- community health, mental health and psychosocial support;
- WASH services;
- places of employment; and
- agricultural extension work.

Target groups: All assessment and programme data for children under five years should be disaggregated by sex and by age 0–5 months, 6–11 months, 12–23 months, and 24–59 months. Disaggregation by disability is recommended from 24 months.

Identify and establish services to provide for the nutritional and care needs of children with disabilities, separated and unaccompanied infants and young children. Refer separated and unaccompanied children to child protection partners. Identify the proportion of pregnant and lactating women.

Consider populations with medium or high HIV prevalence, separated and unaccompanied children, low birth-weight infants, children with disabilities and with feeding difficulties, children under two years not breastfeeding, and those acutely malnourished. Be aware that children of mothers with depression tend to be at higher risk of malnutrition.

Pregnant and breastfeeding women: If the needs of pregnant and breastfeeding women are not met in food, or cash or voucher assistance programmes, target pregnant and breastfeeding women with fortified food. Give micronutrient supplements in accordance with WHO recommendations.

Organise psychosocial support for distressed mothers, including referral to mental health services as necessary. Arrange appropriate support for mothers with disabilities. Create safe places in camp and other collective settings for women to breastfeed, such as baby friendly spaces with exclusive breastfeeding areas.

Breastfed infants: Planning and resource allocation should allow for skilled breast-feeding support in difficult situations. This could include for acutely malnourished infants aged 0–6 months, populations where mixed feeding is common, and infant feeding in the context of HIV.

Non-breastfed infants: In all crises, protect infants and young children who are not breastfed and support them to meet their nutritional needs. The consequences of not breastfeeding vary by the age of the child. The youngest children are most vulnerable to infectious diseases. They depend on access to assured supplies of appropriate breastmilk substitutes, fuel, equipment and WASH conditions.

Infant formula and other breastmilk substitutes: Infant formula is the appropriate breastmilk substitute for infants aged 0–5 months. Give preference to ready-to-use infant formula in liquid form, since it does not require preparation and carries fewer safety risks than powdered infant formula.

Appropriate use, careful storage and hygiene of feeding utensils are essential for ready-to-use infant formula. Ready-to-use infant formula is bulky and therefore expensive to transport and store. In children over six months, use alternative liquid milks. Alternative milks include pasteurised full-cream milk from a cow, goat, sheep, camel or buffalo; ultra-high temperature liquid milk; fermented liquid milk; or yogurt.

Use of infant formula in children over six months will depend on pre-crisis practices, resources available, sources of alternative liquid milks, adequacy of complementary foods and humanitarian organisation policy. Indications for using breastmilk substitutes may be short or longer term. Follow-on, growing-up liquid milks and toddler liquid milks marketed to children over six months are not necessary.

A qualified health or nutrition worker can determine the need for infant formula through individual assessment, follow-up and support. Where individual assessment is not possible, consult with the coordinating authority and technical humanitarian organisations for advice on assessment and targeting criteria. Provide infant formula until the child is breastfeeding or at least six months. When providing breastmilk substitutes to children who need it, do not inadvertently encourage breastfeeding mothers to use it also.

Do not use feeding bottles; they are difficult to clean. Encourage and support cup feeding.

Maintain surveillance of morbidity at individual and population levels, with a focus on diarrhoea.

Complementary feeding is the process that starts when breastmilk alone is no longer sufficient to meet the nutritional requirements of infants and other foods and liquids are needed along with breast milk. Complementary foods and liquids, whether industrially produced or locally prepared, should be provided to children aged 6–23 months.

Pre-existing and existing nutrient gaps are key in determining complementary food support options. Other considerations include the affordability and availability of a nutritious diet, seasonality of food supply and access to locally available complementary foods of good quality. Complementary food response options include:

- cash-based assistance to purchase locally available fortified and nutrient-rich foods;
- distributing nutrient-rich household foods or fortified foods;
- provision of multiple-micronutrient fortified foods to children aged 6–23 months;
- home fortification with micronutrient supplements such as micronutrient powders or other supplements;
- livelihood programmes; and
- safety net programmes.

Consider training or messaging alongside cash-based assistance, to ensure affected people understand the optimal use of cash for nutritional outcomes.

Micronutrient supplementation: Children aged 6–59 months not receiving fortified foods may require multiple micronutrient supplements to meet nutrition requirements. Vitamin A supplements are recommended. In malaria-endemic areas, provide iron in any form, including micronutrient powders, and always in conjunction with malaria diagnosis, prevention and treatment strategies. Examples of malaria prevention strategies are provision of insecticide-treated bed nets and vector-control programmes, prompt diagnosis of malaria illness, and treatment with effective anti-malarial drug therapy. Do not provide iron to children who do not have access to malaria-prevention strategies. Provide iron and folic acid, or multiple micronutrient supplements, to pregnant and lactating women, in accordance with the latest guidance.

HIV and infant feeding: Mothers living with HIV should be supported to breastfeed for at least 12 months and up to 24 months or longer while receiving anti-retroviral therapy. If anti-retroviral drugs are not available, choose the strategy that gives infants the greatest chance of HIV-free survival. This means balancing risks of HIV transmission versus non-HIV causes of child death. Support mothers and caregivers accordingly. Prioritise accelerated access to anti-retroviral drugs ⊕ *see Essential healthcare – sexual and reproductive health standard 2.3.3: HIV.*

Counsel breastfeeding HIV-uninfected mothers and wet nurses, and those whose HIV status is unknown, to breastfeed exclusively for the first six months of the baby's life. After that, introduce complementary foods while continuing breastfeeding until the child is 24 months or more. Infants already established on replacement feeding require urgent identification and support.

Consult existing national and sub-national policies and assess whether they are in line with the latest WHO recommendations. Determine whether they are appropriate for the new crisis context, considering the change in risk exposure to non-HIV infectious disease, the likely duration of the emergency, whether replacement feeding is possible and the availability of anti-retroviral drugs. Updated interim guidance may need to be issued and communicated to mothers and caregivers.

Gender-based violence, child protection and nutrition: Gender-based violence, gender inequality and nutrition are often inter-related. Domestic violence can pose a threat to the health and well-being of women and their children. Nutrition staff should provide supportive and confidential referral for caregivers or children exposed to gender-based violence or child abuse. Other elements to integrate include counselling, working to establish women- and child-friendly treatment sites, and regular monitoring of default rates and failure to respond to treatment. Consider including specialised gender-based violence and child protection case-workers as part of nutrition staff ⊕ *see Protection Principles 3 and 4.*

Public health emergencies: In public health crises, take steps to prevent any interruptions in access to health and feeding support services, to ensure continued household food security and livelihoods, and to minimise disease transmission risks via breastfeeding, as well as to minimise maternal illness and death. Refer to WHO guidance where needed for cholera, Ebola and Zika virus guidance.

5. Food security

Food security exists when all people have physical and economic access to sufficient, safe and nutritious food that meets their dietary needs and food preferences for an active and healthy life.

Food security is influenced by macro-economic, socio-political and environmental factors. National and international policies, processes or institutions can impact affected people's access to nutritionally adequate food. The degradation of the local environment and the increasingly variable and extreme weather caused by climate change also affect food security.

In a humanitarian crisis, food security responses should aim to meet short-term needs and reduce the need for the affected population to adopt potentially damaging coping strategies. Over time, responses should protect and restore livelihoods, stabilise or create employment opportunities and contribute to restoring longer-term food security. They should not have a negative impact on natural resources and the environment.

Household food insecurity is one of four underlying causes of undernutrition, along with poor feeding and care practices, an unhealthy household environment and inadequate healthcare.

The standards in this section consider the resources to meet the food needs of both the general population and people at increased nutritional risk, such as children under five years of age, people living with HIV or AIDS, older people, people with chronic illnesses and people with disabilities.

Responses aimed at treating malnutrition will have a limited impact if the food needs of the general population are not met. People who recover from malnutrition but who cannot maintain an adequate food intake will deteriorate again.

The choice of the most effective and efficient crisis response options requires a thorough analysis of sex-disaggregated needs, household preferences, cost efficiency and effectiveness, protection risks and seasonal changes. It should also identify the specific type and quantity of food required and the optimal way of distributing it.

Food is the major expenditure for vulnerable households. Cash-based assistance can enable people receiving assistance to better manage their overall resources, although this depends on the transfer value provided. Collaborative analysis and programme objectives will guide the targeting, transfer value and any potential conditions placed on the transfer.

Food security responses should progressively aim to work through or support local markets. Decisions on local, national or regional procurement should be based on an understanding of markets, including market and financial service providers.

Market-based programming, such as grants to traders for restocking, can also support markets ⊕ *see Delivering assistance through markets* and *MERS Handbook*.

Food security standard 5:
General food security

People receive food assistance that ensures their survival, upholds their dignity, prevents the erosion of their assets and builds resilience.

Key actions

1⟩ Based on food security assessment data, design the response to meet immediate needs, and consider measures to support, protect, promote and restore food security.

- Consider both in-kind and cash-based options for the food basket.

2⟩ Develop transition and exit strategies for all food security programmes as early as possible.

- Integrate programmes with responses from other sectors.

3⟩ Ensure that people receiving assistance have access to the necessary knowledge, skills and services to cope and support their livelihoods.

4⟩ Protect, preserve and restore the natural environment from further degradation.

- Consider the impact of cooking fuel on the environment.
- Consider livelihoods strategies that do not contribute to deforestation or soil erosion.

5⟩ Monitor the level of acceptance of and access to humanitarian food security interventions by different groups and individuals.

6⟩ Ensure that people receiving food assistance are consulted on the design of the response and are treated with respect and dignity.

- Establish a mechanism for providing feedback.

Key indicators

Percentage of targeted households with acceptable Food Consumption Score

- >35 per cent; if oil and sugar are provided, >42 per cent

Percentage of targeted households with acceptable Dietary Diversity Score

- >5 main food groups regularly consumed

Percentage of targeted households with acceptable Coping Strategy Index

Percentage of people receiving assistance that report complaints or negative feedback related to their treatment with dignity

- All complaints are regularly monitored and quickly responded to.

Guidance notes

Context: Monitor the wider food security situation to assess the continued relevance of a response. Determine when to phase out activities and when to introduce modifications or new projects, and identify any need for advocacy.

In urban settings, take steps to contextualise household food expenditure indicators, particularly in dense low-income settlements. For example, the Food Expenditure Share and its established thresholds may be less accurate in urban contexts, because non-food expenses, such as rent and heating, are relatively higher.

Exit and transition strategies: Start developing exit and transition strategies from the outset of the programme. Before closing a programme or making a transition, there should be evidence of improvement or that another actor can take responsibility. In the case of food assistance, it may mean understanding the existing or planned social protection or long-term safety-net systems.

Food assistance programmes can coordinate with social protection systems or lay the foundation for such a future system. Humanitarian organisations can also advocate for systems that address chronic food insecurity, informed by a chronic food insecurity analysis where available ⊕ *see MERS Handbook*.

At-risk groups: Use community-based risk assessments and other participatory monitoring to counter any patterns that endanger particular groups or individuals. For example, distributing fuel and/or fuel-efficient stoves may reduce the risks of physical and sexual assault for women and girls. Supplemental cash transfers, especially to vulnerable households or individuals, such as women- and child-headed households or households with people with disabilities, can reduce the risk of sexual exploitation and child labour.

Community support structures: Design community support structures together with users, so that they are appropriate and adequately maintained and are more likely to remain after the programme ends. Consider the needs of vulnerable individuals during the design. For example, separated or unaccompanied girls and boys may miss out on the information and skills development that takes place within a family ⊕ *see Core Humanitarian Standard Commitment 4*.

Livelihoods support: ⊕ *See Food security and nutrition – livelihoods standards 7.1 and 7.2, MERS Handbook* and *LEGS Handbook*.

Environmental impact: People living in camps require cooking fuel, which may accelerate local deforestation. Consider options such as fuel distribution, efficient stoves and alternative energy. Take account of the potential environmental benefits of making vouchers more specific to environmentally sustainable goods and services. Look for opportunities to change previous food and cooking customs that may have caused environmental degradation. Consider climate change trends. Prioritise activities that provide relief in the short term and reduce crisis risk in the medium and long term. For example, destocking may locally reduce pressure on pasture during a drought ⊕ *see Shelter and settlement standard 7: Environmental sustainability.*

Access and acceptability: People are more likely to participate in a programme that is easy to access and with acceptable activities. Use participatory design with all members of the affected population to ensure overall coverage without discrimination. While some food security responses target the economically active, responses should be accessible to all people. To overcome constraints for at-risk groups, actively work with them to design activities and set up appropriate support structures.

6. Food assistance

Food assistance is required when the quality and quantity of available food or access to food is not sufficient to prevent excessive mortality, morbidity or malnutrition. It includes humanitarian responses that improve food availability and access, nutrition awareness and feeding practices. Such responses should also protect and strengthen the livelihoods of affected people. Response options include in-kind food, cash-based assistance, support for production and market support. While meeting immediate needs is a priority in the initial stages of a crisis, responses should preserve and protect assets, help to recover assets lost through crises and increase resilience to future threats.

Food assistance may also be used to prevent people adopting negative coping mechanisms such as the sale of productive assets, over-exploitation or destruction of natural resources or the accumulation of debt.

A wide range of tools can be used in food assistance programmes, including:

- general food distributions (provision of in-kind food, cash-based assistance for purchase of food);
- blanket supplementary feeding programmes;
- targeted supplementary feeding programmes; and
- providing relevant services and inputs, including transferring skills or knowledge.

General food distributions provide support to those who need the food most. Discontinue these distributions when the people receiving assistance can produce or access their food through other means. Transitional arrangements may be needed, including conditional cash-based assistance or livelihood support.

People with specific nutrient needs may require supplementary food in addition to any general ration. This includes children aged 6–59 months, older people, persons with disabilities, people living with HIV, and pregnant or breastfeeding women. In many situations, supplementary feeding saves lives. On-site feeding is undertaken only when people do not have the means to cook for themselves. This can be necessary immediately after a crisis, during population movements or where insecurity would put recipients of take-home rations at risk. It can also be used for emergency school feeding, although take-home rations may be distributed through schools. Consider that children not attending school will not access these distributions; plan outreach mechanisms for these children.

Food assistance requires good supply chain management and logistics capabilities to manage commodities effectively.

Management of any cash delivery system needs to be robust and accountable, with systematic monitoring ⊕ *see Delivering assistance through markets.*

Food assistance standard 6.1:
General nutrition requirements

The basic nutritional needs of the affected people, including the most vulnerable, are met.

Key actions

1 ⟩ Measure the levels of access to adequate quantity and the quality of food.

- Assess the level of access on a frequent basis to see whether it is stable or likely to decline.
- Assess affected people's access to markets.

2 ⟩ Design food and cash-based assistance to meet the standard initial planning requirements for energy, protein, fat and micronutrients.

- Plan rations to make up the difference between the nutritional requirements and what people can provide for themselves.

3 ⟩ Protect, promote and support affected people's access to nutritious foods and nutritional support.

- Ensure that children aged 6-24 months have access to complementary foods and that pregnant and breastfeeding women have access to additional nutritional support.
- Ensure households with chronically ill members, people living with HIV and tuberculosis, older people and people with disabilities have appropriate nutritious food and adequate nutritional support.

Key indicators

Prevalence of malnutrition among children <5 years disaggregated by sex, and disaggregated by disability from 24 months

- Use WHO classification system (MAD, MDD-W).
- For disaggregation by disability, use the UNICEF/Washington Group module on Child Functioning.

Percentage of targeted households with acceptable Food Consumption Score

- >35 per cent; if oil and sugar are provided, >42 per cent

Percentage of targeted households with acceptable Dietary Diversity Score

- >5 main food groups regularly consumed

Percentage of targeted households that receive the minimum food energy requirements (2,100kCal per person per day) and recommended daily micronutrient intake

Guidance notes

Monitoring access to food: Consider variables including levels of food security, access to markets, livelihoods, health and nutrition. This will help determine whether the situation is stable or declining, and whether food interventions are necessary. Use proxy indicators such as the Food Consumption Score or dietary diversity tools.

Forms of assistance: Use appropriate forms of assistance (cash, vouchers or in-kind) or a combination to ensure food security. Where cash-based assistance is used, consider complementary food distributions or supplementary food distributions to meet the needs of specific groups. Consider the adequacy of markets to serve particular nutritional needs and use specific methodologies including 'the minimum cost of a healthy diet' assessment tool.

Design of food rations and nutritional quality: A number of ration planning tools are available, for example NutVal. To plan general rations ⊕ *see Appendix 6: Nutritional requirements.* If a ration is designed to provide all the energy content of the diet, then it must contain adequate amounts of all nutrients. If a ration provides only part of the energy requirement of the diet, then design it using one of two approaches:

- If the nutrient content of the other foods available to the population is unknown, design the ration to provide a balanced nutrient content that is proportional to the energy content of the ration.
- If the nutrient content of the other foods available to the population is known, design the ration to complement these foods by filling nutrient gaps.

The following estimates for a population's minimum nutritional requirements should be used for planning general rations and adjusted to context.

- 2,100 kCal per person per day with 10–12 per cent of total energy provided by protein and 17 per cent provided by fat ⊕ *see Appendix 4: Nutritional requirements* for further details.

Ensuring adequate nutrient content of food rations may be challenging where there are limited food types available. Consider access to iodised salt, niacin, thiamine and riboflavin. Options for improving the nutritional quality of the ration include fortifying staple commodities, including fortified blended foods, and encouraging the purchase of locally produced fresh foods using vouchers. Consider using supplementation products such as lipid-based, nutrient-dense, ready-to-use foods, or multiple micronutrient tablets or powders. Provide IYCF-E messages to ensure that optimal breastfeeding and complementary feeding practices are promoted ⊕ *see Infant and young child feeding standards 4.1 and 4.2.*

When planning rations, consult with the community to take account of local and cultural preferences. Choose foods that do not require long cooking if fuel is sparse. Whenever there are changes in rations, share information with entire communities as early as possible to minimise resentment and limit the risk of household violence against women, who may be blamed for reduced rations. Clearly communicate the exit plan from the onset to manage expectations, reduce anxiety and enable households to make relevant decisions.

Link with health programmes: Food assistance can prevent the deterioration of the nutrition status of the affected population, especially when combined with public health measures to prevent diseases such as measles, malaria and parasitic infection ⊕ *see Health systems standard 1.1: Health service delivery* and *Essential healthcare – communicable diseases standard 2.1: Prevention.*

Monitoring food use: Key indicators for food assistance measure access to food but do not quantify food use. Direct measurement of nutrient intake is not realistic. Indirect measurement is a good alternative, using information from various sources including food availability and use at the household level, and assessing food prices, food availability and cooking fuel in local markets. Other options include examining food assistance distribution plans and records, assessing any contribution of wild foods and conducting food security assessments.

At-risk groups: When setting eligibility criteria for food assistance, consult with different groups to identify any particular needs that might otherwise be overlooked. Include adequate and acceptable food such as fortified blended food for young children (aged 6–59 months) in the general ration. Specific population groups that may need attention include older people, people living with HIV, persons with disabilities, and caregivers.

Older people: Chronic disease and disability, isolation, large family size, cold weather and poverty can reduce access to food and increase nutrient requirements. Older people should be able to access food sources and food transfers easily. Foods should be easy to prepare and consume and should meet the additional protein and micronutrient requirements of older people.

People living with HIV: There is a high risk of malnutrition for people living with HIV. This is due to factors such as reduced food intake, poor absorption of nutrients, changes in metabolism, and chronic infections and illness. The energy requirements of people living with HIV vary with the stage of the infection. Milling and fortifying food, or providing fortified, blended or special food supplements are possible strategies for improving access to an adequate diet. In some situations it may be appropriate to increase the overall size of any food ration. Refer malnourished people living with HIV to targeted feeding programmes, when available.

Persons with disabilities, including people with psychosocial disabilities, may be at particular risk of separation from immediate family members and usual caregivers in a crisis. They also may face discrimination. Reduce these risks by ensuring physical access to food, access to energy-dense and nutrient-rich foods, and mechanisms for feeding support. This may include providing manual blenders, spoons and straws, or developing systems for home visiting or outreach. In addition, consider that children with disabilities are less likely to be enrolled in schools, missing school-based food programmes.

Caregivers: It is important to support people caring for vulnerable individuals. Caregivers and those they are caring for may face specific nutritional barriers. For example, they may have less time to access food because they are ill or caring for the ill. They may have a greater need to maintain hygienic practices. They may have fewer assets to exchange for food, due to the costs of treatment or funerals. They may face social stigma and reduced access to community support mechanisms. Use existing social networks to train selected members of the population to support caregivers.

Food assistance standard 6.2:
Food quality, appropriateness and acceptability

The food items provided are of appropriate quality, are acceptable and can be used efficiently and effectively.

Key actions

1 〉 Select foods that conform to the national standards of the host government and other internationally accepted quality standards.

- Perform random sample testing on food stocks.
- Understand and respect national regulations concerning the receipt and use of genetically modified foods when planning to use imported food.

2 〉 Choose appropriate food packaging.

- Provide labels with the date of production, country of origin, expiration or "best before" date, nutritional analysis and cooking instructions in accessible formats and in the local language, especially for less familiar or less commonly used foods.

3 〉 Assess access to water, fuel, stoves and food storage facilities.

- Provide ready-to-eat foods when crises prevent access to cooking facilities.

4 〉 Provide access to adequate milling and processing facilities when whole-grain cereal is provided.

- Meet milling costs of recipients using cash or vouchers, or the less-preferred approach of providing additional grain or milling equipment.

5 〉 Transport and store food in appropriate conditions.

- Follow standards in storage management, with systematic checks on food quality.
- Measure quantities in consistent units; and avoid changing the units and the measuring procedures during the project.

Key indicators

Percentage of affected population that report that food provided is of appropriate quality and meets local preferences

Percentage of affected population that report the mechanism to receive food was appropriate

Percentage of households that report that received food items were easy to prepare and store

Percentage of people receiving assistance that report complaints or negative feedback related to food quality

- All complaints are regularly monitored and quickly responded to.

Percentage of food losses reported by the programme

- Target <0.2 per cent of total tonnage.

Guidance notes

Food quality: Foods must conform to the food standards of the host country's government. Food must also conform to the Codex Alimentarius standards about quality, packaging, labelling and fitness for purpose. When food is not of the quality required for its intended use, it is unfit for the purpose. This is true even if it is fit for human consumption. An example is when the quality of flour may not enable baking at household level even if it is safe to consume. Phytosanitary certificates or other inspection certificates must accompany locally purchased and imported foods. Fumigation should use appropriate products and follow strict procedures. Ensure that independent quality surveyors inspect large-quantity consignments and use independent quality surveyors when there are doubts or disputes about quality.

Ensure that host governments remain involved as much as possible. Obtain information on the age and quality of food consignments from supplier certificates, quality control inspection reports, package labels and warehouse reports. Make a database for certificates of analysis (CoA) issued by a relevant authority to certify the quality and purity of a product.

Assess availability of food commodities on local, national or international markets. If food assistance is sourced locally, it should be sustainable and not further strain local natural resources or distort markets. Factor potential food supply constraints into programme planning.

Food packaging: Food losses can be reported at warehouses and final distribution points. Food losses can be due to poor packaging in the distribution cycle. Packaging should be sturdy and convenient for handling, storage and distribution. It should be accessible for older people, children and persons with disabilities. If possible, packaging should allow direct distribution without requiring re-measuring or repacking.

Food packaging should not carry any messages that are politically or religiously motivated or divisive in nature.

Packaging should not be a hazard, and humanitarian organisations have a responsibility to prevent the environment becoming littered with packaging from items distributed, or bought with cash or vouchers. Use minimal packaging (biodegradable where possible) and locally appropriate materials, if possible by promoting a partnership with the local government and packaging material manufacturers. Provide food receptacles that can be reused, recycled or re-appropriated. Dispose of waste packaging in a way that prevents environmental degradation. Ready-to-use food packaging, such as foil wrappers, may require specific controls for safe disposal.

Where litter occurs, organise regular community clean-up campaigns. These campaigns should be part of community mobilisation and awareness-raising, rather than as cash-for-work ⊕ *see WASH solid waste management standards 5.1 to 5.3.*

Food choice: While nutritional value is the primary consideration in providing food assistance, the commodities should be familiar to the recipients. They should also be consistent with religious and cultural traditions, including any food taboos for pregnant or breastfeeding women. Consult women and girls on food choice, as in many settings they have the primary responsibility for food preparation. Support grandparents, men who are single heads of households, and youth in charge of their siblings without support, as their access to food could be at risk.

In urban contexts, households are likely to access a more diverse range of foods than in rural ones, but the quality of the diet may be limited, requiring different nutritional support.

Infant feeding: Donated or subsidised infant formula, powdered milk, liquid milk or liquid milk products should not be distributed as a separate commodity in a general food distribution. These items should also not be distributed in a take-home supplementary feeding programme ⊕ *see Infant and young child feeding standard 4.2.*

Wholegrain cereal: Where household grinding is traditional or there is access to local mills, distribute wholegrain cereals. Wholegrain cereal has a longer shelf life than its alternatives and may have a higher value to programme participants.

Provide facilities for low-extraction commercial milling that removes germ, oil and enzymes that cause rancidity. Low-extraction commercial milling greatly increases shelf life, although it also reduces protein content. Milled whole maize has a shelf life of only six to eight weeks, so milling should occur shortly before consumption. Milled grain normally requires less cooking time. Milling requirements can sometimes expose women or adolescent girls to increased risk of exploitation. Work with women and girls to identify risks and solutions such as providing support for women-run mills.

Food storage and preparation: Household storage capacity should inform the choice of foods offered. Ensure that people receiving assistance understand how to avoid public health risks associated with food preparation. Provide fuel-efficient stoves or alternative fuels to minimise environmental degradation.

Storage areas should be dry and hygienic, adequately protected from weather and free of chemical or other contamination. Secure storage areas against pests such as insects and rodents. Where appropriate, use Ministry of Health officers to certify the quality of food supplied by vendors and traders.

Food assistance standard 6.3:
Targeting, distribution and delivery

Food assistance targeting and distribution is responsive, timely, transparent and safe.

Key actions

1 > Identify and target food assistance recipients based on need and consultations with appropriate stakeholders.

- Provide clear, publicised details of targeting approaches that are accepted by both recipient and non-recipient populations, to avoid creating tensions and doing harm.
- Initiate formal registration of households to receive food as soon as it is feasible, and update as necessary.

2 > Design food distribution methods or direct cash/voucher delivery mechanisms that are efficient, equitable, secure, safe, accessible and effective.

- Consult women and men, including adolescents and youth, and promote participation by potentially vulnerable or marginalised groups.

3 > Locate distribution and delivery points where they are accessible, safe and most convenient for the recipients.

- Minimise risks to people reaching distributions, regularly monitoring checkpoints or changes in the security situation.

4 > Provide recipients with advance details of the distribution plan and schedule, the quality and quantity of the food ration or the cash or voucher value, and what it is intended to cover.

- Schedule distributions in a way that respects people's travelling and working time and that prioritises at-risk groups as appropriate.
- Define and establish feedback mechanisms with the community before distribution.

Key indicators

Percentage of inclusion and exclusion targeting errors minimised

- Target <10 per cent

Distance from dwellings to final distribution points or markets (in case of vouchers or cash)

- Target <5 kilometres

Percentage of assisted people (disaggregated by sex, age and disability) who report experiencing safety problems travelling (to and from) and at programme sites

Number of cases reported of sexual exploitation or abuse of power related to distribution or delivery practices

Percentage of cases of sexual exploitation or abuse of power related to distribution or delivery practices that are followed up

- 100 per cent

Percentage of targeted households that correctly cite their food assistance entitlement

- Target: >50 per cent of targeted households

Guidance notes

Targeting: Ensure that targeting tools and methods are adapted to context. Targeting should span the intervention, not just the initial phase. Finding the right balance between exclusion errors, which can be life-threatening, and inclusion errors, which are potentially disruptive or wasteful, is complex. In rapid onset crises, inclusion errors are more acceptable than exclusion errors. General food distributions may be appropriate in crises where households have suffered similar losses or where a detailed targeting assessment is not possible due to lack of access.

Children aged 6–59 months, pregnant and lactating women, people living with HIV and other vulnerable groups may be targeted for supplementary foods, or they may be linked to nutrition treatment and prevention strategies. For people living with HIV, this will increase their daily caloric intake and support adherence to anti-retroviral therapy.

Any targeted programme should carefully avoid creating stigma or discrimination. People living with HIV can be included as part of distributions for "people with chronic diseases", for instance, and provided through the health centres where they receive care and treatment. Lists of people living with HIV should never be publicised or shared, and in most contexts community leaders should not be involved as targeting agents for people living with HIV.

Targeting agents/committees: Develop direct contact with affected people and groups in the community, while avoiding community gatekeepers as much as possible. Establish targeting committees that include representatives of the following populations:

- women and girls, men and boys, older people and persons with disabilities;
- locally elected committees, women's groups and humanitarian organisations;
- local and international NGOs;
- youth organisations; and
- local governmental institutions.

The registration processes: Registration can be challenging in camps, especially where displaced people do not have identification documents. Lists from local authorities and community-generated household lists may be useful if an independent assessment proves them accurate and impartial. Encourage the involvement of affected women in designing the registration processes. Include at-risk individuals on distribution lists, especially people with reduced mobility.

If registration is not possible in the initial stages of a crisis, complete it as soon as the situation has stabilised. Establish a feedback mechanism for the registration process that is accessible to all affected people, including women, girls, older people and persons with disabilities. Women have the right to be registered in their own names. Where possible, consult both men and women, separately if necessary, about who should physically collect assistance or receive cash-based assistance on behalf of the household. This consultation should be informed by a risk assessment.

Make special provision for single male- or female-headed households, as well as child- and youth-headed households and separated or unaccompanied children, so that they can safely collect assistance on behalf of their households. Establish childcare adjacent to distribution points to enable single-parent households and women with young children to collect assistance without leaving their children unattended. In contexts where there are polygamous households, treat each wife and her children as a separate household.

Distribution of "dry" rations: General food distributions normally only provide dry rations, which people then cook in their homes. Recipients might include an individual or a household ration-card holder, a representative of a group of households, traditional and women leaders, or leaders of a community-based targeted distribution. The frequency of distribution should consider the weight of the food ration and the recipients' means to carry it home safely. Specific support may be needed to ensure that older people, pregnant and breastfeeding women, separated and unaccompanied children, and persons with disabilities can collect and retain their entitlements. Consider having other community members assist them, or provide them with more frequent, smaller rations.

Distribution of "wet" rations: In exceptional circumstances, such as at the beginning of a rapid-onset crisis, cooked meals or ready-to-eat food may be used for general food distributions. These rations may be appropriate when people are on the move, or when carrying food home would put people receiving assistance at risk of theft, violence, abuse or exploitation. Use school meals and food incentives for education personnel as a distribution mechanism in an emergency.

Distribution points: When locating distribution points, consider the terrain and try to provide reasonable access to other sources of support such as clean and safe water, toilets, health services, shade and shelter, and safe spaces for children and women. The presence of armed checkpoints and military activity must be considered to minimise any risk to civilians and establish safe access to aid. Roads to and from distribution points should be clearly marked, accessible and frequently used by other members of the community. Consider the practicalities and costs of transporting commodities ⊕ *see Protection Principle 2.*

Develop alternative means of distribution to reach those who are located further from the distribution point or who have functional difficulties. Access to distribution is a common source of anxiety for marginalised and excluded populations in a crisis. Provide direct distributions to populations in institutional settings.

Scheduling distributions: Schedule distributions at times that allow travel to distribution points and back home during daylight hours. Avoid creating a requirement for an overnight stay, which creates additional risks. Schedule distributions to minimise disruption to everyday activities. Consider establishing fast-track or prioritisation lines for at-risk groups, and a desk staffed with a social worker who can register any unaccompanied and separated children. Provide advance information on the schedule and distribution through a broad range of communications.

Safety during food, voucher and cash distributions: Take steps to minimise risks to those participating in the distribution. This includes proper crowd control, supervision of distributions by trained staff, and members of the affected population guarding distribution points themselves. If necessary, involve the local police. Inform police officials and officers of the objectives of the food transfers. Carefully plan the site layout at distribution points so that it is safe and accessible for older people, persons with disabilities and people with functional difficulties. Inform all food distribution teams about appropriate expected conduct, including penalties for sexual exploitation and abuse. Include female guardians to oversee off-loading, registration, distribution and post-distribution monitoring of food ⊕ *see Core Humanitarian Standard Commitment 7.*

Providing information: Display ration information prominently at distribution points, in languages and formats accessible to people who cannot read or who have communication difficulties. Inform people through printed, audio, SMS and voice messages about:

- the ration plan, specifying the quantity and type of food rations, or the cash/ voucher value and what it is intended to cover;
- reasons for any changes from earlier plans (timing, quantity, items, other);
- the distribution plan;
- the nutritional quality of the food and, if needed, any special attention required by recipients to protect its nutritional value;

- the requirements for the safe handling and use of the foods;
- specific information for optimum use of food for children; and
- options for obtaining more information or providing feedback.

For cash-based assistance, transfer value should be included in ration information. Information could be provided at the distribution point, displayed at the cash out point or where vouchers can be redeemed, or in a leaflet in the local language.

Changes to the food provided: Changes in rations or the transfer value for cash-based assistance may happen due to a lack of available food, lack of funding or other reasons. When this occurs, convey these changes to the recipients through distribution committees, community leaders and representative organisations. Develop a joint course of action before distributions. The distribution committee should inform people of changes, the reasons behind the changes and the date and plan for resuming normal rations. Options include:

- reducing the rations to all recipients;
- giving a full ration to vulnerable individuals and a reduced ration to the general population; or
- postponing the distribution (as a last resort).

Monitoring of distribution and delivery: Monitor food regularly by randomly weighing rations collected by households to measure the accuracy and equity of distribution. Interview recipients and ensure that the interview sample includes an equal number of women and men, including adolescents and youth, persons with disabilities and older people. Random visits by an interview team made up of at least one male and one female can help determine the acceptability and usefulness of the ration. These visits can identify people who meet the selection criteria but are not receiving food assistance. Such visits can also identify food received from elsewhere, its source and its use. The visits can identify possible use of force to take possessions, forcible recruitments, or sexual or other exploitation ⊕ *see Delivering assistance through markets.*

Food assistance standard 6.4:
Food use

Storage, preparation and consumption of food is safe and appropriate at both household and community levels.

Key actions

1 〉 Protect people receiving assistance from inappropriate food handling or preparation.

- Inform people of the importance of food hygiene and promote good hygiene practices in food handling.

- Where cooked rations are provided, train staff in safe storage, handling and preparation of food, and the potential health hazards of improper practices.

2 > Consult with and advise people receiving assistance on storage, preparation, cooking and consumption of food.

3 > Ensure that households have safe access to appropriate cooking utensils, fuel, fuel-efficient stoves, clean water and hygiene materials.

4 > Ensure that individuals who cannot prepare food or feed themselves have access to caregivers who can support them where possible and appropriate.

5 > Monitor how food resources are used within the household.

Key indicators

Number of cases reported of health hazards from food distributed

Percentage of households able to store and prepare food safely

Percentage of targeted households able to describe three or more hygiene awareness messages

Percentage of targeted households that report having access to appropriate cooking utensils, fuel, drinking water and hygiene materials

Guidance notes

Food hygiene: Crises may disrupt people's normal hygiene practices. Promote food hygiene practices that are adapted to local conditions and disease patterns. Stress the importance of avoiding water contamination, controlling pests and always washing hands before handling food. Inform people receiving food about storing food safely at the household level ⊕ *see WASH hygiene promotion standards.*

Food processing and storage: Access to food-processing facilities, such as cereal-grinding mills, enables people to prepare food in the form of their choice and saves time for other productive activities. Where perishable food items are offered, consider appropriate facilities to store these, such as watertight containers, coolers and freezers. Heat, cold and moisture influence the storage of perishable foods.

Individuals who may require assistance with storage, cooking and feeding include young children, older people, people with disabilities and people living with HIV. Outreach programmes or additional support may be necessary for people who have difficulty providing food to their dependants, such as parents with disabilities.

Intra-house food use monitoring: Humanitarian organisations should monitor and assess intra-house use of food and its appropriateness and adequacy. At the household level, food commodities can either be consumed as intended or be traded or bartered. The goal of the barter could be to access other more-preferred food items, non-food items or payment for services such as school fees or medical bills. Intra-household allocation assessment should also monitor food use by sex, age and disability.

The use of cash and vouchers: It is important to manage the risk of panic buying when households receive cash or vouchers. Prepare traders and people receiving assistance before distribution, at distribution and after distribution. For example, consider whether food will be available throughout the month or whether it would be better to stagger distributions over the course of a month. Vouchers can be issued in small denominations redeemable on a weekly basis, where appropriate. The same principle should apply to cash that is redeemable through automatic teller machines or other forms of digital or manual payment.

7. Livelihoods

People's ability to protect their livelihoods is directly related to their vulnerability to crises. Understanding vulnerabilities before, during and after a crisis makes it easier to provide appropriate assistance, and to identify how communities can rehabilitate and improve their livelihoods.

Crises can disrupt many of the factors that people rely on to maintain their livelihoods. People affected by crises may lose their jobs or have to abandon their land or water sources. Assets may also be destroyed, contaminated or stolen during conflict or natural disasters. Markets may stop functioning.

In the initial stages of a crisis, meeting basic survival needs is the priority. However, over time, rehabilitation of the systems, skills and capacities that support livelihoods will also help people recover with dignity. Promoting livelihoods among refugees often presents unique challenges, such as encampment or restrictive legal and policy frameworks in countries of asylum.

Those who produce food need access to land, water, livestock, support services and markets that can support production. They should have the means to continue production without compromising other resources, people or systems ⊕ *see LEGS Handbook*.

In urban areas, the impact of a crisis on livelihoods is likely to be different from the impact in rural areas. Household composition, skills, disabilities and education will determine the degree to which people may participate in different economic activities. Generally, poorer urban people have a less diverse range of livelihoods coping strategies than their counterparts in rural areas. For example, in some countries, they cannot access land to grow food.

Bringing together those who have lost their livelihoods and those who influence how new opportunities might be created will help to set the priorities of a livelihoods response. This should reflect an analysis of labour, services and associated product markets. All livelihoods interventions should consider how to use and/or support local markets ⊕ *see MERS Handbook*.

Livelihoods standard 7.1:
Primary production
Primary production mechanisms receive protection and support.

Key actions

1 ⟩ Provide access to production inputs and/or assets for farmers.

- Prefer cash or vouchers where markets are functioning and can be supported to recover, to give farmers flexibility to select preferred inputs, seeds, fish stock or livestock species.

- Introduce new technologies after a crisis only if they have been tested in or adapted to similar contexts.

2 〉 Deliver inputs that are locally acceptable, conform to appropriate quality norms and are on time for best seasonal use.

- Favour locally appropriate livestock inputs and local crop varieties that are already in use and in demand for the upcoming season.

3 〉 Ensure inputs and services do not increase vulnerability for recipients or create conflict within the community.

- Assess potential competition for scarce natural resources (such as land or water) as well as potential damage to existing social networks.

4 〉 Involve affected men and women equitably in planning, decision-making, implementing and monitoring of primary production responses.

5 〉 Train producers engaged in crop, fishery, aquaculture, forestry and livestock sectors in sustainable production and management practices.

6 〉 Assess the market and stimulate demand for locally produced crops, vegetables and other agricultural products.

Key indicators

Percentage change in the targeted population's production (food or income source) compared with a normal year

Percentage of households reporting that they have access to adequate storage facilities for their produce

Percentage of targeted households with improved physical access to functioning markets due to programme interventions

Guidance notes

Production strategies: Production strategies must have a reasonable chance of developing and succeeding in context. This can depend on many factors, including access to:

- sufficient natural resources, labour, farm inputs and financial capital;
- good quality seed varieties that are adapted to local conditions; and
- productive animals, which represent a crucial food security asset ⊕ *see LEGS Handbook.*

In addition, the strategy must consider existing livelihood skills, community preferences, the physical environment and potential for scalability.

Promote diverse livelihood activities within a local area, while preventing overuse of natural resources. Environmental damage not only increases the risk of a crisis, but contributes to tensions between communities. Livelihoods interventions should promote adaptation to climate change where possible, such as selecting adapted seed varieties.

Prevent child labour associated with livelihoods initiatives. Be aware of the indirect impact of livelihoods programmes on children, such as missing school because they are required to support the household while a parent is working.

Energy: Consider energy needs for mechanised labour, food processing, communication, cold chains for food preservation and efficient burning devices.

Improvements: Consider introducing improved crop varieties, livestock or fish-stock species, new tools, fertilisers or innovative management practices. Strengthen food production based on the maintenance of pre-crisis patterns and/or links with national development plans.

New technologies: Producers and local consumers must understand and accept the implications of new technologies for local production systems, cultural practices and the natural environment before adopting them. When introducing new technologies, provide appropriate community consultations, information and training. Ensure access for groups at risk of discrimination (including women, older people, minorities and people with disabilities). If possible, coordinate with livelihood experts and government ministries. Ensure ongoing technological support, future accessibility to the technology, and assess its commercial viability.

Cash-based assistance or credit: This can be provided to use at seed and livestock fairs. Understand the potential consequences of a chosen approach on people's nutrition, considering whether it allows people to produce nutrient-rich food themselves or whether it provides cash to purchase food. Assess the feasibility of cash-based assistance for purchasing production inputs, considering availability of goods, access to markets and the existence of a safe, affordable and gender-sensitive cash transfer mechanism ⊕ *see MERS Handbook* and *LEGS Handbook*.

Seasonality and price fluctuations: Provide agricultural inputs and veterinary services to coincide with the relevant agricultural and animal husbandry seasons. For example, provide seeds and tools before the planting season. Destocking of livestock during drought should take place before excess livestock mortality occurs. Restocking should start when the likelihood of recovery is high, for example following the next rainy season. When necessary, or provide food assistance to protect seeds and inputs. Ensure that inputs are sensitive to the different capacities, needs and risks of various groups, including women and persons with disabilities. Extreme seasonal price fluctuations adversely affect poor agricultural producers who sell their produce just after harvest, when prices are at their lowest. These fluctuations also have a negative impact on livestock owners who have to sell during drought. Conversely, consumers who have limited disposable income cannot afford to invest in food stocks. They depend on small but frequent purchases. As a result, they buy food even when prices are high, such as during a drought. For livestock guidance ⊕ *see LEGS Handbook*.

Seeds: Farmers and local agricultural experts should approve specific varieties. Seeds should suit the local agro-ecology and farmers' own management conditions. They should also be disease-resistant and withstand potentially harsh weather conditions due to climate change. Test the quality of seeds originating from outside the region and check that they are appropriate for local conditions. Give farmers access to a range of crops and varieties in any seed-related intervention. This allows them to work out what is best for their particular farming system. For example, farmers growing maize may prefer hybrid seeds to local varieties. Comply with government policies regarding hybrid seeds. Do not distribute genetically modified seeds without the approval of local authorities. Inform farmers if they are provided with genetically modified seeds. When farmers use vouchers or seed fairs, encourage them to buy seeds from local formal suppliers. Farmers may prefer traditional varieties which are adapted to the local context. These will definitely be available at a lower price, meaning they get more seeds for the same voucher value.

Community tensions and security risks: Tensions between the displaced and local population or within the affected community can arise when production requires a change in access to the available natural resources. Competition over water or land can lead to restrictions in their use. Primary food production may not be viable if there is a shortage of vital natural resources over the long term. It is also not feasible if there is a lack of access for certain populations, such as landless people. Providing free inputs can also disrupt traditional social support, compromise redistribution mechanisms or affect private sector operators. This can create tensions and reduce future access to inputs ⊕ *see Protection Principle 1.*

Supply chain: Use existing local, verifiable supply chains to obtain inputs and services for food production, such as veterinary services and seeds. To support the local private sector, use mechanisms such as cash or vouchers that link primary producers directly to suppliers. When designing local purchasing systems, consider the availability of appropriate inputs and suppliers' capacity to increase supply. Assess the risk of inflation and the sustainability of the quality of inputs. Monitor and mitigate the negative effects of responses, including large localised food purchases and distribution, on market prices. Consider the effects of local food purchases and imports on local economies. When working with the private sector, identify and address gender inequalities and share any profits equitably ⊕ *see MERS Handbook*.

Monitor whether producers actually use the provided inputs as intended. Review the quality of the inputs in terms of their performance, their acceptability and producer preferences. Evaluate how the project has affected food availability at household level. For example, consider the quantity and quality of food that is being stocked, consumed, traded or given away. Where the project aims to increase production of a specific food type (animal/fish products or protein-rich legumes), investigate the households' use of these products. Include an analysis of the benefit to different members of the household, such as women, children, older people and people with disabilities.

Post-harvest storage: A significant proportion of produce (estimated average of 30 per cent) is unusable after harvest, due to losses. Support affected people to minimise losses by managing handling, storage, processing, packaging, transportation, marketing and other post-harvest activities. Advise and enable them to store their harvest to avoid moisture and aflatoxins produced by fungi. Enable them to process their crops, especially cereals.

Livelihoods standard 7.2:
Income and employment

Women and men receive equal access to appropriate income-earning opportunities where income generation and employment are feasible livelihood strategies.

Key actions

1 ⟩ Base decisions regarding income-earning activities on a gender-sensitive market assessment.

- Reduce the risk of undernutrition and other public health risks by ensuring that participation in income-earning opportunities does not undermine childcare or other caring responsibilities.
- Understand labour rates for community members and the government minimum wage for unskilled and skilled work.

2 ⟩ Choose types of payment (in-kind, cash, voucher, food or a combination) based on a participatory analysis.

- Understand local capacities, safety and protection benefits, immediate needs, equitable access, existing market systems and the affected people's preferences.

3 ⟩ Base the level of payment on the type of work, local rules, objectives for livelihoods restoration and prevailing approved levels of payment in the region.

- Consider safety-net measures such as unconditional cash and food transfers for households that cannot participate in work programmes.

4 ⟩ Adopt and maintain inclusive, safe and secure working environments.

- Monitor the risk of sexual harassment, discrimination, exploitation and abuse in the workplace and respond quickly to complaints.

215

5 > Promote partnerships with the private sector and other stakeholders to create sustainable employment opportunities.

▪ Provide capital resources equitably to facilitate livelihood recovery.

6 > Choose environmentally sensitive options for income generation whenever possible.

....

Key indicators

Percentage of the target population who improve their net income during a defined period

Percentage of households with access to credit

Percentage of the target population who diversify their income-generating activities

Percentage of the target population employed (or self-employed) in sustainable livelihoods activities for a defined period of time (6–12 months)

Percentage of the affected population with physical and economic access to functioning markets and/or other livelihood support services (formal or informal)

....

Guidance notes

Analysis: A gender-sensitive labour and market analysis is fundamental to justify and define activities, promote recovery and resilience, and sustain outcomes. Understanding the household roles and responsibilities is essential to address any opportunity costs, such as caring for children or older people, or accessing other services such as education or healthcare.

Use existing tools to understand markets and economic systems. Food security responses should be based on market functions before and after the crisis, and their potential for improving the living conditions for poor people. Discuss alternatives or adaptations for at-risk groups (such as youth, persons with disabilities, pregnant women or older people) within the targeted group. Analyse their skills, experience and capacities, and potential risks and mitigation strategies. Explore whether household members normally migrate for seasonal work. Understand how different groups of the affected population may have restricted access to markets and livelihoods opportunities, and support them in getting access.

Safety-net measures: Some women and men may not be able to participate in income-generating activities, such as an elderly couple. The crisis itself may make it impossible for others to participate in employment due to changes in responsibilities or health status. Short-term safety-net measures can support such cases, with links to existing national social protection systems. Recommend new safety nets where needed. Delivery of safety-net measures must support the fair distribution of resources, ensuring that women and girls have direct access to resources where appropriate. At the same time, work with safety-net recipients to find ways for them to transition to safe and sustainable income-generating activities. Whenever possible, cash-based responses should be linked to existing safety-net programmes as part of sustainability and the social protection strategy.

Payments: Conduct a market analysis before implementing any paid work programme. Payment may be in cash or in food or a combination of these and should enable food-insecure households to meet their needs. Communicate project objectives, the humanitarian organisation's expectations of workers, the conditions under which people will be working and the payment amount and process.

Make payment an incentive for people to improve their own situation, rather than compensation for any work in the community. Consider people's purchasing needs and the impact of giving cash or food to create household income to meet basic needs such as school, healthcare and social obligations. Decide on the type and level of payment case by case. Monitor to ensure that all women and men are paid equally for agreed units of work and that there is no discrimination against specific groups.

Consider the impact of resale values on local markets where payment is in-kind and provided as an income transfer. New income-generating activities should enhance rather than replace the existing range of income sources. Payment should not have a negative impact on local labour markets, for example by causing wage inflation, diverting labour from other activities or undermining essential public services.

Purchasing power: Provision of cash may have positive multiplier effects in local economies, but can also cause local inflation for key goods. Food distribution can also affect the purchasing power of people receiving assistance. The purchasing power associated with a given food or combination of foods influences whether the recipient's household eats or sells that food. Some commodities (such as oil) are easier to sell for a good price than others (such as blended food). Establish an understanding of household food sales and purchases when assessing the wider impact of food distribution programmes.

Safety at work: Use practical procedures for minimising public health risk or treating injuries. For example, provide training, protective clothing and first-aid kits where necessary. Minimise the risk of exposure to communicable diseases and HIV. Establish safe access routes to work sites, providing workers with torches where the route is not well lit. Use bells, whistles and radios to warn of threats. Encourage travelling in groups and avoid travelling after dark. Ensure that all participants are aware of emergency procedures and can access early warning systems. Women and girls should be equally protected, and any discriminatory norms in the workplace should be addressed.

Managing household and family duties: Speak regularly with affected people, including women and men separately, to learn their preferences and priorities regarding income generation, cash-for-work opportunities, and other household and family needs. Discuss workloads and any increased tensions in the home due to changes in traditional gender roles and women's increased control over assets.

Cash-for-work activity schedules should consider the physical condition and daily routines of men and women and be culturally appropriate. For example, they should consider prayer times and public holidays. Working hours should not place unreasonable competing demands on people's time. Programmes should not divert household resources away from existing productive activities, nor should they adversely affect access to other employment or education. Participation in income generation should respect national laws on the minimum employment age. This is usually not less than the age of completion of compulsory schooling. Childcare facilities with appropriate financial allocation are recommended at the work sites if caregivers with small children are participating in the programme.

Environmental management: Support people's engagement in environmental activities such as tree planting, camp clean-up and environmental rehabilitation through food and cash-for-work programmes. Though temporary, these activities will increase people's engagement in their surrounding environment.

Consider the accessibility and safety of the working environment. Ensure that any debris to be cleared does not contain hazardous materials. Cash-for-work programmes should not involve any clearance at industrial or waste management sites.

Promote the production of environmentally sustainable construction materials as an income-generating activity and provide associated vocational training. Train people and encourage composting of biodegradable waste for use as fertiliser.

Private sector: The private sector can play an important role in facilitating livelihood protection and recovery. Where possible, establish partnerships to create employment opportunities. These partnerships can also help to establish and grow micro, small and medium enterprises. Business and technology incubators can provide financial capital and opportunities for knowledge transfer ⊕ *see MERS Handbook*.

Appendix 1
Food security and livelihoods assessment checklist

Food security assessments often broadly categorise the affected people into live-lihood groupings according to their sources of, and strategies for, obtaining income or food. This may also include a breakdown of the population according to wealth groups or strata. It is important to compare the current situation with the history of food security before the crisis. Use "average normal years" as a baseline. Consider the specific roles and vulnerabilities of women and men, and the implications of these for household food security.

The following checklist questions cover the broad areas to consider in a food security assessment.

Food security of livelihood groups

- Are there groups in the population who share the same livelihood strategies? How can these be categorised according to their main sources of food or income?

Food security before the crisis (baseline)

- How did the different livelihood groups acquire food or income before the crisis? For an average year in the recent past, what were their sources of food and income?
- How did these different sources of food and income vary seasonally and geographically in a normal year? Constructing a seasonal calendar may be useful.
- Were all groups getting enough food of the right quality to be well nourished?
- Were all groups earning enough income by non-harmful ways to afford their basic needs? Consider food, education, healthcare, soap and other household items, clothing, and productive inputs such as seeds and tools. (The last two questions will indicate whether there were chronic problems. Existing problems may be worsened by a crisis. The appropriate response is influenced by whether the problem is chronic or acute.)
- Looking back over the past five or ten years, how has food security varied from year to year? Constructing a timeline or history of food security may be useful.
- What kind of assets, savings or other reserves do the different livelihood groups own? Examples include food stocks, cash savings, livestock holdings, investments, credit and unclaimed debt.
- Over a period of a week or a month, what do household expenditures include? What proportion is spent on each item?

- Who is responsible for the management of cash in the household and on what is cash spent?
- How accessible is the nearest market for obtaining basic goods? Consider factors such as distance, security, ease of mobility, availability and accessibility of market information, and transport.
- What is the availability and price of essential goods, including food?
- Before the crisis, what were the average terms of trade between basic needs (food, agricultural inputs, healthcare, etc) and income sources (cash crops, livestock, wages, etc)

Food security during crises

- How has the crisis affected the different sources of food and income for each of the livelihood groups identified?
- How has it affected the usual seasonal patterns of food security for the different groups?
- How has it affected access to financial service providers, markets, market availability and prices of essential goods?
- For different livelihood groups, what are the different crisis coping strategies and what proportion of people are engaged in them? How has this changed compared with the situation before the crisis?
- Which group or population is most affected?
- What are the short- and medium-term effects of coping strategies on people's financial and other assets?
- For all livelihood groups, and all people at risk, what are the effects of coping strategies on their health, general well-being and dignity? Are there risks associated with coping strategies?

Appendix 2
Seed security assessment checklist

Below are sample questions for seed security assessments. Assessment of seed security should consider national legislation on hybrid and genetically modified varieties.

Seed security before the crisis (baseline)

- What are farmers' most important crops? What do they use them for – consumption, income or both? Are these crops grown each season? What other crops might become important in times of stress?
- How do farmers usually get seed or other planting material for these crops? Consider all channels.
- What are the sowing parameters for each major crop? What is the average area planted? What are the seeding rates? What are the multiplication rates (ratios of seed or grain harvested to seed planted)?
- Are there important or preferred varieties of specific crops (local climate-adapted varieties)?
- Which production inputs are essential for particular crops or varieties?
- Who in the household is responsible for decision-making, managing crops and disposing of crop products at different stages of production and post-production?

Seed security after a crisis

- Is a farming-related intervention feasible from the point of view of persons receiving assistance?
- Which crops have been affected most by the crisis? Should the focus be on these? Why or why not?
- Are farmers confident the situation is now stable and secure enough that they can successfully cultivate, harvest and sell or consume a crop?
- Do they have sufficient access to fields and other means of production (manure, implements, draught animals)?
- Are they prepared to re-engage in agriculture?

Assessing seed supply and demand: home stocks

- Are adequate amounts of home-produced seed available for sowing? This includes both seed from a farmer's own harvest and seed potentially available through social networks (for example, neighbours).
- Is this a crop that farmers still want to plant? Is it adapted to local conditions? Is there still a demand for it?
- Are the varieties available through a farmer's own production still suitable for planting next season? Does the quality of the seed meet the farmer's normal standards?

Assessing seed supply and demand: local markets

- Are markets generally functioning despite the crisis (are market days being held, are farmers able to move, sell and buy freely)?
- Are current volumes of available seed or grain comparable to those under normal conditions at the same time during previous seasons?
- Are crops and varieties that farmers find suitable for growing found in the markets?
- Are current market prices of seed or grain comparable to the prices at the same time in previous seasons? If there is a price differential, is the magnitude likely to be a problem for farmers?

Assessing seed supply and demand: formal sector

- Are the crops and varieties on offer from the formal sector adapted to particular stress zones? Is there evidence farmers will use them?
- Can the available formal sector seed meet the demand triggered by the crisis? If not, what proportion of farmers' needs will they meet?

Appendix 3
Nutrition assessment checklist

Below are sample questions for assessments examining the underlying causes of undernutrition, the level of nutrition risk and the possibilities for response. The questions are based on the conceptual framework of the causes of undernutrition. ⊕ *See Figure 7 Food security and nutrition: causes of undernutrition.* The information is likely to be available from a variety of sources. Gathering it will require various assessment tools, including key informant interviews, observation and review of secondary data.

Pre-emergency situation

What information already exists on the nature, scale and causes of undernutrition among the affected people? ⊕ *See Food security and nutrition assessments standard 1.1.*

The current risk of undernutrition

What is the risk of undernutrition related to reduced food access?
⊕ See Appendix 1: Food security and livelihoods assessment checklist.

What is the risk of undernutrition related to infant and young child feeding and care practices?

- Is there a change in work and social patterns (due to factors such as migration, displacement or armed conflict) affecting the roles and responsibilities in the household?
- Is there a change in the normal composition of households? Are there large numbers of separated children?
- Has the normal care environment been disrupted (for example, through displacement), affecting access to secondary caregivers, access to foods or access to water?
- Are any infants not breastfed? Are there infants who are artificially fed?
- Has there been any evidence or suspicion of a decline in infant feeding practices in the crisis? In particular, has there been a decrease in breastfeeding initiation or exclusive breastfeeding rates? Has there been an increase in artificial feeding rates and/or any increase in the proportion of infants not breastfed?
- Are age-appropriate, nutritionally adequate, safe complementary foods, and the means to prepare them, hygienically accessible?
- Is there any evidence or suspicion of general distribution of breastmilk substitutes such as infant formula, other milk products, bottles and teats, either donated or purchased?

223

- In pastoral communities, have the herds been away from young children for long? Has access to milk changed from normal?
- Has HIV affected caring practices at household level?
- Has the general food ration been adapted to the needs of older people and people with difficulties feeding? Evaluate its energy composition and micro-nutrient content. Assess the acceptability of the food products (palatability, chewability and digestibility).

What is the risk of undernutrition related to poor public health?

- Are there any reports of disease outbreaks that may affect nutritional status, such as measles or acute diarrhoeal disease? Is there a risk that these outbreaks will occur? ⊕ *See Essential healthcare – communicable diseases standard 2.1.*
- What is the estimated measles vaccination coverage of the affected people? ⊕ *See Essential healthcare – child health standard 2.2.1.*
- Is vitamin A routinely given with measles vaccination? What is the estimated vitamin A supplementation coverage?
- Are there any estimates of mortality rates (either crude or under-five)? What are the estimates and what method has been used to make them? ⊕ *See Essential concepts in health.*
- Is there, or will there be, a significant decline in ambient temperature that is likely to affect the prevalence of acute respiratory infection or the energy requirements of the affected people?
- Is there a high prevalence of HIV?
- Are people already vulnerable to undernutrition due to poverty or ill health?
- Is there overcrowding or a risk of or high prevalence of tuberculosis?
- Are there reported cases of non-communicable diseases such as diabetes, arthritis, cardiovascular diseases and anaemia?
- Is there a high incidence of malaria?
- Have people been in water or in wet clothes or exposed to other harsh environmental conditions for long periods of time?

What formal and informal local structures are currently in place through which potential interventions could be channelled?

- What is the capacity of the Ministry of Health, religious organisations, community support groups, breastfeeding support groups or NGOs with a long- or short-term presence in the area?
- What nutrition interventions or community-based support were already in place and organised by local communities, individuals, NGOs, government organisations, UN agencies or religious organisations? What are the nutrition policies (past, ongoing and lapsed), the planned long-term nutrition responses, and programmes that are being implemented or planned in response to the current situation?

Appendix 4
Measuring acute malnutrition

In major nutritional emergencies, it may be necessary to include infants under six months, pregnant and breastfeeding women, older children, adolescents, adults and older people in nutrition assessments or nutritional programmes.

Infants under six months

While research is ongoing for this age group, there is a limited evidence base for assessment and management. Most guidelines recommend the same anthropometric case definitions of acute infant malnutrition as for older children aged 6–59 months (except for mid upper arm circumference (MUAC), which is not presently recommended for infants under six months). Admission criteria focus on current size rather than an assessment of growth.

The switch from National Center for Health Statistics (NCHS) growth references to WHO 2006 growth standards results in more cases of infants under six months being recorded as wasted. This can result in more infants presenting to feeding programmes, or caregivers becoming concerned about the adequacy of exclusive breastfeeding. It is important to assess and consider the following:

- The infant's longitudinal growth – is the growth rate good, despite body size being small (some infants may be "catching up" following low birth weight)?
- Infant feeding practices – is the infant exclusively breastfeeding?
- Clinical status – does the infant have any medical complications or conditions that are treatable or that make him or her high risk?
- Maternal factors – for example, does the mother lack family support or is she depressed? Inpatient admission to therapeutic feeding programmes should be a priority for high-risk infants.

Children aged 6–59 months

The table below shows the commonly used cut-offs for acute malnutrition among children aged 6–59 months. Calculate weight-for-height (WFH) indices using the WHO 2006 child growth standards. The WFH Z score (according to WHO standards) is the preferred indicator for reporting anthropometric survey results. MUAC is an independent criterion for acute malnutrition and is one of the best predictors of mortality. The prevalence of low MUAC is also used to predict caseloads for supplementary feeding and therapeutic care programmes. The cut-offs commonly used are <11.5 centimetres for severe acute malnutrition and 11.5–12.5 centimetres for moderate acute malnutrition. MUAC is also often used, with a higher cut-off, as part of a two-stage screening process. It should not be used alone in anthropometric surveys, although it can be used as the sole admission criterion for feeding programmes.

	Global acute malnutrition	Moderate acute malnutrition	Severe acute malnutrition
Children 6–59 months	WFH <–2 Z score and/or MUAC <12.5cm and/or nutritional oedema	WFH –3 to –2 Z score and/or MUAC 11.5–12.5cm	WFH <–3 Z score and/or MUAC <11.5cm and/or nutritional oedema
Older people	MUAC 21cm	MUAC 18.5–21.0cm	MUAC 18.5cm
Pregnant and lactating women	MUAC <23cm (may be <210mm in certain contexts)	MUAC 18.5–22.9cm	MUAC <18.5cm
Adults (including people living with HIV or tuberculosis)	BMI <18.5	BMI 16–18.5	BMI <16

Children aged 5–19 years

Use the WHO 2007 growth standards to determine nutrition status in children aged 5–19 years. These growth reference data curves align closely with the WHO child growth standards for children aged 6–59 months and the recommended cut-offs for adults. Consider using MUAC in older children and adolescents, particularly in the context of HIV. As this is a developing technical area, it is important to refer to the latest guidance and technical updates.

Adults (20–59 years)

There is no agreed definition of acute malnutrition in adults, but evidence suggests that the cut-off for severe acute malnutrition could be a body mass index (BMI) lower than 16, and for mild and moderate acute malnutrition lower than 18.5. Surveys of adult malnutrition should aim to gather data on weight, height and sitting height and MUAC measurements. This data can be used to calculate BMI. BMI should be adjusted for the Cormic index (the ratio of sitting height to standing height) only to make comparisons between populations. Such adjustment can substantially change the apparent prevalence of undernutrition in adults and may have important consequences for programming. MUAC measurements should always be taken. If immediate results are needed or resources are severely limited, surveys may be based on MUAC measurements alone.

The lack of validated functional outcome data and benchmarks complicates the interpretation of anthropometric results. Use detailed contextual information when interpreting them. For guidance on assessment ⊕ see References and further reading.

When screening individuals for nutritional care admission and discharge, use a combination of anthropometric indices, clinical signs (particularly weakness, recent weight loss) and social factors (such as access to food, presence of caregivers, shelter). Note that oedema in adults can be caused by factors other than malnutrition, and clinicians should assess adult oedema to exclude other causes. Individual humanitarian organisations should decide on the indicator to determine eligibility for care, taking into account the known shortcomings of BMI, the lack of information on MUAC and the programme implications of the indicators' use. This is a developing technical area, so refer to the latest guidance and technical updates.

MUAC may be used as a screening tool for pregnant women, for example as a criterion for entry into a feeding programme. Given their additional nutritional needs, pregnant women may be at greater risk than other groups in the population. MUAC does not change significantly through pregnancy. A MUAC of less than 20.7 centimetres indicates a severe risk of foetal growth retardation, and less than 23 centimetres indicates a moderate risk. Suggested cut-off points for risk vary by country, but range from 21 to 23 centimetres. Consider less than 21 centimetres as an appropriate cut-off for selection of women at risk during emergencies.

Older people

There is currently no agreed definition of malnutrition in older people, yet this group may be at risk of malnutrition in crises. WHO suggests that the BMI thresholds for adults may be appropriate for people aged over 60 years. However, accuracy of measurement is problematic because of spinal curvature (stooping) and compression of the vertebrae. Arm span or demi-span can be used instead of height, but the multiplication factor to calculate height varies according to the population. Visual assessment is necessary. MUAC may be a useful tool for measuring malnutrition in older people, but research on appropriate cut-offs is still in progress.

Persons with disabilities

No guidelines currently exist for the measurement of individuals with physical disabilities. This lack of guidelines often excludes them from anthropometric surveys. Visual assessment is necessary. MUAC measurements may be misleading in cases where upper arm muscle might build up to aid mobility. There are alternatives to standard measures of height, including length, arm span or demi-span or lower leg length. It is necessary to consult the latest research to determine the most appropriate way of measuring persons with disabilities for whom standard weight, height and MUAC measurement is not appropriate.

Appendix 5
Measures of the public health significance of micronutrient deficiencies

Urgently treat clinical micronutrient deficiencies on an individual basis. Individual cases of clinical micronutrient deficiencies are also usually indicative of an underlying problem of micronutrient deficiency at the population level. Measuring and classifying micronutrient deficiencies at the population level is important for planning and monitoring interventions.

Biochemical tests provide an objective measure of micronutrient status. However, the collection of biological samples for testing often presents logistical, staff training, cold chain and sometimes acceptability challenges. Also, biochemical measurements are not always as sensitive and specific as required. As with acute malnutrition, there may be variations according to the time of day or season of the year when the sample is collected. Good quality control is essential and should always be considered when selecting a laboratory for sample testing.

When assessing micronutrient status, consider the possibility of excessive intakes as well as deficiency. This is of particular concern when multiple highly fortified products or supplements are used to deliver micronutrients.

Micronutrient deficiencies have severe consequences for older people's mental and physical health, their immune system and their functional abilities.

The table below shows classifications of the public health significance of selected micronutrient deficiencies using different indicators. For information about biochemical tests and public health thresholds, consult the latest literature or seek specialist advice.

Micronutrient deficiency indicator	Recommended age group for prevalence surveys	Definition of a public health problem	
		Severity	Prevalence (%)
Vitamin A deficiency			
Night blindness (XN)	24–71 months	Mild	0 ≤ 1
		Moderate	1 ≤ 5
		Severe	5
Bitot's spots (X1B)	6–71 months	Not specified	>0.5
Corneal xerosis/ulceration/keratomalacia (X2, X3A, X3B)	6–71 months	Not specified	>0.01
Corneal scars (XS)	6–71 months	Not specified	>0.05
Serum retinol (≤ 0.7µmol/l)	6–71 months	Mild	2 ≤ 10
		Moderate	10 ≤ 20
		Severe	20
Iodine deficiency			
Goitre (visible and palpable)	School-age children	Mild	5.0–19.9
		Moderate	20.0–29.9
		Severe	30.0
Median urinary iodine concentration (mg/l)	School-age children	Excessive intake	>300
		Adequate intake	100–199
		Mild deficiency	50–99
		Moderate deficiency	20–49
		Severe deficiency	<20
Iron deficiency			
Anaemia (Non-pregnant women haemoglobin <12.0g/dl; children 6–59 months <11.0g/dl)	Women, children 6–59 months	Low	5–20
		Medium	20–40
		High	40
Beriberi			
Clinical signs	Whole population	Mild	1 case and <1%
		Moderate	1–4
		Severe	5

Micronutrient deficiency indicator	Recommended age group for prevalence surveys	Definition of a public health problem	
		Severity	Prevalence (%)
Dietary intake (<0.33mg/l,000kCal)	Whole population	Mild	5
		Moderate	5–19
		Severe	20–49
Infant mortality	Infants 2–5 months	Mild	No increase in rates
		Moderate	Slight peak in rates
		Severe	Marked peak in rates
Pellagra			
Clinical signs (dermatitis) in surveyed age group	Whole population or women >15 years	Mild	≥ 1 case and <1%
		Moderate	1–4
		Severe	5
Dietary intake of niacin equivalents <5mg/day	Whole population or women >15 years	Mild	5–19
		Moderate	20–49
		Severe	50
Scurvy			
Clinical signs	Whole population	Mild	1 case and <1%
		Moderate	1–4
		Severe	5

Appendix 6
Nutritional requirements

Use the following table for planning in the initial stage of a crisis. The minimum nutrient requirements given in the table should be used to assess general rations. They are not intended for assessing the adequacy of supplementary or therapeutic care rations or for assessing rations for particular groups of people such as individuals suffering from tuberculosis or people living with HIV.

Nutrient	Minimum population requirements
Energy	2,100kCal
Protein	53g (10% of total energy)
Fat	40g (17% of total energy)
Vitamin A	550µg retinol activity equivalents (RTE)
Vitamin D	6.1µg
Vitamin E	8.0mg alpha-tocopherol equivalents (alpha TE)
Vitamin K	48.2µg
Vitamin B1 (thiamine)	1.1mg
Vitamin B2 (riboflavin)	1.1mg
Vitamin B3 (niacin)	13.8mg niacin equivalents (NE)
Vitamin B6 (pyridoxine)	1.2mg
Vitamin B12 (cobalamin)	2.2µg
Folate	363µg dietary folate equivalents (DFE)
Pantothenate	4.6mg
Vitamin C	41.6mg
Iron	32mg
Iodine	138µg
Zinc	12.4mg
Copper	1.1mg
Selenium	27.6µg
Calcium	989mg
Magnesium	201mg

Source: RNIs from FAO/WHO (2004), Vitamin and Mineral Requirements in Human Nutrition, *2nd edition, were used for all vitamin and mineral requirement calculations except copper. Requirements for copper are taken from WHO (1996),* Trace Elements in Human Nutrition and Health.

These average population minimum requirements incorporate the requirements of all age groups and both sexes. They are therefore not specific to any single age or sex group and should not be used as requirements for an individual. They are based on an assumed demographic profile, assumptions about the ambient temperature and people's activity levels. They also take into account the additional needs of pregnant and breastfeeding women.

The requirements are expressed as reference nutrient intakes (RNI) for all nutrients except energy and copper.

Updates and further research on macro- and micronutrients are available on the Food and Agriculture Organization of the United Nations (FAO) and WHO websites.

Adjust the population energy requirements (up or down) for the following:

- the demographic structure of the population, in particular the percentage of those under five years, percentage of females and older people, adolescents;
- mean adult weights and actual, usual or desirable body weights;
- activity levels to maintain productive life (requirements will increase if activity levels exceed "light", or 1.6 x basal metabolic rate);
- average ambient temperature, and shelter and clothing capacities (requirements will increase if the mean ambient temperature is less than 20°C);
- the nutritional and health status of the population (requirements will increase if the population is malnourished and has extra requirements for catch-up growth. HIV prevalence may affect average population requirements. Adjust general rations to meet these needs, based on a context analysis and current international recommendations).

For guidance on calculating adjustments, ⊕ *see* UNHCR, UNICEF, WFP and WHO (2002), *Food and Nutrition Needs in Emergencies* and WFP (2001), *Food and Nutrition Handbook* for guidance on calculating adjustments.

If it is not possible to gain this kind of information from assessments, use the figures in the table above as the minimum requirements.

For understanding the population structure, broken down by sex, age and other criteria as needed, use national baseline data or refer to World Population Prospects: https://esa.un.org/unpd/wpp/

References and further reading

General

Child Protection Minimum Standards (CPMS). Global Child Protection Working Group, 2010. http://cpwg.net

Emergency Preparedness and Response Package. WFP, 2012. http://documents.wfp.org

Harvey, P. Proudlock, K. Clay, E. Riley, B. Jaspars, S. *Food Aid and Food Assistance in Emergencies and Transitional Contexts: A Review of Current Thinking*. Humanitarian Policy Group, 2010.

Humanitarian inclusion standards for older people and people with disabilities. Age and Disability Consortium, 2018. www.refworld.org

IASC Framework on Durable Solutions for Internally Displaced Persons. IASC, 2010.

Lahn, G. Grafham, O. *Heat, Light and Power for Refugees: Saving Lives, Reducing Costs*. Chatham House, 2015. https://www.chathamhouse.org

Livestock Emergency Guidelines and Standards (LEGS). LEGS Project, 2014. https://www.livestock-emergency.net

Minimum Economic Recovery Standards (MERS). SEEP Network, 2017. www.seepnetwork.org

Minimum Standards for Child Protection in Humanitarian Assistance. CPWG, 2016. http://cpwg.net

Minimum Standards for Education: Preparedness, Recovery and Response. The Inter-Agency Network for Education in Emergencies [INEE], 2010. www.ineesite.org

Minimum Standard for Market Analysis (MISMA). The Cash Learning Partnership (CaLP), 2017. www.cashlearning.org

Pejic, J. *The Right to Food in Situations of Armed Conflict: The Legal Framework*. International Review of the Red Cross, 2001. https://www.icrc.org

Safe Fuel and Energy Issues: Food Security and Nutrition. Safe Fuel and Energy, 2014. www.safefuelandenergy.org

The Right to Adequate Food (Article 11: 12/05/99. E/C 12/1999/5, CESCR General Comment 12). United Nations Economic and Social Council, 1999. www.ohchr.org

The Sendai Framework for Disaster Risk Reduction. UNISDR. https://www.unisdr.org

Assessment

RAM-OP: Rapid Assessment Method for Older People. www.helpage.org

SMART (Standardized Monitoring and Assessments of Relief and Transition) Guidelines and Methodology. SMART. http://smartmethodology.org

Nutrition

Castleman, T. Seumo-Fasso, E. Cogill, B. *Food and Nutrition Implications of Antiretroviral Therapy in Resource Limited Settings, Food and Nutrition Technical Assistance, technical note no. 7*. FANTA/AED, 2004.

Chastre, C. Duffield, A. Kindness, H. LeJeane, S. Taylor, A. *The Minimum Cost of Diet: Findings from piloting a new methodology in Four Study Locations.* Save the Children UK, 2007. https://resourcecentre.savethechildren.net

Codex Alimentarius. Standards, Guidelines and Advisory Texts. FAO and WHO. www.fao.org

Food and Nutritional Needs in Emergencies. WHO, UNHCR, UN Children's Fund, WFP, 2004. www.who.int

International Code of Marketing of Breast-Milk Substitutes. WHO, 1981. www.who.int

Management of acute malnutrition
Black, RE. Allen, LH. Bhutta, ZA. Caulfield, LE. de Onis, M. Ezzati, M. Mathers, C. Rivera, J. *Maternal and child undernutrition: global and regional exposures and health consequences.* The Lancet, vol. 371, no. 9608, 2008, pp. 243–260. https://doi.org

Participatory methodologies
Bonino, F. *What Makes Feedback Mechanisms Work.* ALNAP, 2014.

Infant and young child feeding
Child Growth Standards and the Identification of Severe Acute Malnutrition in Infants and Children. WHO, 2009.

Early Childhood Development in Emergencies: Integrated Programme Guide. UNICEF, 2014. https://www.unicef.org

Integrating Early Childhood Development Activities into Nutrition Programmes in Emergencies: Why, What and How? UNICEF & WHO Joint statement, 2010. www.who.int

Operational Guidance on Infant and Young Child Feeding in Emergencies. IFE Core Group, 2017. https://www.ennonline.net

Children
Growth reference for school-aged children and adolescents. WHO, 2007. www.who.int

Food security
Coping Strategies Index: CSI Field Methods Manual. CARE, 2008.

Caccavale, O. Flämig, T. *Collecting Prices for Food Security Programming.* World Food Programme, 2015. http://documents.wfp.org

Coates, J. Swindale, A. Bilinsky, P. *Household Food Insecurity Access Scale (HFIAS) for Measurement of Food Access, Indicator Guide, Version 3.* FANTA, 2007.

Food Safety and Quality. FAO and WHO. www.fao.org

Food Security Cluster Urban Group Tools and Pilot Projects. Food Security Cluster. http://fscluster.org

Food Security Cluster Core Indicator Handbook. Food Security Cluster. http://fscluster.org

Humanitarian, Impact areas. Global Alliance for Clean Cookstoves, 2018. http://cleancookstoves.org

Integrated Food Security Phase Classification (IPC) 2018 – Technical Manual Version 3. IPC Global Partners, 2018.

Save Food: Global Initiative on Food Loss and Waste Reduction – Extent, Causes and Reduction. FAO and WHO. http://www.fao.org

Swindale, A. Bilinsky, P. *Household Dietary Diversity Score (HDDS) for Measurement of Household Food Access: Indicator Guide, Version 2.* FANTA, 2006.

Technical Guidance Note: Food Consumption Score Nutritional Quality Analysis (FCS-N). WFP, 2015. https://www.wfp.org

Tier ranking from the IWA interim ISO standards. Global Alliance for Clean Cookstoves. http://cleancookstoves.org

Voluntary Guidelines to Support the Progressive Realization of the Right to Adequate Food in the Context of National Food Security. Committee on World Food Security, 2005.

Food assistance

Guide to Personal Data Protection and Privacy. WFP, 2016. https://docs.wfp.org

Integrated Protection and Food Assistance Programming. ECHO-DG, Final Draft. https://reliefweb.int

NutVal 2006 version 2.2: The planning, calculation, and monitoring application for food assistance programme. UNHCR, WFP, 2006. www.nutval.net

Protection in Practice: Food Assistance with Safety and Dignity. UN-WFP, 2013. https://reliefweb.int

Revolution : From Food Aid to Food Assistance – Innovations in Overcoming Hunger. WFP, 2010. https://documents.wfp.org

Seed interventions

Seed System Security Assessment (SSSA). CIAT and DEV, 2012. https://seedsystem.org

Seeds in Emergencies: A Technical Handbook. FAO, 2010. www.fao.org

Markets and cash-based assistance (CBA)

CaLP CBA quality toolbox: pqtoolbox.cashlearning.org

Cash and Vouchers Manual. WFP, 2014. https://www.wfp.org

E-Transfers in Emergencies: Implementation Support Guidelines. CaLP, 2013. www.cashlearning.org

Emerging Good Practice in the Use of Fresh Food Vouchers. ACF International, 2012. www.actionagainsthunger.org

Guidelines for Integrating Gender-Based Violence Interventions in Humanitarian Action. IASC, 2015. www.gbvguidelines.org

Gender

Guidelines for Integrating Gender-Based Violence Interventions in Humanitarian Action. IASC, 2015. www.gbvguidelines.org

Researching Violence Against Women: A Practical Guide for Researchers and Activists. WHO and Program for Appropriate Technology in Health (PATH), 2005. www.who.int

Persons with disabilities
Including Children with Disabilities in Humanitarian Action, Nutrition booklet. UNICEF. http://training.unicef.org

Module on Child Functioning and Disability. UNICEF, 2018. https://data.unicef.org

Livelihoods
CLARA: Cohort Livelihoods and Risk Analysis. Women's Refugee Commission, 2016. https://www.womensrefugeecommission.org

Sustainable Livelihoods Guidance Sheets. DFID, 2000. http://www.livelihoodscentre.org

Environment
Flash Environmental Assessment Tool. UNOCHA. www.eecentre.org

Handbook on Safe Access to Firewood and Alternative Energy. WFP, 2012.

Integrated Food Security Phase Classification (IPC) 2018 – Technical Manual Version 3. IPC Global Partners, 2018.

Lahn, G. Grafham, O. *Heat, Light and Power for Refugees: Saving Lives, Reducing Costs.* Chatham House, 2015. https://www.chathamhouse.org

Moving Energy Initiative. Chatham House, 2018. https://mei.chathamhouse.org

Further reading
For further reading suggestions please go to
www.spherestandards.org/handbook/online-resources

Shelter and Settlement

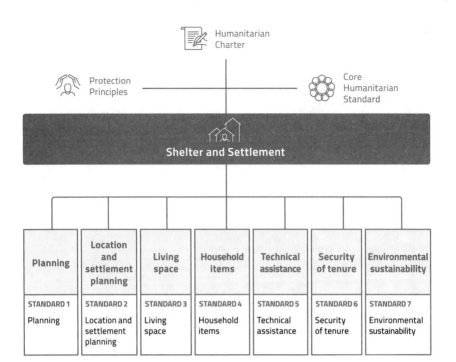

Planning	Location and settlement planning	Living space	Household items	Technical assistance	Security of tenure	Environmental sustainability
STANDARD 1	STANDARD 2	STANDARD 3	STANDARD 4	STANDARD 5	STANDARD 6	STANDARD 7
Planning	Location and settlement planning	Living space	Household items	Technical assistance	Security of tenure	Environmental sustainability

APPENDIX 1 Shelter and settlement assessment checklist
APPENDIX 2 Description of settlement senarios
APPENDIX 3 Additional characteristics of settlement senarios
APPENDIX 4 Assistance options
APPENDIX 5 Implementation options
APPENDIX 6 Potential assistance and implementation options connected to settlement scenarios (online)

Contents

Essential concepts in shelter and settlement

Everyone has the right to adequate housing

The Sphere Minimum Standards for Shelter and Settlement are a practical expression of the right to adequate housing in humanitarian contexts. The standards are grounded in the beliefs, principles, duties and broader rights declared in the Humanitarian Charter. These include the right to life with dignity, the right to protection and security, and the right to receive humanitarian assistance on the basis of need.

A list of the key legal and policy documents that inform the Humanitarian Charter is in Annex 1 with explanatory comments for humanitarian workers.

Shelters and settlements are inter-related and need to be considered as a whole. "Shelter" is the household living space, including the items necessary to support daily activities. "Settlement" is the wider locations where people and community live.

Shelter and settlement responses aim to provide a safe living environment

Timely shelter and settlements support can save lives in the initial stages of a crisis. In addition to providing protection from weather, shelter is necessary to promote health, support family and community life, and provide dignity, security and access to livelihoods ⊕ see Figure 8 below.

The average time that people are displaced has continued to increase over the years. With displacement lasting years or even decades, the location of the shelters and settlement sites, as well as the planning of neighbourhoods and communities where shelters are situated, are important in supporting the dignity and the recovery of people affected by crisis.

Shelter and settlement assistance should support and draw on the existing strengths of affected households, communities, civil society and government. This increases the chance of developing localised strategies that encourage self-sufficiency and self-management by the affected people. A sense of safety, community and social cohesion are essential to begin the process of recovery.

Shelter and settlement response options are not limited to delivering hardware and materials or constructing a shelter. Response options also include providing support to secure land and obtain shelter, housing or household items. This includes technical assistance and quality assurance, which can empower and mobilise an affected population to build back better and more safely. Knowing the national legal framework for land and property is essential. An understanding of the national refugee legislation and associated procedures for determining status is also important.

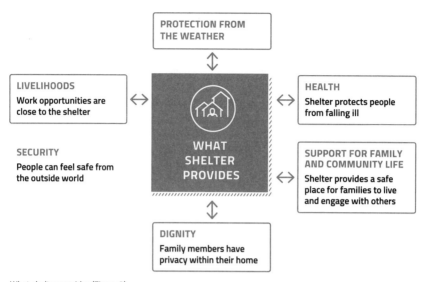

PROTECTION FROM THE WEATHER

LIVELIHOODS
Work opportunities are close to the shelter

HEALTH
Shelter protects people from falling ill

SECURITY
People can feel safe from the outside world

WHAT SHELTER PROVIDES

SUPPORT FOR FAMILY AND COMMUNITY LIFE
Shelter provides a safe place for families to live and engage with others

DIGNITY
Family members have privacy within their home

What shelter provides (Figure 8)

Some of the functions of appropriate emergency shelter. Shelter programmes should support families to meet these needs.

Regardless of the form of support provided, it is important to always respect existing community structures and promote social cohesion.

Each household and community will require different levels and types of support. Security of tenure and adequate civil status documentation is a basic requirement to access safe shelter. However, in conflict settings or where there are unresolved issues related to land tenure, shelter support may be particularly complex ⊕ *see Shelter and settlement standard 6: Security of tenure.*

Increasingly, there is a need to consider long-term displacement and recovery in settlement planning. Displacement can put pressure on existing – often limited – resources and foster tensions with the surrounding host community. Quality programming includes understanding, preventing and mitigating negative environmental impacts. If environmental issues are not taken into account, shelter and settlement programmes may ultimately be inefficient, since short-term outcomes can cause new problems requiring further investment ⊕ *see Shelter and settlement standard 7: Environmental sustainability.*

Shelter and settlement responses in urban settings require specific expertise

Assisting people in urban areas can be complicated because of the high population density, infrastructure needs, government regulations and the social diversity within the community. During and after a crisis, communicating with and assisting highly mobile people is difficult, especially when it comes to finding enough living space. If technically complex infrastructure (such as high-rise buildings) is affected, humanitarian organisations will also need to work with complex tenancy arrangements involving multiple owners, renters or informal settlers.

Working in urban contexts requires expertise in urban planning and design and knowledge of rights, regulations, laws and policies relating to housing, land and property. A strong understanding of local housing and financial markets is crucial. Be prepared to engage with civil society and the private sector. The private sector can play a role in delivering sustainable market-based solutions. The responses should build on local norms and services and avoid creating parallel structures. Developing a holistic response at settlement, neighbourhood or area level is more likely to provide a sustainable contribution to the well-being of affected populations in urban areas ⊕ see Delivering assistance through markets.

Various post-crisis settlement scenarios need to be considered

Where and how affected people find shelter will vary depending on their ability to remain in place or their need to move away. A systematic consideration of the post-crisis context is the first step in planning options for shelter and settlement assistance. It is important to understand the different approaches that may be appropriate for people who are displaced, directly affected but not displaced, or indirectly affected ⊕ see Figure 9 below.

If conditions permit, people may choose to remain in their place of origin as owner-occupier or in rented or informally occupied accommodation or land. Support to non-displaced households could include repair or reconstruction of existing dwellings.

Displaced populations may disperse locally, to other locations within their country of residence, or across international borders. In such situations they are likely to rent accommodation, self-settle or be hosted by others. Some displaced households may choose to gather in collective accommodation or an planned settlement, or to shelter in an unplanned settlement.

An understanding of the crisis through these settlement scenarios will help in planning assistance strategies. This includes selecting the most effective and appropriate type of assistance according to specific categories of the affected populations, and selecting ways of delivering the assistance. It should contribute to an incremental recovery, ideally reaching a durable solution. The standards and appendices in this chapter follow this logic and are meant to be used together ⊕ see Appendix 2: Description of settlement scenarios and Appendix 3: Additional characteristics of settlement scenarios.

These Minimum Standards should not be applied in isolation

The Minimum Standards in this chapter reflect the core content of the right to adequate shelter and contribute to the progressive realisation of this right globally.

The right to adequate shelter is linked to the rights to water and sanitation, food and health. Progress in achieving the Sphere Minimum Standards in one area influences progress in other areas. For a response to be effective, close coordination and

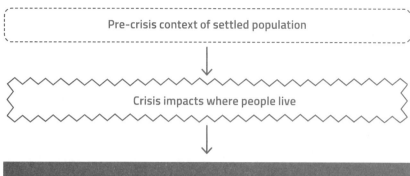

Post-crisis settlement scenarios

NON-DISPLACED POPULATION	DISPLACED POPULATION	INDIRECTLY AFFECTED POPULATION
	DISPERSED	
1. Owner occupied accommodation or land	1. Rental arrangement	1. Host population
	2. Hosted arrangement	
2. Rental accommodation or land	3. Spontaneous arrangement	
3. Informally occupied accommodation or land	COMMUNAL	
	4. Collective accommodation	
	5. Planned settlement	
	6. Unplanned settlement	

Selection of assistance options and implementation

DURABLE SOLUTIONS
Reconstruction
Resettlement
Reintegration

Post-crisis settlement scenarios (Figure 9)

collaboration are required with other sectors. Coordination with local authorities and other responding agencies helps ensure that needs are met, that efforts are not duplicated and that the quality of food security and nutrition responses is optimised. Cross-references throughout the Handbook suggest some potential linkages.

For example, adequate water supply and sanitation facilities in settlements are necessary to ensure the health and dignity of the affected population. Essential cooking and eating utensils and fuel for cooking enable people to use food assistance and meet nutritional requirements.

Where national standards are lower than the Sphere Minimum Standards, humanitarian organisations should work with the government to progressively raise them.

International law specifically protects the right to adequate shelter

The right to access adequate housing is protected by international law. It is the right to live somewhere in security, peace and dignity. This right contains freedoms such as the right to choose one's residence and entitlements such as security of tenure. It enshrines protection principles such as protection from forced eviction. States are obliged to ensure this right when individuals or groups, including refugees and internally displaced persons, are unable to access adequate housing, including in crises ⊕ see Annex 1: Legal foundation to Sphere.

The concept of "adequacy" means that housing is more than four walls and a roof. It underlines the importance of including a settlement lens, cultural identity and the availability of services in a shelter response. "Adequate" housing or other forms of shelter should provide security of tenure and be:

- affordable, allowing the household to attain other essential goods and services to live in dignity;
- habitable, providing physical safety, protected and adequate living space, access to safe drinking water, adequate water, sanitation and hygiene (WASH) facilities, and food preparation and storage;
- culturally acceptable;
- accessible and usable, including for persons facing mobility barriers; and
- located to provide access to livelihoods opportunities and essential community services.

Links to the Protection Principles and Core Humanitarian Standard

Crises can worsen pre-existing inequalities. Therefore, it is important to offer impartial and context-sensitive assistance, in particular to those who have the least capacity to recover from a crisis by themselves ⊕ see Protection Principle 2.

Some people may have difficulties accessing shelter and settlement assistance, due to physical, cultural, economic and social barriers. In understanding and responding to these, pay attention to the following:

- **The legal status of individuals** (for example, refugee, internally displaced, stateless, migrant, asylum seeker, homeless or landless, and others deprived of civil liberties and access to public services or social safety nets); and

- **People facing unique protection risks** and **groups at particular risk of discrimination and social exclusion** due to:
    - their ethnicity, nationality, caste, indigenous group, or religious or political affiliation;
    - their tenure situation, displacement status, informal settler status or renter status;
    - the location of dwellings that are difficult to access, in hazardous areas, insecure areas, urban settlements or informal settlements; and
    - their vulnerability and status within society ⊕ *see What is Sphere* and *Protection Principles*.

Aid workers should be trained on child safeguarding and know how to use referral systems for suspected cases of violence, abuse or exploitation, including of children.

In applying the Minimum Standards, all nine Commitments in the Core Humanitarian Standard should be respected as a foundation for providing an accountable shelter and settlement programme.

1. Planning

Planning is crucial for optimal response outcomes at regional, national, agency or community levels. Understanding the pre- and post-crisis context allows an assessment of both the direct and the indirect impact of the crisis on people's living conditions and any social, economic and political consequences. Identifying needs and then developing appropriate response options, is the basis for a well-planned and coordinated shelter and settlement response.

Shelter and settlement standard 1: Planning

Shelter and settlement interventions are well planned and coordinated to contribute to the safety and well-being of affected people and promote recovery.

Key actions

1 ⟩ Work with the affected population as well as national and local authorities to assess the shelter and settlement needs and capacities.

- Assess changes from the pre-crisis context, identify immediate needs and capacities for the displaced and non-displaced populations, and consider any specific needs of at-risk groups.
- Identify the availability of habitable or occupiable land, buildings, apartments and rooms within the local housing and land rental markets.

2 ⟩ Work with stakeholders to identify the most effective and appropriate assistance options and how to provide these.

3 ⟩ Develop a shelter and settlement plan in coordination with relevant authorities and the affected communities.

- Offer assistance tailored to the needs and preference of the affected population and authorities.
- Optimise cost-efficiency, technical quality, speed and timing, scale of implementation and replicability.

Key indicators

The shelter and settlement plan provides for the essential needs of the target population and is agreed with the population and relevant authorities

Percentage of affected people indicating that shelter and settlement assistance reflects their needs and priorities and contributes to a more durable solution

Guidance notes

Assessment: During assessment, review changes in the shelter and settlement conditions post-crisis and include possible protection risks from the outset. These may include perceptions of the host community, risks associated with access to the settlement, safe access to services or risks of expulsion.

Consider the direct and indirect impact of the crisis on people's living conditions, including social, economic and political consequences.

Crisis affects people in different ways, so different people will have different shelter and settlement needs. Work with groups who may face specific barriers to access shelter, such as persons with disabilities, female-headed house-holds, older people or ethnic and linguistic minorities ⊕ *see Appendix 1: Shelter and settlement assessment checklist, Protection Principle 2* and *Core Humanitarian Standard Commitment 4.*

Assistance and implementation options: Select the most effective options based on context, capacity, resources available, the settlement scenario and the phase of the response. Other factors to consider include location, housing type (including local construction techniques), tenure, and market and legal frameworks. Prioritise support for people's return to their original dwelling (or site of their dwelling) where possible. Assist those who are unable or unwilling to return to their original dwellings to access options tailored to their needs ⊕ *see Appendices 2 to 6.*

Define a timeline to meet immediate needs, considering efficiency, technical quality, scale of implementation, capacities on the ground and replicability. Explore options to increase communities' long-term recovery and resilience to future crises.

Consider different ways to deliver the chosen options, including a combination of:

- financial support;
- in-kind material assistance;
- contracting works/commissioned labour;
- technical assistance/quality assurance support; and
- capacity building.

Review and adjust the combination of options over time as the situation changes.

Displaced people: As well as having immediate needs for shelter, displaced people also require specific support to make informed decisions about shelter solutions available to them. Examples of support include information about whether and when they will return home, how to integrate at the place of displacement or whether to resettle at a third location.

Non-displaced households will need support to return to their original living conditions and should receive appropriate shelter assistance. If reconstruction will take a long time or people are not safe, explore temporary options such as host family assistance, rental assistance, or temporary or transitional shelter. If the crisis has changed the security and safety environment, relocation might be necessary.

Host communities also experience consequences of a crisis, as they share their public and private space. This includes sharing services such as health centres or schools, or acting as a host family. There may be real or perceived competition with displaced people for jobs, services, infrastructure and resources. Solutions need to consider equitable and targeted support that does not create additional risks or threats in the community ⊕ *see Protection Principle 1.*

Market analysis: Understanding the surrounding markets at local, national and regional level is critical for a good quality shelter response. It will inform choices on shelter options and will also capture rent and other settlement-related service information ⊕ *see Delivering assistance through markets, MISMA Handbook and MERS Handbook.*

Debris removal: Initiate debris management immediately after the crisis. Debris can be reused, recycled or identified for separation, collection and/or treatment. It may provide opportunities for cash-for-work programmes. Key issues include the presence of human bodies, structurally dangerous locations and hazardous materials. Removal of debris may require specialised expertise and equipment, so must be planned with other sector specialists ⊕ *see Shelter and settlement standard 7: Environmental sustainability, Health standards and WASH standards.*

Livelihood opportunities: The livelihoods that people engaged in before the crisis, and the opportunities existing after the crisis, are relevant in determining settlement options. Land availability, safe access for cultivation and grazing, access to markets and access to other employment opportunities can affect where people choose to live, even temporarily ⊕ *see Food security and nutrition – Livelihoods standards 7.1 and 7.2, LEGS Handbook and MERS Handbook.*

Return: Returning to their own land and dwellings is a major goal for most crisis-affected people. Affected people should be able to determine the need for repairing their dwellings or upgrading their shelter. Return can support communal coping strategies and retain established settlement patterns and infrastructure. The repair or reconstruction of communal infrastructure such as schools, water systems, clinics or markets is also important to enable displaced people to return. Some circumstances may prevent or delay return, such as security concerns, armed forces occupying the property or land, continuing violent conflict, ethnic or religious tension, fear of persecution, or landmines and unexploded ordnance. Inadequate or discriminatory land and property legislation, or customary procedures may prevent female-headed households, those widowed or orphaned by the crisis, or persons with disabilities from returning. Displaced populations who may not have the ability to undertake reconstruction activities may also be discouraged or prevented from returning.

2. Location and settlement planning

Location and settlement planning should promote safe, acceptable and accessible living spaces that offer access to basic services, livelihoods and opportunities to connect to a broader network.

Shelter and settlement standard 2:
Location and settlement planning

Shelters and settlements are located in safe and secure areas, offering adequate space and access to essential services and livelihoods.

Key actions

1 Work within existing planning processes and regulations and agree terms with host communities and relevant authorities.

- Locate any new settlements a safe distance from actual or potential threats and minimise risks from existing hazards.
- Consider the expected lifespan of the settlement to determine what essential services may need to be expanded or developed.

2 Involve diverse stakeholders, including groups within the affected population, in site selection and settlement planning.

- Identify factors that could affect the location or site layout, considering sex, age, disability, ethnic or linguistic identity, and gender roles and responsibilities.
- In urban contexts, work through a geographically defined, area-based approach to better understand community dynamics.

3 Ensure the affected population has access to essential services and facilities, including livelihoods opportunities.

- Work with other sectors to establish an acceptable distance and safe travel (or transport) to essential services and facilities.
- Coordinate with service providers to prioritise and deliver essential services and livelihoods opportunities where these do not already exist.

4 Plan the use of land to provide sufficient space for all functions, accessibility to all shelters and services, and adequate safety measures throughout the settlement.

- Include planning for shared resources like water and sanitation facilities, communal cooking facilities, child-friendly spaces, gathering areas, religious needs and food distribution points.
- Ensure that the placement of essential services within settlements follows standards for safety, protection and dignity.

5 ⟩ Include rainfall or floodwater drainage planning in site selection and settlement development.

- Provide appropriate drainage facilities so that all dwelling areas and services are kept free of standing water and storm water drains are kept clear.
- Anticipate and manage breeding sites of disease vectors.

Key indicators

Percentage of shelters and/or settlement sites that are located in areas with no or minimal known natural or man-made threats, risks and hazards

Percentage of shelters and/or settlement sites that have safe access to essential services within an acceptable amount of time or distance

Percentage of those receiving settlement assistance who feel safe about the location of their shelter or settlement

Percentage of settlement sites that offer sufficient usable surface area to carry out private and public outdoor activities appropriate to the context

- 45 square metres for each person in camp-type settlements, including household plots
- 30 square metres for each person, including household plots, where communal services can be provided outside the planned settlement area
- Minimum ratio between covered living space and plot size is 1:2; move as soon as possible to 1:3 or more.

Guidance notes

Planning processes and principles: Governments or local authorities often introduce new policies regarding no-build zones, safe zones or buffer zones after a crisis. Advocate for risk-informed planning and appropriate assistance options. A "no-build zone" does not mean a "no-assistance zone", and should not delay shelter or settlement responses.

Understand the ownership situation of any land and property ⊕ *see Shelter and settlement standard 6: Security of tenure.*

Engage the affected people in calculating and organising space to support existing social and cultural practices. Involve women and other at-risk groups in the design and implementation of shelter and settlement planning.

Essential services and facilities: People returning to their original homes and those living in temporary locations or settlements require safe, secure and equitable access to essential services and facilities, such as:

- WASH facilities ⊕ *see WASH water supply standards;*
- communal and household lighting solutions;

- food storage and processing facilities (including stoves and fuel) ⊕ *see Food security and nutrition assessments standard 1.1* and *Food assistance standard 6.4;*
- healthcare facilities ⊕ *see Health systems standard 1.1: Health service delivery;*
- solid waste disposal ⊕ *see WASH solid waste management standards;*
- schools ⊕ *see INEE Handbook;*
- social facilities such as places of worship, meeting points and recreational areas;
- space for culturally appropriate burials and associated rituals; and
- space for livestock accommodation (with adequate separation from residential spaces) ⊕ *see LEGS Handbook.*

Site planning for temporary settlements: Site layouts should be based on urban design and town planning principles, with connecting components such as access points, intersections and public space. These components, informed by physical, social, environmental and economic factors, form the spatial plan of the new settlement. Settlement planning should support existing social networks, allow opportunities for new networks to form, contribute to safety and security, and enable self-management by the affected people.

Maintain the privacy and dignity of separate households when creating the plot layout for temporary settlements. Each household shelter should open onto common space or a screened area, not onto the entrance of another shelter. Provide safe living areas for all potentially vulnerable groups, but avoid clustering them because that can increase their vulnerability. Group together families, extended families and groups from similar backgrounds, to retain social bonds. Consider the needs, preferences and habits of different age, sex and disability groups.

Surface area of planned or self-settled settlements: For planned settlements, the minimum usable surface area is 45 square metres per person in camp-type settlements, including household plots. This includes space for roads and footpaths, external cooking areas or communal cooking areas, education and recreation areas, healthcare facilities, sanitation, firebreaks, administration, water storage, site drainage, religious facilities, food distribution areas, markets, storage and limited kitchen gardens for individual households (excluding significant agricultural activities or livestock). Where communal services can be provided by existing or additional facilities outside the planned settlement, the minimum surface area should be 30 square metres per person. If the minimum surface area cannot be provided, actively take steps to address the consequences of higher-density occupation. Settlement planning should also consider changes in the population.

When operating in an urban area, make use of existing services and housing stock. Ensure adequate separation and privacy between individual households, and reserve space for the required facilities.

Plot size for shelters: A ratio of shelter footprint to plot size of 1:2 or 1:3 is recommended, to allow sufficient space for the most essential outdoor activities of the households. However, a ratio closer to 1:4 or 1:5 is preferable. The ratio should consider cultural and social norms and practical space availability.

Drainage of rainfall and floodwater: Poor drainage of rainfall or floodwater can severely limit people's living spaces, mobility and access to services. Generally, site selection and infrastructure development determine the nature of large-scale drainage systems. Avoid selecting a site that is on a floodplain; it can compromise safety and security, particularly in congested or confined spaces. Water entering and stagnating in people's living, learning and working environments poses a general threat to health, dignity and well-being.

Protect toilets and sewers from flooding, to avoid structural damage and leakage. The main public health threat associated with poor drainage is an increased exposure to diarrhoeal diseases from contact with contaminated water.

Uncontrolled water can also damage other infrastructure, dwellings and belongings, limit livelihood opportunities and cause stress. Poor drainage also provides conditions for vector breeding ⊕ *see WASH vector control standards 4.1 and 4.2.*

Access: Consider the condition of local roads and the proximity to transport hubs for the supply of relief assistance and other goods. The supply of relief assistance must avoid damaging the local road infrastructure. Consider seasonal constraints, hazards and security risks. The site and any primary storage and food distribution points must be accessible by heavy trucks from an all-weather road. Other facilities must be accessible by light vehicles. Provide safe, secure roads and pathways within settlements, and all-weather access to all individual dwellings and communal facilities. Consider the needs of people facing mobility or access barriers.

Fire safety: Fire risk assessments should inform site planning. Include 30-metre firebreaks every 300 metres in built-up areas in camp settings. The space between buildings should be at least 2 metres; ideally it should be double the building height to prevent collapsing structures from touching adjacent buildings.

Consider local cooking and heating practices (such as type of stoves and preferred location). Consider providing safe stoves, fire safety equipment and awareness training to residents. Prefer fire-resistant construction materials and household items. Inform residents (including those facing mobility or accessibility barriers) about fire prevention, management and evacuation plans.

Reducing crime: The design of the settlement can contribute to reducing crime and gender-based violence. Consider the location and accessibility of shelters, buildings and facilities, night lighting, distance to the toilet and bathing area from the shelter, and passive surveillance through visual lines. Buildings used as collective centres must have alternative escape routes.

Changing threats and risks: Undertake regular context, hazard and risk assessments as the situation changes. This may include seasonal hazards, changes in the security situation, unexploded ordnance on the site from previous or current conflicts, or consequences of changing demographics.

Safety of collective centres and community infrastructure: Technical specialists should assess the structural stability of community buildings, collective centres and other structures in inhabited areas affected by crises. Consider actual and potential security or health threats.

Livelihood support: Consider pre-disaster economic activities and potential livelihoods opportunities in the post-disaster context. Identify available land for cultivation and grazing, or access to markets and/or employment opportunities. Shelter and settlement responses have the potential to offer local employment, such as roles in technical assistance, supplies and the labour market. Use training and education programmes to boost local capacity to achieve results within a set time frame ⊕ *see Shelter and settlement standard 5* and *Food security and nutrition – livelihoods standards 7.1 and 7.2.*

Operation and maintenance: Create an operation and maintenance plan to ensure the effective running of any facilities, services and utilities (such as water, sanitation, drainage, waste management, schools). Key components of a plan include community participation, establishing user groups, defining roles and responsibilities, and having a cost recovery or cost sharing plan.

Decommissioning of sites and handover: Appropriate environmental rehabilitation measures can enhance the natural regeneration of the environment in and around temporary settlements. Sites should have a decommissioning plan, ideally developed at the design stage of the intervention ⊕ *see Shelter and settlement standard 7: Environmental sustainability.*

Teaching local populations sustainable land management techniques ensures the recovery of the site and the local environment. Use local labour in clearing and decommissioning activities where possible.

3. Living space

Living space is very important for people's well-being. It is a core human need and right to have a place for a family to dwell, feel safe and perform a variety of essential domestic activities.

Shelter and settlement standard 3:
Living space
People have access to living spaces that are safe and adequate, enabling essential household and livelihoods activities to be undertaken with dignity.

Key actions

1 > Ensure that each affected household has adequate living space to perform basic domestic activities.

- Provide living space that accommodates the diverse needs of members of the household for sleeping, food preparation and eating, respecting local culture and lifestyles.
- Provide a basic roof and walls for occupants and their household assets, offering physical security, dignity, privacy and protection from weather.
- Provide optimal lighting conditions, ventilation and thermal comfort.

2 > Ensure that the space immediately surrounding the living space supports safe access to fundamental activities.

- Include appropriate cooking, toilets, laundry, bathing, livelihoods activities, socialising and play areas.

3 > Promote the use of shelter solutions, construction techniques and materials that are culturally and socially acceptable and environmentally sustainable.

Key indicators

Percentage of the affected population who have adequate living space in and immediately around their shelters to carry out daily activities

- Minimum 3.5 square metres of living space per person, excluding cooking space, bathing area and sanitation facility
- 4.5–5.5 square metres of living space per person in cold climates or urban settings where internal cooking space and bathing and/or sanitation facilities are included
- Internal floor-to-ceiling height of at least 2 metres (2.6 metres in hot climates) at the highest point

Percentage of shelters that meet agreed technical and performance standards and are culturally acceptable

Percentage of people receiving shelter assistance that feel safe in their shelter

....

Guidance notes

Living space: Living space should be adequate for daily activities such as sleeping, preparing and eating food, washing, dressing, storing food and water, and protecting household possessions and other key assets. It must ensure privacy and separation as required between sexes, different age groups and families within a given household according to cultural and social norms ⊕ *see Shelter and settlement standard 2: Location and settlement planning.*

Consider living space for household members to gather, and for the care of infants, children and persons who are ill or injured. Pay attention to changing use of space during day and night, and plan the locations of windows, doors and partitions to maximise the use of internal space and any adjacent external areas such as kitchens or play areas.

To accommodate these activities in dignity, shelters need an enclosed space (walls, windows, doors and roof) with adequate floor area. Overcrowding or exposure to the elements increases the risk of disease outbreak or illness. Reduced space may lead to protection risks, reduced security and privacy.

The minimum living space should reflect cultural and social norms, the context, the phase of response, and guidance by national authorities or the humanitarian response sector. Carefully consider the potential consequences of adopting the minimum calculated space (3.5 square metres per person, 4.5 square metres in cold climates) and agree any adaptation with partners, moving towards the minimum as quickly as possible for all.

Where there is a need to act quickly and save lives, consider initial assistance to either:

- build a roof cover for the minimum living space and follow up with support for walls, doors and windows; or
- build a shelter with a smaller floor area and follow up to increase floor area.

In some situations, the space standard may be dictated by physical limitations. This may be in a confined settlement, dense urban settings or in extreme climatic conditions where shelter materials are not readily available. The minimum space indicated is applicable in the emergency phase and in temporary or transitional shelter solutions. When the duration of stay extends, the habitable space calculations must be revisited. In the recovery phase, acceptable local standards and exit strategies must be taken into account.

Involve affected communities and households as much as possible in determining the type of assistance to be provided. Consult with the people who spend more time in the covered living space and those facing mobility or access barriers.

Ensure that living space is accessible for persons with disabilities and those living with them. Persons with disabilities, particularly those with intellectual and psychosocial disabilities, may need additional space.

Cultural practices, safety and privacy: Respect existing practices and customs and how these affect the need for internal subdivisions (curtains, walls). For example, design the dwelling to accommodate sleeping arrangements for extended family members or different families within the same household.

In collective accommodation, well-planned, well-lit access routes through the living area with partitions to screen personal and household space can provide personal privacy and safety.

In collective accommodation, allow the option for peer groups to share space. For example, some LGBTQI individuals prefer living with friends and peers rather than with their own families.

Protection: Ensure there are multiple exit routes from the dwelling, and that interior spaces open into public areas. Ensure that staff know how to refer any protection concerns around domestic violence or abuse, violence, exploitation or neglect of children. Women, girls and those needing assistance with personal hygiene often require additional space ⊕ *see WASH hygiene promotion standard 1.3: Menstrual hygiene management and incontinence.*

Where temporary collective accommodations are used, take specific actions to prevent sexual exploitation and sexual violence. Work with the community members to understand the risks and address them, and establish a strong complaints system with immediate and verifiable actions.

Psychosocial considerations: Accommodation layout and design should include open public household living spaces that increase options for socialising.

In warm, humid climates, design and orient shelters to maximise ventilation and minimise entry of direct sunlight. A higher ceiling helps air circulation. An attached covered outdoor space helps reduce direct sunlight and protect from rain. Consider the use of adjacent shaded or covered external space for food preparation and cooking, with separate space for other living activities. The roof should be sloped for rainwater drainage with large overhangs, except in locations vulnerable to high winds. The shelter construction material should be lightweight with a low thermal capacity, such as timber. Use raised floors to prevent water entering the covered living area ⊕ *see Shelter and settlement standard 2: Location and settlement planning.*

In hot, dry climates, heavyweight construction material (such as earth or stone) ensures thermal comfort despite changes in night and day temperatures. Alternatively, use a lightweight construction with adequate insulation. Pay attention to the structural design of heavyweight construction in seismic risk areas. Provide shaded and ventilated places where possible and appropriate. If only plastic sheeting or tents are available, provide a double-skinned roof with ventilation between the layers to reduce radiant heat gain. Position door and window openings away from the direction of the prevailing hot wind. Internal flooring should meet the external walling without gaps, to prevent dust and disease vectors entering.

In cold climates, a lower ceiling is preferable to minimise the internal volume that requires heating. Shelters occupied throughout the day require heavyweight construction with high thermal capacity. For shelters only occupied at night, a lightweight construction with low thermal capacity and substantial insulation is more appropriate. Minimise air flow, particularly around door and window openings, to ensure personal comfort while also providing adequate ventilation for space heaters or cooking stoves.

Adequate ventilation helps maintain a healthy internal environment, prevents condensation and reduces the spread of communicable disease. It reduces the effect of smoke from indoor household stoves, which can cause respiratory infections and eye problems. Consider natural ventilation where possible.

Vector control: Low-lying areas, debris and vacant buildings can provide breeding grounds for vectors that can pose public health risks. For communal settlements, site selection and the active mitigation of vector risks are key to reducing the impact of vector-borne diseases ⊕ *see WASH vector control standard 4.2: Household and personal actions to control vectors.*

4. Household items

Household item assistance supports restoring and maintaining health, dignity and safety and undertaking daily domestic activities in and around the home. This standard addresses items for sleeping, food preparation and storage, eating and drinking, thermal comfort, lighting and personal clothing. The WASH chapter gives additional detail about items such as bednets, buckets, water storage and hygiene items.

Shelter and settlement standard 4: Household items

Household item assistance supports restoring and maintaining health, dignity and safety and the undertaking of daily domestic activities in and around the home.

Key actions

1 ⟩ Assess and ensure access to items that enable households to restore and maintain essential domestic activities.

- Consider different needs according to age, sex, disability, social and cultural practices, and family size.
- Prioritise access to items for domestic activities, personal clothing, personal hygiene, and to support safety and health.

2 ⟩ Decide how to deliver the household item assistance effectively and appropriately.

- Consider what can be sourced locally through cash or voucher-based assistance and through local, regional or international procurement for in-kind distribution.
- Consider environmental issues related to how items are packaged or delivered.

3 ⟩ Monitor the availability, quality and use of household items, and adapt as needed.

- Plan to replenish in cases of extended displacement.
- Monitor the chosen markets for availability, price and quality. Adapt the way assistance is provided as the situation evolves.

Key indicators

People have sufficient and appropriate quality clothing

- Minimum two full sets of clothing per person, in the right size and appropriate to culture, season and climate, and adapted to any particular needs

People have sufficient and appropriate quality items for safe, healthy and private sleeping

- Minimum one blanket and bedding (floor mat, mattress, sheeting) per person. Additional blankets/ground insulation required in cold climates
- Long-lasting insecticide-treated nets where needed

People have sufficient and appropriate items to prepare, eat and store food

- Per household or group of four to five individuals: two family-sized cooking pots with handles and lids, one basin for food preparation or serving, one kitchen knife and two serving spoons
- Per person: one dished plate, one set of eating utensils and one drinking vessel

Percentage of the affected population who have access to a sufficient, safe and affordable energy supply to maintain thermal comfort, prepare food and provide lighting

Number of incidents of harm to people using stoves or storing or sourcing fuel

- Establish baseline and measure progress to 0

....

Guidance notes

Essential household items should be available in sufficient quantity and quality for:

- sleeping, thermal comfort and personal clothing;
- water storage, food preparation and storage, eating and drinking;
- lighting;
- cooking, boiling water and heating, including fuel or energy ⊕ *see Food security and nutrition standard 5: General food security*;
- hygiene, including menstrual hygiene or incontinence items ⊕ *see WASH hygiene promotion standards 1.2 and 1.3*;
- protection from vectors; for example, mosquito nets ⊕ *see WASH vector control standard 4.2*; and
- fire and smoke safety.

Selecting appropriate household items: Household items should be provided as part of an overall plan. When specifying the type, quantity and quality of the items, prioritise items that are life-saving. Consider:

- essential daily activities at the individual, household and communal levels;
- cultural norms, appropriateness and traditions;
- safety and ease of use (with minimal additional instruction or technical guidance);
- durability, rate of consumption and need for replenishment;
- current living conditions and arrangements;
- local availability;

- specific needs according to categories of the affected population, including women, girls, men, boys, infants, older people, persons with disabilities and other vulnerable individuals and groups; and
- environmental impact of the selected items ⊕ *see Shelter and settlement standard 7: Environmental sustainability.*

Safety: All plastic items should be made of food-grade plastic. All metallic goods should be stainless steel or enamelled.

Ensure safe separation between the stove and the elements of the shelter. Place internal stoves on a non-flammable base. Install a non-flammable sleeve around the flue where it passes through the shelter to the exterior. Locate stoves away from entrances and to enable safe access during use. Fuel should be stored at a safe distance from the stove itself, and any liquid fuel such as kerosene should be kept out of the reach of children and infants.

Thermal comfort means that people are comfortably warm or cool, covered and dry. Clothes, blankets and bedding provide personal comfort. Sleeping mats and space heaters and coolers will create suitable living conditions. All possible measures should be taken at individual and household level to prevent hypothermia or heat strokes.

Affordable fuel and household energy supply: Fuel and other energy sources are necessary for lighting, cooking, thermal comfort and communication. Collecting or paying for fuel or energy is a recurrent cost and must be planned accordingly. Promote energy-efficient cooking practices, including the use of fuel-efficient stoves, firewood preparation, fire management, food preparation techniques and shared cooking. Consult the crisis-affected people and host community about the location and means of collecting fuel to address issues of personal safety and environmental sustainability.

Artificial lighting should be provided as needed to contribute to personal safety in and around settlements where general illumination is not available. Besides matches and candles, consider the use of energy-efficient artificial lighting such as light-emitting diodes (LEDs) and solar panels.

Market-based programming for household items: Market assessment for household items should form part of a broader market system assessment. Provision of household items should support local markets if possible. Analyse expenditure on these items as part of overall household expenditure patterns. Monitor them over time to adapt and adjust accordingly ⊕ *see Delivering assistance through markets.*

Distribution: Plan efficient and equitable distribution methods in consultation with local authorities and the affected people. Ensure that vulnerable individuals or households are included on distribution lists and can access both the information and the distribution itself. Distribution sites should be chosen carefully, considering walking distance, terrain and the practicalities of transporting larger goods such as shelter support items. Consider including containers for the storage and transportation of personal and household goods.

Post-distribution monitoring: Assess the appropriateness of both the distribution process and the household items themselves. If items are not being used or are being sold in the market, or if there are delays in accessing the items, adapt the process or products. Be aware that needs will change over time and programmes should adapt to those changes.

5. Technical assistance

Technical assistance is an integral part of shelter and settlement responses. It supports the self-recovery of the affected people and improves the quality and safety of their shelter and settlement. It is essential that affected households or communities are actively involved in choosing their accommodation, the design of shelters, the site layout and materials, and in supervising or carrying out work to build the shelters and other construction.

Shelter and settlement standard 5: Technical assistance

People have access to appropriate technical assistance in a timely manner.

Key actions

1 〉 Understand the pre-crisis planning and building practices, available materials, expertise and capacities.

- Consult with affected people, local building professionals and authorities to agree on building practices and materials and to find the required expertise for quality assurance.

2 〉 Involve and support the affected people, local government and local professionals in the building process.

- Comply with the applicable planning and building codes, material specifications and quality standards, as appropriate for the intended lifespan of the shelter, settlement and household intervention.
- Optimise building practices and local livelihood opportunities.

3 〉 Promote safer building practices to meet current shelter needs and reduce future risks.

- For damaged or destroyed houses or shelters, identify the structural risks and hazards, the reasons for any failure, or what may fail in the future.
- Learn from, improve and innovate local building practices and techniques where possible; facilitate effective knowledge transfer to promote appropriate building practices.

4 〉 Ensure that people have access to adequate technical assistance.

- Consider the need for specialised professional expertise, how to adhere to building codes and standards, and how to increase technical capacity among the affected population.

- Pay attention to people who have reduced capacity, ability or opportunity to undertake construction-related activities in a safe and technically sound manner, or negotiate occupancy of an existing safe and technically sound property.

5 〉 Establish appropriate project management of materials, finance, labour, technical assistance and processes for regulatory approval requirements to ensure quality outcomes.

- Follow appropriate tender, bidding, procurement, contract and construction management processes and codes of conduct.
- Encourage the use of locally available, sustainable and familiar technologies, tools and materials and hire labour locally for maintaining and upgrading shelters.

Key indicators

Percentage of programmes where local authorities are involved in defining construction standards and in the monitoring of construction activities

Percentage of construction activities that demonstrate active involvement of the affected population

Percentage of shelter units that are constructed, repaired, retrofitted, upgraded or maintained according to the agreed safe building practices for the specific context and hazards

Percentage of households that report having received appropriate technical assistance and guidance

Guidance notes

Participation and engagement with affected people: Participation in shelter and construction activities should be compatible with existing local practices. Training programmes and apprenticeship schemes can maximise opportunities for participation of all affected people (directly affected people and the host community) during construction. Provide opportunities for women and persons with disabilities to participate. People less able to undertake physical tasks can contribute to activities such as site monitoring, inventory control, administrative support, childcare or food preparation for those engaged in construction work. Be aware that affected people may have other conflicting time constraints. Volunteer community labour teams or contracted labour can support construction efforts of individual households, particularly those headed by women, children, older people or persons with disabilities. Such assistance is important because those groups may be at risk of sexual exploitation when seeking construction assistance.

Engaging young people in construction activities: Being part of a construction project can provide young people with valuable skills, confidence, self-esteem and connectedness to the community.

Ensure children under the minimum working age are not involved in shelter construction or cash-for-work shelter programmes. Children between the minimum working age (usually 14 or 15) and 18 years old should participate in a way that is appropriate for their age and development. Ensure their participation is in line with national legislation in context. Measures must be put into place to ensure international standards and national labour law are adhered to in order to avoid hazardous and underage child labour. Any suspected issues or questions on child labour should be referred to child protection specialists or social services ⊕ *see CPMS Handbook.*

Professional expertise: Provide advice on issues such as site and spatial planning, local construction techniques, damage assessment, demolition and debris removal, construction, site management, assessment of existing building stock and security of tenure. This can ensure that shelters meet established standards. Knowledge of material and labour markets will also be useful, as will legal and administrative support ⊕ *see Shelter and settlement standard 6: Security of tenure.*

Adherence to building codes: Find out whether local or national building codes are usually followed or enforced. If not, advocate for using and complying with them. These codes should reflect local housing culture, climatic conditions, resources, building and maintenance capacities, accessibility and affordability. Ensure that shelter programmes allow households to meet or progressively attain agreed codes and standards, especially in programmes using cash-based assistance to meet shelter needs. Where there are no existing standards, establish Minimum Standards in collaboration with the local authorities and relevant stakeholders (including, where possible, the affected people) to ensure they meet safety and performance requirements.

Increasing technical capacity: Increase community capacity by contributing to training and awareness-raising among the affected populations, local authorities, local building professionals, skilled and unskilled labour, landlords, legal experts and local partners.

In locations vulnerable to seasonal or cyclical crises, involve technical specialists and local experts who have experience with appropriate local solutions or best practices. These people can inform design and building practices and help develop improved solutions.

Sourcing of materials: Where appropriate building materials can be provided quickly, the affected population can construct shelters themselves. These shelter solutions can consist of separate components or a pre-defined kit, with appropriate construction tools. A rapid market assessment and analysis and an environmental impact assessment should inform the selection of materials.

Sourcing materials locally may affect the local economy, workforce or the natural environment. In some situations, adequate quality materials may not be available locally. In those situations, use alternative materials or production processes, or commercial shelter systems, but consider the impact of using materials that are unfamiliar to the local culture. Avoid materials produced through the exploitation of local workers and children.

Safe public buildings: Construct or repair temporary and permanent public buildings such as schools and health centres so that they do not pose a public health risk and are disaster-resilient. Such facilities should comply with building standards and approval procedures. Ensure safety and access for all, including for persons facing barriers to moving and communicating (when possible, coordinate with organisations representing persons with disabilities). Consult with the appropriate authorities when repairing and constructing such buildings. Establish an affordable operation and maintenance strategy.

Procurement and construction management: Develop a construction schedule that includes key target milestones such as start and completion dates, and the dates and duration of the relocation of displaced people. This applies whether the construction is managed by the owner or a contractor. The schedule should note the expected onset of seasonal weather and include a contingency plan for unforeseen events. Establish a construction management and monitoring system for materials, labour and site supervision. This should address sourcing, procurement, transportation, handling and administration throughout the process.

Hire local labour as much as possible to increase their skill set and to support the livelihoods of the affected people. Hire specialist professionals (such as engineers, architects, urban designers, contract managers or lawyers) to carry out specific tasks.

Ensure that environmental concerns are addressed. Promote socially acceptable reuse of salvaged materials where the rights to such material and its quality can be confirmed ⊕ *see Shelter and settlement standard 7: Environmental sustainability.*

Upgrading and maintenance: Initial shelter responses typically only provide a minimum level of covered or enclosed living space. However, the initial construction methods and materials should enable households to maintain, adapt or upgrade the shelter to meet their longer-term needs. Adaptations should be made safely using locally available, familiar and affordable tools and materials, where possible.

Communal tools: Establish procedures that set out how to use, maintain and safely store communal or shared-use tools and materials.

6. Security of tenure

Security of tenure means that people can live in their homes without fear of forced eviction, whether in communal settlement situations, informal settlements, host communities or after return. It is the foundation of the right to adequate housing and many other human rights. In the humanitarian context, an incremental – or step-by-step – approach may be the most appropriate. This recognises that displaced people can be supported to improve their living conditions in different types of accommodation. It does not mean prioritising owners for assistance, nor does it necessarily convey permanence or ownership. Shelter actors have been developing an understanding of what is "secure enough" for the purposes of designing shelter options that support the most vulnerable and tenure-insecure. For more on due diligence and the concept of "secure enough" ⊕ *see References: Payne and Durand-Lasserve (2012).*

Shelter and settlement standard 6:
Security of tenure
The affected population has security of tenure in its shelter and settlement options.

Key actions

1 ⟩ Undertake due diligence in programme design and implementation.

- Achieve as much legal certainty about tenure as possible (the "secure enough" approach), given the context and constraints.
- Coordinate and work with local authorities, legal professionals and interagency forums.

2 ⟩ Understand the legal framework and the reality on the ground.

- Map tenure systems and arrangements for the different post-crisis shelter and settlement scenarios; identify how these affect the most at-risk groups.
- Work with local authorities to understand which regulations will be enforced and which will not, and the related time frames.
- Understand how tenure relations are managed and disputes resolved, and how this may have changed since the onset of the crisis.

3 ⟩ Understand how tenure systems, arrangements and practices affect security of tenure for at-risk groups.

- Include security of tenure as an indicator of vulnerability.
- Understand what documents may be required by people participating in a programme, noting that the most vulnerable may not have, or be able to access, these documents.

- Ensure that the response is not biased towards owner-occupier or freehold arrangements.

4 Implement shelter and settlement programmes to support security of tenure.

- Use local expertise to adapt programming to the different types of tenure, especially for vulnerable groups.
- Ensure that documentation, such as tenure agreements, is properly prepared and reflects the rights of all parties.
- Reduce the risk that the shelter programme may cause or contribute to tensions within the community and with surrounding local communities.

5 Support protection from forced eviction.

- In case of eviction, or risk of eviction, undertake referrals to identify alternative shelter solutions and other sectoral assistance.
- Assist with dispute resolution.

Key indicators

Percentage of shelter recipients that have security of tenure for their shelter and settlement option at least for the duration of a particular assistance programme

Percentage of shelter recipients that have an appropriate agreement for security of tenure for their shelter option

Percentage of shelter recipients with tenure challenges that have accessed, independently or through referral, legal services and/or dispute resolution mechanisms

- ⊕ *See Protection Principle 4.*

Guidance notes

Tenure is the relationship among groups or individuals with respect to housing and land, established through statutory law or customary, informal or religious arrangements. Tenure systems determine who can use what resources, for how long, and under what conditions. There are many forms of tenure arrangements, ranging from full ownership and formal rental agreements to emergency housing and occupation of land in informal settlements. Regardless of the tenure arrangement, all people still retain housing, land and property rights. People living in informal settlements, who are often internally displaced, may not possess a legal right to occupy the land but still possess the right to adequate housing and protection against forced eviction from their home. In order to determine whether an appropriate security of tenure is in place, information such as tenure documentation and organisational use of due diligence methods are required.

Security of tenure is an integral part of the right to adequate housing. It guarantees legal protection against forced eviction, harassment and other threats and enables people to live in their home in security, peace and dignity. All people, including women, should possess a degree of security of tenure. It is important to understand how tenure relations, including dispute resolution mechanisms, are managed and practised, and how they may have changed since the onset of the crisis. Data to assess security of tenure can include numbers of disputes, eviction rates and perceptions of security of tenure.

Incremental tenure: One of the most effective ways to strengthen security of tenure is to build on existing tenure systems that enjoy a degree of social legitimacy ⊕ *see References: UN Habitat and GLTN Social Tenure Domain Model, and Payne and Durand-Lasserve (2012).*

Urban considerations: The majority of the urban displaced live in informal settlements or in rental accommodation without formal ownership, lease and/or use agreements. Therefore, the risk of forced eviction and related forms of exploitation and harassment is a defining feature of their lives. Shelter and settlement assistance options for urban areas should address complex tenure situations and consider incremental tenure approaches for renters, informal settlers, squatters and others.

Do no harm: In some contexts, a humanitarian shelter intervention can lead to the eviction of vulnerable groups. In others, highlighting security of tenure issues can increase the risk of eviction for vulnerable groups. A due diligence approach will identify security of tenure risks facing different groups. In some cases where the risks to security of tenure are too great, it may be best to do nothing at all.

Common triggers for eviction: The threat of eviction comes from a complex inter-action of factors, most of which are also triggers for exploitation and abuse. They include:

- inability to pay rent, often due to restrictions on livelihoods such as the right to work;
- absence of written lease agreements with landlords, making people vulnerable to price increase and eviction;
- disputes with landlords;
- discrimination against affected people;
- restrictions on improving the housing environment, with those in breach of building permissions coming under constant threat of eviction;
- users or occupants of buildable areas being unable to regularise their situation with the civil administration;
- housing transactions taking place within customary or religious frameworks, and therefore not being recognised by statutory law, or vice versa;
- for women: divorce, intimate partner violence and other forms of domestic violence, or the death of their husband; and

- a lack of civil documentation for women (they may be included in their father's or husband's documentation) and for other marginalised or persecuted groups.

Evictions and relocation: Resettlement may be consistent with human rights law to protect the health and safety of inhabitants exposed to natural disasters, environmental hazards or to preserve critical environmental resources. However, misusing regulations aimed at protecting public health and safety or the environment to justify eviction in the absence of genuine risk, or when other options are available, is contrary to international human rights law.

7. Environmental sustainability

Environmental sustainability addresses responsible programming that meets the needs of the present without compromising the ability of future generations to meet their own needs. Ignoring environmental issues in the short term can compromise recovery, worsen existing problems or cause new ones ⊕ *see Protection Principle 1* and *Core Humanitarian Standard Commitments 3 and 9.*

Shelter and settlement standard 7: Environmental sustainability

Shelter and settlement assistance minimises any negative programme impact on the natural environment.

Key actions

1 ⟩ Integrate environmental impact assessment and management in all shelter and settlement planning.

- Assess the environmental impacts of the crisis, and environmental risks and vulnerabilities, to minimise negative effects of the shelter and settlement options.
- Incorporate an environmental management plan into operations and monitoring procedures.

2 ⟩ Select the most sustainable materials and techniques among the viable options.

- Prefer those that do not deplete local natural resources or contribute to long-term environmental damage.
- Salvage and reuse, recycle or re-purpose available materials, including debris.

3 ⟩ Manage solid waste in a safe, timely, culturally sensitive and environmentally sustainable way in all settlements.

- Coordinate with WASH, health, public works and other authorities, the private sector and other stakeholders to establish or re-establish sustainable waste management practices.

4 ⟩ Establish, restore and promote safe, reliable, affordable and environmentally sustainable energy supply systems.

- Determine whether existing energy supply systems have a negative environmental impact on natural resources, pollution, health and safety.
- Ensure any new or revised energy supply options meet user needs, and provide training and follow-up as needed.

5 ▷ Protect, restore and improve the ecological value of operational sites (such as temporary settlements) during and after use.

- Assess environmental baseline conditions and available local natural resources for each site and identify environmental hazards, including those due to previous commercial or industrial use.
- Remove immediate and obvious hazards from the area and repair any serious environmental degradation, while keeping the removal of natural vegetation and the disruption of natural drainage at a minimum.
- Leave the site in a state that will allow the local population to use it immediately, where possible in better condition than before.

Key indicators

Percentage of shelter and settlement activities that are preceded by an environmental review

Number of recommendations from the environment management and monitoring plan that have been implemented

Percentage of shelter constructions using low carbon emission construction materials and procurement methods

Percentage of solid waste on the site that is reused, re-purposed or recycled

- Target > 70 per cent by volume

Percentage of temporary settlement sites that are restored to better environmental conditions than before use

Guidance notes

Environmental impact assessment consists of three elements: a baseline description of the local environment against which the assessment is occurring; an understanding of the proposed activity and its potential threat to the environment; and an understanding of the consequences if the threat occurs.

It may be helpful to consult with appropriate environmental agencies. Key points to consider in an environmental impact assessment include:

- pre-crisis access to and use of local natural resources, including fuel and construction materials, water sourcing and waste management;
- the extent of locally available natural resources and the impact of the crisis on these assets; and
- social, economic and cultural issues (including gender roles) that may influence the sustainability of the response and improve its overall effectiveness and efficiency.

Sourcing materials: When sourcing natural resources such as water, timber, sand, soil and grasses, and fuel for firing bricks and roof tiles, be aware of the environmental impact. Promote the use of multiple sources, the reuse of salvaged materials and the production of alternative materials. Reforestation can be a good way to produce sustainable building materials. Avoid using materials that have been produced through exploitation of adults and children ⊕ *see Delivering assistance through markets.*

Site selection: Environmental impact assessments should inform site selection. For example, locating settlements close to existing infrastructure can reduce the environmental impacts associated with building new infrastructure. Consider exposure to climate-related risks ⊕ *see Shelter and settlement standard 2: Location and settlement planning.*

Erosion: Retain trees and other vegetation to stabilise the soil and maximise shade and protection from the climate. Using natural contours for services such as roads, pathways and drainage networks minimises erosion and flooding. If necessary, establish drainage channels, piped drainage runs under roadways or planted earth banks to prevent soil erosion. Where the slope is more than 5 per cent, engineering techniques must be applied to prevent excessive erosion.

Debris management and waste reuse or re-purposing: Debris management planning immediately after the crisis promotes the salvaging of debris for reuse, re-purposing or safe disposal.

There is potential to reuse or re-purpose solid waste found in humanitarian settings. Reuse of materials in humanitarian settings as part of a more systematic solid waste management strategy depends on cultural attitudes to the handling of waste and the proximity of businesses willing to purchase the separated materials. Humanitarian settings provide opportunities for inventive reuse of materials ⊕ *see WASH excreta management standard 3.1 and WASH solid waste management standards 5.1 and 5.3.*

Energy: When working on energy consumption, consider climate, available natural resources, indoor and outdoor pollution, health impact, safety, and user preferences. Where possible, programmes should reduce household energy needs. Energy-efficient design, using passive approaches to the heating or cooling of structures, and using energy efficient household items such as solar lamps reduces household costs and environmental impacts ⊕ *see Food security and nutrition standard 5: General food security.*

Identify the risks to the public caused by damaged energy supplies, for example damaged power lines and leaking propane or fuel oil storage tanks. Coordinate with local government and energy vendors to restore, deliver and maintain the energy services. Subsidies or other incentives may be an option for assuring safety and reducing pollution or demands on natural resources.

Management of natural resources: Where there are limited natural resources to support a substantial increase in human habitation, a resource management plan is essential. If necessary, consult external experts. The resource management plan may suggest external fuel supplies and options for livestock grazing, agricultural production and other income streams that depend on natural resources. Large, well-managed settlements may be more environmentally sustainable than numerous smaller, dispersed settlements that are not as easy to manage or monitor. However, large communal settlements may put more pressure on nearby host communities than smaller, dispersed settlements. Shelter actors should always consider the impact of their interventions on the host population's needs for natural resources ① *see Core Humanitarian Standard Commitment 9* and *LEGS Handbook.*

Urban and rural contexts: People in rural areas are generally more dependent on the natural resources in their immediate surroundings, compared with urban dwellers. However, urban areas absorb large quantities of natural resources such as timber, sand and cement, bricks and other natural building materials, coming from a much larger catchment area. Informed decisions should be taken when using large quantities of construction materials in urban or other large-scale shelter programmes, where environmental impacts may go far beyond the programme implementation area.

Appendix 1
Shelter and settlement assessment checklist

This list of questions serves as a checklist to ensure that appropriate data is obtained to inform the post-crisis shelter and settlement response. The list of questions is not mandatory. Use and adapt it as appropriate.

Information on the underlying causes of the crisis, the security situation, the basic demographics of the displaced and any host population, and the key people to consult and contact, will need to be obtained separately.

Assessment and coordination

- Has an agreed coordination mechanism been established by the relevant authorities and humanitarian organisations?
- What baseline data are available on the affected people and what are the known hazards and shelter and settlement risks and vulnerabilities?
- Is there a contingency plan to inform the response?
- What initial assessment information is already available?
- Is an interagency and/or multi-sectoral assessment planned and does this include shelter, settlement and household items?

Demographics

- How many people comprise an average household?
- How many affected people are living in different types of households? Consider groups living outside of family connections, such as groups of unaccompanied children, households that are not average size, or others. Disaggregate by sex, age, disability and ethnicity, linguistic or religious affiliation as appropriate in context.
- How many affected households lack adequate shelter, and where are these households?
- How many people, disaggregated by sex, age and disability, who are not members of individual households have no or inadequate shelter, and where are they located?
- How many affected households that lack adequate shelter have not been displaced and can be assisted at the site of their original homes?
- How many affected households that lack adequate shelter are displaced and require shelter assistance with host families or in temporary settlements?
- How many people, disaggregated by sex and age, lack access to communal facilities such as schools, healthcare facilities and community centres?

Risks

- What are the immediate risks to life, health and security resulting from the lack of adequate shelter, and how many people are at risk?

- What are the less immediate risks to people's lives, health and security resulting from the lack of adequate shelter?
- How do tenure systems, arrangements and practices affect security of tenure for vulnerable and marginalised populations?
- What are the particular risks for vulnerable people, including women, children, unaccompanied minors, and persons with disabilities or chronic illnesses, due to the lack of adequate shelter, and why?
- What is the impact on any host populations of the presence of displaced people?
- What are the potential risks for conflict or discrimination among or between groups within the affected population, particularly for women and girls?

Resources and constraints

- What are the material, financial and human resources of the affected people that are available to meet some or all of their urgent shelter needs?
- What are the issues regarding land availability, ownership and usage that affect people's ability to meet urgent shelter needs, including temporary communal settlements where required?
- What risks may potential host populations face in accommodating displaced people within their own dwellings or on adjacent land?
- What are the opportunities and constraints affecting the use of existing available and unaffected buildings or structures to accommodate displaced people temporarily?
- Is accessible vacant land suitable for temporary settlements, considering topography and other environmental constraints?
- What regulatory requirements and constraints may affect the development of shelter solutions?

Materials, design and construction

- What initial shelter solutions or materials have the affected people, affected populations or other actors provided?
- What existing materials can be salvaged from the damaged site for use in the reconstruction of shelters?
- What are the typical building practices of the affected people and what materials do they use for the structural frame, roof and external wall enclosures?
- What alternative solutions for design or materials are potentially available and familiar or acceptable to the affected people?
- What design features will ensure safe and ready access to and use of shelter solutions by all affected people?
- How can the identified shelter solutions minimise future risks and vulnerabilities?
- How are shelters typically built, and by whom?

- How are construction materials typically obtained, and by whom?
- How can women, youths, persons with disabilities and older people be trained or assisted to participate in the building of their own shelters, and what are the constraints?
- Where individuals or households lack the capacity or opportunity to build their own shelters will additional assistance be required to support them? Examples include the provision of voluntary or contracted labour or technical assistance.

Household and livelihood activities

- What household and livelihood support activities typically take place in or near the shelters of the affected people, and how does the resulting space provision and design reflect these activities?
- What legal and environmentally sustainable livelihood support opportunities can be provided through the sourcing of materials and the construction of shelter and settlement solutions?

Essential services and communal facilities

- What is the current availability of water for drinking and personal hygiene, and what are the possibilities and constraints in meeting the anticipated sanitation needs?
- What is the current provision of social facilities (such as health clinics, schools and places of worship), and what are the constraints to and opportunities for accessing these facilities?
- Where communal buildings, particularly schools, are used for sheltering displaced people, what is the process and timeline for returning them to their intended use?

Host population and environmental impact

- What are the issues of concern for the host population?
- What are the organisational and physical constraints related to accommodating the displaced people within the host population or within temporary settlements?
- What are the environmental concerns regarding the local sourcing of construction materials?
- What are the environmental concerns regarding the needs of the displaced people for fuel, sanitation, waste disposal, and grazing for animals, among others?

Household item needs

- What are the critical non-food items required by the affected people?
- Can any of the required non-food items be obtained locally?
- Is the use of cash or vouchers possible?
- Will technical assistance be required to complement the provision of shelter support items?

Clothing and bedding

- What types of clothing, blankets and bedding do women, men, children and infants, pregnant and lactating women, persons with disabilities and older people typically use? Are there particular social and cultural considerations?
- How many women and men of all ages, children and infants have inadequate or insufficient clothing, blankets or bedding to provide protection from the negative effects of the climate and to maintain their health, dignity and well-being?
- What are the potential risks to the lives, health and personal safety of the affected people if their need for adequate clothing, blankets or bedding is not met?
- What vector-control measures, particularly the provision of mosquito nets, are required to ensure the health and well-being of households?

Cooking and eating, stoves and fuel

- What cooking and eating utensils did a typical household have access to before the crisis?
- How many households do not have access to sufficient cooking and eating utensils?
- How did affected people typically cook and heat their dwellings before the crisis, and where did the cooking take place?
- What fuel was typically used for cooking and heating before the crisis, and where was this obtained?
- How many households do not have access to a stove for cooking and heating, and why?
- How many households do not have access to adequate supplies of fuel for cooking and heating?
- What are the opportunities and constraints (in particular environmental concerns) of sourcing adequate supplies of fuel for the crisis-affected and neighbouring populations?
- What is the impact on affected people, and in particular women of all ages, of sourcing adequate supplies of fuel?
- Are there cultural issues regarding cooking and eating to take into account?

Tools and equipment

- Which basic tools to repair, construct or maintain a shelter are available to the households?
- What livelihood support activities can also utilise the basic tools for construction, maintenance and debris removal?
- What training or awareness-raising activities will enable the safe use of tools?

Appendix 2
Description of settlement scenarios

Settlement scenarios allow for a first-level categorisation of where and how affected people are living. An understanding of the crisis through these settlement scenarios will help when planning assistance strategies. Gather additional details to inform detailed planning ⊕ *see Appendix 3: Additional characteristics of settlement scenarios.*

Population group	Settlement scenario	Description	Examples
Non-displaced people	Owner-occupied accommodation or land	The occupant owns his or her property and/or land (ownership may be formal or informal) or is a part or joint owner.	Houses, apartments, land
	Rental accommodation or land	Renting allows an individual or household to use housing or land for a specified period of time at a given price, without transfer of ownership, on the basis of a written or verbal contract with a private or public owner.	
	Informally occupied accommodation or land	Households occupy the property and/or land without the explicit permission of the owner or appointed representative of the premises.	Empty houses, apartments, vacant land
Displaced people Dispersed	Rental arrangement	Rental allows an individual or household to use housing or land for a specified period of time at a given price, without transfer of ownership. It is based on a written or verbal contract with a private or public owner. This can be self-funded individually or communally or subsidised by the government or humanitarian community.	Houses, apartments, land from existing housing stock

Population group	Settlement scenario	Description	Examples
Displaced people	Hosted arrangement	Host populations provide shelter for displaced populations or individual families.	Houses, apartments, land already occupied or made available by the host population
	Spontaneous arrangement	Displaced households spontaneously settle in a location without agreement with the relevant actors (such as owner, local government, humanitarian organisations and/or the host population).	Empty houses, empty apartments, vacant land, road side
Communal	Collective accommodation	Pre-existing facility or structure where multiple households take shelter. Infrastructure and basic services are provided on a communal basis or access to them is made possible.	Public buildings, evacuation, reception and transit centres, abandoned buildings, company compounds, unfinished buildings
	Planned settlement	A purpose-built settlement for displaced people where the site layout is planned and managed, and where infrastructure, facilities and services are available.	Formal settlements managed by government, UN, NGOs or civil society. Can include transit or reception centres or evacuation sites
	Unplanned settlement	Multiple households spontaneously and collectively settle in a location, creating a new settlement. Households or the collective might have rental agreements with the landowner. This is often without prior arrangement with the relevant actors (such as owner, local government and/or the host population). On-site basic services are initially not planned.	Informal sites and settlements

Appendix 3
Additional characteristics of settlement scenarios

This table sets out secondary characteristics that expand the settlement scenarios outlined in ⊕ *Appendix 2 Description of settlement scenarios*. Using it to understand the crisis in more detail should inform detailed planning processes.

Note: The choice of characteristics and their definition vary by context and should align to the relevant guidance. Create additional characteristics as needed for a particular context.

Category	Examples	Notes
Types of displaced populations	Refugees, asylum seekers, internally displaced persons (IDPs), refugee returnees, IDP returnees, others of concern (for example, migrants)	⊕ *See Humanitarian profile support guidance (www.humanitarianresponse. info)*
Indirectly affected	Pre-existing populations, host populations	Host populations are often impacted by directly affected populations, for example by sharing communal services such as schools, or acting as host families.
Geographic context	Urban, peri-urban, rural	Peri-urban: an area between consolidated urban and rural regions.
Damage level	No damage, partial damage, fully destroyed	Categorising damage level should inform whether the house or shelter is safe to occupy.
Duration/phase	Short-term, medium-term, long-term, permanent Emergency, transitional, recovery, durable	Definitions of these terms vary and should be set at response level.
Tenure systems	Statutory, customary, religious, hybrid	Informal land or housing arrangements are those that include regularised and unregulated squatting Unauthorised subdivisions on legally owned land, and various forms of unofficial rental arrangements. In some cases, several forms of tenure may coexist on the same plot, with each party entitled to certain rights.
Forms of housing tenure	Ownership, use rights, rental, collective tenure	
Forms of land tenure	Private, communal, collective, open access, state/public	

Category	Examples	Notes
Shelter type	Tents, makeshift shelters, transitional shelter, core shelter, houses, apartments, rented space within a bigger unit, garages, caravans, containers	⊕ *See Appendix 4: Assistance options.*
Site management	Managed, remote or mobile managed, self-managed, no management	Managed: with no objection from landowner, and endorsed by authorities. Remote or mobile managed: in cases where a team is managing a number of sites. Self-managed: by community leadership structure or internal committees.

Appendix 4
Assistance options

A range of context-specific assistance options can be combined to meet the needs of affected people. Consider the advantages and disadvantages of each and develop the most appropriate programme.

Assistance option	Description
Household items	⊕ see Shelter and settlement standard 4: Household items.
Shelter kits	Construction material, tools and fixtures needed to create or improve living space. Consider whether to supply structural materials such as poles and pegs or if they can be supplied by the households. Consider the need for additional instruction, promotion, education or awareness-raising.
Shelter toolkits	Construction tools and hardware needed to create or improve living space and settlement.
Tents	Premanufactured portable shelters with a cover and a structure.
Return and transit support	Support for affected people who choose to return to their place of origin or relocate to a new location. Such support may include a wide range of services such as providing transport, transport fares or vouchers, or items such as tools, materials and seed stocks.
Repairs	Repair describes restoring a building from damage or decay to a sound working condition where it meets the required standards and specifications. If buildings have suffered minor damage, it is possible to repair them without a more major retrofit. For displaced people it may be necessary to repair collective centres or to upgrade pre-existing buildings such as schools for mass shelter.
Retrofitting	Retrofit of the buildings involves strengthening and/or structural system modification of the buildings' structure. The goal is to make a building more resistant to future hazards by having safety features installed. Buildings that were damaged by the crisis may need to be retrofitted in addition to being repaired. For displaced people, it may be necessary to retrofit houses of host families, if they are at risk from a hazard.
Host assistance	People who are unable to return to their original homes often stay with family and friends or communities with shared historical, religious or other ties. Supporting the host to continue to shelter affected people includes support to expand or adapt an existing host family shelter, or financial and material support for running costs.
Rental assistance	Assistance to affected households to rent accommodation and land can include financial contributions, support to obtain a fair agreement or advice on property standards. Rent is an ongoing expense, thus plan exit strategies, promoting self-sufficiency or connecting livelihood activities early ⊕ see Shelter and settlement standard 3: Living space and standard 6: Security of tenure. (Note: Rental assistance can inject cash into the host population or it can exhaust the market and cause inflation.)

Assistance option	Description
Temporary shelters	Short-term shelter solutions, which are intended to be removed once the next stage of shelter solution is offered. Usually these are constructed with limited costs.
Transitional shelters	Rapid shelters designed from materials and techniques that are designed to transition into more permanent structures. The shelter should be upgradeable, reusable, resaleable or moveable from temporary sites to permanent locations.
Core housing	Housing units planned, designed and constructed to be eventually part of a permanent house, but not completing it. Core housing allows the future process of extension by the household through its own means and resources. The aim is to create a safe and adequate living space of one or two rooms together with water and sanitation facilities and the necessary household items ⊕ *see Shelter and settlement standard 3: Living space and standard 4: Household items.*
Reconstruction/ rebuilding	Demolishing and rebuilding structures that cannot be repaired.
Information centres	Information centres offer advice and guidance to affected people. Information provided through local centres may clarify rights to advice and assistance, options and processes for return; rights to land, access to compensation, technical advice and assistance, return, integration and relocation; and channels to offer feedback; and ways to seek redress, including arbitration and legal aid.
Legal and adminis-trative expertise	Providing legal and administrative expertise helps the affected people to be aware of their rights and to receive the administrative support they need free of charge or at a reduced cost. Particular attention should be paid to the needs of the most vulnerable groups.
Securing tenure	Support in securing housing and/or land occupation rights for the affected people guarantees legal protection against forced eviction, harassment and other threats, and provides security, peace and dignity ⊕ *see Shelter and settlement standard 6: Security of tenure.*
Infrastructure and settlement planning	Infrastructure and settlement planning support is used to improve the services of a community and support the planning of sustainable transitional settlement and reconstruction solutions. Infrastructure and settlement planning support may be divided into two categories: that which is coordinated primarily by the shelter sector and those that are primarily coordinated by other sectors.
Collective accommodation support	Existing buildings can be used as collective centres or evacuation centres and to provide rapid shelter. These can be schools, community buildings, covered playgrounds, religious facilities or vacant properties. Such prop-erties may require adaptation or upgrading for habitation ⊕ *see Shelter and settlement standard 3: Living space.* When using school buildings to accommodate crisis-affected people, identify and utilise alternative structures immediately to enable schooling to continue ⊕ *see Collective Centre Guidelines and INEE Handbook*
Managing settle-ments and collective centres	⊕ *See Collective Centre Guidelines*

Assistance option	Description
Debris removal and management of the dead	Debris removal helps improve public safety and access to the affected people. Consider environmental impact as well ⊕ *see Shelter and settlement standards 2 and 7.* Handle and identify the dead appropriately ⊕ *see Health 1.1 and WASH 6.*
Rehabilitate and/ or install common infrastructure	Rehabilitate or construct infrastructure such as water supply, sanitation, roads, drainage , bridges and electricity ⊕ *See WASH chapter for guidance, and Shelter and settlement standard 2: Location and settlement planning.*
Rehabilitate and/or construct community facilities	***Education:*** Schools, child-friendly spaces, safe play areas ⊕ *see INEE Handbook;* ***Health service:*** Health centres and hospitals ⊕ *see Health systems standard 1.1: Health service delivery;* ***Security:*** Police posts or community watch structures; ***Communal activities:*** Meeting places for decision-making, recreation and worship, fuel storage, cooking facilities and solid waste disposal; and ***Economic activities:*** Markets, land and space for livestock, space for livelihoods and business.
Urban/village planning and zoning	When re-planning residential areas after a crisis, involve local authorities and urban planners, so that regulations and mutual interests of all stakeholders are respected ⊕ *see Shelter and settlement standard 2: Location and settlement planning.*
Relocation	Relocation is a process that involves rebuilding a family's or a community's housing, assets and public infrastructure in a different location.

Appendix 5
Implementation options

The assistance delivery method influences the quality, timing, scale of delivery and cost. Select implementation options based on an understanding of local markets, including commodity, labour and rental markets, in support of economic recovery ⊕ *see Delivering assistance through markets*. Consider the impact of the selected implementation options on the degree of participation and sense of ownership, gender dynamics, social cohesion and livelihoods opportunities.

Implementation option	Description
Technical assistance and quality assurance	Technical assistance is an integral part of any shelter and settlement response, regardless of the assistance ⊕ *see Shelter and settlement standard 5: Technical assistance*.
Financial support	Through financial support, households and communities can access goods or services or meet their shelter and settlement needs. According to the risk and complexities of the task, complement financial support with technical assistance and capacity building. Market-based transfers include the following options: **Conditional cash transfers:** Useful when it is vital to meet specific conditions; for example, Tranche system. **Restricted cash or vouchers:** Useful for specific goods or engaging vendors. **Unconditional, unrestricted or multipurpose.** **Access to financial services** such as savings groups, loans, micro-credit, insurance and guarantees. ⊕ *see Delivering assistance through markets*.
In-kind material support	Procuring and then distributing items and materials directly to affected households is an option when local markets are not able to supply the appropriate quality or quantity or in a timely manner ⊕ *see Delivering assistance through markets*.
Commissioned labour and contracting	Commissioning or contracting labour to achieve shelter and settlement goals through owner-driven, contractor-driven or agency-driven models ⊕ *see Shelter and settlement standard 5: Technical assistance*.
Capacity building	Skills enhancement and training offer opportunities for stakeholders to increase their ability to respond, individually and collectively, and also to interact and consider together common challenges and tools such as developing and implementing building standards and codes ⊕ *see Shelter and settlement standard 5: Technical assistance*. Successful capacity building should allow experts to concentrate on supervising activities undertaken by local stakeholders and to provide their assistance to a higher number of persons receiving assistance.

For a table with potential assistance and implementation options connected to settlement scenarios please go to www.spherestandards.org/handbook/online-resources

References and further reading

International legal instruments

Article 25 Universal Declaration of Human Rights. Archive of the International Council on Human Rights Policy, 1948. www.claiminghumanrights.org

General Comment No. 4: The Right to Adequate Housing (Art. 11.1 of the Covenant). UN Committee on Economic, Social and Cultural Rights, 1991. www.refworld.org

General Comment 7: The right to adequate housing (Art. 11.1 of the Covenant): forced evictions. UN Committee on Economic, Social and Cultural Rights, 1997. www.escr-net.org

Guiding Principles on Internal Displacement. OCHA, 1998. www.internal-displacement.org

Pinheiro, P. *Principles on Housing and Property Restitution for Refugees and Displaced Persons.* OHCHR, 2005. www.unhcr.org

Refugee Convention. UNHCR, 1951. www.unhcr.org

General

Camp Closure Guidelines. Global CCCM Cluster, 2014. www.globalcccmcluster.org

Child Protection Minimum Standards (CPMS). Global Child Protection Working Group, 2010. http://cpwg.net

Emergency Handbook, 4th Edition. UNHCR, 2015. emergency.unhcr.org

Humanitarian Civil-Military Coordination: A Guide for the Military. UNOCHA, 2014. https://docs.unocha.org

Humanitarian inclusion standards for older people and people with disabilities. Age and Disability Consortium, 2018. www.refworld.org

Livestock Emergency Guidelines and Standards (LEGS). LEGS Project, 2014. https://www.livestock-emergency.net

Minimum Economic Recovery Standards (MERS). SEEP Network, 2017. https://seepnetwork.org

Minimum Standards for Education: Preparedness, Recovery and Response. The Inter-Agency Network for Education in Emergencies [INEE], 2010. www.ineesite.org

Minimum Standard for Market Analysis (MISMA). The Cash Learning Partnership (CaLP), 2017. www.cashlearning.org

Post-Disaster Settlement Planning Guidelines. IFRC, 2012. www.ifrc.org

UN-CMCoord Field Handbook. UN OCHA, 2015. https://www.unocha.org

Settlement scenarios

Humanitarian Profile Support Guidance. IASC Information Management Working Group, 2016. www.humanitarianresponse.info

Shelter after Disaster. Shelter Centre, 2010. http://shelterprojects.org

Temporary communal settlement
Collective Centre Guidelines. UNHCR and IOM, 2010. https://www.globalcccmcluster.org

Cash, vouchers, market assessments/Disabilities
All Under One Roof: Disability-inclusive Shelter and Settlements in Emergencies. IFRC, 2015. www.ifrc.org

CaLP CBA quality toolbox. http://pqtoolbox.cashlearning.org

Gender and gender-based violence
Guidelines for Integrating Gender-Based Violence Interventions in Humanitarian Action. Inter-Agency Standing Committee (IASC), 2015. Part 3, section 11: Shelter, Settlement and Recovery. https://gbvguidelines.org

IASC Gender Handbook for Humanitarian Action. IASC, 2017. https://reliefweb.int

Security of Tenure in Humanitarian Shelter Operations. NRC and IFRC, 2014. www.ifrc.org

Child protection
Minimum Standards for Child Protection in Humanitarian Action: Standard 24. Alliance for Child Protection in Humanitarian Action, Global Protection Cluster, 2012. http://cpwg.net

Schools and public buildings
Guidance Notes on Safer School Construction (INEE Toolkit). INEE, 2009. http://toolkit.ineesite.org

Urban context
Urban Informal Settlers Displaced by Disasters: Challenges to Housing Responses. IDMC, 2015. www.internal-displacement.org

Urban Shelter Guidelines. NRC, Shelter Centre, 2010. http://shelterprojects.org

Security of tenure
Land Rights and Shelter: The Due Diligence Standard. Shelter Cluster, 2013. www.sheltercluster.org

Payne, G. Durand-Lasserve, A. *Holding On: Security of Tenure – Types, Policies, Practices and Challenges.* 2012. www.ohchr.org

Rapid Tenure Assessment Guidelines for Post-Disaster Response Planning. IFRC, 2015. www.ifrc.org

Securing Tenure in Shelter Operations: Guidance for Humanitarian Response. NRC, 2016. https://www.sheltercluster.org

The Right to Adequate Housing, Fact Sheet 25 (Rev.1). OHCHR and UN Habitat, 2014. www.ohchr.org

The Right to Adequate Housing, Fact Sheet 21 (Rev.1). OHCHR and UN Habitat, 2015. www.ohchr.org

Further reading
For further reading suggestions please go to
www.spherestandards.org/handbook/online-resources

Health

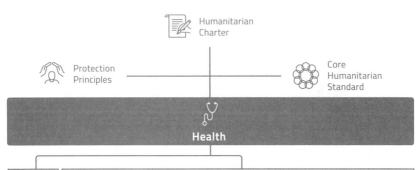

Health systems	Essential Healthcare						
	Communiable diseases	Child health	Sexual and reproductive health	Injury and trauma care	Mental health	Non-communicable diseases	Palliative care
STANDARD 1.1 Health service delivery	STANDARD 2.1.1 Prevention	STANDARD 2.2.1 Childhood vaccine-preventable diseases	STANDARD 2.3.1 Reproductive, maternal and newborn healthcare	STANDARD 2.4 Injury and trauma care	STANDARD 2.5 Mental health care	STANDARD 2.6 Care of non-communicable diseases	STANDARD 2.7 Palliative care
STANDARD 1.2 Health workforce	STANDARD 2.1.2 Surveillance and outbreak detection and early response	STANDARD 2.2.2 Management of newborn and childhood illness	STANDARD 2.3.2 Sexual violence and clinical management of rape				
STANDARD 1.3 Essential medicines and medical devices	STANDARD 2.1.3 Diagnosis and case management		STANDARD 2.3.3 HIV				
STANDARD 1.4 Health financing	STANDARD 2.1.4 Outbreak preparedness and response						
STANDARD 1.5 Health information							

APPENDIX 1   Health assessment checklist
APPENDIX 2   Sample weekly surveillance reporting forms
APPENDIX 3   Formulas for calculating key health indicators
APPENDIX 4   Poisoning

Contents

Essential concepts in health

Everyone has the right to timely and appropriate healthcare

The Sphere Minimum Standards for Healthcare are a practical expression of the right to healthcare in humanitarian contexts. The standards are grounded in the beliefs, principles, duties and rights declared in the Humanitarian Charter. These include the right to life with dignity, the right to protection and security, and the right to receive humanitarian assistance on the basis of need.

For a list of the key legal and policy documents that inform the Humanitarian Charter, including explanatory comments for humanitarian workers, ⊕ *see Annex 1: Legal foundation to Sphere.*

The aim of healthcare in a crisis is to reduce excess morbidity and mortality

Humanitarian crises have a significant impact on the health and well-being of affected populations. Access to life-saving healthcare is critical in the initial stages of an emergency. Healthcare may also include health promotion, prevention, treatment, rehabilitation and palliative care at any stage of the response.

The public health impact of a crisis can be both direct (injury or death from the crisis itself) and indirect (changes in living conditions, forced displacement, lack of legal protection or decreased access to healthcare).

Overcrowding, inadequate shelter, poor sanitation, insufficient water quantity and quality, and reduced food security all increase the risk of malnutrition and outbreaks of communicable diseases. Extreme stressors can also trigger mental health conditions. Eroding social support mechanisms and self-help systems can lead to negative coping mechanisms and reduced help-seeking behaviour. Reduced access to healthcare and interrupted medicine supply can disrupt ongoing treatment such as maternal healthcare and treatment for HIV, diabetes and mental health conditions.

The primary goal of a health response during a crisis is to prevent and reduce excess mortality and morbidity. Patterns of mortality and morbidity, and hence healthcare needs, will vary according to the type and extent of each crisis.

The most useful indicators to monitor and evaluate the severity of a crisis are the crude mortality rate (CMR) and the more sensitive under-five crude mortality rate (U5CMR). A doubling or more of the baseline CMR or U5CMR indicates a significant public health emergency and requires an immediate response ⊕ *see Appendix 3: Formulas for calculating key health indicators.*

In the absence of a known baseline, the following constitutes an emergency threshold:

- CMR >1/10,000/day
- U5CMR >2/10,000/day

Emergency thresholds must be decided at country level. Where a baseline U5CMR already exceeds emergency thresholds, for instance, waiting for it to double would be unethical.

Support and develop existing health systems

A health systems approach will progressively realise the right to health during the crisis and recovery so it is important to consider how to support existing systems. Hiring staff (national and international) will have short- and long-term implications for national health systems. Following analysis, well-planned health interventions can enhance existing health systems, their future recovery and their development.

In the first phase of a crisis, prioritise targeted health and multi-sectoral rapid assessments. Incomplete information and inaccessible areas should not impede timely public health decision-making. Undertake more comprehensive assessments as soon as possible.

Urban crises require a different approach to health responses

Urban responses must consider the population density, built environment policies, social structures and existing social services. Identifying people at risk or without access to healthcare is challenging. The scale of need can quickly outstrip what can be provided. People seeking refuge in towns and cities rarely know about existing health services or how to access them, risking a further increase in communicable diseases. Outreach will help people cope with new urban stresses such as inadequate access to shelter, food, healthcare, jobs or social support networks.

Rumours and misinformation spread quickly in cities. Use technology to immediately supply accurate information on healthcare and services. Secondary and tertiary healthcare providers are often more active in cities, so increase these providers' capacity to deliver primary healthcare. Engage them in early warning and response systems for communicable diseases and increase their capacity to deliver their usual specialised services.

These Minimum Standards should not be applied in isolation

The Minimum Standards in this chapter reflect the core content of the right to adequate healthcare and contribute to the progressive realisation of this right globally. This right is linked to rights to water and sanitation, food, and shelter. Achieving the Sphere Minimum Standards in one area influences progress in other areas. Coordinate and collaborate closely with other sectors.

Coordinate with local authorities and other responding agencies to ensure that needs are met, efforts are not duplicated, and healthcare response quality is optimised. Coordination between healthcare actors is also important to meet needs impartially and ensure that people who are hard to reach, at risk or marginalised also have access to care. Cross-references throughout the Handbook suggest some potential linkages.

Where national standards are lower than Sphere minimums, work with the government to progressively raise them.

Priorities should be decided on the basis of sound information shared between sectors and be reviewed as the situation evolves.

International law specifically protects the right to healthcare

Healthcare must be provided without discrimination and must be accessible, meaning: available, acceptable, affordable and of good quality. States are obliged to ensure this right during crises ⊕ *see Annex 1: Legal foundation to Sphere.*

The right to healthcare can be assured only if the:

- population is protected;
- professionals responsible for the health system are well trained and committed to universal ethical principles and professional standards;
- health system meets Minimum Standards; and
- state is able and willing to establish and maintain safe and stable conditions in which healthcare can be delivered.

Attacks, threats and other violent obstructions of the work of healthcare personnel, facilities and medical transport are a violation of international humanitarian law. These protections are derived from the basic obligations to respect and protect the wounded and sick.

Humanitarian organisations should carefully consider the nature of any threat and how to address it. For example, an attack by a national army may be treated differently from a threat from the local community ⊕ *see Special considerations to protect healthcare* below.

Links to the Protection Principles and Core Humanitarian Standard

Healthcare actors must care for the wounded and the sick humanely, delivering impartial care without distinction, based on need. Ensuring confidentiality, data protection and privacy is crucial to protect individuals from violence, abuse and other problems.

Medical staff are often first responders in cases of violence against individuals, including gender-based violence and child abuse and neglect. Train staff to identify and refer cases to social welfare or protection actors using confidential communication and referral systems. An unaccompanied or separated child in need of critical healthcare but without a legal guardian to consent poses a particular protection challenge. Consult with the child and relevant local authorities if possible. The right to life and healthcare is essential to meet the child's best interests and may outweigh the right to consent. Decisions must be sensitive to the context and to cultural norms and practices. International medical evacuation and the referral and movement of unaccompanied children requires stringent documentation as well as the involvement of protection services and local authorities.

Increasingly, healthcare must be provided at sea, including international waters, or once individuals are brought ashore. This brings specific protection challenges and political complexities and requires careful planning, preparedness and mitigation of protection risks.

Carefully evaluate civil–military cooperation, particularly in conflicts. Military and armed groups can be important providers of healthcare, even for civilians. Humanitarian agencies may – as a last resort – have to use military capabilities such as infrastructure support to re-establish power supplies to health facilities or provide logistics assistance such as transporting health items or medical evacuation. However, reliance on the military should be considered in the context of access to healthcare and perceptions of neutrality and impartiality ⊕ *see Humanitarian Charter* and *Settings with domestic or international military forces* in *What is Sphere?*

In applying the Minimum Standards, all nine Commitments in the Core Humanitarian Standard should be respected. Feedback mechanisms must be put in place during healthcare responses ⊕ *see Core Humanitarian Standard Commitment 5.*

Special considerations to protect healthcare

Preventing attacks on healthcare facilities, ambulances and healthcare workers requires sustained effort at international, state and community levels. The nature of threats will vary greatly by context and should be addressed and reported. To protect healthcare, health actors should consider the following issues in their work and in supporting ministries of health or other relevant parties.

During all emergencies – and especially during a conflict – health actors must present themselves as neutral and impartial and act according to these principles, as this may not be well understood by the parties to the conflict, the community or the patients.

When providing critical life-saving medical services, follow humanitarian principles and provide impartial healthcare based on need alone. To promote neutrality, care for the wounded and the sick without distinction, ensure patient safety and maintain confidentiality of medical information and personal data.

Acceptance from local communities, officials and parties to a conflict may help protect healthcare. Health actors should both educate those around them and maintain the perception of impartiality and neutrality. A healthcare facility's standard of care, quality of services, and location (for example, if situated near a military camp) will also influence these perception.

Healthcare facilities typically apply a 'no weapons' policy, with weapons left outside a facility or ambulance. This promotes a neutral environment, can help avoid tensions or escalation of conflict within the facility, and can prevent the facility from becoming a target itself.

Take physical security measures to protect the facility and staff from hazards. At the same time, understand how security measures can affect the general public's perception and acceptance of the healthcare facility.

Humanitarian organisations must consider the risks and advantages in how they profile their services and how this affects community trust and acceptance. Keeping a low profile (for example by not branding assets or locations) may be appropriate in some operations, while in others it might be better to display large logos on assets or locations.

1. Health systems

A well-functioning health system can respond to all healthcare needs in a crisis so that even during a large-scale health crisis such as an Ebola outbreak, other healthcare activities can continue. Easily treatable conditions will still be treated, and maternal and child health primary care programmes will continue, reducing excess mortality and morbidity. Any actor promoting, restoring or maintaining health contributes to the overall health system. The health system encompasses all levels, from national, regional, district and community to household carers, the military and the private sector.

In a crisis, health systems and the provision of healthcare are often weakened, even before demand increases. Healthcare workers may be lost, medical supplies interrupted or infrastructure damaged. It is important to understand the impact of the crisis on health systems to determine priorities for humanitarian response.

Humanitarian actors rarely operate in an emergency where there is no pre-existing health system. Where a system is weak, it will need to be strengthened or developed (for example through referral pathways, health information collation and analysis).

The standards in this section address five core aspects of a well-functioning health system:

- delivery of quality health services;
- a trained and motivated healthcare workforce;
- appropriate supply, management and use of medicines, diagnostics material and technology;
- appropriate financing of healthcare; and
- good health information and analysis.

These aspects affect each other in many ways. For instance, insufficient health-care workers or lack of essential medicines will affect service delivery.

Leadership and coordination are vital to ensure needs are addressed in an impartial manner. The ministry of health (MoH) usually leads and coordinates the response and may request support from other health actors. Sometimes the ministry lacks capacity or willingness to assume the role in an efficient and impartial manner, so another agency should take this responsibility. If the MoH does not have access or would not be accepted in all areas of the country, humanitarian actors should seek to support the accepted existing system, especially in an acute emergency. Carefully determine how to work with non-state actors and others, and their ability to provide or coordinate healthcare for the population.

Access to the population is important but must be considered with a clear understanding of the humanitarian principles and implications for impartial and neutral assistance. Coordination should occur at and between all levels of healthcare from national to community and with other sectors such as WASH, nutrition and education, as well as with cross-sectoral technical working groups such as mental health and psychosocial support, gender-based violence (GBV) and HIV.

Health systems standard 1.1:
Health service delivery

People have access to integrated quality healthcare that is safe, effective and patient-centred.

Key actions

1 ⟩ Provide sufficient and appropriate healthcare at the different levels of the health system.

- Prioritise health services at country level or at the closest operational level in acute emergencies, based on type of crisis, epidemiological profile and health system capacity.
- Identify different types of care that should be available at different levels (household, community, healthcare facility and hospital).

2 ⟩ Establish or strengthen triage mechanisms and referral systems.

- Implement protocols for triage at healthcare facilities or field locations in conflict situations, so that those requiring immediate attention are identified and quickly treated or stabilised before being referred and transported elsewhere for further care.
- Ensure effective referrals between levels of care and services, including protected and safe emergency transport services and between sectors such as nutrition or child protection.

3 ⟩ Adapt or use standardised protocols for healthcare, case management and rational drug use.

- Use national standards, including essential medicines lists, and adapt to the emergency context.
- Use international guidelines if national guidelines are outdated or not available.

4 ⟩ Provide healthcare that guarantees patients' rights to dignity, privacy, confidentiality, safety and informed consent.

- Ensure safety and privacy so that everyone may access care, including people with conditions often associated with stigma, such as HIV or sexually transmitted infections (STIs).

5 〉 Provide safe healthcare and prevent harm, adverse medical events
or abuse.

- Implement a system to report and review adverse medical events.
- Establish a policy to report any abuse or sexual violence.

6 〉 Use appropriate infection prevention and control (IPC) measures, including
minimum WASH standards and medical waste disposal mechanisms, in all
healthcare settings.

- During disease outbreaks such as cholera or Ebola, seek comprehensive
guidance from specialist bodies such as the World Health Organization
(WHO) UNICEF and Médecins Sans Frontières (MSF).

7 〉 Manage or bury the dead in a safe, dignified, culturally appropriate manner,
based on good public health practice.

Key indicators

Percentage of population that can access primary healthcare within one hour's walk from dwellings

- Minimum 80 per cent

Percentage of healthcare facilities that deliver prioritised health services

- Minimum 80 per cent

Number of inpatient beds (excluding maternity beds) per 10,000 people

- Minimum 18

Percentage of population requiring a referral seen at the next level of healthcare

Percentage of patients referred in adequate time

Guidance notes

Access to healthcare depends on availability of healthcare, including physical reach, acceptability and affordability for all.

Availability: Healthcare can be delivered through a combination of community-level, mobile and fixed healthcare facilities. The number, type and location of each will vary by context. A broad guideline for planning coverage of fixed healthcare facilities is:

- One healthcare facility per 10,000 people; and
- One district or rural hospital per 250,000 people.

These do not ensure adequate healthcare coverage in all settings, however. In rural areas, a better target may be one facility for 50,000 people, combined with community case management programmes and mobile clinics. In urban areas, secondary healthcare facilities may be the first point of access and therefore cover primary care for a larger population than 10,000.

Providing surge capacity for healthcare is critical in emergencies. Avoid duplicating existing services, which can waste resources and reduce trust in existing facilities. People need to confidently return to those facilities when temporary facilities close.

Monitor the utilisation rate of services. Low rates may indicate poor quality, direct or indirect cost barriers, preference for other services, overestimation of the population or other access problems. Higher rates may suggest a public health problem or underestimation of the target population, or may indicate access problems elsewhere. All data should be analysed by sex, age, disability, ethnic origin and other factors that may be relevant in context. To calculate utilisation rate ⊕ *see Appendix 3.*

Acceptability: Consult with all sections of the community to identify and address obstacles to accessing services by different parts of the community and all sides in a conflict, especially at-risk groups. Work with women, men, children, people living with and at high risk of HIV, persons with disabilities, and older people to understand health-seeking behaviour. Engaging with people in the design of healthcare will build patient engagement and improve timeliness of care.

Affordability: ⊕ *See Health systems standard 1.4: Health financing.*

Community-level care: Primary healthcare includes household and community care. Access to primary healthcare may be through community health workers (CHWs) or volunteers, peer educators, or in collaboration with village health committees to increase patient and community engagement. Care may range from prevention programmes to health promotion or case management and depends on context. All programmes should establish links with the nearest primary healthcare facility to ensure integrated care, clinical supervision and programme monitoring. If CHWs are screening for acute malnutrition, referral to nutrition services at healthcare facilities or other locations is needed ⊕ *see Food security and nutrition assessments standard 1.2: Nutrition assessment.* Integrate care with community programmes in other sectors such as WASH and nutrition ⊕ *see WASH hygiene promotion standard 1.1* and *Food security and nutrition – management of malnutrition standard 2.1.*

Emergency referral systems with pre-determined, safe and protected transport mechanisms should be available 24 hours a day, seven days a week. There should be a clinical handover between referrer and receiving healthcare provider.

Patients' rights: Design healthcare facilities and services to ensure privacy and confidentiality, such as with separate consultation rooms. Seek informed consent from patients or their guardians before medical or surgical procedures. Address any special considerations that can influence informed consent and safety, such as age, gender, disability, language or ethnicity. Establish patient feedback mechanisms as early as possible. Protect patient data ⊕ *see Health systems standard 1.5: Health information.*

Appropriate and safe facilities: Apply rational drug-use protocols and safe management of medicines and devices ⊕ *see Health systems standard 1.3: Essential medicines and medical devices.*

Ensure that facilities are suitable, even in emergencies. Ensure private spaces for consultations, organised patient flow, a 1-metre space between beds, ventilation, a sterilisation room (not open air) for hospitals, sufficient energy supply to support critical equipment, and adequate WASH structures. During disease outbreaks, review infrastructure requirements and guidance including, for example, triage, observation and isolation zones.

Devise measures to make healthcare facilities safe, protected and accessible during a crisis such as flooding or conflict.

Infection prevention and control (IPC) is key in all settings to prevent disease and antimicrobial resistance. Even in a non-crisis setting, globally 12 per cent of patients will develop an infection while receiving healthcare, and 50 per cent of infections after surgery are resistant to well-known antibiotics.

Core IPC components include producing and implementing guidelines (on standard precautions, transmission-based precautions and clinical aseptic techniques), having an IPC team in each setting, training healthcare workforce, monitoring programmes and incorporating detection of healthcare-associated infections and antimicrobial resistance into surveillance systems. Healthcare settings should have appropriate staffing and workload, bed occupancy (not more than one patient per bed), built environment and should maintain safe hygiene practice ⊕ *see Health systems standard 1.2: Healthcare workforce,* ⊕ *see Appropriate and safe facilities above,* WASH infrastructure and equipment, ⊕ *see WASH standard 6: WASH in healthcare settings.*

Standard precautions are a part of IPC measures and include:

- *Prevention of injuries from sharps:* Handle needles, scalpels and other sharps with care, for example when cleaning used instruments or disposing of used needles. Anyone with a sharps injury should be offered post-exposure prophylaxis (PEP) for HIV within 72 hours ⊕ *see Essential healthcare – sexual and reproductive health standard 2.3.3: HIV.*
- *Use of personal protective equipment (PPE):* Provide appropriate PPE based on risk and the task to be performed. Assess the type of exposure anticipated (for example, splash, spray, contact or touch) and the category of transmission of disease, the durability and appropriateness of the PPE for the task (such as fluid-resistant or fluid-proof), and the fit of the equipment. Additional PPE will depend on the type of transmission: contact (for example, gown or gloves), droplet (surgical masks need to be worn when within 1 metre of the patient)

or airborne (particulate respirators). ⊕ *See WASH standard 6: WASH in healthcare settings.*

- Other measures include hand hygiene, healthcare waste management, maintaining a clean environment, cleaning medical devices, respiratory and cough hygiene, and understanding principles of asepsis ⊕ *see WASH standard 6: WASH in healthcare settings.*

Adverse events: Globally, 10 per cent of hospital patients suffer an adverse event (even outside a humanitarian crisis), mostly from unsafe surgical procedures, medication errors and healthcare-associated infections. An adverse events register should be maintained at every healthcare facility and audited to promote learning.

Management of the dead: Use local customs and faith practices to respectfully manage the dead and identify and return remains to families. Whether an epidemic, natural disaster, conflict or mass killing, management of the dead requires coordination between health, WASH, legal, protection and forensic sectors.

Dead bodies rarely represent an immediate health risk. Certain diseases (for example cholera or Ebola) require special management. Recovery of the dead may require PPE, equipment for recovery, transportation and storage, as well as documentation. ⊕ *See WASH standard 6: WASH in healthcare settings.*

Healthcare systems standard 1.2:
Healthcare workforce
People have access to healthcare workers with adequate skills at all levels of healthcare.

Key actions

1 ⟩ Review existing staffing levels and distribution against national classifications to determine gaps and under-served areas.

- Track staffing levels per 1,000 people by function and place of employment.

2 ⟩ Train staff for their roles according to national standards or international guidelines.

- Recognise that staff in acute emergencies may have expanded roles and need training and support.
- Introduce refresher training where turnover is high.

3 ⟩ Support healthcare workers to operate in a safe working environment.

- Implement and advocate for all possible measures to protect healthcare workers in conflicts.

- Provide occupational health training and immunisations for hepatitis B and tetanus for clinical workers.
- Supply adequate IPC and PPE to carry out staff duties.

4 ⟩ Develop incentive and salary strategies that minimise pay differences and inequitable distribution of healthcare workers between MoH and other healthcare providers.

5 ⟩ Share healthcare workforce data and readiness information with MoH and other relevant bodies locally and nationally.

- Be aware of displacement and departure of healthcare workers during conflict.

Key indicators

Number of community health workers per 1,000 people

- Minimum 1–2 community health workers

Percentage of births attended by skilled personnel (doctors, nurses, midwives)

- minimum 80 per cent

Number of skilled birth attendant personnel (doctors, nurses, midwives) per 10,000 people

- minimum 23 per 10,000 people

All health staff performing clinical work have received training in clinical protocols and case management

Guidance notes

Availability of healthcare workers: The healthcare workforce includes medical doctors, nurses, midwives, clinical officers, laboratory technicians, pharmacists and CHWs, as well as management and support staff. The number and profile of workers should match the population and service needs. Understaffing can result in excessive workloads and unsafe healthcare. Integrate existing healthcare workers into the emergency response.

When recruiting and training local staff, follow national guidelines (or international if national are unavailable). International staff recruitment should follow national and MoH regulations (for example evidence of qualifications, especially for clinical practice).

Consider care for people in hard-to-reach rural and urban areas, including those close to conflict. Staff must provide care to people of all ethnicities, languages and affiliations. Recruit and train lower-level healthcare workers for community outreach, case management in mobile teams or health posts, and develop strong referral mechanisms. Incentive packages may be needed to work in difficult areas.

Community health workers (CHWs): Community programming with CHWs (including volunteers) increases access to hard-to-reach populations, including marginalised or stigmatised populations. If there are geographical constraints or acceptability issues in diverse communities, one CHW may only practically be able to serve 300 people rather than 500.

CHWs' work will vary. They may be trained in first aid or case management or may conduct health screening. They must be linked to the nearest healthcare facility to ensure appropriate oversight and integrated care. Often CHWs cannot be absorbed into the health system once the emergency subsides. In some contexts, CHWs may usually work only in rural settings, so a different model may be needed in urban crises.

Acceptability: Meeting people's sociocultural expectations will increase patient engagement. Staff should reflect the population's diversity with a mix of different socioeconomic, ethnic, language and sexual orientation groups, and an appropriate gender balance.

Quality: Organisations must train and supervise staff to ensure their knowledge is up to date and their practice is safe. Align training programmes with national guidelines (adapted for emergencies) or agreed international guidelines.

Include training on:

- clinical protocols and case management;
- standard operating procedures (such as IPC, medical waste management);
- security and safety (adapted to the level of risk); and
- codes of conduct (such as medical ethics, patients' rights, humanitarian principles, child safeguarding, protection from sexual exploitation and abuse) ⊕ *see Essential healthcare – sexual and reproductive health standard 2.3.2: Sexual violence and clinical management of rape* and *Protection Principles.*

Regular supervision and quality monitoring will encourage good practice. One-off training will not ensure good quality. Share records of who has been trained, in what, by whom, when and where with the MoH.

Health systems standard 1.3:
Essential medicines and medical devices
People have access to essential medicines and medical devices that are safe, effective and of assured quality.

Key actions

1 ⟩ Establish standardised essential medicine and medical device lists for priority healthcare.

- Review existing national essential medicines and medical device lists early in the response and adapt to the emergency context.

- Pay special attention to controlled medicines that may require special advocacy to ensure availability.

2 ⟩ Establish effective management systems to ensure availability of safe essential medicines and medical devices.

- Include transport, storage and cold chain for vaccines as well as for the collection and storage of blood products.

3 ⟩ Accept donations of medicine and medical devices only if they follow internationally recognised guidelines.

Key indicators

Number of days essential medicines are not available

- Maximum 4 days out of 30 days

Percentage of health facilities with essential medicines

- Minimum 80 per cent

Percentage of health facilities with functional essential medical devices

- Minimum 80 per cent

All medicines dispensed to patients are within the expiry date

Guidance notes

Managing essential medicines: Essential medicines include drugs, vaccines and blood products. Good medicine management ensures availability but also prohibits unsafe or expired medicines. The main management elements are selection, forecasting, procurement, storage and distribution.

Selection should be based on the national essential medicines list. Advocate to close any gaps such as for non-communicable diseases, reproductive health, pain relief for palliative care and surgery, anaesthesia, mental health, controlled drugs (see below) or others.

Forecasting should be based on consumption, morbidity data and context analysis. National medicine supplies may be disrupted if local manufacturing is affected, warehouses are damaged or international procurement is delayed, among other factors.

Procurement methods should adhere to national laws, customs regulations and quality assurance mechanisms for international procurement. Advocate for improved mechanisms if delays occur (through the MoH, lead agency, national disaster management authority or humanitarian coordinator). If systems do not exist, procure prequalified products, within expiry date and in the language of the country and healthcare workforce.

Storage: Medicines should be safely stored throughout the drug supply cycle. Requirements vary between products. Medicines should not be stored directly on the floor. Ensure separate areas for expired items (locked), flammable products (well ventilated, with fire protection), controlled substances (with added security) and products requiring cold chain or temperature control.

Distribution: Establish safe, protected, predictable and documented transport mechanisms from central stocks to healthcare facilities. Partners may use a push (automatic supply) or pull (supply on demand) system.

Safe disposal of expired medicines: Prevent environmental contamination and hazards to people. Comply with national regulations (adapted to emergencies) or international guidance. Ultra-high temperature incineration is costly, and pharmaceutical stockpiling works only in the short term ⊕ *see WASH standard 6: WASH in healthcare settings.*

Essential medical devices: Define and procure necessary devices and equipment (including laboratory reagents, larger machines) at each level of healthcare that are nationally or internationally compliant. Include assistive devices for persons with disabilities. Ensure safe use of devices, including regular maintenance and spare parts supply, preferably locally. Decommission devices safely. Distribute or replace lost assistive devices and provide clear information on use and maintenance. Refer to rehabilitation services for appropriate size, fitting, use and maintenance. Avoid one-off distribution.

Prequalified kits are useful in the early stages of a crisis or in pre-positioning for preparedness. They contain prequalified essential medicines and medical devices and vary according to health intervention. WHO is the lead provider for Interagency Emergency Health Kits and non-communicable disease kits, in addition to kits to manage diarrhoea, trauma and others. The United Nations Population Fund (UNFPA) is the lead provider of sexual and reproductive health kits.

Controlled drugs: Medicines for pain relief, mental health and post-partum bleeding are usually controlled. As 80 per cent of low-income countries do not have access to adequate pain relief medicines, advocate with the MoH and government to improve availability for controlled drugs.

Blood products: Coordinate with the national blood transfusion service, where it exists. Only collect blood from volunteers. Test all products for HIV, hepatitis B and C, and syphilis as a minimum, with blood grouping and compatibility testing. Store and distribute products safely. Train clinical staff in the rational use of blood and blood products.

Health systems standard 1.4:
Health financing

People have access to free priority healthcare for the duration of the crisis.

Key actions

1 ⟩ Plan for user fees to be abolished or temporarily suspended where they are charged through government systems.

2 ⟩ Reduce indirect costs or other financial barriers to reach and use services.

Key indicators

Percentage of healthcare facilities that do not charge user fees for priority healthcare (including consultations, treatment, investigations and provision of medicines)

- Target 100 per cent

Percentage of people not making any direct payment when accessing or using healthcare (including consultations, treatment, investigations and provision of medicines)

- Target 100 per cent

Guidance notes

User fees: Requiring payment for services during an emergency impedes access and may prevent people from seeking healthcare.

Suspending user fees for government healthcare providers will necessarily cause financial strain. Consider supporting MoH facilities or those of other responsible providers with staff salaries and incentives, extra medicines, medical devices and assistive devices. If user fees are temporarily suspended, ensure users get clear information about the timing and reasons, and monitor accessibility and service quality.

Indirect costs can be minimised by providing adequate services in communities and using planned mechanisms for transport and referral.

Cash-based assistance: The Universal Health Coverage 2030 targets state that people should receive healthcare without undue financial hardship. There is no clear evidence that using cash-based assistance specifically for health responses in humanitarian contexts has a positive impact on health outcomes, as of this edition ⊕ *see What is Sphere? including Delivering assistance through markets.*

Experience suggests that using cash-based assistance for health responses *may* help if:

- the emergency has stabilised;
- there is a predictable service to support, such as ant-enatal care or chronic disease management;
- there is existing positive health-seeking behaviour and high demand; and
- other critical household needs such as food and shelter have been met.

Health systems standard 1.5:
Health information

Healthcare is guided by evidence through the collection, analysis and use of relevant public health data.

Key actions

1 > Strengthen or develop a health information system that provides sufficient, accurate and up-to-date information for effective and equitable health response.

- Ensure the health information system includes all stakeholders, is simple to implement and simple to collect, analyse and interpret information to steer response.

2 > Strengthen or develop disease Early Warning, Alert and Response (EWAR) mechanisms for all hazards that require an immediate response.

- Decide which priority diseases and events to include based on the epidemiological risk profile and context of the emergency.
- Incorporate both indicator- and event-based components.

3 > Agree on and use common operating data and definitions.

- Consider denominator figures, such as population, family size and age disaggregation.
- Establish administrative areas and geographic codes.

4 > Agree standard operating procedures for all health actors when using health information.

5 > Ensure mechanisms to protect data to guarantee the rights and safety of individuals, reporting units and/or populations.

6 > Support the lead actor to compile, analyse, interpret and disseminate health information to all stakeholders in a timely and regular manner, and to guide decision-making for health programmes.

- Include coverage and utilisation of health services, and analysis and interpretation of epidemiological data.

Key indicators

Percentage of complete Early Warning, Alert and Response (EWAR)/surveillance reports submitted on time

- Minimum 80 per cent

Frequency of health information reports produced by the lead health actor

- Minimum monthly

Guidance notes

Health information system: A well-functioning health information system ensures the production, analysis, dissemination and use of reliable and timely information on health determinants, health systems performance and health status. Data may be qualitative or quantitative and collected from various sources such as census surveys, vital registration, population surveys, perceived needs surveys, individual records and healthcare facility reports (such as health management information systems). It should be flexible enough to incorporate and reflect unexpected challenges such as outbreaks or the total collapse of the health system or services. Information will identify problems and needs at all levels of the health system.

Collect missing information through further assessment or surveys. Consider cross-border movement of people, and the information needed or available. Provide regular analysis on who is doing what and where.

Health management information systems (HMIS) or routine reporting use health information generated from healthcare facilities to assess healthcare delivery performance. An HMIS monitors delivery of specific interventions, treatment of conditions, resources such as tracer drug availability, human resources and utilisation rates.

Health surveillance is the continuous and systematic collection, analysis and interpretation of health data. Disease surveillance specifically monitors different diseases and patterns of progression and is often captured in HMIS reporting.

Early Warning Alert and Response (EWAR) is part of a routine health surveillance system. It detects and generates an alert for any public health event that needs an immediate response, such as chemical poisoning or epidemic prone diseases ⊕ *see Essential healthcare – communicable diseases standard 2.1.2: Surveillance, outbreak detection and early response.*

Standard operating procedures: Establish common definitions and ways of conveying information across geographical locations, levels of care and health actors. As a minimum, agree on:

- case definitions;
- indicators of what to monitor;
- reporting units (such as mobile clinics, field hospitals, health posts);

- reporting pathways; and
- frequency of data submission, analysis and reporting.

Disaggregation of data: Health information data should be disaggregated by sex, age, disability, displaced and host populations, context (such as camp/non-camp situation) and administrative level (region, district) to guide decision-making and detect inequity for at-risk groups.

For EWAR, disaggregate mortality and morbidity data for children under and over age five years. The aim is to quickly generate an alert; less detailed data is acceptable. Outbreak investigations data, contact tracing, line listing and further monitoring of disease trends must have disaggregated data.

Data management, security and confidentiality: Take adequate precautions to protect the safety of the individual and the data. Staff should never share patient information with anyone not directly involved in the patient's care without the patient's permission. Give consideration to persons with intellectual, mental or sensory impairment that may affect their ability to give informed consent. Be aware that many people living with conditions such as HIV may not have disclosed their status to their close family members. Treat data that relates to injury caused by torture or other human rights violations, including sexual assault, with care. Consider passing such information to appropriate actors or institutions if the individual gives informed consent ⊕ *see Protection Principle 1* and *Core Humanitarian Standard Commitment 4*.

Threats to healthcare: Threats to healthcare workers, or any violent incidents involving healthcare workers should be reported using agreed local and national mechanisms ⊕ *see Essential concepts in health (above)* and *References and further reading (below)*.

2. Essential healthcare

Essential healthcare addresses the major causes of mortality and morbidity in a crisis-affected population. Coordinate with the ministries of health and other official health actors to agree on which services to prioritise, when and where. Base priorities on context, risk assessment and available evidence.

A crisis-affected population will have new and different needs, which will continue to evolve. People may face overcrowding, multiple displacements, malnutrition, lack of access to water, or continuing conflict. Age, gender, disability, HIV status, linguistic or ethnic identity can further influence needs and may be significant barriers to accessing care. Consider the needs of those living in under-served or hard-to-reach locations.

Agree on priority services with the MoH and other health actors, focusing on those risks most likely to occur and cause the greatest morbidity and mortality. Health programmes should provide appropriate, effective care, taking into account the context, logistics and resources that will be needed. Priorities may change as the context improves or deteriorates further. This exercise should be conducted regularly, based on available information and as the context changes.

Once mortality rates have declined or a situation has stabilised, more comprehensive health services may be feasible. In protracted settings this may be an essential package of health services, defined at country level.

This section outlines the essential minimum healthcare in key areas of emergency response: communicable diseases, child health, sexual and reproductive health, injury and trauma care, mental health, non-communicable diseases and palliative care.

2.1 Communicable diseases

A humanitarian crisis, whether caused by a natural disaster, conflict or famine, often brings increased morbidity and mortality from communicable diseases. People moving into crowded communal settlements or shelters means that diseases such as diarrhoea and measles spread easily. Damage to sanitation facilities or a lack of clean water means that water- and vector-borne diseases are transmitted rapidly. Reduced population immunity results in increased susceptibility to disease. A breakdown of health systems can interrupt long-term treatment, such as for HIV and tuberculosis (TB) provision of routine immunisations, and treatment of simple conditions such as respiratory infections.

Acute respiratory infections, diarrhoea, measles and malaria still account for the largest morbidity in crisis-affected populations. Acute malnutrition worsens these diseases, especially in children under age five years, and in older people.

The objective in a crisis is to prevent communicable diseases from the beginning, to manage any cases, and to ensure a rapid and appropriate response if there is an outbreak. Interventions to address communicable diseases should include prevention, surveillance, outbreak detection, diagnosis and case management, and outbreak response.

Communicable diseases standard 2.1.1: Prevention

People have access to healthcare and information to prevent communicable diseases.

Key actions

1 ⟩ Determine the risk of communicable diseases in the affected population.

- Review pre-existing health information if available and surveillance data as well as nutritional status and access to safe water and sanitation.
- Conduct risk assessments with the affected population, including local leaders and health professionals.

2 ⟩ Work with other sectors to develop general prevention measures and establish integrated health promotion programmes at community level.

- Address specific fears, rumours and common beliefs that could undermine healthy behaviour.
- Coordinate with other sectors performing outreach, such as hygiene promoters or community nutrition workers, to ensure harmonised messaging.

3 ⟩ Implement vaccination measures to prevent disease.

- Determine the need for vaccination campaigns for specific communicable diseases based on risk, feasibility and context.
- Resume delivery of routine vaccination via pre-existing immunisation programme as soon as possible.

4 ⟩ Implement disease-specific prevention measures as needed.

- Provide and ensure all inpatients use long-lasting insecticide-treated nets (LLINs) in any malaria zone.

5 ⟩ Implement infection prevention and control (IPC) measures at all levels of healthcare according to risk ⊕ *see Health systems standard 1.1* and WASH support in *WASH standard 6: WASH in healthcare settings*.

Key indicators

Percentage of people who adopt key practices promoted in health education activities and messages

Percentage of affected households who report that they have received appropriate information on communicable disease-related risks and preventive action

Percentage of affected households who can describe three measures they are taking to prevent communicable diseases

All inpatients in healthcare settings use long-lasting insecticide nets (LLINs) in malarial zones

Incidence of major communicable diseases is stable or not increasing against pre-crisis level

Guidance notes

Risk assessments: Conduct risk assessments with the affected population, local leaders and health professionals. Analyse risks posed by the context and environment, such as in crowded communal settlements and urban areas. Actively consider different segments of the population for disease-specific factors, low immunity or other risks.

Inter-sectoral prevention measures: Develop general prevention measures such as appropriate hygiene, waste disposal, safe and sufficient water and vector management. Adequate shelter, spacing of shelters and ventilation can help reduce transmission. Exclusive breastfeeding and access to adequate nutrition contributes directly to health status ⊕ *see Core Humanitarian Standard Commitment 3, WASH hygiene promotion standard 1.1, WASH water supply standards 2.1 and 2.2, WASH solid waste management standards 5.1 to 5.3, Shelter and settlement standard 2* and *Food security and nutrition – infant and young child feeding standards 4.1 and 4.2.*

Health promotion: Engage communities to provide information in formats and languages that are accessible for older people, persons with disabilities, women and children. Take the time to test and validate messages on sensitive issues.

Vaccination: The decision to implement a vaccination campaign will be based on three factors:

- An **assessment of general risk factors** such as malnutrition, high burden of chronic disease, overcrowding, inadequate WASH conditions, and disease-specific risks such as geography, climate, season and population immunity.
- The **feasibility of a campaign**, based on an assessment of the characteristics of the vaccine, including availability, efficacy, safety, whether it is single or multiple antigens, oral or injection, and its stability. Consider operational factors such as access to population, time constraints, transport, material requirements, cost and the ability to gain informed consent.
- The **general context**, including ethical and practical constraints such as community opposition, inequities due to lack of resources and political or security constraints, or known threats against vaccinators.

⊕ *See Essential healthcare – child health standard 2.2.1: Childhood vaccine-preventable diseases* and *Vaccination in Acute Humanitarian Crises: A Framework for Decision Making, WHO, 2017*, which covers 23 antigens, including cholera, meningitis, measles and rotavirus.

Prevention of malaria: Where there is high to moderate malaria transmission, provide LLINs to severely malnourished people and households, pregnant women, children under age five years, unaccompanied children and people living with HIV. Then prioritise people in supplementary feeding programmes, households with children under age five and households of pregnant women. Give pregnant women chemoprophylaxis according to national protocols and resistance patterns. In areas with high malnutrition and measles mortality, consider targeted seasonal malaria chemoprophylaxis.

Aedes mosquito-transmitted diseases: Dengue fever, chikungunya, Zika virus and yellow fever are spread by the *Aedes* mosquito. Prevent disease through integrated vector management. Individuals should wear clothing to prevent being bitten, and households should use good water and waste management practices and repellents or LLINs for young children and infants sleeping during the day ⊕ *see WASH vector control standard 4.2: Household and personal actions to control vectors.*

Communicable diseases standard 2.1.2:
Surveillance, outbreak detection and early response
Surveillance and reporting systems provide early outbreak detection and early response.

Key actions

1 〉 Strengthen or establish a context-specific disease Early Warning Alert and Response (EWAR) mechanism.

- Decide priority diseases and events to be included, based on epidemiological risk.
- Train healthcare workers at all levels about priority diseases and mechanisms to notify health authorities and generate an alert.
- Disseminate weekly EWAR reports to all stakeholders to take necessary action.

2 〉 Establish outbreak investigation teams.

- Ensure actions are triggered rapidly when an alert is generated.
- Initiate remote investigation where teams do not have access to the affected populations, such as in active conflict areas.

3 〉 Ensure samples can be tested by rapid diagnostic tests or laboratories to confirm an outbreak ⊕ *see Essential healthcare – communicable diseases standard 2.1.3: Diagnosis and case management.*

Key indicators

Percentage of alerts being reported within in 24 hours

- 90 per cent

Percentage of reported alerts being verified within 24 hours

- 90 per cent

Percentage of verified alerts being investigated within 24 hours

- 90 per cent

Guidance notes

Early Warning Alert and Response (EWAR): In coordination with all stakeholders, including MoH, partners and community, strengthen or establish an EWAR system representative of the affected population ⊕ *see Health systems standard 1.5: Health information.* The system should be able to capture rumours, unusual events and community reports.

Surveillance and early warning: Strengthen the EWAR system with partners, and agree on reporting units, data flow, reporting tools, data analysis tools, case definitions and frequency of reporting.

Alert generation and reporting: Alerts are unusual health events that may signal the early stages of an outbreak. Define alert thresholds specific to each disease and report as quickly as possible. Use event-based immediately notifiable reporting by healthcare workers or analyse indicator-based reports (weekly or more frequently). Log all alerts immediately and relay them to outbreak investigation teams to verify.

Alert verification: Verify the alert information within 24 hours. Verification can be done remotely, such as by phone, and involves collecting further data and analysing the case(s) based on symptoms, date of onset, place, sex, age, health outcomes and differential diagnoses.

Outbreak detection: If an alert is verified, conduct a field investigation within 24 hours. Ensure teams have sufficient skills to verify alerts, perform field investigation, detect a suspected outbreak and take laboratory samples. The investigation will confirm an outbreak if an epidemic threshold has been reached or determine whether the alert reflects sporadic cases or seasonal peaks.

Review cases, take samples and conduct a risk assessment. Possible outcomes are:

- it is not a case;
- a case is confirmed, but it is not an outbreak; or
- a case is confirmed and an outbreak is suspected/confirmed.

Some outbreaks can only be confirmed by laboratory analysis; however, even suspected outbreaks may still need immediate action.

Alert and outbreak thresholds

	Alert threshold	Outbreak threshold
Cholera	2 cases with acute watery diarrhoea and severe dehydration in people age 2 or above, or dying from acute watery diarrhoea in the same area within one week of each other 1 death from severe acute watery diarrhoea in a person age 5 or above 1 case of acute watery diarrhoea, testing positive for cholera by rapid diagnostic tests in an area	1 confirmed case
Malaria	Decided at country level depending on context	Decided at country level depending on context
Measles	1 case	Defined at country level
Meningitis	2 cases in one week (in a population <30,000) 3 cases in a week (in a population of 30,000–100,000)	5 cases in a week (in a population of <30,000) 10 cases per 100,000 people in a week (in a population of 30,000–100,000) 2 confirmed cases in one week in a camp
Viral haemorrhagic fevers	1 case	1 case
Yellow fever	1 case	1 case

Outbreak investigation and early response: Investigate further if an outbreak is confirmed or suspected. Determine the cause/source, who has been affected, modes of transmission and who is at risk, in order to take appropriate control measures.

Perform descriptive epidemiology investigations, including:

- cases, deaths and person, time and place of onset, to develop an epidemic curve and spot map;
- line listings which follow each case and analyse the extent of outbreak, for example number of hospitalisations, complications, case fatality rate; and
- calculating attack rates based on agreed population figures.

Develop a hypothesis that explains exposure and disease. Consider pathogen, source and route of transmission.

Evaluate the hypothesis and agree an outbreak case definition. This may be more specific than a case definition used for surveillance. Once laboratory investigations have confirmed an outbreak from numerous sources, follow the outbreak case definition; there may be no need to continue to collect samples.

Communicate and update findings promptly and regularly. Implement population-based control measures as soon as possible.

All of these activities may occur at the same time, especially during an ongoing outbreak ⊕ *see Essential healthcare – communicable diseases standard 2.1.4: Outbreak preparedness and response.*

Communicable diseases standard 2.1.3: Diagnosis and case management

People have access to effective diagnosis and treatment for infectious diseases that contribute most significantly to morbidity and mortality.

Key actions

1 ⟩ Develop clear messages that encourage people to seek care for symptoms such as fever, cough and diarrhoea.

- Develop written materials, radio broadcasts or mobile phone messages using accessible formats and languages.

2 ⟩ Use approved standard case management protocols to provide healthcare.

- Consider implementing community-based case management such as for malaria, diarrhoea and pneumonia.
- Refer severe cases to higher levels of care or isolation.

3 ⟩ Provide adequate laboratory and diagnostic capacity, supplies and quality assurance.

- Determine the use of rapid diagnostic tests or laboratory testing for pathogens, and at which level of healthcare it should be provided (for example, rapid diagnostic tests in the community).

4 ⟩ Ensure treatment is not disrupted for people receiving long-term care for communicable diseases such as TB and HIV.

- Introduce TB control programmes only after recognised criteria are met.
- Coordinate with HIV programmes to ensure healthcare provision for those with HIV–TB co-infection.

Key indicators

Percentage of health centres supporting a crisis-affected population using standardised treatment protocols for a specified illness

- Use monthly record review to monitor trends

Percentage of suspected cases confirmed by a diagnostic method as determined by an agreed protocol

Guidance notes

Treatment protocols: Protocols should include a package of diagnosis, treatment and referral. If no such package is available in a crisis, consider international guidance. Understand local drug-resistance patterns (also considering displacement), especially for malaria, TB and typhoid. Consider clinically high-risk groups such as children under age two years, pregnant women, older people, people living with HIV and acutely malnourished children, who are at higher risk for certain communicable diseases.

Acute respiratory infections: In crises, vulnerability is increased by overcrowding, indoor smoke and poor ventilation, and malnutrition and/or vitamin A deficiency. Reduce case fatality rates through timely identification, oral antibiotics and referral of severe cases.

Diarrhoea and bloody diarrhoea: Control mortality rates through increased access to and use of oral rehydration therapy and zinc supplementation at household, community or primary healthcare level. Treatment can be at community oral rehydration points.

Community case management: Patients with malaria, pneumonia or diarrhoea can be treated by trained CHWs. Ensure all programmes are linked and overseen from the nearest healthcare facility. Ensure equitable and impartial access for all.

Laboratory testing: Establish a referral network of national, regional and international laboratory facilities to test specimens. Ensure rapid diagnostic testing for malaria, cholera and dengue fever, plus testing of blood haemoglobin level. Provide appropriate transport media for samples to be tested for other pathogens (such as Cary-Blair medium for cholera).

Train healthcare workers in diagnostic methods, quality assurance, and specimen collection, transport and documentation. Develop a protocol for definitive testing at reference laboratories nationally, regionally or internationally. Definitive testing includes cultures from specimens, serological and antigen testing or RNA testing for yellow fever, viral haemorrhagic fevers and hepatitis E. Establish protocols on safe transport mechanisms for pathogens, especially for viral haemorrhagic fever, plague or similar. Consider aviation regulations for transport of specimens by air.

Tuberculosis (TB) control is complex because of increasing drug resistance. Only establish programmes if continuous access to the population and provision of care is assured for at least 12–15 months. Multi-drug-resistant TB (MDR TB, resistant to two core anti-TB drugs, isoniazid and rifampicin) and extensively drug-resistant TB (EDR TB, resistant to four core anti-TB drugs) have been identified. Both these types require longer, more expensive and more complex treatments. In crises, it is often difficult to access the diagnostic and sensitivity testing necessary to ensure correct selection and use of TB medications.

Communicable diseases standard 2.1.4:
Outbreak preparedness and response

Outbreaks are adequately prepared for and controlled in a timely and effective manner.

Key actions

1 > Develop and disseminate an integrated outbreak preparedness and response plan in partnership with all stakeholders and sectors.

- Focus training on key staff in high-risk areas.
- Pre-position essential medicines, medical devices, rapid tests, PPE and kits (such as for cholera and diarrhoeal disease) in epidemic-prone areas and areas with limited access.

2 > Implement disease-specific control measures once an outbreak is detected.

- Determine the need for a targeted vaccination campaign.
- Scale up IPC measures, including providing isolation areas for cholera, hepatitis E or other outbreaks.

3 > Create and coordinate outbreak-specific logistic and response capacity.

- Ensure transport and storage capacity for medicines and supplies, including cold chain for vaccines.
- Add healthcare facility capacity, such as cholera or meningitis tents.
- Ensure access and transport to laboratories at local, national and international levels to test samples.

4 > Coordinate with other sectors as needed, including child protection.

Key indicators

Percentage of health staff in high-risk areas trained on outbreak response plan and protocols

Case fatality rate is reduced to an acceptable level

- Cholera <1 per cent
- Meningitis <15 per cent
- Hepatitis E <4 per cent in general population, 10–50 per cent in pregnant women in third trimester
- Diphtheria (respiratory) <5–10 per cent
- Pertussis <4 per cent in children aged one year, <1 per cent in those aged one to four years
- Dengue <1 per cent

Guidance notes

Outbreak preparedness and response plan: Develop this with health partners, MoH, community members and leaders. WASH, nutrition, shelter and education partners, the host government, prisons and military (if relevant) should also be involved. Ensure that other critical health services are not compromised when responding to the outbreak.

The plan should define:

- outbreak response coordination mechanism at national, subnational and community level;
- mechanisms for community mobilisation and risk communication;
- strengthening EWAR: disease surveillance, outbreak detection, outbreak (epidemiological) investigation;
- case management;
- control measures specific to disease and context;
- cross-sectoral measures;
- protocols on safe transport and referral pathways of samples for laboratory investigation;
- contingency plans for scaling up services at different levels of care, including establishing isolation areas in treatment centres;
- outbreak control team capacities and surge healthcare worker requirements; and
- availability of essential medicines, vaccines, medical devices, laboratory supplies and PPE for healthcare workers, including international procurement (for example, global stockpile of vaccines).

Outbreak control relies on adequate risk communication and dedicated outbreak control teams. Contain the outbreak comprehensively so it does not spread to new areas and to reduce the number of new cases where an outbreak is occurring. This will require active case finding and prompt diagnosis and case management. Provide isolation areas as needed (for example, for cholera or hepatitis E). Improve vector control to reduce exposure to infection, use LLINs and improved hygiene behaviour.

Vaccination campaigns

Meningitis: Serogroups A, C, W and Y can cause outbreaks in crises. Vaccines for A and C are available for use in epidemics. Routine vaccination in crises is not recommended and not possible for serogroups C and W. Target vaccination at specific age groups based on known attack rates, or at those aged six months to 30 years. Given the need for lumbar puncture for a definitive diagnosis, establish a clear case definition.

Viral haemorrhagic fever: The management and diagnosis of viral haemorrhagic fevers, such as Ebola or Lassa fever, are based on stringent national and international guidelines. This includes protocols on new vaccines and innovative treatment methods. Effective community engagement during these outbreaks is vital.

Yellow fever: Mass vaccination is recommended once a single case is confirmed in a settlement for displaced and host populations. Combine this with *Aedes* vector control measures and strict isolation of cases.

Polio: Polio is included in the WHO Expanded Programme on Immunization (EPI), and vaccination should be restarted following the initial stages of an emergency. Initiate mass vaccination if a case of paralytic polio is detected.

Cholera: Clear treatment and outbreak protocols should be available and coordinated across sectors. Use cholera vaccines according to the WHO framework and complement existing strategies for cholera control.

Hepatitis A and E: These present a significant risk, particularly in refugee camps. Prevent and control outbreaks using improved sanitation and hygiene and access to safe water.

Measles: ⊕ *See Essential healthcare – child health standard 2.2.1: Childhood vaccine-preventable diseases.*

Pertussis or diphtheria: Pertussis outbreaks are common when people are displaced. Due to concerns about risks among older recipients of the whole-cell diphtheria, pertussis and tetanus (DPT) vaccine, be careful about a pertussis outbreak-related vaccination campaign. Use an outbreak to address routine immunisation gaps. Case management includes antibiotic treatment of cases and early prophylactic treatment of contacts in households where there is an infant or a pregnant woman. Diphtheria outbreaks are less common but still a threat in crowded settings with low diphtheria immunity. In camps, mass diphtheria vaccination campaigns with three separate doses of vaccine are not unknown. Case management includes the administration of both antitoxin and antibiotic.

Case fatality rates: The acceptable case fatality rate CFR for specific diseases varies with context and existing immunity. Aim to reduce case fatality rates as much as possible. High case fatality rates may indicate a lack of access to appropriate healthcare, late presentation and case management, significant co-morbidities in the population, or poor-quality healthcare. Monitor the case fatality rate frequently and take immediate corrective steps if higher than expected.

Care of children: During outbreaks, consider children to be a specific group when designing and implementing programmes. Coordinate and refer between the health and child protection sectors. Address the risks of separating children from their parents. The risks may be caused by morbidity and mortality of the parents or by programme design. Focus on preventing family separation and ensure parental or child consent for treatment. Take measures to keep education facilities open, being mindful of necessary control measures and health education.

2.2 Essential healthcare – child health

During crises, children are even more vulnerable to infections, diseases and other risks to their health and lives. Not only have living conditions deteriorated, but immunisation programmes are also interrupted. The risks are even higher for unaccompanied and separated children.

A concerted child-focused response is required. Initially this will focus on life-saving care, but ultimately interventions must alleviate suffering and promote growth and development. Programmes should address the major causes of morbidity and mortality. Globally these risks are acute respiratory infections, diarrhoea, measles, malaria, malnutrition and neonatal causes of morbidity and mortality.

Child health standard 2.2.1:
Childhood vaccine-preventable diseases
Children aged six months to 15 years have immunity against disease and access to routine Expanded Programme on Immunization (EPI) services during crises.

Key actions

1 > Determine whether there is a need for vaccinations, and the appropriate approach for the emergency.

- Base this on an assessment of risk (for example population, season), feasability of a campaign (including need for mutliple doses, availibility), and context (such as security, competing needs). This should be an ongoing process as a crisis evolves ⊕ *see Essential healthcare – communicable diseases standard 2.1.1: Prevention.*

2 > Conduct a mass measles vaccination campaign for children aged six months to 15 years, regardless of measles vaccination history, when estimated measles coverage is less than 90 per cent or unknown.

- Include vitamin A for children age 6–59 months.
- Ensure that all infants vaccinated between six and nine months receive another dose of measles vaccine at nine months.

3 > Re-establish the EPI defined on p.401 and 402 EPI as soon as possible.

- Aim for primary healthcare facilities or systems of mobile teams/outreach to offer the national immunisation schedule for vaccine-preventable diseases at least 20 days per month.

4 > Screen children attending healthcare facilities or mobile clinics for vaccination status and administer any needed vaccinations.

Key indicators

Percentage of children aged six months to 15 years who have received measles vaccination, on completion of a measles vaccination campaign

- >95 per cent

Percentage of children aged six to 59 months who have received an appropriate dose of vitamin A, on completion of measles vaccination campaign

- >95 per cent

Percentage of children aged 12 months who have had three doses of DPT

- >90 per cent

Percentage of primary healthcare facilities that offer basic EPI services at least 20 days/month

Guidance notes

Vaccination: Vaccines are vital in preventing excess deaths in acute crises. National guidance may not cover emergencies or people who have crossed borders, so work without delay to determine needed vaccines and create an implementation plan that includes procurement processes. ⊕ *See Essential healthcare – communicable diseases standard 2.1.1* for guidance on risk assessment and vaccination decisions and *Health systems standard 1.3: Essential medicines and medical devices* on the procurement and storage of vaccines.

Measles vaccination: Measles immunisation is a priority health intervention in crises.

- *Coverage:* Review coverage data for displaced and host populations to assess if routine measles immunisation coverage or measles campaign coverage has been higher than 90 per cent for the preceding three years. Carry out a measles campaign if vaccination coverage is less than 90 per cent, unknown or in doubt. Administer vitamin A supplementation at the same time. Ensure that at least 95 per cent of newcomers to a settlement aged between six months and 15 years are vaccinated.
- *Age ranges:* Some older children may have missed routine vaccination, measles campaigns and the measles disease itself. These children remain at risk of measles infection and can infect infants and young children, who are at higher risk of dying from the disease. Therefore, vaccinate up to the age of 15 years. If this is not possible, prioritise children aged 6–59 months.
- *Repeat vaccinations:* All children aged nine months to 15 years should receive two doses of measles vaccine as part of standard national immunisation programmes. Children between six and nine months who have received the measles vaccine (for example, in an emergency

campaign) should receive a further two doses at the recommended ages according to the national schedule (usually nine months and 15 months in high-risk areas).

Polio: Consider polio campaigns where polio outbreaks or threats to eradication programmes exist, as determined in *Vaccination in Acute Humanitarian Crises: A Framework for Decision Making* ⊕ *see Essential healthcare – communicable diseases standard 2.1.1: Prevention.*

National EPI programme: Re-establish EPI promptly to protect children against measles, diphtheria and pertussis and reduce the risk of respiratory infections. National EPI programmes may need supplemental vaccines ⊕ *see Essential healthcare – communicable diseases standard 2.1.4: Outbreak preparedness and response.*

Vaccine safety: Ensure the safety of vaccines at all times. Follow the manufacturer's instructions for storage and refrigeration ⊕ *see Health systems standard 1.3: Essential medicines and medical devices.*

Informed consent: Obtain informed consent from parents or guardians to administer vaccine. This includes an understanding of risks and potential side effects.

Child health standard 2.2.2:
Management of newborn and childhood illness

Children have access to priority healthcare that addresses the major causes of newborn and childhood morbidity and mortality.

Key actions

1 〉 Provide appropriate healthcare at different levels (facility, mobile clinics or community programmes).

- Use 'Newborn Health in Humanitarian Settings' guidelines for essential newborn care ⊕ *see References.*
- Consider adopting integrated community case management (iCCM) and Integrated Management of Childhood Illness (IMCI).

2 〉 Establish a standardised system of assessment and triage at all facilities that provide care for sick newborns or children.

- Ensure that children with danger signs (unable to drink or breastfeed, vomits everything, convulsions, and lethargic or unconscious) receives immediate treatment.
- Include assessment of trauma and chemical poisoning in contexts where there is increased risk.

3 〉 Make essential medicines available in the appropriate dosages and formulations for treating common childhood illnesses at all levels of care.

4 〉 Screen children for their growth and nutritional status.

- Refer all malnourished children to nutritional services.
- Provide facility-based treatment for children suffering from severe acute malnutrition with complications.

5 〉 Establish an appropriate case management protocol for treating childhood and vaccine-preventable diseases, such as diphtheria and pertussis, in situations where the risk of outbreak is high.

- Use existing protocols where possible.

6 〉 Design health education messages to encourage families to engage in healthy behaviour and disease preventive practices.

- Promote actions such as exclusive breastfeeding, infant feeding, handwashing, keeping infants warm and encourage early childhood development.

7 〉 Design health education messages to encourage people to seek early care for any illness such as fever, cough or diarrhoea among children and newborns.

- Take steps to reach children who do not have an adult or parent caring for them.

8 〉 Identify children with a disability or developmental delay.

- Provide advice on and referrals to care or rehabilitation services.

....

Key indicators

Under-five crude mortality rates

- Fewer than 2 deaths per 10,000 per day ⊕ *see Appendix 3 for calculations*

Effective anti-malarial treatment provided in a timely manner to all children under age five years presenting with malaria

- Within 24 hours of the onset of symptoms
- Exception for children under age five years experiencing severe acute malnutrition

Oral rehydration salts (ORS) and zinc supplementation provided in a timely manner to all children under age five years presenting with diarrhoea

- Within 24 hours of the onset of symptoms

Appropriate care provided in a timely manner to all children under age five years presenting with pneumonia

- Within 24 hours of the onset of symptoms

Guidance notes

Essential newborn care: Provide all newborns with skilled care at birth, preferably in a healthcare facility and according to the ⊕ *see* 'Integrated Management of Pregnancy and Childbirth' (IMPAC) and 'Newborn Health in Humanitarian Settings' guidelines. Whether the birth takes place with or without skilled care, essential newborn care consists of:

- thermal care (delay bathing, and keep the baby dry and warm with skin-to-skin contact);
- infection prevention (promote clean birth practices, handwashing, clean cord, and skin and eye care);
- feeding support (immediate and exclusive breastfeeding, not discarding colostrum);
- monitoring (assess for danger signs of infections or conditions that may need referral); and
- post-natal care (provide it at or close to home in the first week of life, with the first 24 hours being the most critical for a post-natal care visit; aim for three home visits in the first week of life).

Integrated management of childhood illness (IMCI) focuses on the care of children under age five years at a primary healthcare level. After establishing IMCI, incorporate clinical guidelines into standard protocols and train health professionals properly.

Integrated community case management (iCCM) is an approach to provide timely and effective treatment of malaria, pneumonia and diarrhoea to people with limited access to healthcare facilities, especially to children under age five years.

Management of diarrhoea: Treat children with diarrhoea with low osmolality oral rehydration salts (ORS) and zinc supplementations. Zinc shortens the duration of diarrhoea, and ORS prevents dehydration. Encourage caregivers to continue or increase breastfeeding during the episode, and to increase all feeding after.

Management of pneumonia: If children have a cough, assess for fast or difficult breathing and chest indrawing. If present, treat with an appropriate oral antibiotic. Refer those with danger signs or severe pneumonia for priority care.

Fast breathing rates are age-specific:

Birth – 2 months: >60/min	12 months: >50/min
1–5 years: >40/min	5 years: >20/min

HIV: Where HIV prevalence is greater than 1 per cent, test all children with severe acute malnutrition. Mothers and caregivers of HIV-exposed infants require adapted support and advice ⊕ *see Food security and nutrition standards.*

Feeding separated children: Arrange supervised feeding for separated or unaccompanied children.

Child protection concerns: Use routine health services to identify child neglect, abuse and exploitation. Refer cases to child protection services. Integrate identification and gender-sensitive case management procedures into routine health services for mothers and infants, children and adolescents.

Nutrition referrals: ⊕ *See Food security and nutrition standard 3: Micronutrient deficiencies*, and *Management of malnutrition standard 2.2: Severe acute malnutrition.*

Household air pollution: Consider providing alternative cooking stoves to reduce smoke and fumes and the respiratory illness they cause ⊕ *see Shelter and settlement standard 3: Living space and standard 4: Household items.*

Poisoning: ⊕ *See Appendix 4.*

2.3 Sexual and reproductive health

From the onset of a crisis, critical life-saving sexual and reproductive care must be available. Establish comprehensive services as soon as feasible.

These critical services are part of an integrated health response and aided by the use of reproductive health kits ⊕ *see Health systems standard 1.3: Essential medicines and medical devices.*

Comprehensive sexual and reproductive healthcare involves upgrading existing services, adding missing services and enhancing quality. Understanding the health systems architecture will help determine how to support this ⊕ *see Health systems standards 1.1 to 1.5.*

All individuals, including those in humanitarian settings, have the right to sexual and reproductive health. Sexual and reproductive healthcare must respect the cultural backgrounds and religious beliefs of the community while meeting universally recognised international human rights standards. Be sensitive to the needs of adolescents, older people, persons with disabilities and at-risk populations, regardless of sexual orientation or gender identity.

Emergencies elevate risks of sexual violence, including exploitation and abuse. All actors should work together to prevent and respond, in close coordination with the protection sector. Compile information safely and ethically. Share data only according to agreed protocols ⊕ *see Protection Principles* and *Health systems standard 1.5: Health information.*

Sexual and reproductive health standard 2.3.1: Reproductive, maternal and newborn healthcare

People have access to healthcare and family planning that prevents excessive maternal and newborn morbidity and mortality.

Key actions

1 ⟩ Ensure that clean and safe delivery, essential newborn care, and emergency obstetric and newborn care services are available at all times.

- Establish a referral system with communication and transportation from the community to the healthcare facility or hospital that functions at all times.

2 ⟩ Provide all visibly pregnant women with clean delivery packages when access to skilled health providers and healthcare facilities cannot be guaranteed.

3 ⟩ Consult the community to understand local preferences, practices and attitudes towards contraception.

- Involve men, and women, and adolescent boys and girls in separate and private discussions.

4 ⟩ Make a range of long-acting reversible and short-acting contraceptive methods available at healthcare facilities based on demand, in a private and confidential setting.

- Provide counselling that emphasises informed choice and effectiveness.

Key indicators

Skilled care is available for emergency obstetrics and newborn care at all times

- Basic emergency obstetric and newborn care: minimum five facilities per 500,000 people
- Comprehensive emergency obstetric and newborn care: minimum one facility per 500,000 people

Percentage of births attended by skilled personnel

- Minimum target: 80 per cent

Referral system for obstetric and newborn emergencies available

- Available 24 hours/day and 7 days/week

Percentage of deliveries in health facilities by caesarean section

- Target: 5–15 per cent

All primary health centres report availability of at least four methods of contraception between three and six months after the onset of the crisis.

Guidance notes

Emergency obstetric and newborn care: About 4 per cent of any population will be pregnant women, and about 15 per cent of those will experience an unpredictable obstetric complication during pregnancy or at the time of delivery that will require emergency obstetric care. About 5–15 per cent of deliveries will require surgery such as caesarean section. Globally 9–15 per cent of newborns will require life-saving emergency care. About 5–10 per cent of newborns do not breathe spontaneously at birth and require stimulation, and half of those require resuscitation. The major reasons for failure to breathe include pre-term birth and acute intrapartum events resulting in severe asphyxia ⊕ *see Essential healthcare – child health standard 2.2.2: Management of newborn and childhood illness.*

Basic emergency obstetrics and newborn care includes parenteral antibiotics, uterotonic drugs (parenteral oxytocin, misoprostol), parenteral anticonvulsant drugs (magnesium sulphate), removal of retained products of conception using appropriate devices, manual removal of placenta, assisted vaginal delivery (vacuum extraction), and maternal and newborn resuscitation.

Comprehensive emergency obstetric and newborn care includes all of the above as well as surgery under general anaesthesia (caesarean section, laparotomy), and rational and safe blood transfusion with standard precaution measures. Post-abortion care is a life-saving intervention that is part of emergency obstetric and newborn care and aims to reduce death and suffering from the complications of miscarriage (spontaneous abortion) and unsafe abortions. Treatment includes managing bleeding (possibly through surgical intervention) and sepsis, and providing tetanus prophylaxis.

It is essential that both basic and comprehensive emergency obstetric and newborn care services are available at all times.

The referral system should ensure that women or newborns have the means to travel to and from a primary healthcare facility with basic emergency obstetric and newborn care and to a hospital with comprehensive emergency obstetric and newborn care.

Family planning: Engage with various groups in the community to understand preferences and cultural attitudes. Ensure the community is aware of where and how to access contraception. Share information in multiple formats and languages to ensure accessibility. Engage community leaders to disseminate the information.

Trained providers who understand the client's preferences, culture and context should give contraceptive counselling. Counselling should emphasise confidentiality and privacy, voluntary and informed choice and consent, method effectiveness for medical and non-medical methods, possible side effects, management and follow-up, and guidance on removal if needed.

A range of contraceptive types should be available immediately to meet antici-pated demand. Providers should be trained to remove long-active reversible contraceptives.

Other services: Initiate other maternal and newborn care as soon as possible, including ante-natal and post-natal care.

Coordination with other sectors: Coordinate with the nutrition sector to ensure that pregnant and breastfeeding women are referred to nutrition services as appropriate, such as for targeted supplementary feeding ⊕ *see Food security and nutrition – management of malnutrition standards 2.1 and 2.2.*

Sexual and reproductive health standard 2.3.2: Sexual violence and clinical management of rape

People have access to healthcare that is safe and responds to the needs of survivors of sexual violence.

Key actions

1 ⟩ Identify a lead organisation to coordinate a multi-sectoral approach to reduce the risk of sexual violence, ensure referrals and provide holistic support to survivors.

- Coordinate with other sectors to strengthen prevention and response.

2 ⟩ Inform the community of available services and the importance of seeking immediate medical care following sexual violence.

- Provide post-exposure prophylaxis for HIV as soon as possible (within 72 hours of exposure).
- Provide emergency contraception within 120 hours.

3 ⟩ Establish safe spaces in healthcare facilities to receive survivors of sexual violence and to provide clinical care and referral.

- Display and use clear protocols and a list of patients' rights.
- Train healthcare workers in supportive communication, maintaining confidentiality and protecting survivor information and data.

4 ⟩ Make clinical care and referral to other supportive services available for survivors of sexual violence.

- Ensure referral mechanism for life-threatening, complicated or severe conditions.
- Establish referral mechanisms between health, legal, protection, security, psychosocial and community services.

Key indicators

All health facilities have trained staff, sufficient supplies and equipment for clinical management of rape survivor services based on national or international protocols

All survivors of sexual violence state they received healthcare in a safe and confidential manner

All eligible survivors of sexual violence receive:

- Post-exposure prophylaxis within 72 hours of an incident or from exposure
- Emergency contraception within 120 hours of an incident or from exposure

Guidance notes

Prevention of sexual violence and rape requires action across all sectors ⊕ *see WASH water supply standard 2.1* ⊕ *see WASH excreta management standard 3.2* ⊕ *see Food security and nutrition – food assistance standard 6.3 and Livelihoods standard 7.2; Shelter and settlement standards 2 and 3* ⊕ *see Protection Principle 1* and *Core Humanitarian Standard Commitments 4 and 8.* ⊕ *See Health systems standard 1.1 to 1.3* for further information on making healthcare facilities safe and providing safe care.

Clinical care, including mental healthcare and referral for survivors, must be in place in all primary healthcare facilities and mobile teams ⊕ *see Healthcare systems 1.2* and *Essential healthcare standard 2.5*. This includes skilled staff to provide compassionate, timely and confidential treatment and counselling to all children, adults and older people on:

- emergency contraception;
- pregnancy testing, pregnancy options information and safe abortion referral to the full extent of the law;
- presumptive treatment of STIs;
- post-exposure prophylaxis to prevent HIV transmission ⊕ *see Health standard 2.3.3: HIV*
- prevention of hepatitis B;
- care of wounds and prevention of tetanus; and
- referral for further services, such as other health, psychological, legal and social services.

Ensure equal gender distribution of healthcare workers fluent in local and patient languages, and coach female and male chaperones and interpreters to provide non-discriminatory and unbiased services. Train healthcare workers on clinical care for survivors of sexual violence, focusing on supportive communication, history and examination, treatment and counselling. Where feasible and needed, provide training on the medico-legal system and forensic evidence collection.

Child survivors of sexual violence: Children should be cared for by healthcare workers trained in post-rape management of children. Allow children to choose the gender of the healthcare worker. Involve specialised protection actors quickly in all cases.

Community engagement: Work with patients and the community to improve accessibility and acceptability of care and to deliver prevention programmes throughout a crisis. Ensure confidential feedback mechanisms and swift feedback. Involve women, men, adolescent girls and boys, and at-risk populations such as persons with disabilities and LGBTQI groups.

Legal frameworks: Be aware of the national medico-legal system and relevant laws on sexual violence. Inform survivors of any mandatory reporting laws that could limit the confidentiality of the information patients disclose to healthcare providers. This may influence their decision to continue to seek care, but must be respected.

In many countries, induced abortion is legal under circumstances such as rape. Where this is the case, access or referrals should be provided without discrimination.

While addressing sexual violence is critical, forms of gender-based violence (GBV) such as intimate partner violence, child and forced marriage and female genital mutilation are also not only prevalent in humanitarian crises, but in some scenarios may increase during a crisis and have significant unique health impacts (physical, sexual, mental) on individuals that require specific responses. Other international guidelines are increasingly recognising not only sexual violence, but these other forms of GBV and their impacts on health ⊕ *see IASC Guidelines for Integrating Gender-Based Violence Interventions in Humanitarian Action*.

Sexual and reproductive health standard 2.3.3: HIV

People have access to healthcare that prevents transmission and reduces morbidity and mortality due to HIV.

Key actions

1⟩ Establish and follow standard precautions and procedures for the safe and rational use of blood transfusion.

2⟩ Provide anti-retroviral therapy (ART) to everyone who is already on it, including women in prevention of mother-to-child transmission programmes.

- Actively trace people living with HIV to continue treatment.

3 Provide lubricated male condoms and, where already used by the population, female condoms.

- Work with leaders and the affected population to understand local use, increase acceptance and ensure that condom distribution is culturally appropriate.

4 Offer testing to all pregnant women where HIV prevalence is greater than 1 per cent.

5 Initiate post-exposure prophylaxis (PEP) as soon as possible, but within 72 hours of exposure for survivors of sexual violence and occupational exposure.

6 Provide co-trimoxazole prophylaxis for opportunistic infections for:
   a. patients living with HIV; and
   b. children born to mothers living with HIV, at four to six weeks of age; continue until HIV infection is excluded.

7 Ensure primary healthcare facilities have antimicrobials and provide syndromic management to patients with symptoms of an STI.

Key indicators

All transfused blood is screened and is free of transfusion-transmissible infections, including HIV

Percentage of people previously on anti-retroviral therapy (ART) who continue to receive ART medicines

- 90 per cent

Percentage of women accessing health services who are tested for HIV, where HIV prevalence is greater than 1 per cent

- 90 per cent

Percentage of individuals potentially exposed to HIV reporting to health facilities who receive PEP within 72 hours of exposure

- 100 per cent

Percentage of HIV-exposed infants receiving co-trimoxazole at four to six weeks of age

- 95 per cent

Guidance notes

The key actions above should apply in all humanitarian crises, regardless of the local HIV epidemiology.

Involve the affected community and key populations (healthcare workers, leaders, women, LGBTQI people, persons with disabilities) in HIV service delivery, and ensure they know where to access anti-retroviral (ARV) medicines. If there is already an association of people living with HIV, consult with and involve them in programme design and delivery.

Community-led distribution of condoms within peer groups is useful. Key populations and adolescents will often know where their peers congregate, and volunteers can distribute to peers. Educate key populations with culturally appropriate messages about correct use and disposal of used condoms. Make condoms available to the community, aid agency staff, uniformed staff, aid delivery truck drivers and others.

Blood transfusion: ⊕ *See Health systems standards 1.1 and 1.3.*

Post-exposure care and treatment should include counselling, HIV exposure risk assessment, informed consent, assessment of the source, and provision of anti-retroviral medicines. Do not give PEP to a person known to be living with HIV. Although counselling and testing is recommended before starting PEP, if not feasible do not delay the initiation of PEP ⊕ *see Essential healthcare – sexual and reproductive health standard 2.3.2: Sexual violence and clinical management of rape.*

Comprehensive HIV-related activities in crises: Establish the following activities as soon as feasible:

HIV awareness: Provide accessible information to the public, particularly to populations at higher risk, about preventing HIV and other STIs.

HIV prevention: Provide high-risk populations with harm-reduction services such as sterile injecting equipment and opioid substitution therapy for people who inject drugs, where these services already existed ⊕ *see Essential healthcare standard 2.5: Mental health care.*

HIV counselling and testing: Provide (or re-establish) counselling and testing services linked to ART initiation. Priority groups for HIV testing are pregnant women and their partners, children with severe acute malnutrition where the HIV prevalence is greater than 1 per cent, and other at-risk groups.

Stigma and discrimination: It is crucial to ensure that strategies and programmes do not increase stigma. Aim to actively decrease stigma and discrimination in areas known to have high stigma index and discriminatory behaviours.

ART interventions: Extend anti-retroviral therapy to all who need it – not only those who were previously enrolled – as soon as possible.

Prevention of mother-to-child transmission: Test pregnant women and their partners and provide early infant HIV diagnosis. Provide ART to women who

Note: Caritas Internationalis and its Members do not promote the use of, or distribute any form of, artificial birth control.

are already known to be positive for or who newly test positive for HIV. Refer infants who test positive to paediatric HIV services. Provide infant feeding guidance specific to women living with HIV, and retention and adherence support ⊕ *see Food security and nutrition – Infant and young child feeding standards 4.1 and 4.2.*

Services for HIV/TB co-infection: Provide TB screening and referral for people living with HIV. Provide TB treatment to people previously enrolled on a treatment programme ⊕ *see Essential healthcare – Communicable disease standard 2.1.3: Diagnosis and case management.* Link testing services for TB and HIV in high – prevalence settings and establish TB infection control in healthcare settings.

2.4 Injury and trauma care

In any crisis, a high burden of morbidity and mortality is attributable to injury. Increased demand for trauma care services is likely to quickly exceed the capacities of local health systems. To reduce the impact of injuries and the risk of health system collapse, provide systematic triage and mass casualty management alongside basic emergency, safe operative and rehabilitative care. This section addresses the health system response to physical injury. Specific guidance on poisoning, mental health and sexual violence are addressed elsewhere ⊕ *see Appendix 4: Poisoning; Essential healthcare standard 2.5* and *Essential healthcare – Sexual and reproductive health standard 2.3.2.*

Injury and trauma care standard 2.4:
Injury and trauma care

People have access to safe and effective trauma care during crises to prevent avoidable mortality, morbidity, suffering and disability.

Key actions

1 ⟩ Provide care for trauma at all levels for all patients.

- Quickly establish safe referral systems between facilities and from affected communities to facilities.
- Establish mobile clinics or field hospitals if care in fixed structures is not accessible to the population.

2 ⟩ Ensure that healthcare workers have the skills and knowledge to address injuries.

- Include all levels from first responders to those providing definitive surgical and anaesthetics care.

3 > Establish or strengthen standardised protocols for triage and injury and trauma care.

- Include referral systems for child protection, survivors of sexual violence, and those requiring mental health and psychosocial support.

4 > Provide tetanus prophylaxis to anyone at risk of injury, to injured people with open wounds and those involved in rescue and clean-operations.

5 > Ensure minimum safety and governance standards for all facilities providing trauma and injury care, including field hospitals.

6 > Ensure timely access to rehabilitation services, priority assistive devices and mobility aids for injured patients.

- Confirm that assistive devices such as wheelchairs and crutches or other mobility aids can be repaired locally.

7 > Ensure timely access to mental health services and psychosocial support.

8 > Establish or strengthen the health information systems to include injury and trauma data.

- Prioritise basic clinical documentation such as individual medical records for all trauma patients.
- Use standard definitions to integrate injury into the health information system data sets.

Key indicators

Percentage of health facilities that have a disaster plan including management of mass casualties, reviewed and rehearsed on a regular basis

Percentage of health facilities with protocols for the acutely injured including formal triage instruments

Percentage of health facilities with staff that have received basic training in the approach to the acutely injured

Percentage of health facilities implementing quality improvement measures to reduce baseline morbidity and mortality according to available data

Guidance notes

Training and skills development for injury and trauma care should include:

- mass casualty management, for those responding and coordinating response;
- basic first aid;
- standardised triage in the field and at healthcare facilities; and
- early recognition, resuscitation, wound management, pain control and time-sensitive psychosocial support.

Standardised protocols should exist or be developed to cover the following:

- acuity-based triage classification for routine and surge situations that includes assessment, prioritisation, basic resuscitation and criteria for emergency referral;
- frontline emergency care at the point of access; and
- referrals for emergency and advanced care, including surgery, post-operative care and rehabilitation.

Minimum safety and quality standards: Even where trauma care is being provided in response to an acute event or ongoing conflict, Minimum Standards must be assured. Areas to be addressed include:

- the safe and rational use of medications, devices and blood products, including supply chain;
- infection prevention and control;
- sufficient power supply for lighting, communications and operating essential medical devices such as emergency resuscitation equipment and sterilisation autoclaves; and
- medical waste management.

Community-based first aid: Timely and appropriate first aid by non-professionals saves lives if done in a safe and systematic manner. All first aiders should use a structured approach to the injured. Basic wound management training, such as in cleaning and dressing, is vital.

Include household- and community-level first aid, and guidance on when and where to seek medical help. Raise awareness of context-specific risks such as unstable infrastructure or risk of injury during rescue attempts.

Triage is the process of categorising patients according to the severity of their injuries and their need for care. It identifies those who would most benefit from immediate medical intervention. Several triage systems exist. One widely used system applies five colours: red for highest priority patients, yellow for medium, green for lower, blue for patients beyond the technical capacity of the facility or who require palliative care, and grey for the deceased.

Frontline professional emergency care: All higher-level healthcare workers, such as doctors, should be skilled in a systematic approach to the acutely ill and injured ⊕ *see the ABCDE approach in the IFRC International First Aid and Resuscitation Guidelines*. Initial resuscitation and life-saving interventions, such as fluid and anti-biotic administration, haemorrhage control and treatment of pneumothorax, can be delivered in many settings before transferring the patient to advanced services.

Anaesthesia, trauma and surgical care: Emergency, operative and rehabilitative care should be undertaken only by organisations with appropriate expertise. Providers should act within their professional scope of practice, with adequate resources to sustain their activities. Inappropriate or inadequate care may do more harm than doing nothing. Surgery provided without appropriate pre- and post-operative care and ongoing rehabilitation can result in a failure to restore functional capacities of the patient.

Field hospitals: The use of temporary field hospitals may be necessary, especially in acute crises, and should be coordinated with MoH or lead agencies and other health actors. Standards and safety of care should meet national and international standards ⊕ *see References* for further guidance.

Rehabilitation and social reintegration: Early rehabilitation can increase survival, maximise the impact of medical and surgical interventions and enhance quality of life for injured survivors. Medical teams with inpatient capacity must be able to provide early rehabilitation. Map existing rehabilitation capacities and referral pathways and understand the links between existing social welfare systems and cash-based assistance. Establish links with local rehabilitation centres or community-based rehabilitation organisations for ongoing care.

Prior to discharge, consider the ongoing needs of trauma and injury patients, including those with a pre-existing disability. Ensure medical and rehabilitation follow-up, patient and caregiver education, essential assistive devices (such as crutches or wheelchairs), mental health and psychosocial support, and access to other essential services. Establish multi-disciplinary care plans and teams including physical rehabilitation specialists and staff skilled in mental healthcare and psychosocial support. Mental health and psychosocial support for those with life-changing injuries should begin as when they are inpatients. Links to ongoing support services are essential ⊕ *see Essential healthcare standard 2.5: Mental health care.*

Special management considerations – pain control: Good pain management after injury reduces the risks of pneumonia and deep vein thrombosis and helps the patient start physiotherapy. It reduces the physiological stress response, leading to a reduction in cardiovascular morbidity, and reduces psychological stress. Acute pain from trauma should be treated following the reverse WHO pain ladder. Neuropathic pain resulting from nerve injury may be present from the outset and should be treated appropriately ⊕ *see Health systems standard 1.3: Essential medicines and medical devices* and *Essential healthcare standard 2.7: Palliative care* ⊕ *see WHO pain ladder.*

Special management considerations – wound management: In most crises, many patients will present for care more than six hours after injury. Delayed presentation greatly increases the risk of wound infection and associated mortality. Healthcare workers must know protocols to manage wounds (including burns) and prevent and treat infection, for both acute and delayed presentations. These protocols include providing appropriate antibiotics, surgical removal of foreign material and dead tissue, and dressing.

Tetanus: In sudden-onset natural disasters the risk of tetanus can be relatively high. Administer tetanus toxoid-containing vaccine (DT or Td – diphtheria and tetanus vaccines – or DPT, depending on age and vaccination history) to those with open wounds. Individuals with dirty or highly contaminated wounds should also receive a dose of tetanus immune globulin (TIG) if they are not vaccinated against tetanus.

2.5 Mental health

Mental health and psychosocial problems are common among adults, adolescents and children in all humanitarian settings. The extreme stressors associated with crises place people at increased risk of social, behavioural, psychological and psychiatric problems. Mental health and psychosocial support involves multisectoral actions. This standard focuses on actions by health actors ⊕ *see* the Core Humanitarian Standard and Protection Principles for more information on psychosocial interventions across sectors.

Mental health standard 2.5:
Mental health care
People of all ages have access to healthcare that addresses mental health conditions and associated impaired functioning.

Key actions

1 〉 Coordinate mental health and psychosocial supports across sectors.

- Set up a cross-sectoral technical working group for mental health and psychosocial issues. It may be co-led by a health organisation and a protection humanitarian organisation.

2 〉 Develop programmes based on identified needs and resources.

- Analyse existing mental health systems, staff competencies, and other resources or services.
- Conduct needs assessments, keeping in mind that mental health conditions may be pre-existing, induced by the crisis or both.

3 〉 Work with community members, including marginalised people, to strengthen community self-help and social support.

- Promote community dialogue on ways to address problems collaboratively, drawing on community wisdom, experience and resources.
- Preserve or support re-initiation of pre-existing support mechanisms such as groups for women, youth and people living with HIV.

4 〉 Orient staff and volunteers on how to offer psychological first aid.

- Apply the principles of psychological first aid to manage acute stress after recent exposure to potentially traumatic events.

5 〉 Make basic clinical mental healthcare available at every healthcare facility.

- Organise brief training and supervise general healthcare workers to assess and manage priority mental health conditions.
- Organise a referral mechanism among mental health specialists, general healthcare providers, community-based support and other services.

6 〉 Make psychological interventions available where possible for people impaired by prolonged distress.

- Where feasible, train and supervise non-specialists.

7 〉 Protect the rights of people with severe mental health conditions in the community, hospitals and institutions.

- Visit psychiatric hospitals and residential homes for people with severe mental health conditions on a regular basis from early in the crisis.
- Address neglect and abuse in institutions and organise care.

8 〉 Minimise harm related to alcohol and drugs.

- Train staff in detection and brief interventions, harm reduction, and management of withdrawal and intoxication.

9 〉 Take steps to develop a sustainable mental health system during early recovery planning and protracted crises.

....

Key indicators

Percentage of secondary healthcare services with trained and supervised staff and systems for managing mental health conditions

Percentage of primary healthcare services with trained and supervised staff and systems for managing mental health conditions

Number of people participating in community self-help and social support activities

Percentage of health services users who receive care for mental health conditions

Percentage of people who have received care for mental health conditions who report improved functioning and reduced symptoms

Number of days for which essential psychotropic medicines were not available in the past 30 days

- Less than four days

....

Guidance notes

Multi-level support: Crises affect people in different ways, requiring different kinds of support. A key to organising mental health and psychosocial support is to develop a layered system of complementary supports that meets different needs,

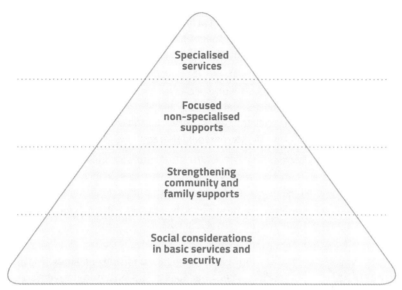

Pyramid of multi-layered services and supports (Figure 10)
Source: IASC Reference Group for Mental Health and Psychosocial Support in Emergency Settings (2010)

as illustrated in the diagram below. This pyramid shows how different actions complement each other. All layers of the pyramid are important and should ideally be implemented concurrently.

Assessment: Rates of mental health conditions are substantial in any crisis. Prevalence studies are not essential to initiate services. Use rapid participatory approaches and, where possible, integrate mental health in other assessments. Do not limit assessment to one clinical issue.

Community self-help and support: Engage community health workers, leaders and volunteers to enable community members, including marginalised people, to increase self-help and social support. Activities could include creating safe spaces and the conditions for community dialogue.

Psychological first aid: Psychological first aid needs to be available to people exposed to potentially traumatic events such as physical or sexual violence, witnessing atrocities and experiencing major injuries. This is not a clinical intervention. It is a basic, humane and supportive response to suffering. It includes listening carefully, assessing basic needs and ensuring they are met, encouraging social support and protecting from further harm. It is non-intrusive and does not press people to talk about their distress. After brief orientation, community leaders, healthcare workers and others involved in the humanitarian response can provide psychological first aid to people in distress. Although psychological first aid should be widely available, the overall mental health and psychosocial support response should not be limited to it alone.

Single-session psychological debriefing promotes venting by encouraging people to briefly but systematically recount perceptions, thoughts and emotional reactions experienced during a recent stressful event. It is at best ineffective and should not be used.

Other psychological interventions: Non-specialised healthcare workers can deliver psychological interventions for depression, anxiety and post-traumatic stress disorder when they are well trained, supervised and supported. This includes cognitive behaviour therapy or interpersonal therapy.

Clinical mental healthcare: Brief all health staff and volunteers about available mental healthcare. Train health providers according to evidence-based protocols such as the. Where possible, add a mental health professional such as a psychiatric nurse to general healthcare facilities. Arrange private space for consultations ⊕ *see mhGAP Humanitarian Intervention Guide*.

The most frequent conditions presented to health services in emergencies are psychosis, depression and a neurological condition, epilepsy. Maternal mental health is of specific concern because of its potential impact on care for children.

Integrate mental health categories into the health information system ⊕ *see Appendix 2: Sample HMIS form*.

Essential psychotropic medicines: Organise an uninterrupted supply of essential psychotropic medicines with at least one from each therapeutic category (anti-psychotic, anti-depressant, anxiolytic, anti-epileptic, and medicines to counter side effects of anti-psychotics. ⊕ *See the Interagency Emergency Health Kit for suggested psychotropic medicines* and *Health systems standard 1.3: Essential medicines and medical devices*.

Protecting the rights of people with mental health conditions: During humanitarian crises, people with severe mental health conditions are extremely vulnerable to human rights violations such as abuse, neglect, abandonment and lack of shelter, food or medical care. Designate at least one agency to address the needs of people in institutions.

Transition to post-crisis: Humanitarian crises increase the long-term rates of many mental health conditions, so it is important to plan for sustained increased treatment coverage across the affected area. This includes strengthening existing national mental health systems and fostering inclusion of marginalised groups (including refugees) in these systems. Demonstration projects, with short-term emergency funding, can provide proof-of-concept and create momentum to attract further support and funds for mental health system development.

2.6 Non-communicable diseases

The need to focus on non-communicable diseases (NCDs) in humanitarian crises reflects increased global life expectancy combined with behavioural risk factors such as tobacco smoking and unhealthy diets. About 80 per cent of deaths from NCDs occur in low- or middle-income countries, and emergencies exacerbate this.

Within an average adult population of 10,000 people, there are likely to be 1,500–3,000 people with hypertension, 500–2,000 with diabetes, and 3–8 acute heart attacks over a normal 90-day period.

Diseases will vary but often include diabetes, cardiovascular disease (including hypertension, heart failure, strokes, chronic kidney disease), chronic lung disease (such as asthma and chronic obstructive pulmonary disease) and cancer.

Initial response should manage acute complications and avoid treatment interruption, followed by more comprehensive programmes.

Mental health and palliative care are specifically addressed in ⊕ *Essential healthcare standards 2.5: Mental healthcare* and *2.7: Palliative care.*

Non-communicable diseases standard 2.6: Care of non-communicable diseases

People have access to preventive programmes, diagnostics and essential therapies for acute complications and long-term management of non-communicable diseases.

Key actions

1 ⟩ Identify the NCD health needs and analyse the availability of services pre-crisis.

- Identify groups with priority needs, including those at risk of life-threatening complications such as insulin-dependent diabetes or severe asthma.

2 ⟩ Implement phased-approach programmes based on life-saving priorities and relief of suffering.

- Ensure patients diagnosed with life-threatening complications (for example, severe asthma attack, diabetic ketoacidosis) receive appropriate care. If appropriate care is not available, offer palliative and supportive care.
- Avoid sudden treatment disruption for patients diagnosed before the crisis.

3 ⟩ Integrate NCD care into the health system at all levels.

- Establish a referral system to manage acute complications and complex cases in secondary or tertiary care, and to palliative and supportive care.
- Refer patients for nutrition or food security responses where required.

4 〉 Establish national preparedness programmes for NCDs.

- Include essential medicines and supplies in pre-positioned or contingency emergency medical supplies.
- Prepare individual patients with a backup supply of medications and instructions on where to access emergency care should a crisis occur.

Key indicators

Percentage of primary healthcare facilities providing care for priority NCDs

Number of days essential medicines for NCDs were not available in the past 30 days

- Less than four days

Number of days for which basic equipment for NCDs was not available (or not functional) in the past 30 days

- Less than four days

All healthcare workers providing NCD treatment are trained in NCD management

Guidance notes

Needs and risk assessment to identify priority NCDs: Design according to context and phase of emergency. This could involve reviewing records, using pre-crisis data, and conducting household surveys or epidemiological assessment with a cross-sectional survey. Gather data regarding specific NCD prevalence and incidence and identify life-threatening needs or severely symptomatic conditions.

Analyse pre-crisis service availability and use, especially for complex cases such as cancer or chronic renal disease, to assess expectations and health system capacity in the context. The medium- to long-term aim is to support and reinstate such services.

Complex treatment needs: Provide continuity of care for patients with complex needs such as renal dialysis, radiotherapy and chemotherapy, if possible. Give clear and accessible information about referral pathways. Provide referrals to palliative care support if available ⊕ *see Essential healthcare standard 2.7: Palliative care.*

Integration of NCD care into the health system: Provide basic treatment for NCDs at primary healthcare level in line with national standards, or in line with international emergency guidance where national standards do not exist.

Work with communities to improve early detection and referrals. Integrate CHWs into primary care facilities, and engage with community leaders, traditional healers and the private sector. Outreach services can provide NCD health services to isolated populations.

Adapt the existing health information system for the crisis setting, or develop a new one, to include monitoring of main NCDs: hypertension, diabetes, asthma, chronic obstructive pulmonary disease, ischaemic heart disease and epilepsy ⊕ *see Health systems standard 1.5: Health information and appendix 2.*

Medicines and medical devices: Review the national list of essential medicines and devices, including technologies and core laboratory tests, to manage NCDs. Focus on primary healthcare ⊕ *see Health systems standard 1.3: Essential medicines and medical devices.* If needed, advocate for the inclusion of key essential medicines and medical devices in line with international and emergency guidance on NCDs. Provide access to essential medicines and medical devices at the appropriate levels of care. NCD kits may be used in conjunction with inter-agency emergency health kits in the early stages of the crisis to increase availability of essential medicines and equipment. Do not use these kits to provide long-term supplies.

Training: Train all levels of clinical staff on case management of NCD conditions and train all staff in priority NCD management, including standard operating procedures on referral ⊕ *see Health systems standard 1.2: Health care workforce.*

Health promotion and education: Provide information about NCD services and where to access care. Information should be accessible to all, including older people and persons with disabilities, to promote healthy behaviours, modifying risk factors, and improving self-care and adherence to treatment. Healthy behaviours can include regular physical activity or reducing alcohol and tobacco consumption, for example. Work with different parts of the community to develop messages and distribution strategies so that they are age, gender and culturally appropriate. Adapt prevention and control strategies to the context, considering constraints such as limited food supply or overcrowding.

Prevention and preparedness plans: Include NCD management in national disaster and emergency plans, ensuring it is specific to the different types of healthcare facilities (for example, small health centres or major hospitals with dialysis units). Health centres in unstable or disaster-prone contexts should be prepared for NCD service delivery.

Form a registry of patients with complex conditions and critical needs and create standardised operating protocols for referring them if a crisis occurs.

2.7 Palliative care

Palliative care is the prevention and relief of suffering and distress associated with end-of-life care. It includes identifying, assessing and treating pain as well as other physical, psychosocial and spiritual needs. Integrate physiological, psychological and spiritual care based solely on patient or family request, and include support systems to help patients, families and caregivers. This end-of-life care should be provided regardless of the cause.

Palliative care standard 2.7:
Palliative care

People have access to palliative and end-of-life care that relieves pain and suffering, maximises the comfort, dignity and quality of life of patients, and provides support for family members.

Key actions

1 > Establish guidelines and policies to support consistent palliative care.

- Include national or international guidelines for pain and symptom control at healthcare facilities.
- Develop triage guidelines based on the patient's medical condition and prognosis and availability of resources.

2 > Develop a care plan and provide palliative care to patients who are dying.

- Ensure pain relief and dignity in death in an acute emergency, as a minimum.
- Explore the patient's or family's understanding of the situation as well as their concerns, values and cultural beliefs.

3 > Integrate palliative care into all levels of health system.

- Establish strong referral networks to provide continuity of support and care.
- Prioritise community-based management involving home-based care.

4 > Train healthcare workers to provide palliative care, including pain and symptom control, and mental health and psychosocial support.

- Meet national standards, or international standards where national standards do not exist.

5 > Provide essential medical supplies and equipment.

- Stock palliative medicines and appropriate medical devices such as incontinence pads and catheters at healthcare facilities.
- Be aware of controlled drugs regulations that may delay availability of essential medicines.

6 > Work with local systems and networks to support patients, caregivers and families in the community and at home.

- Provide supplies for home care needs, such as incontinence pads, urinary catheters and dressing packs.

Key indicators

Number of days for which essential palliative care medicines were not available in the past 30 days

- Less than 4 days

Percentage of staff trained in basic pain and symptom control or palliative care in each health centre, hospital, mobile clinic and field hospital

Percentage of patients identified by the healthcare system as in need that have received end-of-life care

Guidance notes

Humanitarian health actors should be aware of and respect local ways of making medical decisions and local values related to illness, suffering, dying and death. Relief of suffering is important, and dying patients should receive comfort-oriented care, whether their illness is from fatal injuries, infectious disease or any other cause.

Developing a care plan: Identify relevant patients and respect their right to make informed decisions about their care. Provide unbiased information and take account of their needs and expectations. The care plan should be agreed and be based on patient preferences. Offer access to mental health and psychosocial support.

Availability of medicines: Some palliative care medicines such as pain relief are included in the basic and supplementary modules of the inter-agency emergency health kit, and in the Essential Medicines List. Inter-agency emergency health kits (IEHK) are useful for early phases of a crisis but are not suitable for protracted situations where more sustainable systems should be established ⊕ *see Health systems standard 1.3: Essential medicines and medical devices* and *References and further reading.*

Family, community and social support: Coordinate with other sectors to agree a referral pathway for patients and their families to have integrated support. This includes accessing national social and welfare systems or organisations that offer assistance in shelter, hygiene and dignity kits, cash-based assistance, mental health and psychosocial support, and legal assistance to ensure that basic daily needs are met.

Coordinate with relevant sectors to trace separated families so that patients may communicate with them.

Work with existing networks of community care, who often have trained home-based care facilitators and community psychosocial workers, to provide additional support for patients and family members and help provide home-based care if required (such as for people living with HIV).

Spiritual support: All support should be based on patient or family requests. Work with local faith leaders to identify spiritual care providers who share the patient's faith or belief. These providers can act as a resource for patients, carers and humanitarian actors.

Orient local faith leaders on key principles of psychosocial support for patients facing major health issues.

Establish reliable mechanisms for bilateral referral between the healthcare system and spiritual leaders for any patient, caregiver or family member who requests it.

Ensure support for safe and dignified burial practices in collaboration with the local community, according to national or international guidance ⊕ *see Health systems standard 1.1: Health service delivery.*

Appendix 1
Health assessment checklist

Preparation

- Obtain available information on the crisis-affected population.
- Obtain available maps, aerial photos or satellite images, and geographic information system (GIS) data of the affected area.
- Obtain demographic, administrative and health data.

Security and access

- Determine the existence of the ongoing natural or human-made hazards.
- Determine the overall security situation, including the presence of armed forces.
- Determine the access that humanitarian organisations have to the crisis-affected population.

Demographics and social structure

- Determine the size of the crisis-affected population, disaggregated by sex, age and disability.
- Identify groups at increased risk, such as women, children, older people, persons with disabilities, people living with HIV or marginalised groups.
- Determine the average household size and estimates of the number of female- and child-headed households.
- Determine the existing social structure and gender norms, including positions of authority and/or influence in the community and the household.

Background health information

- Identify health problems that existed in the crisis-affected area before the emergency.
- Identify pre-existing health problems in the country of origin for refugees, or the area of origin for internally displaced persons.
- Identify existing risks to health, such as potential epidemic diseases.
- Identify pre-existing and existing barriers to healthcare, social norms and beliefs, including positive and harmful practices.
- Identify previous sources of healthcare.
- Analyse the various aspects of the health system and their performance ⊕ *see Health systems standards 1.1 to 1.5.*

Mortality rates

- Calculate the crude mortality rate.
- Calculate the age-specific mortality rates (such as under-five mortality rate).

- Calculate cause-specific mortality rates.
- Calculate proportional mortality rate.

Morbidity rates

- Determine incidence rates of major health conditions that have public health importance.
- Determine age- and sex-specific incidence rates of major health conditions where possible.

Available resources

- Determine the capacity of the MoH of the country affected by the crisis.
- Determine the status of national health facilities, including total number by type of care provided, degree of infrastructure damage, and access.
- Determine the numbers and skills of available healthcare staff.
- Determine the available health budgets and financing mechanism.
- Determine the capacity and functional status of existing public health programmes such as Extended Programme on Immunisation.
- Determine the availability of standardised protocols, essential medicines, medical devices and equipment, and logistics systems.
- Determine the status of existing referral systems.
- Determine the level of IPC standards in health facilities.
- Determine the status of the existing health information system.

Data from other relevant sectors

- Nutritional status.
- Environmental and WASH conditions.
- Food basket and food security.
- Shelter – quality of shelter.
- Education – health and hygiene education.

Appendix 2
Sample weekly surveillance reporting forms

2.1 Mortality surveillance form (aggregate)*

Site: ....

Date from Monday: .... To Sunday: ....

Total population at beginning of this week: ....

Births this week: .... Deaths this week: ....

Arrivals this week (if applicable): .... Departures this week: ....

Total population at end of week: .... Total under 5 years population: ....

	<5 Years		≥5 Years		Total
	Male	Female	Male	Female	
Immediate cause					
Acute lower respiratory infection					
Cholera (suspected)					
Diarrhoea – bloody					
Diarrhoea – watery					
Injury – non-accidental					
Malaria					
Maternal death – direct					
Measles					
Meningitis (suspected)					
Neonatal (0–28 days)					
Other					
Unknown					
Total by age and sex					
Underlying cause					
AIDS (suspected)					
Malnutrition					
Maternal death – indirect					
Non-communicable diseases (specify)					
Other					
Total by age and sex					

*This form is used when there are many deaths and therefore more detailed information on individual deaths cannot be collected due to time limitations.

–Other causes of mortality can be added according to context and epidemiological pattern.

–Age can be further disaggregated as feasible, for example 0–11 months, 1–4 years, 5–14 years, 15–49 years, 50–59 years, 60–69 years, 70–79 years, 80+ years.–

–Deaths should not be reported solely from health facilities, but should include reports from site and religious leaders, community workers, women's groups and referral hospitals.

–Whenever possible, case definitions should be put on the back of this form.

2.2 Mortality surveillance form (individual records) *

Site: ....

Date from Monday: .... To Sunday: ....

Total population at beginning of this week: ....

Births this week: .... Deaths this week: ....

Arrivals this week (if applicable): .... Departures this week: ....

Total population at end of week: .... Total under 5 years population: ....

No	Sex (m, f)	Age (days=d, months=m, yrs=y)	Direct cause of death												Underlying causes				Date (dd/mm/yy)	Location in site (e.g. block no.)	Died in hospital or at home
			Acute lower respiratory infection	Cholera (suspected)	Diarrhoea – bloody	Diarrhoea – watery	Injury – non-accidental	Malaria	Maternal death – direct	Measles	Meningitis (suspected)	Neonatal (0–28 days)	Non-communicable dis. (specify)	Other (specify)	Unknown	AIDS (suspected)	Malnutrition	Maternal death (indirect)	Other (specify)			
1																						
2																						
3																						
4																						
5																						
6																						
7																						
8																						

*This form is used when there is enough time to record data on individual deaths; it allows analysis by age, location and facility utilisation rates.

–Frequency of reporting (that is, daily or weekly) depends upon the number of deaths.
–Other causes of death can be added as appropriate in the situation.
–Deaths should not be reported solely from site health facilities, but should include reports from site and religious leaders, community workers, women's groups and referral hospitals.
–Whenever possible, case definitions should be put on the back of this form.
–Age can be further disaggregated as feasible, for example 0–11 months, 1–4 years, 5–14 years, 15–49 years, 0–59 years, >60 years.

2.3 Sample early warning alert and response (EWAR) early warning reporting form

This form is used in the acute phase of the crisis when the risk of public health events, such as trauma, poisoning, or outbreaks from epidemic-prone diseases, are high.

Date from Monday: .... To Sunday: ....

Town/village/settlement/camp:..

Province: .... District: ....

Subdistrict: .... Site name: ....

▪ Inpatient ▪ Outpatient ▪ Health centre ▪ Mobile clinic

Supporting agency(ies): ....

Reporting officer & contact number: ....

Total population: .... Total under 5 years population: ..

A. WEEKLY AGGREGATE DATA

New cases of:	Morbidity		Mortality		Total
	<5 Years	5 Years and over	<5 Years	5 Years & over	
TOTAL ADMISSIONS					
TOTAL DEATHS					
Acute respiratory infection					
Acute watery diarrhoea					
Acute bloody diarrhoea					
Malaria – suspected/confirmed					
Measles					
Meningitis – suspected					
Acute haemorrhagic fever syndrome					
Acute jaundice syndrome					
Acute flaccid paralysis (AFP)					
Tetanus					
Other fever >38.5°C					
Trauma					
Chemical poisoning					
Others					
Total					

– More than one diagnosis is possible; the most important should be recorded. Each case should be counted only once.
– Include only those cases that were seen (or deaths that occurred) during the surveillance week.
– Write "0" (zero) if you had no case or death during the week for one of the syndromes listed in the form.
– Deaths should be reported only in the mortality section, NOT in the morbidity section.
– Case definitions for each condition under surveillance should be written on the back of this form.
– Causes of morbidity can be added or subtracted according to the epidemiology and risk assessment of disease.
– The purpose of EWAR surveillance is the early detection of public health events that need immediate response.
– Data on conditions such as malnutrition should be obtained through surveys (prevalence), rather than surveillance (incidence).

B. OUTBREAK ALERT

At any time you suspect any of the following diseases, please SMS or phone ....
or email .... with maximum information on time, place and number of cases and
deaths: cholera, shigellosis, measles, polio, typhoid, tetanus, hepatitis A or E, dengue,
meningitis, diphtheria, pertussis, haemorrhagic fever, trauma and chemical poisoning.
This list of diseases will vary depending on the disease epidemiology of the country.

2.4 Sample routine health management information system (HMIS) surveillance reporting form

Site: ....

Date from Monday: .... To Sunday: ....

Total population at beginning of this week/month: ....

Births this week/month: .... Deaths this week/month: ....

Arrivals this week/month (if applicable): ....

Departures this week/month: ....

Total population at end of week/month: ....

Total under 5 years population: ....

Morbidity	Under 5 years (new cases)		5 years and over (new cases)		Total		Repeat cases	
Diagnosis	Male	Female	Total	Male	Female	Total	New cases	Total
Acute respiratory infection								
Acute watery diarrhoea								
Acute bloody diarrhoea								
Malaria – suspected/confirmed								
Measles								
Meningitis – suspected								
Acute haemorrhagic fever syndrome								
Acute jaundice syndrome								
Acute flaccid paralysis (AFP)								
Tetanus								
Other fever >38.5°C								
HIV/AIDS								
Eye diseases								
Skin diseases								
Acute malnutrition								
Sexually Transmitted Infection								
Genital ulcer disease								
Male urethral discharge								
Vaginal discharge								
Pelvic inflammatory disease (PID)								
Neonatal conjunctivitis								

Morbidity	Under 5 years (new cases)			5 years and over (new cases)			Total		Repeat cases	
Diagnosis	Male	Female	Total	Male	Female	Total			New cases	Total
Congenital syphili										
Non-communicable diseases										
Hypertension										
Ischaemic heart disease										
Diabetes										
Asthma										
Chronic obstructive pulmonary disease										
Epilepsy										
Other chronic NCD										
Mental Health										
Alcohol or other substance use disorder										
Intellectual disability and development disorders										
Psychotic disorder (including bipolar disorder)										
Dementia or delirium										
Moderate-severe emotional disorder/ depression										
Medically unex- plained somatic complaint										
Self-harm (including suicide attempt)										
Other psychological complaint										
Injuries										
Major head/spine injury										
Major torso injury										
Major extremity injury										
Moderate injury										
Minor injury										
Total										

Age can be further disaggregated as feasible, for example 0–11 months, 1–4 years, 5–14 years, 15–49 years, 50–59 years, >60 years

Appendix 3
Formulas for calculating key health indicators

Crude mortality rate (CMR)

Definition: The rate of death in the entire population, including both women and men and all ages.

Formula:

$$\frac{\text{Total number of deaths during time period}}{\text{Mid-period population at risk x Number of days in time period}} \times 10{,}000 \text{ persons} = \text{Deaths}/10{,}000 \text{ persons/day}$$

Under-5 mortality rate (U5MR)

Definition: The rate of death among children below five years of age in the population.

Formula:

$$\frac{\text{Total number of deaths in children <5 years during time period}}{\text{Total number of children <5 years x Number of day in time period}} \times \frac{10{,}000}{\text{persons}} = \text{Deaths}/10{,}000 \text{ children under 5 years/day}$$

Incidence rate

Definition: The number of new cases of a disease that occur during a specified period of time in a population at risk of developing the disease.

Formula:

$$\frac{\text{Number of new cases due to specific disease in time period}}{\text{Population at risk of developing disease x Number of months in time period}} \times 1{,}000 \text{ persons} = \text{New cases due to specific disease}/1{,}000 \text{ persons/month}$$

Case fatality rate (CFR)

Definition: The number of people who die of a disease divided by the number of people who have the disease.

Formula:

$$\frac{\text{Number of people dying from disease during time period}}{\text{People who have the disease during time period}} \times 100 = x\%$$

Health facility utilisation rate

Definition: The number of outpatient visits per person per year. Whenever possible, draw a distinction between new and old visits. **New** visits should be used to calculate this rate. However, it is often difficult to differentiate between new and old visits, so they are frequently combined as total visits during a crisis.

Formula:

$$\frac{\text{Total number of visits in one week}}{\text{Total population}} \times 52 \text{ weeks } = \text{Visits/person/year}$$

Number of consultations per clinician per day

Definition: Average number of total consultations (new and repeat cases) seen by each clinician per day.

Formula:

$$\frac{\text{Total number of consultations in one week}}{\text{Number of FTE* clinicians in health facility}} \div \frac{\text{Number of days health facility}}{\text{open per week}}$$

*FTE (full-time equivalent) refers to the equivalent number of clinicians working in a health facility. For example, if there are six clinicians working in the outpatient department but two of them work half-time, then the number of FTE clinicians = 4 full-time staff + 2 half-time staff = 5 FTE clinicians.

Appendix 4
Poisoning

Poisoning can occur when people are exposed to toxic chemicals through the mouth, nose, skin, eyes or ears or through ingestion. Children are at higher risk because they breath more quickly, have a large surface area relative to body mass, have more permeable skin, and are closer to the ground. Toxic exposures can affect a child's development, including causing growth retardation and impaired nutrition, and can lead to illness or death.

Initial management
On presentation to the health facility, if the patient is known to have been exposed to or has signs and symptoms of chemical exposure:

- take precautions for healthcare staff, including wearing appropriate personal protective equipment (PPE);
- triage patients;
- perform life-saving interventions;
- decontaminate (for example, remove the patient's clothes, or rinse affected areas with soapy water), ideally outside the health facility to prevent further exposures; then
- follow further treatment protocols, including supportive treatment.

Treatment protocols
These may vary by country. In general, providing an antidote, and supportive treatment (such as for breathing), is needed.

The table below shows symptoms of chemical exposure and common antidotes given.

Symptoms of exposure to toxic chemicals and possible treatment

Class of toxic chemical	Common features of exposure	Antidotes (country guidelines will vary)
Nerve agents such as sarin, tabun or VX	Pinpoint pupils; blurred vision; headache; copious secretions; tight chest and breathing difficulty; nausea; vomiting; diarrhoea; muscle twitching; seizures; loss of consciousness.	Atropine Oximes (pralidoxime, obidoxime) Benzodiazepines (for seizures)
Blister agents such as mustard gas	Tearing; eye irritation; conjunctivitis; corneal damage; redness and blisters of the skin with pain; respiratory distress.	Supportive treatment +/- sodium thiosulphate For example, eye irrigation, topical antibiotic, skin washing, bronchodilators, Use sodium thiosulphate in severe cases
Cyanide	Gasping for air; asphyxiation; seizures; confusion; nausea.	Amyl nitrite (first aid) Sodium thiosulphate and sodium nitrite or with 4 DMAP or Hydroxocobalamin or Dicobalt edetate
Incapacitating agents such as BZ	Dry mouth and skin; tachycardia; altered consciousness; delusions; hallucinations; hyperthermia; incoordination; dilated pupils.	physostigmine
Tear gas and riot control agents.	Stinging and burning of mucous membranes; lacrimation; salivation; runny nose; tight chest; headache; nausea.	Mainly supportive treatment
Chlorine	Eye redness and lacrimation; nose and throat irritation; cough; suffocation or choking sensation; shortness of breath; wheezing; hoarse voice; pulmonary oedema.	N acetylcysteine (NAC)
Thallium (rat poison)	Abdominal pain; nausea; vomiting; diarrhoea; constipation; seizures; delirium; depression; scalp and body hair loss; painful peripheral neuropathy and distal motor weakness; ataxia; neurocognitive deficits.	Prussian blue
Lead	Anorexia; vomiting; constipation; abdominal pain; pallor; inattentiveness; weakness; peripheral palsies.	Chelation
Organophosphates (includes some insecticides and nerve gas)	Salivation; lacrimation; urination; defaecation; gastric cramps; vomiting.	Atropine Oximes (pralidoxime, obidoxime)

Modified from WHO, Environmental Health in Emergencies guidance.

References and further reading

Health and human rights
The Right to Health: Fact Sheet No.31. OHCHR and WHO, 2008.
http://www.ohchr.org

Civil–military coordination
Civil Military Coordination during Humanitarian Health Action. Global Health Cluster, 2011. www.who.int

Humanitarian Civil-Military Coordination: A Guide for the Military. UN OCHA, 2014.
http://www.unocha.org

Protection and international humanitarian law
Ambulance and pre-hospital services in risk situations. ICRC, 2013. www.icrc.org

Common Ethical principles of health care in times of armed conflict and other emergencies. ICRC, Geneva, 2015. https://www.icrc.org

Ensuring the preparedness and security of health care facilities in armed conflict and other emergencies. ICRC, 2015. www.icrc.org

Guidance Note on Disability and Emergency Risk Management for Health. World Health Organization, 2013. http://www.who.int

Health Care in Danger: The responsibilities of health care personnel working in armed conflicts and other emergencies. ICRC, 2012. www.icrc.org

Minimum Standards for Child Protection in Humanitarian Action: Standard 24 Shelter and Child Protection. Child Protection Working Group (now the Alliance for Child Protection in Humanitarian Action), 2012.
https://resourcecentre.savethechildren.net

Monitoring and Reporting Mechanism (MRM) on Grave Violations Against Children in situations of Armed Conflict. UN and UNICEF, 2014. http://www.mrmtools.org

Coordination
Health Cluster Guide. Global Health Cluster, 2009. http://www.who.int

Reference module for cluster coordination at the country level. IASC, 2015.
www.humanitarianresponse.info

Health in emergencies
Blanchet, K et al *Evidence on public health interventions in humanitarian crises.* The Lancet, 2017: http://www.thelancet.com

Classification and Minimum Standards for foreign medical teams in sudden onset disasters. WHO, 2013. http://www.who.int

Ensuring Access to Health Care Operational Guidance on Refugee Protection and Solutions in Urban Areas. UNHCR, 2011. http://www.unhcr.org

Public Health Guide in Emergencies. The Johns Hopkins and Red Cross Red Crescent, 2008. http://pdf.usaid.gov

Refugee Health: An approach to emergency situations. Médecins Sans Frontières, 1997. http://refbooks.msf.org

Spiegel et. al. *Health-care needs of people affected by conflict: future trends and changing frameworks.* The Lancet, 2010. http://www.thelancet.com

Clinical guidelines
Clinical Guidelines - Diagnosis and Treatment Manual. MSF, 2016. http://refbooks.msf.org

Health systems
Analysing Disrupted Health Sectors. A Modular Manual. WHO, 2009. http://www.who.int

Elston et al. *Impact of the Ebola outbreak on health systems and population health in Sierra Leone.* Journal of Public Health, 2015. https://academic.oup.com

Everybody's Business. Strengthening Health Systems to Improve Health Outcomes. WHO, 2007. http://www.who.int

The Health System Assessment Approach: A How to Manual 2.0. USAID, 2012. www.hfgproject.org

Parpia et al. *Effects of Response to 2014-2015 Ebola Outbreak on Deaths from Malaria, HIV / AIDS and Tuberculosis West Africa. Emerging Infection Diseases Vol 22.* CDC, 2016. https://wwwnc.cdc.gov

Recovery Toolkit: Supporting countries to achieve health service resilience. WHO, 2016. http://www.who.int

Toolkit assessing health system capacity to manage large influx of refugees, asylum-seekers and migrants. WHO/UNHCR/IOM, 2016. http://www.euro.who.int

Safety
Comprehensive Safe Hospital Framework. WHO, 2015. http://www.who.int

Patient Safety: Making Health Safer. WHO, 2017. http://www.who.int

Infection prevention and control
Essential environmental health standards in health care. WHO,2008. http://www.who.int

Essential Water and Sanitation Requirements for Health Structures. MSF, 2009. http://oops.msf.org

Guideline for Isolation Precautions: Preventing Transmission of Infectious Agents in Healthcare Settings. CDC, 2007 updated 2017. https://www.cdc.gov

Guidance for the selection and use of Personal Protective Equipment (PPE) in healthcare settings. CDC, 2004. https://www.cdc.gov

Guidelines for safe disposal of unwanted pharmaceuticals in and after emergencies. WHO, 1999. http://apps.who.int

Guidelines on Core Components of Infection Prevention and Control Programmes at the National and Acute Health Care Facility level. WHO, 2016. http://www.who.int

Management of Dead Bodies after Disasters: A field Manual for First Responders, Second Edition. ICRC, IFRC, 2016. www.icrc.org

Safe management of wastes for health-care activities, Second edition. WHO, 2014. http://www.who.int

Healthcare workforce

Classifying health workers: mapping occupations to the international standards. WHO. http://www.who.int

Global strategy on human resources for health. Workforce 2030. WHO, 2016. http://www.who.int

Human resources for Health Information System, Minimum Data Set for Health Workforce Registry. WHO, 2015. *http://www.who.int*

Health workforce requirement for universal health coverage and the SDGs. WHO, 2016. http://www.who.int

International Standard Classification of Occupation: Structure, group definitions and correspondence tables. ILO, 2012. http://www.ilo.org

WISN Workload indicators of staffing need, user's manual. WHO, 2010. http://www.who.int

Working together for health. World Health Report 2006. WHO 2006. http://www.who.int

Medicines

Emergency Reproductive Health Kit. UNFPA, 2011. https://www.unfpa.org

Guidelines of Medicine Donations. WHO, 2010. http://www.who.int

Interagency Emergency Health Kit. WHO, 2015. http://www.who.int

Model Formulary for children. WHO, 2010. http://apps.who.int

Model List of Essential Medicines 20th List. WHO, 2017. http://www.who.int

Non-Communicable Diseases Kit. WHO, 2016. http://www.who.int

Revised Cholera Kits. WHO, 2015. http://www.who.int

The Interagency Emergency Health Kit 2017: Medicines and Medical Devices for 10 000 People for Approximately Three Months. WHO. 2017.

Medical devices including assistive devices

Core Medical Equipment. WHO, 2011. http://www.who.int

Decommissioning Medical Equipment and Devices. WHO http://www.who.int

Global Atlas of Medical Devices. WHO, 2017. http://www.who.int

Guidelines on the provision of Manual Wheelchairs in less resourced settings. World Health Organization, 2008. http://www.who.int

Medical Device technical series: Medical device regulations, medical devices by health care facilities, needs assessment for medical devices, procurement process resource guide, medical device donations, medical equipment maintenance programme overview. WHO, 2011. http://www.who.int

Priority Assistive Products List. The GATE Initiative, WHO and USAID, 2016. http://www.who.int

Controlled medicines
Access to Controlled Medications Programme, WHO Briefing Note. WHO, 2012. http://www.who.int

Availability of Internationally Controlled Drugs: Ensuring Adequate Access for Medical and Scientific Purposes. International Narcotics Control Board and WHO, 2010. http://www.incb.org

Availability of narcotic drugs and psychotropic substances in emergency situations, INCD report, pages 36-37. International Narcotics Control Board, 2014. www.incb.org

Ensuring Balance in National Policies on Controlled Substances. Guidance for availability and accessibility of controlled medicines. WHO, 2011. http://www.who.int

Blood products
Blood safety and availability. WHO, 2017. http://www.who.int

Guidelines on management of blood and blood components as essential medicines, Annex 3. WHO, 2017. http://apps.who.int

Universal Access to Safe Blood Transfusion. WHO, 2008. http://www.who.int

Health financing
Cash-based Interventions for Health Programmes in Refugee Settings: A Review. UNHCR, 2015. http://www.unhcr.org

Cash for Health: Key Learnings from a cash for health intervention in Jordan. UNHCR, 2015. http://www.unhcr.org

Monitoring progress towards universal health coverage at country and global levels. WHO, 2014. http://apps.who.int

Removing user fees for primary health care services during humanitarian crises. Global Health Cluster and WHO, 2011. http://www.who.int

Health information
IASC Guidelines: Common Operating Datasets in Disaster Preparedness and Response. IASC, 2011 https://interagencystandingcommittee.org

Global Reference List of 100 Core Health Indicators. WHO, 2015. http://www.who.int

Standards for Public Health Information Services in Activated Health Clusters and Other Humanitarian Health Coordination Mechanisms. Global Health Cluster, 2017. www.humanitarianresponse.info

Health needs assessments and prioritisation of health care services
Assessment Toolkit: Practical steps for the assessment of health and humanitarian crises. MSF, 2013. http://evaluation.msf.org

Global Health Observatory Data Repository: Crude birth and death rate by country. World Health Organization, 2017. http://apps.who.int

Rapid Risk Assessments of Acute Public Health Events. WHO, 2012.

http://www.who.int
SARA Service Availability and Readiness Assessment Survey. WHO/USAID, 2015. http://www.who.int

Communicable disease prevention
Integrated Vector Management in Humanitarian Emergencies Toolkit. MENTOR Initiative and WHO, 2016. http://thementorinitiative.org

Vaccination in Acute Humanitarian Crises: A Framework for Decision Making. WHO, 2017. http://www.who.int

Communicable diseases (specific diseases)
Dengue: Guidelines for Diagnosis, Treatment, Prevention and Control: New Edition. WHO, 2009. http://www.who.int

Guidelines for the control for shigellosis. WHO, 2005. http://www.who.int

Interim Guidance Document on Cholera surveillance. Global Task Force on Cholera Control and WHO, 2017. http://www.who.int

Liddle, K et al. *TB Treatment in a Chronic Complex Emergency: Treatment Outcomes and Experiences in Somalia.* Trans R Soc Trop Med Hyg, NCBI, 2013. www.ncbi.nlm.nih.gov

Managing Meningitis Epidemics in Africa. WHO, 2015. http://apps.who.int

Management of a measles epidemic. MSF, 2014. http://refbooks.msf.org

Meningitis Outbreak Response in Sub-Saharan Africa. WHO, 2014. http://www.who.int

Pandemic Influenza Preparedness (PIP) Framework for the sharing of influenza viruses and access to vaccines and other benefits. WHO, 2011. http://apps.who.int

Outbreak detection and early response
Early detection, assessment and response to acute public health events, Implementation of Early Warning and Response with a focus on Event-Based Surveillance. WHO, 2014. http://www.who.int

"Early warning, alert and response (EWAR): a key area for countries preparedness for Health Emergencies. WHO, 2018. Weekly Epidemiological Record. WHO. http://www.who.int

Early warning, alert and response (EWAR) a key area for countries preparedness for Health Emergencies. WHO, 2018. http://apps.who.int

Weekly Epidemiological Record. WHO. http://www.who.int

Outbreak Surveillance and Response in Humanitarian Crises, WHO guidelines for EWARN implementation. WHO, 2012. http://www.who.int

Outbreak preparedness and response
Communicable disease control in emergencies, A field Manual. WHO, 2005.
http://www.who.int

Epidemic Preparedness and Response in Refugee Camp Settings, Guidance for Public health officers. UNHCR, 2011. http://www.unhcr.org

Outbreak Communication Planning Guideline. WHO, 2008. http://www.who.int

Child and newborn health
IMCI Chart Booklet. WHO, 2014. http://www.who.int

Integrated Community Case Management in Acute and Protracted Emergencies: case study for South Sudan. IRC and UNICEF, 2017. https://www.rescue.org

Newborn Health in Humanitarian Settings Field Guide Interim Version. IAWG RH in Crises, 2016. http://iawg.net

Overview and Latest update on iCCM: Potential for Benefit to Malaria Programs. UNICEF and WHO, 2015. www.unicef.org

Polio vaccines: WHO position Paper Weekly epidemiological record. WHO, 2016.
http://www.who.int

Updates on HIV and infant feeding. UNICEF, WHO, 2016. http://www.who.int

Sexual and reproductive health
Adolescent Sexual and Reproductive Health Toolkit for Humanitarian Settings. UNFPA and Save the Children, 2009. http://iawg.net

Inter-Agency Reproductive Health Kits for Crisis Situations, 5th Edition. UNFPA/IAWG, 2011. http://iawg.net

Inter-agency Field Manual on Sexual and Reproductive Health in Humanitarian Settings. IWAG on Reproductive Health in Crises and WHO, 2018.
http://www.who.int

Medical eligibility criteria wheel for contraceptive use. WHO, 2015. http://who.int

Minimum Initial Service Package (MISP) for Reproductive Health in Crisis Situations: A distance learning module. IWAG and Women's Refugee Commission. 2011.
http://iawg.net

Selected practice recommendations for contraceptive use, Third Edition. WHO, 2016.
http://www.who.int

Safe abortion: Technical & policy guidance for health systems. WHO, 2015.
http://www.who.int

Sexual violence and clinical management of rape
Clinical Care for Sexual Assault Survivors. International Rescue Committee, 2014.
http://iawg.net

Caring for Child Survivors of Sexual Abuse Guidelines for health and psychosocial service providers in humanitarian settings. IRC and UNICEF, 2012. https://www.unicef.org

Clinical Management of Rape Survivors: Developing protocols for use with refugees and internally displaced persons, Revised Edition, pp.44–47. WHO, UN Population Fund, and UNHCR, 2004. www.who.int

Clinical Management of Rape Survivors: E-Learning. WHO 2009. http://apps.who.int

Guidelines for Integrating Gender-Based Violence Interventions in Humanitarian Action, Reducing Risk, promoting resilience and aiding recovery. Inter-Agency Standing Committee, 2015. https://gbvguidelines.org

Guidelines for Medico-Legal Care of Victims of Sexual Violence. WHO, 2003. http://www.who.int

HIV
Consolidated Guidelines on the Use or ART Drugs for Treating and Preventing HIV Infection: Recommendations for a public health approach - Second edition. WHO, 2016. www.who.int

Guidelines for Addressing HIV in Humanitarian Settings. UNAIDS and IASC, 2010. http://www.unaids.org

Guidelines for the delivery of antiretroviral therapy to migrant and crisis-affected populations in Sub Saharan Africa. UNHCR, 2014. http://www.unhcr.org

Guidelines for management of sexually transmitted infections. WHO, 2003. www.emro.who.int

Guidelines on post-exposure prophylaxis for HIV and the use of Cotrimoxazole prophylaxis for HIV-related infections among adults, adolescents and children. WHO, 2014. http://www.who.int

HIV prevention in emergencies. UNFPA, 2014. http://www.unfpa.org

PMTCT in Humanitarian Settings Inter-Agency Task Team to Address HIV in Humanitarian Emergencies Part II: Implementation Guide. Inter-Agency Task Team, 2015. http://iawg.net

WHO policy on collaborative TB/HIV activities Guidelines for national programmes and other stakeholders. WHO, 2012. http://www.who.int

Injury and trauma care
American Heart Association Guidelines for CPR & ECC. American Heart Association, 2015 and 2017. https://eccguidelines.heart.org

Anaesthesia Handbook, Annex 3: ICRC Pain Management. Reversed WHO pain management ladder. ICRC, 2017. https://shop.icrc.org

Child Protection in Humanitarian Action Review: Dangers and injuries. Alliance for Child Protection in Humanitarian Action, 2016. https://resourcecentre.savethechildren.net

Classification and Minimum Standards for Foreign Medical Teams in Sudden Onset Minimum Technical Standards and Recommendations for Rehabilitation. WHO, 2016. http://apps.who.int

Disasters. WHO, 2013. http://www.who.int

eCBHFA Framework Community Based Health and First Aid. ICRC, 2017. http://ifrc-ecbhfa.org

EMT minimum data set for reporting by emergency medical teams. WHO, 2016. https://extranet.who.int

Guidelines for trauma quality improvement programmes. World Health Organization, 2009. http://apps.who.int

International First Aid and Resuscitation Guidelines. IFRC, 2016. www.lfrc.org

Interagency initiative comprising a set of integrated triage tools for routine, surge and prehospital triage allowing smooth transition between routine and surge conditions. WHO and ICRC. http://www.who.int

Recommended Disaster Core Competencies for Hospital Personnel. California Department of Public Health, 2011. http://cdphready.org

Technical Meeting for Global Consensus on Triage. WHO and ICRC, 2017. https://www.humanitarianresponse.info/sites/www.humanitarianresponse.info

The European Resuscitation Council Guidelines for Resuscitation. European resuscitation council, 2015. https://cprguidelines.eu

The WHO Trauma Care Checklist. WHO, 2016. http://www.who.int

von Schreeb, J et al. *Foreign field hospitals in the recent sudden-onset disasters in Iran, Haiti, Indonesia, and Pakistan.* Prehospital Disaster Med, NCBI, 2008. https://www.ncbi.nlm.nih.gov

War Surgery, Working with limited resources in armed conflict and other situations of violence. International Committee of the Red Cross, 2010. https://www.icrc.org

Mental health

A faith-sensitive approach in humanitarian response: Guidance on mental health and psychosocial programming. The Lutheran World Federation and Islamic Relief Worldwide, 2018. https://interagencystandingcommittee.org

A Common Monitoring and Evaluation Framework for Mental Health and Psychosocial Support in Emergency Settings. IASC, 2017. https://reliefweb.int

Assessing Mental Health and Psychosocial Needs and Resources: Toolkit for Humanitarian Settings. WHO and UNHCR, 2012. http://www.who.int

Building back better: sustainable mental health care after emergencies. WHO, 2013. http://www.who.int

Facilitate community self-help and social support (action sheet 5.2) in guidelines on Mental Health and Psychosocial Support in Emergency Settings. IASC, 2007. https://interagencystandingcommittee.org

Group Interpersonal Therapy (IPT) for Depression. WHO, 2016. http://www.who.int

Inter-Agency Referral Form and Guidance Note for Mental Health and Psychosocial Support in Emergency Settings. IASC, 2017. https://interagencystandingcommittee.org

mhGAP Humanitarian Intervention Guide: Clinical Management of Mental, Neurological and Substance Use Conditions in Humanitarian Settings. WHO and UNHCR, 2015. http://www.unhcr.org

Problem Management Plus (PM+): Individual psychological help for adults impaired by distress in communities exposed to adversity. WHO, 2016. http://www.who.int

Psychological First Aid: Guide for Field Workers. WHO, War Trauma Foundation and World Vision International, 2011. http://www.who.int

Psychological First Aid Training Manual for Child Practitioners. Save the Children, 2013. https://resourcecentre.savethechildren.net

Reference Group for Mental Health and Psychosocial Support in Emergency Settings in Mental Health and Psychosocial Support in Humanitarian Emergencies: What Should Humanitarian Health Actors Know. IASC, 2010. http://www.who.int

Non-communicable diseases
Disaster Risk Management for Health: Non-Communicable Diseases Fact Sheet 2011. WHO, 2011. http://www.who.int

Jobanputra, K. Boulle, P. Roberts, B. Perel, P. *Three Steps to Improve Management of Noncommunicable Diseases in Humanitarian Crises.* PLOS Medicine, 2016. http://journals.plos.org

Lozano et al. *Global and regional mortality from 235 causes of death for 20 age groups in 1990 and 2010: a systemic analysis for the Global Burden of Disease Study 2010.* The Lancet, 2012. https://www.ncbi.nlm.nih.gov

NCD Global Monitoring Framework. WHO, 2013. http://www.who.int

NCDs in Emergencies – UN Interagency Task Force on NCDs. WHO, 2016. http://www.who.int

Slama, S et al. *Care of Non-Communicable Diseases in Emergencies.* The Lancet, 2016. http://www.thelancet.com

WHO Package of Essential Non-Communicable Disease Interventions, Tools for implementing WHO PEN. WHO, 2009. http://www.who.int

Palliative care
Caring for Volunteers Training Manual. Psychosocial Centre IFRC, 2015. http://pscentre.org

Disaster Spiritual Care Handbook. Disaster Services, American Red Cross, 2012. https://interagencystandingcommittee.org

Guidance for managing ethical issues in infectious disease outbreaks. WHO, 2016. http://apps.who.int

IASC guidelines on mental health and psychosocial support in emergency settings. IASC, 2007. http://www.who.int

IAHPC List of Essential Medicines for Palliative Care. International Association for Hospice and Palliative Care, 2007. https://hospicecare.com

Matzo, M et al. *Palliative Care Considerations in Mass Casualty Events with Scarce Resources.* Biosecurity and Bioterrorism, NCBI, 2009.
https://www.ncbi.nlm.nih.gov

Powell, RA. Schwartz, L. Nouvet, E. Sutton, B. et al. *Palliative care in humanitarian crises: always something to offer.* The Lancet, 2017. http://www.thelancet.com

Palliative Care, Cancer control: knowledge into action: WHO guide for effective programmes. WHO, 2007. http://www.who.int

Silove, D. *The ADAPT model: a conceptual framework for mental health and psychosocial programming in post conflict settings.* War Trauma Foundation, 2013.
https://www.interventionjournal.com

Nouvet, E. Chan, E. Schwartz, LJ. *Looking good but doing harm? Perceptions of short-term medical missions in Nicaragua.* Global public health, NCBI, 2016.
https://www.ncbi.nlm.nih.gov

19th WHO Model List of Essential Medicines chapter 2 2, Medicines for pain and palliative care. WHO, 2015. http://www.who.int

Poisoning
Initial Clinical management of patients exposed to chemical weapons. WHO, 2015. http://www.who.int

Further reading
For further reading suggestions please go to
www.spherestandards.org/handbook/online-resources

A Annexes

Contents

Annex 1
Legal Foundation to Sphere

The Humanitarian Charter sets out shared beliefs and common principles concerning humanitarian action and responsibilities in situations of disaster or conflict, and notes that these are reflected in international law. The following annotated list of key documents includes the most relevant international legal instruments relating to international human rights law, international humanitarian law (IHL), refugee law and humanitarian action. It does not attempt to represent regional law and developments. Further resources and web links to a number of other guidelines, principles, standards and frameworks that support implementation are available on the Sphere website, www.spherestandards.org. Notes are provided only for the documents that require explanation, are newer additions, or have specific sections concerning disaster or conflict.

The Sphere Handbook reflects specific concerns that are part of the international legal framework. Generally, these include the right to personal safety and dignity; freedom from discrimination; and the rights to water and sanitation, shelter, food security and nutrition, and healthcare. While some of these rights are spelled out in specific international covenants, they are all included in one of the general human rights instruments on either civil and political rights or economic, social and cultural rights.

This annex includes documents which are organised thematically in four categories:

1. **Human rights, protection and vulnerability**
2. **Armed conflict and humanitarian assistance**
3. **Refugees and internally displaced persons**
4. **Disasters and humanitarian assistance**
5. **Humanitarian policy frameworks, guidelines and principles on human rights, protection and vulnerability in emergency preparedness and response** www.spherestandards.org/handbook/online-resources

To ensure clarity about the status of each document within these categories, they are classified as a) treaties and customary law or b) UN and other formally adopted intergovernmental guidelines and principles.

1. International instruments on human rights, protection and vulnerability

The following documents relate primarily to the human rights recognised in universal treaties and declarations. A number of key documents relating to age (children and older people), sex and disability are also included, because these are some of the most common bases of vulnerability in disaster or conflict.

1.1 Treaties and customary law on human rights, protection and vulnerability

Human rights treaty law applies to states that are parties to the relevant treaty, but customary law (for example, the prohibition on torture) applies to all states. Human rights law applies at all times, with two possible exceptions:

- Some limited civil and political rights may be suspended during declared national emergencies, consistent with Article 4 of the International Covenant on Civil and Political Rights ("derogation").
- During recognised armed conflicts, IHL applies first if there is any inconsistency with human rights law.

1.1.1 Universal human rights

The Universal Declaration of Human Rights 1948 (UDHR), adopted by UN General Assembly Resolution 217 A(III) of 10 December 1948. www.un.org

> **Comment:** Proclaimed by the UN General Assembly in 1948, the UDHR set out, for the first time, fundamental human rights to be universally protected. It is not a treaty but is generally agreed to have become part of customary international law. The first sentence of the preamble introduces the concept of the "inherent dignity" of human beings as a fundamental basis for human rights, and Article 1 states, "All human beings are born free and equal in dignity and rights."

International Covenant on Civil and Political Rights 1966 (ICCPR), adopted by UN General Assembly Resolution 2200A (XXI) of 16 December 1966, entry into force 23 March 1976, United Nations, Treaty Series, vol. 999, p. 171 and vol. 1057, p. 407. www.ohchr.org

Second Optional Protocol to ICCPR 1989 (aiming at the abolition of the death penalty), adopted by UN General Assembly Resolution 44/128 of 15 December 1989, entry into force 11 July 1991, United Nations, Treaty Series, vol. 1642, p. 414. www.ohchr.org

> **Comment:** States parties to the ICCPR must respect and ensure the rights for all individuals within their territory or under their jurisdiction, while

recognising the right of "peoples" to self-determination and the equal rights of men and women. Some rights (marked with asterisk*) may never be suspended, even in the most dire national emergency.

ICCPR Rights: right to life;* no torture or other cruel, inhuman or degrading treatment;* no slavery;* no arbitrary arrest or detention; humanity and dignity in detention; no imprisonment for breach of contract;* freedom of movement and residence; only lawful expulsion of aliens; equality before the law, fair trial and presumption of innocence in criminal trials; no retrospectivity in criminal offences;* equal recognition before the law;* private life; free thought, religion and conscience;* free opinion, expression and peaceful assembly; freedom of association; right to marriage and family life; protection of children; right to vote and participate in public affairs; minorities' right to enjoy their own culture, religion and language.*

International Covenant on Economic, Social and Cultural Rights 1966 (ICESCR), adopted by UN General Assembly Resolution 2200A (XXI) of 16 December 1966, entry into force 3 January 1976, United Nations, Treaty Series, vol. 993, p. 3. www.ohchr.org

Comment: States parties agree to commit the maximum of their available resources to "achieving progressively" the covenant rights, which are to be enjoyed equally by men and women.

ICESCR Rights: to work; to receive just remuneration; to join trade unions; to have social security or insurance; to family life, including protection of mothers after childbirth and protection of children from exploitation; to an adequate standard of living, including food, clothing and housing; to physical and mental health; to education; and to participate in cultural life and enjoy the benefits of scientific and cultural progress.

International Convention on the Elimination of All Forms of Racial Discrimination 1969 (ICERD), adopted by UN General Assembly Resolution 2106 (XX) of 21 December 1965, entry into force 4 January 1969, United Nations, Treaty Series, vol. 660, p. 195. www.ohchr.org

Convention on the Elimination of All Forms of Discrimination Against Women 1979 (CEDAW), adopted by UN General Assembly Resolution 34/180 of 18 December 1979, entry into force 3 September 1981, United Nations, Treaty Series, vol. 1249, p. 13. www.ohchr.org

Convention on the Rights of the Child 1989 (CRC), adopted by UN General Assembly Resolution 44/25 of 20 November 1989, entry into force 2 September 1990, United Nations, Treaty Series, vol. 1577, p. 3. www.ohchr.org

Optional Protocol to CRC on the Involvement of Children in Armed Conflict 2000, adopted by UN General Assembly Resolution A/RES/54/263 of 25 May 2000, entry into force 12 February 2002, United Nations, Treaty Series, vol. 2173, p. 222. www.ohchr.org

Optional Protocol to CRC on the Sale of Children, Child Prostitution and Child Pornography 2000, adopted by UN General Assembly Resolution A/RES/54/263 of 25 May 2000, entry into force 18 January 2002, United Nations, Treaty Series, vol. 2171, p. 227. www.ohchr.org

> **Comment:** The CRC has almost universal state accession. It restates the basic human rights of children and identifies when they need special protection (for example, when separated from their families). The protocols require positive action on specific child protection issues for states that are parties to them.

Convention on the Rights of Persons with Disabilities 2006 (CRPD), adopted by UN General Assembly Resolution A/RES/61/106 of 13 December 2006, entry into force 3 May 2008, United Nations, Treaty Collection, Chapter IV, 15. www.ohchr.org

> **Comment:** The CRPD supports the rights of people with disabilities under all other human rights treaties, as well as dealing specifically with aware-ness-raising regarding persons with disabilities, non-discrimination and accessibility of services and facilities. There is also special mention of "situations of risk and humanitarian emergencies" (Article 11).

1.1.2 Genocide, torture and other criminal abuse of rights

Convention on the Prevention and Punishment of the Crime of Genocide 1948, adopted by UN General Assembly Resolution 260 (III) of 9 December 1948, entry into force 12 January 1951, United Nations, Treaty Series, vol. 78, p. 277. www.ohchr.org

Convention against Torture and Other Cruel, Inhuman or Degrading Treatment or Punishment 1984, adopted by UN General Assembly Resolution 39/46 of 10 December 1984, entry into force 26 June 1987, United Nations, Treaty Series, vol. 1465, p. 85. www.ohchr.org

> **Comment:** This convention has a very high number of states parties. The prohibition on torture is also now generally recognised as part of customary international law. No kind of public emergency or war may be invoked to justify torture. States must not return (refoul) anyone to a terri-tory where the person has reasonable grounds to believe he or she would be in danger of torture.

Rome Statute of the International Criminal Court 1998, adopted by the Diplomatic Conference in Rome, 17 July 1998, entry into force 1 July 2002, United Nations, Treaty Series, vol. 2187, p. 3. www.icrc.org

> **Comment:** Article 9 of the Statute (Elements of Crimes), adopted by the International Criminal Court (ICC) in 2002, describes in detail war crimes,

crimes against humanity and genocide, thus codifying much of customary international criminal law. The ICC can investigate and prosecute matters referred to it by the UN Security Council (even if the accused person's state is not a party to the treaty), as well as crimes allegedly committed by nationals of states parties to the treaty, or in their territory.

1.2 United Nations and other formally adopted intergovernmental principles and guidelines on human rights, protection and vulnerability

Madrid International Plan of Action on Ageing 2002, UN Second World Assembly on Ageing, Madrid, 2002, endorsed by UN General Assembly Resolution 37/51 of 3 December 1982. www.ohchr.org

United Nations Principles for Older Persons 1991, UN General Assembly Resolution 46/91 of 16 December 1991. www.ohchr.org

2. International instruments on armed conflict, international humanitarian law and humanitarian assistance

2.1 Treaties and customary law on armed conflict, international humanitarian law and humanitarian assistance

International humanitarian law (IHL) specifies the thresholds of when violent conflict becomes "armed conflict" and thus makes this special legal regime applicable. The International Committee of the Red Cross (ICRC) is the official repository of the IHL treaties and provides extensive information and resources on its website, including the official commentary on the Geneva Conventions and their Protocols, and the rules of the Customary International Humanitarian Law Study. www.icrc.org

2.1.1 Core IHL treaties

The Four Geneva Conventions of 1949

Protocol Additional to the Geneva Conventions, Protection of Victims of International Armed Conflicts 1977 (Protocol I)

Protocol Additional to the Geneva Conventions, Protection of Victims of Non-International Armed Conflicts 1977 (Protocol II). www.icrc.org

> **Comment:** The four Geneva Conventions – to which all states are parties and which are also generally accepted as part of customary law – concern protection and treatment of the wounded and sick in land warfare (I) and at sea (II), treatment of prisoners of war (III) and protection of civilians during armed conflict (IV). They apply primarily to international armed conflicts, except for Article 3 common to the conventions which concerns non-international conflicts, and some other elements now accepted as customary law in non-international conflicts. The two 1977 protocols updated the conventions at that time, especially the definitions of combatants and codifying of non-international conflicts. A number of states have not acceded to the protocols.

2.1.2 Treaties on restricted weapons, landmines and cultural property

In addition to the "Geneva law" outlined above, there is also the body of law often described as the "Hague law" on armed conflict. This includes the convention on protection of cultural property and a number of conventions on the types of weapons that are restricted or prohibited, including gases and other chemical and biological weapons, conventional weapons that are indiscriminate or cause unnecessary suffering, as well as anti-personnel landmines and cluster munitions. www.icrc.org

2.1.3 Customary IHL

Customary IHL refers to the law of armed conflict that is accepted by states, through their statements, policies and practices, as representing customary rules that apply to all states, regardless of their accession to the IHL treaties. There is no agreed list of customary rules, but the most authoritative interpretation is the study below.

Customary International Humanitarian Law (CIHL) Study, ICRC, Henckaerts, J-M. and Doswald-Beck, L., Cambridge University Press, Cambridge and New York, 2005. www.icrc.org

> **Comment:** The study covers almost the full ambit of the law of armed conflict. It lists 161 specific rules and whether each applies in international armed conflict and/or non-international armed conflict. While some legal commentators criticise its methodology, the CIHL study emerged from a broadly consultative and rigorous research process over ten years, and its authority as a collection and interpretation of the customary rules is widely recognised.

2.2 UN and other formally adopted intergovernmental principles and guidelines on armed conflict, IHL and humanitarian assistance

UN Security Council "Aide Memoire" on Protection 2002, as updated 2003 (S/PRST/2003/27). undocs.org

> **Comment:** This is not a binding resolution on states, but a guidance document for the UN Security Council relating to peacekeeping and urgent situations of conflict, resulting from consultations with a range of UN agencies and inter-agency standing committees (IASC).

UN Security Council resolutions on sexual violence and women in armed conflict, especially the first such resolution, number 1325 (2000) on women, peace and security, which was a milestone in addressing violence against women in situations of armed conflict, and subsequently Res. 1820 (2008), Res. 1888 (2009), Res. 1889 (2009) and Res. 1325 (2012). All UN Security Council resolutions by year and number are available at: www.un.org

3. International instruments on refugees and internally displaced persons (IDPs)

3.1 Treaties on refugees and IDPs

In addition to the international treaty, this section includes two African Union (formerly Organization of African Unity, or OAU) treaties, because they both set historic precedents.

Convention relating to the Status of Refugees 1951 (as amended), adopted by the United Nations Conference of Plenipotentiaries on the Status of Refugees and Stateless Persons, Geneva, 2 to 25 July 1951, entry into force 22 April 1954, United Nations, Treaty Series, vol. 189, p. 137. www.unhcr.org

Protocol Relating to the Status of Refugees 1967, noted by the UN General Assembly, in Resolution 2198 (XXI) 2 of 16 December 1966, United Nations, Treaty Series, vol. 606, p. 267. www.unhcr.org

> **Comment:** The first international agreement on refugees, the Convention defines a refugee as a person who, "owing to a well-founded fear of being persecuted for reasons of race, religion, nationality, membership of a particular social group or political opinion, is outside the country of his nationality, and is unable to or, owing to such fear, is unwilling to avail himself of the protection of that country or return there because there is a fear of persecution..."

OAU Convention Governing the Specific Aspects of Refugee Problems in Africa, 1969, adopted by the Assembly of Heads of State and Government at its Sixth Ordinary Session, Addis Ababa, 10 September 1969. www.unhcr.org

> **Comment:** This accepts and expands the 1951 Convention definition to include people who have been compelled to leave their country not only as a result of persecution but also owing to external aggression, occupation, foreign domination or events seriously disturbing public order. It also recognises non-state groups as perpetrators of persecution and it does not require that refugees show a direct link between themselves and the future danger.

African Union Convention for the Protection and Assistance of Internally Displaced Persons in Africa (Kampala Convention) 2009, adopted by a Special Summit of the African Union, held in Kampala, entry into force 6 December 2012. au.int/en/treaties/african-union-convention-protection-and-assistance-internally-displaced-persons-africa

> **Comment:** This is the first multilateral convention concerning IDPs.

3.2 UN and other formally adopted intergovernmental principles and guidelines on refugees and IDPs

Guiding Principles on Internal Displacement 1998, recognised in September 2005 by heads of state and governments assembled at the World Summit in New York in UN General Assembly Resolution 60/L.1 (132, UN Doc. A/60/L.1) as "an important international framework for the protection of internally displaced persons". www.ohchr.org

> **Comment:** These principles are based on international humanitarian and human rights law and analogous refugee law, and are intended to serve as an international standard to guide governments, international organisations and all other relevant actors in providing assistance and protection to IDPs.

4. International instruments on disasters and humanitarian assistance

4.1 Treaties on disasters and humanitarian assistance

Convention on the Safety of United Nations and Associated Personnel 1994, adopted by UN General Assembly Resolution 49/59 of 9 December 1994, entry into force 15 January 1999, United Nations, Treaty Series, vol. 2051, p. 363.

Optional Protocol to the Convention on the Safety of United Nations and Associated Personnel 2005, adopted by UN General Assembly Resolution A/60/42 of 8 December 2005, entry into force 19 August 2010, United Nations, Treaty Series, vol. 2689, p.59. www.un.org

> **Comment:** In the Convention, protection is limited to UN peacekeeping unless the UN has declared "exceptional risk" – an impractical requirement. The Protocol corrects this major flaw in the Convention and expands the legal protection to all UN operations, from emergency humanitarian assistance to peacebuilding and the delivery of humanitarian, political and development assistance.

Tampere Convention on the Provision of Telecommunication Resources for Disaster Mitigation and Relief Operations 1998, approved by the Intergovernmental Conference on Emergency Telecommunications 1998, entry into force 8 January 2005, United Nations, Treaty Series, vol. 2296, p. 5. www.itu.int

UN Framework Convention on Climate Change 1992 (UNFCCC), adopted by the United Nations Conference on Environment and Development, Rio de Janeiro, 4 to 14 June 1992, welcomed by the UN General Assembly in Resolution 47/195 of 22 December 1992, entry into force 21 March 1994, United Nations, Treaty Series, vol. 1771, p. 107. unfccc.int

- **Kyoto Protocol to the UNFCCC 1997**, adopted at the third session of the Conference of the Parties (COP-3) to the Framework Convention, Kyoto, Japan, 1997, entry into force 16 February 2005, United Nations, Treaty Series, vol. 2303, p. 148. unfccc.int
- **Paris Agreement 2015**, adopted at the 21st session of the Conference of the Parties to the Framework Convention (COP-21), Paris, France, December 2015, entry into force November 2016. unfccc.int

> **Comment:** The UNFCCC, the Kyoto Protocol and the Paris Agreement are all part of one treaty framework. They address the urgent need for implementing climate change adaptation and risk reduction strategies, and building local capacity and resilience, especially in countries that are prone to natural disasters. They emphasise disaster reduction strategies and risk management, especially with regard to climate change.

4.2 UN and other formally adopted intergovernmental principles and guidelines on disasters and humanitarian assistance

Strengthening of the coordination of humanitarian emergency assistance of the United Nations, with Annex, Guiding Principles, General Assembly Resolution 46/182 of 19 December 1991. www.unocha.org

> **Comment:** This led to the creation of the UN Department of Humanitarian Affairs, which became the UN Office for the Coordination of Humanitarian Affairs (OCHA) in 1998.

Sendai Framework for Disaster Risk Reduction 2015–2030 (Sendai Framework). www.unisdr.org

> **Comment:** The Sendai Framework is the successor instrument to the Hyogo Framework for Action (HFA) 2005–2015: Building the Resilience of Nations and Communities to Disasters. It was adopted by declaration at the 2015 Third UN World Conference on Disaster Risk Reduction, and endorsed by the UN General Assembly (in Resolution 69/283). The United Nations Office for Disaster Risk Reduction (UNISDR) supports implementation. It is a 15-year voluntary non-binding agreement with the goal to substantially reduce disaster risk and losses in lives, livelihoods and health.

Guidelines for the domestic facilitation and regulation of international disaster relief and initial recovery assistance, (IDRL Guidelines) 2007, adopted by the 30th International Conference of the Red Cross and Red Crescent (which includes states parties to the Geneva Conventions). www.ifrc.org

Annex 2
The Code of Conduct for the International Red Cross and Red Crescent Movement and Non-governmental Organisations (NGOs) in Disaster Relief

Prepared jointly by the International Federation of Red Cross and Red Crescent Societies and the International Committee of the Red Cross[1]

Purpose

This Code of Conduct seeks to guard our standards of behaviour. It is not about operational details, such as how one should calculate food rations or set up a refugee camp. Rather, it seeks to maintain the high standards of independence, effectiveness and impact to which disaster response NGOs and the International Red Cross and Red Crescent Movement aspires. It is a voluntary code, enforced by the will of the organisation accepting it to maintain the standards laid down in the Code.

In the event of armed conflict, the present Code of Conduct will be interpreted and applied in conformity with international humanitarian law.

The Code of Conduct is presented first. Attached to it are three annexes, describing the working environment that we would like to see created by Host Governments, Donor Governments and Inter-governmental Organisations in order to facilitate the effective delivery of humanitarian assistance.

Definitions

NGOs: NGOs (Non-Governmental Organisations) refers here to organisations, both national and international, which are constituted separately from the government of the country in which they are founded.

NGHAs: For the purposes of this text, the term Non-Governmental Humanitarian Agencies (NGHAs) has been coined to encompass the components of the International Red Cross and Red Crescent Movement – The International Committee of the Red Cross, The International Federation of Red Cross and Red Crescent Societies and its member National Societies – and the NGOs as defined

---

1 *Sponsored by: Caritas Internationalis,* Catholic Relief Services,* International Federation of Red Cross and Red Crescent Societies,* International Save the Children Alliance,* Lutheran World Federation,* Oxfam,* World Council of Churches,* International Committee of the Red Cross (* members of the Steering Committee for Humanitarian Response).*

above. This code refers specifically to those NGHAs who are involved in disaster response.

IGOs: IGOs (Inter-Governmental Organisations) refers to organisations constituted by two or more governments. It thus includes all United Nations Agencies and regional organisations.

Disasters: A disaster is a calamitous event resulting in loss of life, great human suffering and distress, and large scale material damage.

The Code of Conduct

Principles of Conduct for The International Red Cross and Red Crescent Movement and NGOs in Disaster Response Programmes

1. The humanitarian imperative comes first

The right to receive humanitarian assistance, and to offer it, is a fundamental humanitarian principle which should be enjoyed by all citizens of all countries. As members of the international community, we recognise our obligation to provide humanitarian assistance wherever it is needed. Hence the need for unimpeded access to affected populations is of fundamental importance in exercising that responsibility. The prime motivation of our response to disaster is to alleviate human suffering amongst those least able to withstand the stress caused by disaster. When we give humanitarian aid it is not a partisan or political act and should not be viewed as such.

2. Aid is given regardless of the race, creed or nationality of the recipients and without adverse distinction of any kind. Aid priorities are calculated on the basis of need alone

Wherever possible, we will base the provision of relief aid upon a thorough assessment of the needs of the disaster victims and the local capacities already in place to meet those needs. Within the entirety of our programmes, we will reflect considerations of proportionality. Human suffering must be alleviated whenever it is found; life is as precious in one part of a country as another. Thus, our provision of aid will reflect the degree of suffering it seeks to alleviate. In implementing this approach, we recognise the crucial role played by women in disaster-prone communities and will ensure that this role is supported, not diminished, by our aid programmes. The implementation of such a universal, impartial and independent policy, can only be effective if we and our partners have access to the necessary resources to provide for such equitable relief, and have equal access to all disaster victims.

3. Aid will not be used to further a particular political or religious standpoint

Humanitarian aid will be given according to the need of individuals, families and communities. Not withstanding the right of NGHAs to espouse particular political or religious opinions, we affirm that assistance will not be dependent on the adherence of the recipients to those opinions. We will not tie the promise, delivery or distribution of assistance to the embracing or acceptance of a particular political or religious creed.

4. We shall endeavour not to act as instruments of government foreign policy

NGHAs are agencies which act independently from governments. We therefore formulate our own policies and implementation strategies and do not seek to implement the policy of any government, except in so far as it coincides with our own independent policy. We will never knowingly – or through negligence – allow ourselves, or our employees, to be used to gather information of a political, military or economically sensitive nature for governments or other bodies that may serve purposes other than those which are strictly humanitarian, nor will we act as instruments of foreign policy of donor governments. We will use the assistance we receive to respond to needs and this assistance should not be driven by the need to dispose of donor commodity surpluses, nor by the political interest of any particular donor. We value and promote the voluntary giving of labour and finances by concerned individuals to support our work and recognise the independence of action promoted by such voluntary motivation. In order to protect our independence we will seek to avoid dependence upon a single funding source.

5. We shall respect culture and custom

We will endeavour to respect the culture, structures and customs of the communities and countries we are working in.

6. We shall attempt to build disaster response on local capacities

All people and communities – even in disaster – possess capacities as well as vulnerabilities. Where possible, we will strengthen these capacities by employing local staff, purchasing local materials and trading with local companies. Where possible, we will work through local NGHAs as partners in planning and implementation, and co-operate with local government structures where appropriate. We will place a high priority on the proper co-ordination of our emergency responses. This is best done within the countries concerned by those most directly involved in the relief operations, and should include representatives of the relevant UN bodies.

7. Ways shall be found to involve programme beneficiaries in the management of relief aid

Disaster response assistance should never be imposed upon the beneficiaries. Effective relief and lasting rehabilitation can best be achieved where the intended beneficiaries are involved in the design, management and implementation of the assistance programme. We will strive to achieve full community participation in our relief and rehabilitation programmes.

8. Relief aid must strive to reduce future vulnerabilities to disaster as well as meeting basic needs

All relief actions affect the prospects for long-term development, either in a positive or a negative fashion. Recognising this, we will strive to implement relief programmes which actively reduce the beneficiaries' vulnerability to future disasters and help create sustainable lifestyles. We will pay particular attention to environmental concerns in the design and management of relief programmes. We will also endeavour to minimise the negative impact of humanitarian assistance, seeking to avoid long-term beneficiary dependence upon external aid.

9. We hold ourselves accountable to both those we seek to assist and those from whom we accept resources

We often act as an institutional link in the partnership between those who wish to assist and those who need assistance during disasters. We therefore hold ourselves accountable to both constituencies. All our dealings with donors and beneficiaries shall reflect an attitude of openness and transparency. We recognise the need to report on our activities, both from a financial perspective and the perspective of effectiveness. We recognise the obligation to ensure appropriate monitoring of aid distributions and to carry out regular assessments of the impact of disaster assistance. We will also seek to report, in an open fashion, upon the impact of our work, and the factors limiting or enhancing that impact. Our programmes will be based upon high standards of professionalism and expertise in order to minimise the wasting of valuable resources.

10. In our information, publicity and advertising activities, we shall recognise disaster victims as dignified humans, not hopeless objects

Respect for the disaster victim as an equal partner in action should never be lost. In our public information we shall portray an objective image of the disaster situation where the capacities and aspirations of disaster victims are highlighted, and not just their vulnerabilities and fears. While we will cooperate with the media in order to enhance public response, we will not allow external or internal demands for publicity to take precedence over the principle of maximising overall relief assistance. We will avoid competing with other disaster response agencies for media coverage in situations where such coverage may be to the detriment of the service provided to the beneficiaries or to the security of our staff or the beneficiaries.

The working environment

Having agreed unilaterally to strive to abide by the Code laid out above, we present below some indicative guidelines which describe the working environment we would like to see created by donor governments, host governments and the inter-governmental organisations – principally the agencies of the United Nations – in order to facilitate the effective participation of NGHAs in disaster response.

These guidelines are presented for guidance. They are not legally binding, nor do we expect governments and IGOs to indicate their acceptance of the guidelines through the signature of any document, although this may be a goal to work to in the future. They are presented in a spirit of openness and cooperation so that our partners will become aware of the ideal relationship we would seek with them.

Annex I: Recommendations to the governments of disaster affected countries

1. Governments should recognise and respect the independent, humanitarian and impartial actions of NGHAs

NGHAs are independent bodies. This independence and impartiality should be respected by host governments.

2. Host governments should facilitate rapid access to disaster victims for NGHAs

If NGHAs are to act in full compliance with their humanitarian principles, they should be granted rapid and impartial access to disaster victims, for the purpose of delivering humanitarian assistance. It is the duty of the host government, as part of the exercising of sovereign responsibility, not to block such assistance, and to accept the impartial and apolitical action of NGHAs. Host governments should facilitate the rapid entry of relief staff, particularly by waiving requirements for transit, entry and exit visas, or arranging that these are rapidly granted. Governments should grant over-flight permission and landing rights for aircraft transporting international relief supplies and personnel, for the duration of the emergency relief phase.

3. Governments should facilitate the timely flow of relief goods and information during disasters

Relief supplies and equipment are brought into a country solely for the purpose of alleviating human suffering, not for commercial benefit or gain. Such supplies should normally be allowed free and unrestricted passage and should not be subject to requirements for consular certificates of origin or invoices, import and/or export licences or other restrictions, or to importation taxation, landing fees or port charges.

The temporary importation of necessary relief equipment, including vehicles, light aircraft and telecommunications equipment, should be facilitated by the receiving host government through the temporary waving of licence or registration restrictions. Equally, governments should not restrict the re-exportation of relief equipment at the end of a relief operation.

To facilitate disaster communications, host governments are encouraged to designate certain radio frequencies, which relief organisations may use in-country and for international communications for the purpose of disaster communications, and to make such frequencies known to the disaster response community prior to the disaster. They should authorise relief personnel to utilise all means of communication required for their relief operations.

4. Governments should seek to provide a coordinated disaster information and planning service

The overall planning and coordination of relief efforts is ultimately the responsibility of the host government. Planning and coordination can be greatly enhanced if NGHAs are provided with information on relief needs and government systems for planning and implementing relief efforts as well as information on potential security risks they may encounter. Governments are urged to provide such information to NGHAs.

To facilitate effective coordination and the efficient utilisation of relief efforts, host governments are urged to designate, prior to disaster, a single point-of-contact for incoming NGHAs to liaise with the national authorities.

5. Disaster relief in the event of armed conflict

In the event of armed conflict, relief actions are governed by the relevant provisions of international humanitarian law.

Annex II: Recommendations to donor governments

1. Donor governments should recognise and respect the independent, humanitarian and impartial actions of NGHAs

NGHAs are independent bodies whose independence and impartiality should be respected by donor governments. Donor governments should not use NGHAs to further any political or ideological aim.

2. Donor governments should provide funding with a guarantee of operational independence

NGHAs accept funding and material assistance from donor governments in the same spirit as they render it to disaster victims; one of humanity and independence of action. The implementation of relief actions is ultimately the responsibility of the NGHA and will be carried out according to the policies of that NGHA.

3. Donor governments should use their good offices to assist NGHAs in obtaining access to disaster victims

Donor governments should recognise the importance of accepting a level of responsibility for the security and freedom of access of NGHA staff to disaster sites. They should be prepared to exercise diplomacy with host governments on such issues if necessary.

Annex III: Recommendations to inter-governmental organisations

1. IGOs should recognise NGHAs, local and foreign, as valuable partners

NGHAs are willing to work with UN and other inter-governmental agencies to effect better disaster response. They do so in a spirit of partnership which respects the integrity and independence of all partners. Inter-governmental agencies must respect the independence and impartiality of the NGHAs. NGHAs should be consulted by UN agencies in the preparation of relief plans.

2. IGOs should assist host governments in providing an overall coordinating framework for international and local disaster relief

NGHAs do not usually have the mandate to provide the overall coordinating framework for disasters which require an international response. This responsibility falls to the host government and the relevant United Nations authorities. They are urged to provide this service in a timely and effective manner to serve the affected state and the national and international disaster response community. In any case, NGHAs should make all efforts to ensure the effective co-ordination of their own services.

In the event of armed conflict, relief actions are governed by the relevant provisions of international humanitarian law.

3. IGOs should extend security protection provided for UN organisations, to NGHAs

Where security services are provided for inter-governmental organisations, this service should be extended to their operational NGHA partners where it is so requested.

4. IGOs should provide NGHAs with the same access to relevant information as is granted to UN organisations

IGOs are urged to share all information, pertinent to the implementation of effective disaster response, with their operational NGHA partners.

Annex 3
Abbreviations and Acronyms

ART	anti-retroviral therapy
BMI	body mass index
CBA	cash-based assistance
CDC	Centers for Disease Control and Prevention
CHS	Core Humanitarian Standard on Quality and Accountability
CHW	community health worker
cm	centimetre
CMR	crude mortality rate
CPMS	Child Protection Minimum Standards
CRPD	Convention on the Rights of Persons with Disabilities
DPT	diphtheria, pertussis and tetanus
EPI	Expanded Programme on Immunization
EWAR	Early warning alert and response
FANTA	Food and Nutrition Technical Assistance
FAO	Food and Agriculture Organization of the United Nations
FRC	free residual chlorine
GBV	gender-based violence
HMIS	health management information system
HWTSS	household-level water treatment and safe storage
IASC	Inter-agency standing committee
iCCM	Integrated Community Case Management
ICCPR	International Covenant on Civil and Political Rights
ICRC	International Committee of the Red Cross
IDP	internally displaced person
IFRC	International Federation of Red Cross and Red Crescent Societies
IHL	international humanitarian law
IMCI	integrated management of childhood illness
INEE	Inter-Agency Network for Education in Emergencies
IPC	infection prevention and control
IYCF	infant and young child feeding
km	kilometre
LEGS	Livestock Emergency Guidelines and Standards
LGBTQI	Lesbian, gay, bisexual, trans, queer, intersex
LLIN	long-lasting insecticide-treated net
MAM	moderate acute malnutrition
MEAL	monitoring, evaluation, accountability and learning
MERS	Minimum Economic Recovery Standards
MISMA	Minimum Standard for Market Analysis
MOH	ministry of health

MSF	*Médecins sans Frontières* (Doctors without Borders)
MUAC	mid upper arm circumference
NCDs	non-communicable diseases
NGO	non-governmental organisation
NTU	nephelometric turbidity units
OAU	Organization of African Unity (now African Union)
OCHA	United Nations Office for the Coordination of Humanitarian Affairs
OHCHR	Office of the United Nations High Commissioner for Human Rights
PEP	post-exposure prophylaxis
PPE	personal protective equipment
RNI	reference nutrient intakes
SEEP	Small Enterprise Education and Promotion (Network)
STIs	sexually transmitted infections
TB	tuberculosis
U5CMR	under-5 crude mortality rate
UN	United Nations
UNFPA	United Nations Population Fund
UNHCR	Office of the United Nations High Commissioner for Refugees (UN Refugee Agency)
UNICEF	United Nations Children's Fund
WASH	water supply, sanitation and hygiene promotion
WFH	weight for height
WFP	World Food Programme
WHO	World Health Organization

I Index

Index

A

abattoir waste 130
abbreviations 393
abuse 61. *See also* gender-based violence; *see also* protection; *see also* sexual exploitation and abuse (SEA)
acceptability
food security 196
healthcare workers 304
access
food 199
humanitarian assistance 40
justice systems 44
legal support 44
settlements/shelter 252
toilets 115
water 105
accountability
general 388
Minimum Standards 10
references/further reading 85
acronyms 393
admission criteria
feeding programmes 225
malnutrition management 175, 179
adults. *see also* people
malnutrition 226
adverse events 302
aedes mosquito-transmitted diseases 314
AIDS. *See* HIV/AIDS
aid workers. *See* staff members; *See* community health workers (CHWs); *See* healthcare workers
air pollution 327
anaesthesia 337
anthropometric surveys 170
anti-retroviral therapies 334
armed conflicts
disaster relief 390
guidelines 380
legal provision 30
treaties and customary laws 379
artificial feeding, infants and young children 187, 190, 203
artificial lighting 260
ART interventions 334
ARV interventions 334
assessments
mental health conditions 341
NCDs 344
references/further reading 86
shelter and settlement planning 247
at-risk groups
food assistance 200
food security 167, 195

hygiene promotion 101
auditing 84

B

bathing facilities 109
beneficiaries, involvement 387
blood products 306
blood transfusions 334
bottled water 109
breastfeeding 180, 190
breastmilk substitutes 190
building codes 264
building materials 264

C

camps. *See* communal settlements
caregivers, food assistance 201
care plans 347
case fatality rates (CFR) 319, 321, 356
cash-based assistance
checklist 22
general 9
references/further reading 26, 86
WASH 156
CFR (case fatality rates) 319, 321, 356
checklists
food security 219
hygiene promotion 139
livelihoods 219
nutrition assessment 223
seed security assessment 221
solid waste management 143
vector control 142
WASH general 139
water supply 140
children. *see also* healthcare; *see also* infants and young children
faeces 115
feeding 185, 327
feeding, artificial 187, 190
feeding, reference/further reading 3
gender-based violence 192
healthcare 322
illnesses 324
malnutrition 225
protection 12, 327
references/further reading 3, 86
separated 327
sexual violence 332
vaccination 322, 323
WASH 98
chlorine solutions 135
cholera 321